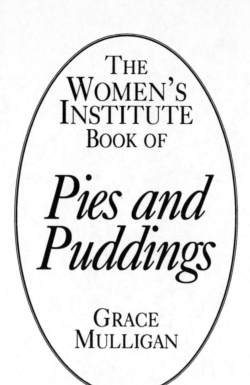

THE
WOMEN'S
INSTITUTE
BOOK OF

*Pies and
Puddings*

GRACE
MULLIGAN

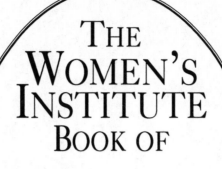

THE WOMEN'S INSTITUTE BOOK OF

Pies and Puddings

GRACE MULLIGAN

HarperCollins*Publishers*

For Brian

First published in 1995 by
HarperCollins*Publishers* London

Text © Grace Mulligan 1995
All rights reserved

Editor: Lewis Esson
Text designer: Siân Keogh
Illustrator: Ray Barnett
Indexer: Susan Bosanko

For HarperCollins*Publishers*
Editorial Director: *Polly Powell*
Commissioning Editor: *Barbara Dixon*
Design Manager: *Ray Barnett*

A catalogue record for this book is available
from the British Library

ISBN 0 00 412758 7

Typeset in Garamond
Printed and bound in Great Britain by Butler & Tanner Ltd, Frome and London

Front Cover: Chris Brown

About The Author

From Dundee in the old county of Angus, Grace Mulligan trained originally as a home economics teacher at Edinburgh's famous cookery school in Atholl Crescent. She taught for three years in a large secondary school and then moved south to Yorkshire with her new husband and to a job in general practice.

Four children later, Grace's passion for all aspects of food and cooking was undimmed. She continued to perfect her skills in preservation, baking and meal cookery. She became a national judge in the Women's Institute and taught at their Denman college in Oxfordshire. Travel too opened new opportunities for experiment and learning. It was through her work with the home economics committee of the old Yorkshire Federation and demonstrating at the Great Yorkshire show that she was approached by Mary Watts, the producer of ITV's cookery series *Farmhouse Kitchen* and invited to become a guest presenter.

Eventually the then presenter Dorothy Sleightholme retired, having been with the series for eleven years. Grace took her place and stayed for just under ten years. The programme was made at Yorkshire Television and was networked throughout the UK. It won the Glenfiddich Award as the best TV food programme as well as the overall trophy in the same year. The eight books for the series introduced Grace to recipe writing and she took part in four then went on the publish three under her own name. Grace also contributes to several newspapers and magazines on a regular basis. Many groups and organizations invite Grace to speak on the making of a TV cookery programme and are astonished to hear about the huge amount of preparation and rehearsal which is needed to fill a 30–minute slot.

Now, as a member of the Guild of Food Writers, Grace takes a lively interest in all that is going on in the food world. One of her main concerns is that so many children are growing up unable to prepare a simple meal for themselves from fresh ingredients. The craft of cooking must be encouraged for it is a satisfying skill which anyone can learn.

About The WI

If you enjoy this book, the chances are you would enjoy belonging to the largest women's organization in the country – the WI.

We are women who receive enormous satisfaction from all the organisation has to offer; the list is long. You can make new friends, enjoy companionship, visit new places, develop new skills, take part in community services, fight local campaigns, become a WI Market producer, and play an active role in an organisation which has a national voice. The WI is unique in owning a residential adult education establishment. At Denman College, you can take a course in anything from advanced motoring to paper sculpture, from book-binding to yoga, from cordon bleu cookery to fly fishing.

For more information about the WI, write to the **National Federation of Women's Institutes, 104 New Kings Road, London SW6 4LY** or telephone 0171 371 9300. **The NFWI Wales Office is at 19 Cathedral Road, Cardiff CF1 9LJ,** telephone 01222 221712.

CONTENTS

INTRODUCTION

The making of pies and puddings should be one of the delights of the kitchen and a chance to enjoy the odd flight of fancy at weekends or on high days and holidays. Some people are convinced, however, that baking and pastry-making are particularly difficult; but providing you follow a few basic tips on techniques and ingredients as follows you can be sure of good results every time.

PASTRY AND BAKING

Fats

One look at the diversity on supermarket shelves and the choice of fat for pastry and baking can be extremely difficult. We now have many variations on spreads that look very like margarine and butter. Some are not at all suitable for the pies and puddings in this book, others are. As always, the answer is usually printed on the wrapper – 'Suitable for Baking' or 'Suitable for Pastry'.

For everyday shortcrust pastry my own preference is for a mixture of half block margarine and half white vegetable fat – 2 oz (50 g) block margarine plus 2 oz (50 g) white fat to 8 oz (225 g) sifted plain white flour.

In the long run the choice of fats is a matter of what sort of taste and you want. The addition of butter instead of margarine will improve the flavour and give you a much crisper pastry. An all-butter pastry, however, is very rich indeed, but it is also less easy to rub in. Use all margarine or all vegetable fat and taste the difference for yourself.

All fats are easier to rub in by hand if they are at room temperature. By this I mean not rock-hard, but also not sloppy. If you use a food processor to rub in, then I find it is better to use the fats straight out of the fridge.

Flour

The type of flour you use for pastry is again a personal choice. Lots of people prefer the slightly aerated – almost cake-like – texture of self-raising flour. I use plain white flour or a mixture of plain white and brown flour. Wholewheat flour is heavier and I usually mix that with half wholewheat and half brown flour. Do also try to sift your flour before you start mixing as flour is often very compacted in the bag.

Other Ingredients

Cold – or even iced – water is best for mixing pastry, since you are trying to keep everything as cool as possible.

Using an egg yolk to mix pastry will give a crisper finish too. I find it easier to use if this egg yolk is first mixed with a tablespoon of water.

EQUIPMENT FOR MAKING PASTRY

I like to use a jug to dribble the water over my rubbed-in mixture. I also prefer a round bladed knife – an old-fashioned one with a long blade – to mix the pastry. My other preference is for a tall narrow bowl rather than a wide flattish bowl. My own mixing bowls are made of melamine.

One last point on making pastry: I think it is easier to mix just 8 oz (225 g) of pastry at a time rather than larger quantities.

GREASING TINS

I almost always use a white vegetable fat for this job. In fact, I keep a small jar of it in my fridge at all times. I melt it in the microwave and apply with a brush also kept for this purpose. You can use oil if you wish, but I find that after several uses this eventually builds up to a very tacky surface that is very hard to clean.

Thinking back to my training days we were told not to use butter or margarine for greasing because the salt content would make our baking stick. Nowadays we have extra aids like non-stick paper for lining the bases of tins (not all that easy with pies, but useful for cakes). We also have non-stick tins, which work extremely well when new but do deteriorate with use. They do not like to be scoured, nor should you use a knife in them to cut up your tart.

The other 'magic' lining material sold in

sheets for you to cut and fit into your tins works beautifully, washes well and can be used indefinitely.

LINING TINS

Of all jobs associated with baking this is the one which most people loathe. There are a few short-cuts. Always use greaseproof paper and use the tin as a pattern to make your cut-out circles by drawing round it. I tend to do a bundle at once and keep them firmly clipped together in a drawer. You can cut out about ten circles at once by folding the paper over and over. It is, of course, cheaper to buy a roll of greaseproof than a pack of sheets. You can also pay more and buy ready-made cut-out circles.

Lining square tins is easiest of all since you can use two strips of paper the width of your tin and set them in the tin across each other.

To line a round tin, grease your tin well then just line the base with a circle and the side with a straight strip. The other, more complicated method is to use a double strip of paper for the side and fold it up about 1 in (5 cm) from the bottom. Now cut diagonally to the fold about every ½ in (1 cm). This should now sit along the inside of the tin and the cut border will overlap on the base of the tin. Finish the lining with a circle of paper that will help to hold the side lining paper down.

PIE AND PUDDING CONTAINERS

Heavy traditional pie dishes are usually in stoneware, nearly always oval ion shape and with a generous lip for the pastry to sit on. The sizes are very variable indeed, but roughly they contain anything from about 3 pints (1.75 litres) of filling down to ¾ pint (450 ml). The traditional oblong enamelled pie dishes are very long-lasting too. The ones I have are white with a dark blue edge. You can make pies in a variety of deep dishes, but the lack of a wide lip means that the pastry sometimes slides into the filling.

Plate pie tins are always shallow and almost always made in metal – aluminium, tin or enamelled.

Pork pie tins are usually deep with loose bases. A small deep cake tin will usually work well too, but do get the pie out before it is really cold.

Metal flan and quiche tins are sold in a bewildering range of sizes and depths. The loose-bottomed ones are the best, so that your flan or quiche reaches the table in one piece. Once baked stand the quiche on something like a tin of beans so that the outside of the flan tin falls down. You can then slide the flan on to a flat plate. It is often easier to leave the flan on the base and recover it later. The 'French' flan tins which are very shallow and usually have

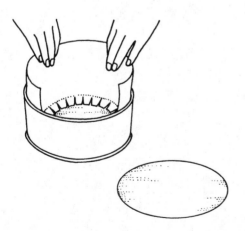

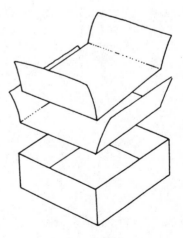

scalloped edges look very nice but do take care as the sharp edges play havoc with your pastry as you line the tin and you may find that you have to seal up the holes.

You can also buy miniature flan tins which are excellent for individual portions, but Yorkshire pudding tins make a good substitute.

PUDDING BASINS

The traditional basins are in stoneware, have a narrow base and a definite rim round the outside top edge. They are sold in a large number of sizes. I also use small handle-less cups for mini puddings. Pudding tins are also on sale as well as handy disposable foil pudding basins for use in a freezer.

I always grease pudding basins well, then also set a small circle of greaseproof paper in the base. This ensures that you do not leave half of the pudding inside the tin when you turn it out.

To cover a pudding basin I use first greaseproof paper, then foil. Lots of old recipes say to make a pleat in the covering paper to allow the pudding to expand. There is only need for this if your basin is really full. I tend to use a larger basin to avoid this and I also then have a flatter top that will stand and not wobble on turning out.

You can buy aluminium basins and enamel ones. I also have in my cupboard an aluminium basin with a matching twist-on lid as well as a pottery basin with a lid. I do not see them in the shops now, but we used to be able to buy cotton pudding basin covers which could be pulled up tight with tape at the side to give a tight fit. They also had a tape handle which facilitated easier lifting of the hot pudding basin out of the pan.

STEAMING PUDDINGS

I have always maintained that steaming a pudding is a much easier procedure than many others. Apart from the length of cooking time and the necessity of watching the water level, nothing could be simpler.

A purpose-built steamer consists of two pans, one on top of the other. The top pan has holes in the base to allow steam through from the pan of simmering water below. If you are really into economical cooking you can also cook your potatoes, rice or vegetables in the bottom pan – but obviously not for the same length of time, of course.

To improvise a steamer you need a pan large enough to hold the pudding basin comfortably. Just put an old plate in the base with the pudding on it. Fill up with boiling water and away you go. The water level can be up to halfway up the sides of the basin and it is best to simmer gently rather than boil furiously. If the pan boils dry, the plate will protect your pudding for a little longer and will also stop rattling, thus providing you with an ominous warning silence.

WEIGHTS AND MEASURES

Conversion Chart

Metric grammes (g)	Imperial ounces (oz)	Metric grammes (g)	Imperial pounds (lb)
7	¼	675	1½
15	½	900	2
25	1		
50	2	kilogrammes (kg)	
75	3	1.1	2½
125	4	1.3	3
150	5		
175	6		
200	7		
225	8 (½ pound)		
250	9		
275	10		
300	11	Metric millilitres (ml)	Imperial fluid ounces (fl oz)
325	12	150	5 (¼ pint)
350	13	300	10 (½ pint)
400	14	450	15 (¾ pint)
425	15	575	20 (1 pint)
450	16 (1 pound)		

Follow *either* the metric or the imperial measures – never mix the two.

Spoon Measures

All spoon measures used in this book are level unless otherwise stated.

Oven Temperature Chart

Description	Gas	Fahrenheit °F	Centigrade °C
Very low	¼	225	110
Low	½	250	120
Slow	1	275	140
Cool	2	300	150
Moderate	3	325	160
	4	350	180
Moderately hot	5	375	190
Fairly hot	6	400	200
Hot	7	425	220
	8	450	230
Very hot	9	475	250

The oven temperatures used throughout this book are for a conventional oven. For fan-assisted ovens, refer to the manufacturer's handbook as temperatures and cooking times are generally reduced.

SECTION 1

PIES, TARTS & FLANS

'Simple Simon met a pieman,
Going to the fair;
Says Simple Simon to the pieman,
Let me taste your ware.'

1

Basic
Pastry Recipes

Flour-and-water mixtures go back to Roman times. They were wrapped around meat prior to cooking to seal in juices and prevent scorching. It was much later that this outside crust was found to be quite tasty. Later still, the crust was improved further with fat and later on still with additions like cheese and herbs.

It used to be thought that pastry-making was a hard-to-learn skill. With a food processor, however, the much-hated rubbing-in process can be eliminated. Anybody can make pastry by following the instructions on page 17.

If making pastry by hand, try to keep everything cool and use ice-cold water for mixing. The fat you use can be all butter, which gives a very crisp pastry but is also rather expensive for everyday use. I like an equal parts mix of hard (block) margarine and white fat. Plain flour is preferable to self-raising, and it is also a good idea to sieve it. I also prefer a tall narrow bowl, rather than a wide flat bowl and I use a long-bladed old-fashioned dinner knife for mixing. The addition of an egg yolk or whole egg enriches the flavour, adds a crisp texture and, of course, you need less water. It does pay to let mixed pastry rest in a lump for just 30 minutes, and then again when it has been rolled out and fitted into a pie tin. I prefer to rest pastry in a cool place rather than the fridge, which sometimes sets it like a rock and you have to wait again for it to soften up.

SHORTCRUST PASTRY

This is probably the most versatile of all pastries. It is usually made with a proportion of half the weight of fat to that of the flour.

4 oz (125 g) plain flour, plus more for dusting
1 oz (25 g) hard block margarine, cut into pieces
1 oz (25 g) white fat, cut into pieces
about 2 tablespoons ice-cold water

1   Sift the flour into a bowl.
2   Stir the fats into the flour and, using your fingertips, rub the fat into the flour. Lift your hands up and out of the flour to allow it to be aired. Stop when the mixture looks like damp breadcrumbs.
3   Sprinkle the water, a little at a time, over the mixture and start to draw it together with a long-bladed knife, pressing the mixture on the side of the bowl.
4   Once the mixture looks as if it is coming together, use you hands to gather it up. You should be able to leave the bowl clean if the pastry is at the correct texture.
5   Knead gently in the bowl, then sprinkle a little flour over and put the lump in a polythene bag. Set aside in a cool place for 30 minutes.

Variations

Sweet Shortcrust Almond Pastry
Stir in 1 oz (25 g) ground almonds with 2–3 drops of almond essence and 1 teaspoon caster sugar.

Herby Shortcrust Pastry
This is the basic mixture with the addition of fresh or dried herbs to the bowl after the rubbing-in process. The amount of herbs could be about 1 heaped tablespoon of finely chopped fresh herbs like parsley or thyme. If you use dry herbs use only 1 level teaspoon, since dried herbs are more pungent.

Cheese Pastry
This is the basic shortcrust mixture again, but add grated cheese to the bowl after the rubbing in has been done. The quantity rather depends on the cheese – you would need much less of a mature Cheddar than a mild one. I find if the cheese, when grated, is rather waxy or soft it is better if it is left to dry out a little. Just spread it out on a plate for a couple of hours.

WHOLEWHEAT PASTRY

Wholewheat flour is heavier than white and a good mixture of half whole wheat and half white gives a nice flavour, using the method in the basic Shortcrust Pastry mixture. For an entirely whole-wheat pastry mixture it is better to use this recipe. It is based on a Sarah Brown recipe which she used on television's *Farmhouse Kitchen*. It is easy to roll and is not at all unmanageable. You can also roll it out very thinly.

8 oz (225 g) 100%-wholewheat flour, plus more for dusting
pinch of salt
pinch of baking powder
1 teaspoon soft brown sugar
2 oz (50 g) vegetable fat
1 oz (25 g) butter
1 teaspoon vegetable oil
3–4 tablespoons cold water

1   Sift the flour into a bowl and add the bran back into it from the sieve.
2   Stir the salt, baking powder and sugar into the flour and whizz the fats into the mixture in a food processor.
3   When the flour looks like damp breadcrumbs, slow down the speed and add the oil and water.
4   Stop the machine the minute the mixture comes into a rough lump. Turn this out and knead lightly to a smooth ball. Dust with flour and set the pastry in a plastic bag to rest for 30 minutes.

RICH SWEET SHORTCRUST PASTRY

This is excellent for dessert and tartlets.

8 oz (225 g) plain white flour, sieved, plus
    more for dusting
1 oz (25 g) caster sugar
5 oz (150 g) softened butter
1 teaspoon lemon juice
1 egg yolk from a size-1 or size-2 egg
2–3 tablespoons ice-cold water

1   Sieve the flour again into a bowl, adding the
sugar. Rub in the butter until the mixture looks
like damp breadcrumbs.
2   In a small bowl, add the lemon juice and egg
yolk to 2 tablespoons of the cold water. Sprinkle
this mixture over the flour and, using a long-
bladed knife, mix to a dough adding more water
if needed. Use your hand to bring the pastry
together in a rough lump.
3   Knead lightly, dust with flour and set aside
for 30 minutes in a plastic bag.

FOOD PROCESSOR PASTRY

8 oz (225 g) plain white flour, plus more for
    dusting
2 oz (50 g) hard block margarine, cut into
    pieces
2 oz (50 g) white vegetable fat, cut into
    pieces
pinch of salt

1   Put the flour, fats and salt into the processor
and whizz until the mixture looks sandy.
2   Turn down the speed and add 2-3 tablespoons
of water, a little at a time. Stop machine as soon
as mixture comes together into a rough lump.
3   Turn out, sprinkle with a little flour and
gather into a ball. Set aside to rest in a cool place
for 30 minutes.

RICH CHEESE PASTRY

Use for savoury flans and quiches.

8 oz (225 g) plain white flour (or half white
    and half brown)
pinch of cayenne pepper
2 fat pinches of salt
2 fat pinches of dry mustard powder
3 oz (75 g) block margarine or solid white
    fat or a mixture
3 oz (75 g) strongly flavoured cheese, finely
    grated
1 egg yolk from a size-1 or size-2 egg
about 2 tablespoons ice-cold water

1   Sieve the flour into a bowl, adding the
cayenne pepper, salt and mustard.
2   Rub in the fat or fat mixture, until the mixture
looks like damp breadcrumbs. Stir in the cheese.
3   Mix the egg yolk and water and sprinkle this
over the pastry crumbs. Using a long-bladed
dinner knife, mix the pastry together. Add more
water if you need to.
4   Use your hand finally to gather all the
mixture together, leaving a clean bowl. Knead
gently, dust with flour and set aside in a plastic
bag for about 30 minutes to rest before using.

SUET PASTRY

The easiest pastry of all to make, it is most
suitable for savoury pies and pastries.

8 oz (225 g) self-raising white flour
1 teaspoon baking powder
4 oz (125 g) prepared packet suet
1 size-3 egg, beaten
1 tablespoon cold water

1   Sift the flour and baking powder into a bowl
and stir in the suet.
2   Mix the beaten egg and water and use to mix
the flour to a firm dough.
3   Gather the dough into a ball and set it aside
in a plastic bag for about 5 minutes before use.

HOT-WATER CRUST

This is the traditional pastry used for raised pork pies. It is made in a very different way.

4 fl oz (125 ml) water
4 oz (125 g) lard
10 oz (275 g) strong plain white flour (bread flour)
$\frac{1}{2}$ level teaspoon salt

1   In a large pan, boil the water with the lard. Watch out as it often spits.
2   Sift the flour and salt into a bowl and pour the boiling fat and water over. Mix first with a wooden spoon and then with your hands until quite smooth.
3   Use as soon as the pastry is cool enough to handle.
4   If the pastry gets stiff and cool, a quick 2–3 second blast in a microwave will make it go pliable again.

RICH PIE PASTRY

This recipe came to me via another Scot, Anne Wallace of Stewarton, Ayrshire.

10 oz (275 g) plain white flour
1 teaspoon salt
$4\frac{1}{2}$ (140 g) lard
1 small egg (size-2 or size-3), beaten
about $2\frac{1}{2}$ fl oz (65 ml) water

1   Sieve the flour and salt into a bowl.
2   Rub in the lard.
3   Mix the egg and the water and mix this into the flour to make a soft elastic dough. You may need a very little more water.
4   Set the dough aside in a plastic bag for 1 hour. Roll out and use.

ROUGH PUFF PASTRY

This pastry is not as popular as it once was, but I think it makes a good substitute for the even more slowly made flaky pastry.

8 oz (225 g) strong white flour (bread flour)
pinch of salt
3 oz (75 g) block margarine (cold, but not rock-hard), cut into small pieces.
3 oz (75 g) lard or white vegetable fat (cold, but not rock-hard), cut into small pieces
$\frac{1}{4}$ pt (150 ml) water
1 teaspoon lemon juice

1   Sieve the flour and salt into a bowl.
2   Stir in the fats and mix lightly.
3   Use the water and lemon juice to mix to a lumpy dough.
4   On a floured board, form this dough into a brick-shaped block. Cool the block for 10 minutes in a plastic bag in the fridge.
5   On a well-floured board, roll this block out to a rectangle about $\frac{1}{4}$ inch (7 mm) thick and about three times as long as it is wide. Fold the pastry by turning the bottom one-third up and the top third down (you now have three layers). Use the rolling pin to seal the open edges together. Wrap this block in a plastic bag and cool for 10 minutes.
6   Put the pastry on the board again with the sealed edges top and bottom. Repeat the rolling, folding, sealing and cooling sequence three times more.
7   Cool again for 30 minutes before using.

NEW FLAKY PASTRY

This is another variation on flaky pastry.

8 oz (225 g) plain flour, plus extra
6 oz (175g) butter, hardened in the fridge
pinch of salt
about 3–4 tablespoons ice-cold water

1 Sift the flour and salt into a large mixing bowl.
2 Put extra flour in a small cup.
3 Using a piece of foil, grip the butter and grate it on the largest holes on a grater straight into the flour, using the spare flour for dipping the block when it becomes sticky.
4 Stir the butter gently through the flour.
5 Using a long-bladed knife, mix and stir the butter and flour with enough cold water to make a firm dough.
6 As the dough comes together, use your hand to knead it gently into a ball.
7 Wrap the dough in a plastic bag and cool for 30 minutes before using.

CHOUX PASTRY

This airy pastry is almost always associated with eclairs and profiteroles. It also makes an excellent container for savoury fillings.

2½ oz (65 g) plain white flour
pinch of salt
2 oz (50 g) butter
4 fl oz (125 ml) water
2 size-3 or size-4 eggs, beaten

1 Sieve the flour and salt in a heap on a square of greaseproof paper.
2 Cut up the butter and put it into the water in a saucepan. Bring to the boil.
3 When the butter has melted, lift the flour and salt on the piece of greaseproof paper and shoot it into the water, all at once. Remove the pan from the heat and beat with a wooden spoon until free of lumps.
4 Allow this mixture to cool slightly, then beat in the eggs. Start by adding half of the eggs and then, having beaten this mixture until smooth, add the rest of the eggs a little at a time.
5 The mixture should be shiny and slack enough to pipe easily, but firm enough to retain its shape. Cover and allow the mixture to cool again before using.

'I do like a bit of butter to my bread!'

The Kings Breakfast, A. A. Milne

2

FIRST COURSES AND SNACKS

TARTLETS

The most important point in baking tartlets is that the tins should be non-stick or very well greased. Be sure to ease the pastry well down into the base.

RED PEPPER & GOATS' CHEESE TARTLETS

Makes about 30 mini-tartlets or about 10 lunch-size (4 in/10 cm) tartlets.

Herby Pastry
6 oz (175 g) plain white flour, plus more for dusting
3 oz (75 g) butter and lard mixed plus more for greasing
1 level teaspoon dried herbs
½ teaspoon fresh thyme leaves (or 1 pinch of dried thyme)
ice-cold water

Red Pepper Filling
3 large red peppers (about 16 oz/450 g)
dash of oil
1 small garlic clove
2 rounded teaspoons of finely chopped pickled gherkins or pickled onions
2 dessertspoons of tomato purée
1 round of firm goats' cheese (or any fairly strongly flavoured cheese)
4 oz (125 g) cream cheese
salt and pepper

First Make The Pastry
1 Either whizz the flour and fats together in a food processor or sift flour into a bowl and rub in fats until mixture looks like damp breadcrumbs.
2 Stir in the dried herbs and thyme.
3 Put some ice-cold water in a jug and sprinkle it over the surface of the 'crumbs'. Using a long-bladed knife, stir the 'crumbs' together, pressing them against the side of the bowl.
4 At this point, use your hand to gather the pastry mixture together into a ball, turning it over and over and kneading it until it is fairly smooth. Set the pastry aside in a plastic bag to

rest for about 20 minutes.
5 Sprinkle flour lightly on a smooth surface and cut the pastry into two pieces. Roll each piece out thinly on the floured surface and cut out circles to fit whichever tins you are using. Gather up the trimmings and re-roll them to make more rounds.

Make the Red Pepper Filling
1 Cut the peppers into four, deseed them and remove the green stalk.
2 Chop the flesh into tiny pieces. I find it easier to use scissors and cut the peppers over the frying pan, cutting them first into long strips and then across into tiny dice.
3 Put some oil into the pan with the peppers and then grate the garlic clove on the biggest holes of a grater into the pan. Cook gently until the peppers are soft and almost mushy, stirring often. Season with salt and pepper.
4 Add the chopped pickled gherkins or onions along with the tomato purée. Cook for a couple of minutes more. Set aside.

To Bake the Pastry Cases
1 Preheat the oven to gas4/350°F/180°C. Grease the patty tins with melted fat (it is easier to use a brush). Ease the pastry circles into the tins and prick the pastry all over with a sharp skewer or small fork.
2 Bake the cases for about 20 minutes or until they are a light gold. Remove them from the oven.

To Finish
1 De-rind the goats' or other strong cheese, grate it into a bowl and then work it into the cream cheese.
2 Spoon a small amount of cheese mixture into the pastry cases and top with a thick layer of the red pepper.
3 Reheat carefully and serve warm. If you have to let everything go cold, reheat the tartlets with a sheet of foil over the top.

MINI FILO TARTLETS FOR PRE-DINNER DRINKS

You need very small patty tins or mini muffin tins for these bite-sized morsels.

To make the tiny pastry cases you need to melt some butter and grease the inside of each tin with it. Use 3 sheets of filo pastry at a time and stick them on top of each other using melted butter between each sheet. Cut the triple layer into approximately 3 in (6 cm) squares (the size will vary depending on your tins) and press each triple layer into a tin.

Bake in a moderate oven (gas4/350°F/ 180°C) for about 10 minutes. Keep an eye on this pastry as it burns easily. Remove from the tins while still warm.

Cream Cheese Base Fillings

These should not be added until the last minute before serving.

- Beat finely chopped chutney into the cream cheese
- Mix cream cheese with finely chopped chives or any other green herb
- Mix cream cheese with finely chopped walnuts or pecans
- Add a dash of tomato purée to the cream cheese

Note: The cream cheese should be quite soft but not wet.

Toppings

These should be dainty, bright and neat.

- Finely chopped avocado
- Finely chopped mixed coloured peppers
- Finely chopped tomato flesh
- Wafer-thin slices of radish or cucumber
- Grated carrot
- Toasted flaked almonds
- Toasted coconut
- Grated coloured cheese
- Tiny slices of smoked ham
- Grilled and chopped bacon

MINI PASTRY PIZZAS FOR PRE-DINNER DRINKS

In many ways these simple circles or squares of puff pastry are the easiest of all pre-dinner nibbles.

Use ready-made puff pastry and allow it to thaw. It should be soft but still chilly to touch. Do not try to roll out half-frozen pastry.

Preheat the oven to gas7/425°F/220°C. Roll the pastry out very thinly indeed. Cut it into small circles or squares and set them on greased baking sheets.

Bake for about 12 minutes, or until golden and crisp. Cool on a wire tray.

Tomato Base for the Pizzas

1 small onion, peeled and finely chopped
dash of oil
1 small tin (8 oz/225 g) Italian tomatoes
pinch of fennel seed, lightly bruised in a
    mortar
1 level teaspoon sugar
1 dessertspoon tomato purée

Make Tomato Base

1 In a small pan, fry the onion gently with a dash of oil until fairly soft, stirring often.
2 Chop up the tomatoes and add them to the pan with their liquid and the fennel seed, sugar and tomato purée.
3 Simmer this mixture uncovered until it reduces to a jam-like consistency. It must not be runny. Allow to cool.
4 Spread a layer of tomato mixture on each piece of pastry.

Toppings

Cheese is always good, especially if at the last minute you flash the pizzas under a hot grill and serve them warm.

Grate the cheese and vary both the colour and flavour, eg Gruyère, mature Cheddar, mild Wensleydale and red Leicester.

BREAD TARTLETS OF STUFFED TOMATO & MUSTARD SAUCE

Serves 6

Stuffed tomatoes make good starters, but often collapse on reheating. These toasted cases hold the tomatoes together and give a nice texture.

Bread Tartlets
2 oz (50 g) melted butter
6 slices of medium-cut white or brown bread
1 teaspoon sesame seeds
salt and pepper

Stuffed Tomatoes
3 firm but ripe tomatoes (judge the size by the capacity of your bread tartlets)
½ oz (25 g) butter
1 tablespoon oil
1 small onion, peeled and very finely chopped
3 oz (75 g) breadcrumbs
3 oz (75 g) grated cheese (I like Emmental and Parmesan mixed)
2 teaspoons of chopped fresh parsley

Grainy Mustard Sauce
3–4 large tablespoons fromage frais or thick Greek yoghurt
1 teaspoon thin honey
2 large teaspoons grainy mustard

To make bread tartlet cases
1   Preheat the oven to gas5/375°F/190°C.
2   Grease your patty tins very thoroughly with some of the butter.
3   Cut each bread slice into a square, discarding crusts. Using a pastry brush, apply the melted butter to one side of each. Season and sprinkle a few sesame seeds over. Turn slices over and repeat process. Now press the bits of bread into each tin quite hard to make them stick.
4   Bake until crisp but not brittle, 10–12 minutes. Remove from tins and transfer to a wire rack before they cool down.

To make stuffed tomatoes
1   Cut each tomato across the middle. Scoop out seeds and drain upside down on kitchen paper.
2   Melt the butter with the oil in a pan and fry the onion carefully until soft. Set aside to cool.
3   Mix breadcrumbs, cheese and parsley well in a bowl. Stir in cooled onions and season. Stuff mixture into tomatoes – not too tightly.
4   Set on a greased baking tin and bake at gas4/350°F/180°C, until softish but not disintegrating.

To make grainy mustard sauce
Beat or whisk all the ingredients together, taste and adjust the seasoning with salt and pepper.

To serve
Set a tomato in each case, reheat gently and serve with a spoonful of warmed sauce on the plate.

SWEET & SOUR ONION TARTLETS

Serves 6

6 sun-dried tomatoes, chopped small
3½ fl oz (100 ml) olive oil
4 fl oz (125 ml) sherry vinegar
1 tablespoon sesame oil
8 oz (225 g) Shortcrust Pastry (see page 16)
2 oz (50 g) butter, plus more for greasing
2 large Spanish onions, thinly sliced
3 oz (75 g) caster sugar
flour for dusting

Topping
1 round fresh goats' cheese

1   About 2 hours ahead, put the chopped sun-dried tomatoes to soak in a mixture of 5 tablespoons of the olive oil, 5 tablespoons of the sherry vinegar and the sesame oil.
2   Roll out the pastry thinly on a floured board and cut out six 5 in (13 cm) circles of pastry. Ease the pastry into 4 inch (10 cm) Yorkshire pudding tins which have been well greased with butter. If

you do not have a 5 in (13 cm) cutter, look for a saucer about the same size and use that as a template.

3   Chill the pastry cases for 30 minutes and prick them all over with a fork or skewer.

4   Bake blind in a fairly hot oven (gas5/375°F/190°C) for about 12–15 minutes. Keep an eye on the tartlet cases and, if the pastry starts to rise from the base, use the handle of a knife to pat it down again. Remove from the oven.

5   Now cook the onions: melt the butter with the remaining oil in a pan and cook the onions for about 15 minutes, or until soft. Stir often.

6   Add the remaining sherry vinegar and the sugar. Remove from the heat and stir until the sugar has dissolved. Return to the heat and cook gently until the juices become thick and syrupy.

7   To fill the pastry cases: wait until the onion mixture is almost cold, then spoon it into each case. Next spoon a little of the sun-dried tomato mixture over each and finally top with a thin slice of goats' cheese. Reheat the tartlets with care.

Caramelized Onion & Feta Cheese Boats

It is not easy to find pastry boat shapes which will hold a good amount of filling. I usually use my eclair tins, which are much deeper. It just means that my boats have round ends! The number you make will, of course, depend on the size of your boats.

Cheesy Pastry

6 oz (175 g) brown flour, plus more for dusting
1 oz (25 g) grated Parmesan cheese
3 oz (75 g) butter and lard mixed, plus more for greasing

Onion & Feta Cheese Filling

1 oz (25 g) butter
1 tablespoon oil
½ oz (15 g) caster sugar
2 large onions, peeled and thinly sliced
6 oz (175 g) Feta cheese, crumbled

1 oz (25 g) sun-dried tomato, finely chopped and soaked in boiling water for at least 10 minutes
2 size-3 eggs, beaten
¼ pt (150 ml) single cream
white pepper

Make the cheesy pastry

1   Sift the flour into a bowl and stir in the Parmesan cheese. Rub the fats in until the mixture looks like damp breadcrumbs.

2   Using a long-bladed knife to draw the pastry together, sprinkle in enough cold water to bind the dough until it comes together.

3   Use your hand to knead and turn the pastry until it comes together in a smooth ball. Set the pastry aside for 30 minutes.

4   Preheat the oven to gas4/350°F/180°C. Grease the boat shapes carefully with lard. If you are worried about the pastry sticking, place a narrow strip of foil or greaseproof paper in the base of each tin. Roll the pastry thinly on a floured board. Cut an oblong of pastry for each boat. Ease the pastry in and press it against the sides. Trim away excess. Prick the pastry all over.

5   Bake for about 15–20 minutes, or until pastry is cooked but still quite pale. Remove from the oven and turn the oven up to gas6/400°F/200°C.

Make the filling

1   Melt the butter with the oil in a roomy pan, add the sugar and then the onion. Fry gently for about 10 minutes, stirring often.

2   Let the onion cool down a little, then spoon it into the pastry cases, followed by the crumbled Feta cheese and the drained sun-dried tomato.

3   Whisk the eggs into the cream, season with pepper and pour this mixture into each boat. Do not fill to the brim until you get the boats in the oven or to be exact, on the shelf.

4   Bake for a further 20–25 minutes, or until the filling has risen up and set. Eat while still warm.

PUFF PESTO TARTS

Serves 4

These easy tarts are best when good-quality tomatoes are in season, as well as aromatic basil.

1 packet of frozen puff pastry, thawed
little melted butter
1 jar of green or red pesto sauce
6 ripe tomatoes (firm but not under-ripe)
olive oil
fresh basil leaves, finely chopped
salt and freshly ground black pepper

1   Preheat oven to the highest it will go and set a baking sheet inside.
2   Roll pastry very thinly. Cut into four 7 in (17.5 cm) squares. With a knife, score another square 1 in (5 cm) in from the edge – not cutting right through. Prick inner squares with a fork. Mark borders lightly too and brush with a little butter.
3   Spread pesto thinly on the inside squares only. Lay tomato slices over in closely packed squares. Brush generously with oil. Season.
4   Bake for 15–20 minutes, until pastry is puffed and golden. Sprinkle basil over tomatoes. Dribble over a little more oil and serve at once.

SWEET SPANISH ONION & CHEESE TARTLETS

Serves 8

10 oz (275 g) Shortcrust Pastry (see page 16)
1 oz (25 g) butter, plus more for greasing
1 tablespoon oil
2 large Spanish onions, peeled and chopped
6 fl oz (175 ml) single cream
2 size-1 or size-2 eggs, beaten
1 level teaspoon made mustard
3 oz (75 g) mature Cheddar cheese, grated
1 oz (25 g) Parmesan cheese, grated

1   Roll out pastry thinly and cut out eight 5 in (13 cm) circles. Press into Yorkshire pudding tins which have been buttered. Set aside in fridge.
2   Melt the butter with the oil in a roomy pan and toss onions in it over a high heat for 5 minutes. Turn down heat and cook onions slowly for 20–25 minutes. Season well and let cool a little.
3   Preheat the oven to gas5/375°F/190°C.
4   Divide onions between the cases and level. Put cream, eggs and mustard in a jug and whisk well. Season and pour over the onions, not quite filling each to the brim. Sprinkle over the mixed cheese and bake for about 30 minutes. Serve warm.

PARMESAN PASTRY TARTS WITH PRAWN & EGG

Serves 6

Parmesan Pastry Tarts
3 oz (75 g) mixed butter and lard, plus more
    for greasing
6 oz (175 g) plain flour, sifted
2 teaspoons grated Parmesan cheese

Prawn & Egg Filling
4 oz (125 g) frozen prawns
1 heaped dessertspoon white flour
about ¼ pt (150 ml) milk
½ oz (15 g) butter, plus more for finishing
1 tablespoon chopped fresh parsley
6 tiny eggs (size-6), hard-boiled
salt and pepper

To make the Parmesan pastry tarts
1   Rub the fats into the flour and stir in the Parmesan cheese. Sprinkle 3–4 tablespoons cold water over the pastry crumbs and use a long-bladed knife to bind them together. Knead the pastry lightly in the bowl. Put the ball of pastry aside in a plastic bag for about 25 minutes.
2   Carefully grease Yorkshire pudding tins about 4 in (10 cm) across and ½ in (1 cm) deep with lard.
3   Cut the pastry into two pieces and roll each one out thinly. Cut out circles big enough for the tins and ease a circle of pastry into each. Prick

the pastry all over to prevent it rising. Set the tartlet cases in the fridge for about 10 minutes and preheat the oven to gas6/400°F/200°C.
4   Bake the chilled tartlet cases for 15 minutes, or until crisp and golden. Remove from the oven.

To make the prawn filling

1   Drain the prawns and reserve the liquid. Chop the prawns up, but not too small.
2   Whisk the dry flour into a generous $^1/_4$ pt (150 ml) of milk. Add the prawn liquid.
3   Cook, stirring well, over a moderate heat until the milk thickens. Add the butter, salt and pepper and the parsley. The mixture should be fairly thick, but not stiff. Add more milk if necessary.

To assemble the tarts

1   I prefer to do this by heating the pastry tartlets and the filling independently.
2   Set the warm tartlets on the serving plates. Spoon in the prawn filling. Shell the eggs and cut each one in two. Push two halves into the centre of each tart, yolks up.
3   Dot with butter and reheat briefly in the oven.
4   Serve with a few salad leaves.

BREAKFAST TARTLETS WITH SCRAMBLED EGG & BACON

Serves 2 or 3

The best way, but also the slowest way, to make perfect creamy scrambled eggs is in a bowl set in a pan of hot water – a bain-marie.

3 size-1 eggs
knob of butter
3–4 tablespoons of milk or cream
6 warm baked bread tartlets (see page 24)
3 rashers of smoked streaky bacon, grilled
    until crisp and then chopped very small
salt and pepper

1   Set a bowl in a pan of hot water. Break the eggs into it and whisk them with a fork. Add the butter and milk or cream. Stir often, scraping the egg from round the edges of the bowl. Be prepared to add a little more milk or cream if necessary. Season when creamy and set.
2   Spoon into the warmed bread tartlets and sprinkle the bacon on top. Serve at once.

HAM & PEASE PUDDING TARTS

Serves 6

7 oz (225 g) yellow split peas (soaked
    overnight)
1 small onion, peeled and chopped
1 small carrot, peeled and chopped
6 parsley stalks
1 bay leaf
1 sprig of thyme
1 small sprig of rosemary
4 oz (125 g) cooked ham or bacon scraps,
    chopped
2 oz (50 g) butter
1 small egg, beaten
6 baked shortcrust pastry tartlet cases (see
    pages 24–5, Sweet & Sour Onion Tartlets)
salt and pepper

1   Drain the split peas and tie them in a loose cloth bundle, allowing plenty of room to swell.
2   Put in a roomy pan of water with the onion, carrot and herbs. Bring to boil, then reduce heat and simmer until peas are very soft, about 2 hours. Drain peas, reserving liquid to make soup. Set meat in a warm oven, covered.
3   Put peas in a food processor and whizz until smooth, adding half the butter and the egg halfway through. Taste and adjust seasoning. Add rest of butter if mixture is too thick and pour into a dish. Set in warm oven to keep warm.
4   To serve, heat pastry cases. Spoon in warm pease pudding and top with the chopped meat.

QUICHES

A savoury quiche is endlessly useful and hugely popular. Like all pastry-based cooking, they are at their best freshly made. Storing a quiche in the fridge is hygienic, but it does the quiche no good at all unless it is given enough time to come back to room temperature before being eaten.

In the quiche recipes which follow, I recommend using flan rings, which to my mind are more useful than flan tins, but they are not quite so easy to find. The ring is greased and set on a greased baking sheet. Once cooked the ring slips off easily. You do not have to struggle to move the quiche. Another tip is to turn the baking sheet upside down and grease the underside. The quiche does not then have to slide off and over a border on the tin.

The reason for my instruction to have the empty baking sheet warming up in the oven is to help prevent that prevalent disease of quiche – soggy bottom. The flan is put straight on to the hot flat baking sheet and starts to cook at once. The idea of painting raw egg on to the bottom of each tart again is to help the pastry to stay crisp. The flan case is then returned to the oven to allow the egg white to seal the pastry and dry out.

WENSLEYDALE CHEESE & ONION QUICHE

Serves 6–9

The combination of cheese and onion is an old one for a packed lunch. One of my viewers once wrote and told me that long ago there was an onion mild enough to be eaten like an apple. He wondered if I had any idea of the variety in question. I don't, but if any of you do, please let me know.

Pastry
8 oz (225 g) Shortcrust Pastry (see page 16)

Filling
3 medium onions
1½ oz (40 g) butter, plus more for greasing
1 oz (25 g) plain white flour
¼ pt (150 ml) milk, warmed
grated nutmeg
6 oz (175 g) Wensleydale cheese, grated

1   Preheat the oven to gas7425°F/220°C. Grease with butter an 8 in (20 cm) flan tin or a flan ring set on a greased baking sheet.
2   Roll out the pastry thinly and ease it into the flan tin or the flan ring. Trim off the excess pastry. With a skewer or a sharp fork, prick the pastry all over the base and up the sides.
3   Bake blind for about 10 minutes, then lower the heat to gas5/375°F/190°C and continue baking blind for a further 5 minutes. By pricking the pastry this does stop it rising, but if it does just knock it down again with something blunt like the handle of a knife. Set aside.
4   Make the filling: peel and chop the onions fairly finely. Melt the butter in a pan and cook the onions over a high heat for the first 5 minutes. Turn the heat down a little and cook gently until they are really soft, 10 minutes.
5   Sprinkle over the flour and stir it in along with the warm milk. Continue cooking and stirring until the mixture thickens. Season with salt and pepper, nutmeg and half the cheese.
6   Pour the onion mixture into the pastry cases. Sprinkle over the rest of the cheese and bake at gas5/375°F/190°C until the topping is browned.

TRUE QUICHE LORRAINE

Serves 6–9

The true *quiche lorraine* from France is very like our own bacon-and-egg pie and the filling is just bacon, eggs and cream. No cheese and no onion. The pastry is mixed with an egg and this gives a really crisp finish.

Pastry
3 oz (75 g) unsalted butter, plus more for
    greasing
6 oz (175 g) plain flour
1 (size-1) egg

Filling
6 thin streaky bacon rashers
1 whole egg plus 3 extra egg yolks
1/2 pt (300 ml) double cream
pepper

1   Preheat the oven to gas5/375°F/190°C and put a baking sheet inside to warm up. Grease with butter an 8 in (20 cm) flan tin or a flan ring set on a greased baking sheet.
2   Make up the pastry by rubbing the butter into the flour until the mixture looks like damp breadcrumbs. Beat the egg and use that to bind the pastry together. Knead it gently then place it in a plastic bag to sit on one side for at least 30 minutes.
3   Roll out the pastry so that it is smooth and thin. Lift it on your rolling pin and ease it into the flan tin. Fit it carefully and trim off the surplus pastry. Put to chill in the fridge.
4   To prepare the filling: cut the bacon rashers into small strips and cook them in a hot dry pan until the fat runs.
5   Prick the chilled pastry base all over, then set the bacon pieces inside and season with pepper.
6   Whisk the egg and egg yolks with the double cream. Season with salt and pepper. Take the quiche flan over to the oven and set it on the hot tray. Now pour in the custard.
7   Bake for 30–40 minutes, until the filling is fairly firm. Serve at once.

ONION QUICHE WITH A WHOLEMEAL HERB PASTRY

Serves 6–9

Spanish onions are very mild and juicy and are particularly nice with Gruyère cheese.

Wholemeal Herb Pastry
3 oz (75 g) plain white flour
3 oz (75 g) plain fine wholemeal flour
1 small teaspoon finely chopped rosemary
    and thyme leaves
3 oz (75 g) butter or margarine

Filling
3 tablespoons olive oil
2 large Spanish onions, peeled and sliced
4 oz (100 g) Gruyère cheese, grated
3 eggs
1/4 pt (150 ml) single cream
freshly grated nutmeg

1   Preheat oven to gas6/400°F/200°C. Butter 9 in (23 cm) flan tin or ring on a greased baking sheet.
2   Make the pastry: mix the two flours with the herbs and add the margarine, cut into little pieces. Rub in the fat to the 'breadcrumb' stage. Add roughly 2 large tablespoons of cold water. Mix to a firm dough, cover and set aside for 30 minutes.
3   Knead and roll out the pastry on a floured board and use to line the flan tin or flan ring. Prick the pastry bottom and line it with greaseproof paper. Weight with baking beans.
4   Bake for 10 minutes. Remove paper and beans and return pastry case to the oven for 5 minutes.
5   Make the filling: heat the oil in a roomy pan and fry the onions slowly for at least 10 minutes. Allow to go cold, then spread into the flan case and top with the grated cheese.
6   Reduce the oven temperature to gas4/350°F/ 180°C. Take the flan to the oven and set it on the hot baking sheet. Whisk together the eggs, cream, salt and pepper, pour this into the flan. Grate some fresh nutmeg over the surface and bake for another 25 minutes, or until the custard is set.

FETA CHEESE & ONION QUICHE

Serves 6–9

Feta cheese is a highly salted crumbly cheese, originally from Greece. It goes particularly well with onions which have been fried long enough for the sweetness to surface.

Pastry
6 oz (175 g) plain white flour
pinch of salt
3 oz (75 g) unsalted butter, plus more for
  greasing

Filling
1 oz (25 g) sun-dried tomatoes
1 tablespoon oil
2 large onions, peeled and thinly sliced
2 teaspoons caster sugar
6 oz (175 g) Feta cheese, crumbled
2 (size-1) eggs
¼ pt (150 ml) single cream

1 Preheat the oven to gas6/400°F/200°C and put a baking sheet inside to heat up. Grease with butter an 8 in (20 cm) flan tin or a flan ring set on a greased baking sheet.
2 To make the pastry: sift the flour and salt into a bowl. Cut the butter into tiny pieces then rub into the flour. It will soon begin to look like damp breadcrumbs. Stir in just enough cold water to bring the crumbs together. Knead gently in a bowl and, when smooth, set it aside for 10–15 minutes to rest.
3 Now roll the pastry out very thinly and ease it into the flan tin and ring. Trim off the surplus and set aside in the fridge for 10 minutes.
4 Lightly prick the raw pastry and line it with a circle of greaseproof paper. Weigh this down with baking beans and bake blind for about 10 minutes. Remove the beans and the paper, then bake the pastry for 5 minutes more.
5 Pour boiling water over the sun-dried tomatoes and leave for 10 minutes.

6 Heat the oil in a frying pan, stir in the sugar then the onions. Fry gently for 5–10 minutes, stirring often, until the onions are soft.
7 Allow the onions to cool, then spread them in the pastry base. Follow that with a layer of the drained and finely chopped tomato, then the crumbled cheese. Season these ingredients with pepper only.
8 Whisk together the eggs and cream. Season with pepper and pour this into the flan. Set the tin on the hot baking sheet in the oven. Bake for 20–25 minutes until the filling is set.

MEDITERRANEAN VEGETABLE QUICHE

Serves 6–9

This quiche is based on pastry made with olive oil and enriched with an egg. You will need a traditional loose-bottomed flan tin, about 11 in (28 cm) across and quite shallow.

Olive Oil Pastry
8 oz (225 g) plain white flour, sieved
pinch of salt
4 tablespoons (60 ml) olive oil
1 egg, beaten
butter or lard, for greasing

Filling
10 oz (275 g) aubergines
1 small red pepper, cored and seeded
1 tablespoon olive oil
3 ripe but firm tomatoes
1 tablespoon mixed chopped fresh herbs
1 garlic clove, peeled and crushed
4 or 5 black olives
2 heaped teaspoons French mustard
3 egg yolks
12 fl oz (350 ml) rich milk (or milk and
  cream mixed)
6 oz (175 g) mature Cheddar cheese,
  grated
salt and pepper

1   Sieve the flour and salt into a roomy bowl. Make a well in the flour and pour in the olive oil and about 3 tablespoons of warm water.
2   Add the egg and use a fork to beat the egg and oil together with the water, gradually bringing in the flour until you have a pastry dough.
3   Use your hand to knead the dough until smooth. Set it aside covered for 20 minutes.
4   Preheat the oven to gas6/400°F/200°C and put in a baking sheet to heat up. Grease an 11 in (28 cm) shallow fluted loose-bottomed flan tin with butter or lard.
5   Roll out the pastry thinly and use to line the flan tin. Prick the pastry all over.
6   Bake for about 15 minutes. Now brush the pastry with a little of the beaten egg and continue baking for a further 5 minutes. Remove from the oven.
7   Slice the aubergines very thinly. Chop the pepper into long thin slices. Brush a big baking sheet or tray with oil and spread the aubergine on this. Cover with the slices of green pepper, dribble over a little more oil and bake in the hot oven for 20 minutes or until the vegetables are just beginning to go brown round the edges. Remove from the oven.
8   Slice the tomatoes and squeeze out the seeds and lay the slices in a layer on the bottom of the quiche. Sprinkle with half of the chopped fresh herbs and grate the garlic clove over. Now arrange the aubergine slices on top of the tomatoes and the pepper strips on top of that. Season with salt and pepper. Cut up the olives and dot these about.
9   In a jug, whisk together the mustard, egg yolks and the rich milk (or milk and cream). Season generously. Take the quiche over to the oven and sit it on the hot baking sheet. Pour the egg and milk mixture over, allowing it to sink in before adding the rest. Bake for 30 minutes.
10 Sprinkle over the rest of the herbs and the cheese and continue baking for a further 15 minutes, or until the quiche has set.
11 Serve warm or cold.

SPRING ONION & CHUNKY GAMMON QUICHE

Serves 6–9

This is a good way to use pieces of gammon from a home-boiled ham shank. You must also have good green parsley so that the finished quiche looks pink and green.

Pastry
6 oz (175 g) Shortcrust Pastry (see page 16)

Filling
1 bunch of spring onions
1 oz (25 g) butter, plus more for greasing
5–6 oz (150–175 g) cooked gammon, cut into small chunks
1 tablespoon chopped fresh green parsley
2 large eggs
1/4 pt (150 ml) stock and milk mixed (use some of the water in which the ham was boiled or 1/2 of a ham stock cube dissolved in water)

1   Preheat the oven to gas6/400°F/200°C and put in an empty baking sheet. Grease with butter an 8 in (20 cm) flan tin or a flan ring set on a greased baking sheet.
2   Roll out the pastry on a floured board and use to line the tin or ring.
3   Prepare the spring onions and chop into 1/2 in (1 cm) pieces. Melt the butter in a small pan and fry the spring onions gently until they wilt and soften. Remove from the heat.
4   Scatter the gammon chunks in the flan, follow this with the spring onion and the parsley. Grind some pepper over everything.
5   Whisk up the eggs with the stock and milk. Season with pepper. Take the quiche to the oven and set it on the hot baking sheet. Pour the savoury custard into the quiche. Bake for 20–25 minutes or until the custard is set.
6   Serve warm.

CARROT & SILKEN TOFU QUICHE

Serves 6–9

This quiche uses wholemeal flour and soya margarine.

Wholemeal Soy Pastry
8 oz (225 g) plain fine wholemeal flour
¼ teaspoon ground cumin
4 oz (125 g) soya margarine, plus more for greasing

Filling
8 oz (225 g) carrots, scraped and grated
2 oz (50 g) roasted and salted peanuts
2 tablespoons chopped fresh coriander
1 size-1 or size-2 egg, beaten
2 fl oz (50 ml) milk
6 oz (175 g) smooth tofu

1   Preheat the oven to gas5/375°F/190°C and set a baking sheet in to get hot. Grease with margarine an 8 in (20 cm) flan tin or flan ring set on a greased baking tray
2   Make the pastry: sieve the flour and cumin into a bowl and return the bran to the bowl. Rub 2 oz (50 g) of the margarine into the flour. Melt the remaining margarine and stir this into the flour with enough water to make a smooth dough. Set this aside for 20 minutes.
3   Roll out the pastry and use to line the tin or ring.
4   To make the filling: mix the carrot, peanuts, coriander and egg. Beat the milk into the tofu or pass them through a food mixer. Stir into the carrot mixture and spoon the whole lot into the flan.
5   Set the flan in the oven on the hot baking sheet and bake for about 40 minutes or until the pastry is cooked and the filling set.
6   Serve hot or cold.

QUICHE OF RED PEPPER & LEEK WITH LOW-FAT PASTRY

Serves 6–9

Low-fat Pastry
½ level teaspoon sweet paprika
4 oz (125 g) plain white flour, sieved
4 oz (125 g) fine plain wholemeal flour, sieved
2 oz (50 g) butter, warm and soft
4 fl oz (100 ml) warm water

Filling
2 tablespoons oil
2 medium red peppers, deseeded and chopped small
1 lb (500 g) young thin leeks, cleaned and topped and tailed
2 size-1 eggs, beaten
1 oz (25 g) grated Parmesan cheese
½ pt (300 ml) milk
salt and pepper

1   Put a baking sheet in the oven and preheat to gas4/350°F/180°C/. Butter a 9 in (23 cm) flan tin or flan ring set on a greased baking sheet.
2   Make the pastry: mix the paprika with the sieved flours. Use a fork to mix in the soft butter and warm water. Mix to a soft dough. Wrap this up and set it aside for 15 minutes.
3   Make the filling: heat the oil in a small pan and cook peppers gently until soft (10 minutes or so). Season well and purée with a stick blender.
4   Cut leeks into 1 in (2 cm) lengths. Cook in boiling salted water for 5 minutes. Drain.
5   Roll out the pastry so that it is smooth and thin. Lift it on your rolling pin and ease it into the flan tin. Fit it carefully and trim off the surplus pastry. Prick with a fork.
6   Bake the pastry case blind for 10 minutes, then reduce the heat slightly. Spread the pepper purée in the bottom and top with the leeks. These look better if you can manage to get them to sit up on their ends. Whisk the eggs with the Parmesan and milk. Pour over the vegetables.
7   Bake for about 25 minutes until set.

SPINACH & BACON QUICHE

Serves 6–9

This quiche uses shortcrust pastry. Fresh spinach is best for this recipe, but a packet of frozen and thawed whole leaves (as opposed to chopped) will do almost as well. Cook the fresh washed leaves by melting a knob of butter in a small pan. Fold and twist the spinach leaves to fit in the pan. Crush the lid on and cook and shake the spinach for about 3 minutes. Chop the leaves roughly. I find this easier if I put the spinach leaves in a narrow jug, then use my scissors.

Pastry
6 oz (175 g) Shortcrust Pastry (see page 16)
butter or lard, for greasing

Filling
4 oz (125 g) lean cooked bacon
1 lb (450 g) fresh spinach leaves (or frozen),
    drained and chopped as above
2 (size-1) eggs, beaten
2 Baby Bel cheeses (tiny round cheese with
    a red coating which comes away easily)
¼ pt (150 ml) single cream
generous grating of nutmeg
salt and pepper

1   Preheat the oven to gas5/375°F/190°C and place a baking sheet inside.
2   Roll out pastry thinly. Grease an 8 in (20 cm) flan tin or a flan ring set on a greased sheet. Line the tin carefully with the pastry, easing it in and pushing down into the sides. Trim off excess pastry and set flan in the fridge.
3   Fry or grill bacon and cut it into pieces. When it is cold, arrange pieces in the bottom of pastry case. Drain the spinach of most of the moisture and layer on top of the bacon. Season.
4   Whisk the eggs into the cream and pour over.
5   Take the red wax covering from the Baby Bels and slice them thinly horizontally. Set them over the top. Grate the nutmeg over the top.
6   Bake the quiche for about 35–40 minutes.

WILD MUSHROOM & PESTO PASTRY TART

Serves 6–9

If you are lucky enough to live where you can gather mushrooms for free this recipe will show off their rich flavour beautifully. Almost any kind of mushroom will do or just mix two or three varieties. Pesto is a famous sauce for pasta and can be bought in jars, it is a mixture of basil, pine kernels, Parmesan cheese and olive oil.

Pesto Pastry
3 oz (75 g) butter, plus more for greasing
6 oz (175 g) plain white flour sifted
1 teaspoon ready–made pesto sauce

Filling
8 oz (225 g) wild or cultivated mushrooms
1½ oz (40 g) butter
2 (size-1) eggs
just over ¼ pt (150 ml) double cream
2 oz (50 g) freshly grated Parmesan cheese
pinch of cayenne pepper
salt and pepper

1   Make the pastry: rub the butter into the flour. Put pesto in a jug with a very small amount of cold water. Use to bind to a smooth dough. Knead gently and set aside for 20 minutes.
2   Roll out the pastry thinly on a floured board. Line a greased 8 in (20 cm) flan tin or flan ring set on a greased baking sheet. Fit the pastry neatly, pressing into the bottom of the border. Trim off the excess pastry by running a rolling pin over the top of the edges. Set the flan in the fridge.
3   Preheat the oven to gas5/375°F/180°C and place a metal baking sheet to heat up inside.
4   Make the filling: wipe and chop the mushrooms. Melt the butter in a frying pan and fry the mushrooms very briefly. Drain them well, season and set them in the flan.
5   Whisk the eggs with the cream and the cheese, reserving about one teaspoon of cheese. Season with some salt, pepper and cayenne. Pour into the flan and sprinkle the reserved cheese on top.
6   Bake for about 40 minutes.

ARBROATH SMOKIE TART WITH OLIVE OIL PASTRY

Serves 6–9

Pastry
8 oz (225 g) Olive Oil Pastry (see
   Mediterranean Vegetable Quiche, page 30)

Filling
1 pair of medium Arbroath smokies
3 size-1 eggs
12 fl oz (350 ml) milk and cream mixed
white pepper
1 tablespoon chopped fresh parsley

1   Make the pastry as instructed on page 30.
Follow the instructions for making a 10–11 in
(25–27 cm) baked pastry shell. Leave the oven at
gas6/400°F/200°C.
2   Gently open out the smokies and remove as
much flesh as possible without bones. Break the
flesh up a little and spread it over the base of the
flan case (which should still be sitting in its tin).
3   Whisk the eggs into the milk and cream
mixture and season with pepper only, stir in the
parsley. Pour over the smokie flesh and stop short
of filling the flan to the brim. Set flan on the hot
baking sheet and pour in remaining custard.
4   Bake for about 30–40 minutes or until the
custard is set. Serve warm.

'The cook was a good cook, as cooks go;
and as cooks go, she went.'

Reginald on Besetting Sins, Saki

YOGHURT & ZUCCHINI QUICHE

Serves 6–9

Zucchini are, of course, what the Italians and
Americans call courgettes!

Pastry
8 oz (225 g) Shortcrust Pastry (see page 16)

Filling
1¼ lb (625 g) young courgettes
little oil
3 size-1 eggs
½ pt (300 ml) natural yoghurt
3 oz (75 g) grated Parmesan cheese
nutmeg
1 tablespoon brown breadcrumbs
salt and pepper

1   Preheat the oven to gas6/400°F/200°C.
Grease an 8 in (20 cm) flan tin or a flan ring
sitting on a greased baking sheet.
2   First roll out the pastry and use to line the
flan tin or flan ring. Trim the pastry with
scissors, leaving the pastry standing up beyond
the rim of the tin a little. Prick the pastry base
all over with a skewer or a sharp fork.
3   Set the flan on the hot baking sheet in the
oven and bake blind for 10–15 minutes. The
pastry should be set but not coloured. Remove
from the oven and set aside.
4   Make the filling: wipe the courgettes and top
and tail them. Cut into long strips and then into
chunky pieces. Heat a little oil in a roomy frying
pan and toss in the courgettes. Fry over a high
heat, stirring frequently. Season with salt and
pepper. Do not allow the courgettes to go soggy.
Drain in a nylon sieve and set aside.
5   Whisk the eggs into the yoghurt and stir in
half of the cheese. Set the courgettes in the pastry
case and pour the egg and milk mixture over.
Grate some nutmeg over the top and scatter with
the remaining cheese and the breadcrumbs.
6   Set the flan tin on the hot baking sheet again
and bake for about 30–40 minutes or until the
custard is set and golden.

TARRAGON, CREAM CHEESE & COURGETTE QUICHE

Serves 6–9

This is another quiche made with shortcrust pastry.

Tarragon is a herb which marries perfectly with a cream cheese. To strip the long thin leaves from the stem, run your thumb and forefinger down the stalk from top to bottom. Hold on to the leaves tightly and then snip them into the bowl. The very young growth can be used stalks and all, since they are soft. Hard stems are still a good source of flavour, but remember to retrieve them before you are finished.

Courgettes are usually very wet, so having steamed them it is worthwhile to dry them with kitchen roll.

Pastry
6 oz (175 g) Shortcrust Pastry (see page 16)

Filling
2 large firm wrinkle-free courgettes (about 1½ lb / 675 g)
8 oz (225 g) cream cheese (drained if wet)
1 tablespoon chopped fresh tarragon
¼ pt (150 ml) milk
3 large (size-1) eggs
salt and pepper

1 Preheat the oven to gas7/425°F/220°C and place a baking sheet inside. You will need a shallow flan tin measuring about 9–10 in (23–25 cm) across.
2 Make the shortcrust pastry as instructed on page 16. Give it a rest for about 30 minutes, then roll it out fairly thinly. Lift it over the flan tin on the rolling pin and try to drop it in the middle. These shallow tins have very sharp edges so you may have to do a patching job. Trim off the overlapping edges.
3 Prick the pastry all over with a skewer or fork, set the flan tin on the hot baking sheet and bake for 15–20 minutes. Then take a little egg white from your eggs and paint the inside of the pastry case. Set the flan tin back in the oven for just 4–5 minutes. Take it out of the oven and allow it to cool down.
4 To prepare the filling: first wipe the courgettes and then top and tail them. Cut into ½ in (1 cm) slices, then chop each slice into four. Set the pieces and the chopped tarragon stems in a steamer over a pan of simmering water for 6–7 minutes. The chunks are better if they stay fairly firm. Lift the pieces into a sieve and leave to drain and cool.
5 To make up the rich custard, put the cream cheese into a bowl and beat it until creamy. Then add the milk a little at a time and follow this with the beaten eggs and the tarragon. Season well with salt and pepper.
6 Dry off the courgettes, discard the tarragon stalks and set the courgettes in the pastry case, which is still sitting in the flan tin. Pour the savoury custard over, stopping short at filling quite to the brim. Set the tin back in the oven on the hot baking sheet and pour in the rest of the custard.
7 Bake at a slightly lower temperature for about 30–40 minutes, or until the custard has set. Allow to cool down a little before serving.

SMOKY BACON & SHREDDED LEEK QUICHE

Serves 6–9

Pastry
3 oz (75 g) wholewheat flour
3 oz (75 g) plain white flour
3 oz (75 g) mixed butter and lard
salt and pepper

Filling
about 5 big leeks
5 slices of smoked streaky bacon, grilled
and cut into pieces
4 size-3 eggs, beaten
$\frac{1}{2}$ pt (300 ml) milk (or milk and single cream)
knob of butter
1 tablespoon grated mature Cheddar cheese

1   First make the pastry in the usual way. Mix the two flours, season lightly and rub in the two fats. Use cold water to sprinkle over and a long knife to stir and press the crumbs together. Now use your hand to gather up all the flour so that the bowl is clean. Knead the pastry gently then set the ball aside to rest for about 30 minutes.
2   Preheat the oven to gas4/375°F/180°C (wholewheat pastry is better in a not-too-hot oven) and grease a 10 in (25 cm) shallow flan tin.
3   Roll the pastry out thinly and carefully use to line the tin. Trim off excess pastry. Prick all over with a skewer or sharp fork.
4   Set the tin on the hot baking sheet and bake for about 15 minutes. Take the flan out and brush some of the egg white from your beaten eggs all over the pastry. Set the flan back in the oven for another 5–6 minutes. Remove the tin from the oven and turn the temperature up a little.
5   Prepare filling: clean the leeks and cut each down lengthwise and then across into 3 in (7.5 cm) strips. Shred each strip of leek lengthwise. Set the shredded leeks in a steamer over a pan of simmering water. Allow them to become soft, then remove from the steamer and let cool.

6   Lay the shredded and steamed leeks in the flan case (it should still be in its tin). Season well and scatter the bacon pieces on top.
7   Whisk the eggs into the milk or milk and cream. Pour over the filling, stopping short of the brim. Lift the flan over to the oven and place on the hot baking sheet. Top up with any remaining custard, add the butter and sprinkle over the cheese.
8   Bake for a further 30–40 minutes, or until the custard has just set. Serve warm.

LEMON CHICKEN WHOLEWHEAT QUICHE

Serves 6–9

Wholewheat Pastry
3 oz (75 g) butter and vegetable fats mixed
8 oz (225 g) wholemeal flour
1 teaspoon soft brown sugar
pinch of salt
pinch of baking powder
$\frac{1}{2}$ teaspoon dry mustard
1 teaspoon oil

Filling
1 small onion, peeled and finely chopped
1 tablespoon oil
1 oz (25 g) plain flour
7 oz (190 g) can of sweetcorn
$\frac{1}{4}$ pt (150 ml) milk
$\frac{1}{2}$ chicken stock cube (optional)
4 oz (125 g) chopped cooked chicken
grated rind and juice of 1 lemon
2–3 tablespoons cream
2 oz (50 g) grated mature Cheddar cheese
salt and pepper

1   Preheat the oven to gas6/400°F/200°C and put a baking sheet inside. Grease an 8 in (20 cm) flan tin or a flan ring set on a greased metal sheet.
2   Make the pastry: rub the fats into the flour or put them in a food processor and whizz together. Add the sugar, salt, baking powder and mustard.

3   Mix in 4 fl oz (125 ml) of water and the oil. This will look very wet at first, but gradually the flour swells to give a manageable dough. Roll out about two-thirds and use to line the greased flan tin or flan ring. Press dough well into the angle and trim off the extra. Set in the fridge to firm up for a few minutes, then prick pastry all over.

4   Place flan case on the hot baking sheet and bake blind for 20 minutes. Remove from oven.

5   Make the filling: fry the onion in the oil until it is soft but not brown. Shake the flour, salt and pepper over the hot onion and stir for about 1 minute. Add the liquid drained from the tin of sweetcorn to the milk and gradually stir this into the flour and onion mixture. Bring to the boil and cook for about 2 minutes. Take this sauce off the heat and taste it. If the chicken taste is not strong enough you could crumble half of a chicken stock cube into the sauce. Stir in well and add the drained sweetcorn, chicken, lemon juice and rind and cream. Season with pepper and pour into the baked flan case. Sprinkle over the cheese.

6   Return the flan to the moderately hot oven, set it on the hot baking sheet and bake for a further 15 minutes or so. It is good both hot and cold.

RED PEPPER & TOMATO SKINNY QUICHE

Serves 6–9

Red peppers taste so much better once they have been roasted and they also retain their brilliant colour.

This is just a flat pastry with a double edge and made for instant eating – really a pizza, but with a herb-flavoured pastry base.

Herb Pastry

3 oz (75 g) margarine and white vegetable fat mixed, plus more for greasing
6 oz (175 g) plain flour, sieved, plus more for dusting
1 teaspoon mixed dried herbs
1 fat pinch of fresh thyme leaves
1 fat pinch of dried oregano

Filling

2 large red peppers (about ³/₄ lb / 350 g)
1 medium onion, peeled and finely chopped
1 tablespoon oil, plus more for greasing
15 oz (425 g) can chopped Italian tomatoes
1 tablespoon tomato purée
2 large teaspoons sugar
1 garlic clove, peeled and crushed
1 pinch of fennel seeds
1 size-1 egg, beaten
salt

1   Make the pastry: rub the fats into the sieved flour until it looks like damp sand. Stir in the herbs. Sprinkle a little cold water on top, stir and press the mixture with a long-bladed knife. Now use your hands to gather the dough together and knead it lightly. Set the pastry aside covered for about 20 minutes.

2   Preheat the oven to gas4/350°F/180°C.

3   Sprinkle flour on a flat surface and have ready a greased heavy baking sheet. Roll the pastry out to a neat circle or rectangle, with the pastry about 1/8 in (3 mm) thick. Paint a narrow strip all round the edge with water. Turn the pastry back on itself to make a thick edge and press it down to stick together. Pinch this wall all round with two fingers to make a scalloped edge. Prick the pastry all over with a sharp skewer.

4   Bake for about 20 minutes, or until the pastry is golden. Remove from the oven.

5   Make the filling: put the two red peppers in the hot oven until their skins look blistered and starting to go dark brown and black. Take the peppers out of the oven and allow them to cool.

6   In a roomy pan, fry the onions in the oil until soft. Add the tomatoes, tomato purée, sugar, garlic and fennel seeds. Stir well and cook over a low heat until the consistency becomes jam-like and very thick.

7   Peel the skins from the roasted peppers and chop the flesh (this is a messy job). Add this to the tomato mixture and cook again until the mixture is as thick as before. Season and stir in the beaten egg and spread thickly over the pastry.

8   Bake in the hot oven until heated through and set. Serve warm.

LANARK BLUE CHEESE & CHIVE QUICHE

Serves 6–9

Lanark Blue cheese is Scotland's answer to the famous French Roquefort. The man who makes it, in the hills north of Biggar, gave me some to try at the Highland Show in Edinburgh where I was demonstrating. I melted just 2 oz (50 g) of the cheese in a little white wine and after taking the pan away from the heat, I stirred in a little cream. The rich sauce was then poured over some freshly cooked penne pasta with a tablespoon of chopped parsley. It was delicious.

Pastry
12 oz (325 g) Shortcrust Pastry (see page 16)
butter or lard, for greasing

Filling
1 tablespoon oil
6 shallots, finely chopped
6 oz (175 g) strongly flavoured cheese, such as Lanark Blue
1 large tablespoon chopped chives
2 eggs plus 2 extra yolks
1 pt (600 ml) milk
salt and pepper

1   Grease a 10 in (25 cm) shallow flan tin about 2 in (5 cm) deep. Roll out the pastry on a lightly floured board and use to line the flan tin, working the pastry well into the baseline. Prick all over and chill for 30 minutes.
2   Preheat the oven to gas6/400°F/200°C with a large baking sheet in it.
3   Set the flan tin on the hot baking sheet and bake blind for about 20 minutes. Remove from the oven and allow to cool, but do not remove from the tin.
4   Make the filling: heat the oil in a frying pan and fry the shallots until soft. Set aside to cool.
5   Spread the cooked shallots in the bottom of the flan. Crumble or chop the cheese into tiny bits and add this to the flan too with about half of the chives.
6   Beat together the eggs, extra yolks, milk and

seasoning. Pour into the case, but do not fill the flan up to the brim. Hold some back and after you have taken the flan to the oven and put it on the hot sheet add a little more custard and sprinkle with the remaining chives.
7   Finally bake again for 20 minutes, until the filling is set and lightly coloured.

MUSHROOM & ANCHOVY SQUARE WITH PAPRIKA PASTRY

Serves 6–9

This recipe was sent to me ages ago and I do think that the anchovy with the mushrooms is a fine and unusual combination.

Paprika Pastry
6 oz (175 g) plain white flour
pinch of salt
1/2 teaspoon paprika
fat pinch of mustard powder
3 oz (75 g) butter or margarine

Filling
1 medium onion, peeled and finely chopped
1–2 tablespoons oil
8 oz (225 g) firm button mushrooms, wiped and halved
4 oz (125 g) red cheese grated
1 small can (2 oz / 50 g) anchovy fillets, drained and rinsed
3 size-1 eggs, beaten
1/2 pt (300 ml) single cream
1/4 pt (150 ml) milk
pepper

1   Preheat the oven to gas6/400°F/200°C. Put a large baking sheet in the oven to heat up.
2   Make the pastry: sift the flour, salt, paprika and mustard powder into a roomy bowl. Rub in the butter or margarine until it resembles breadcrumbs. Sprinkle over just enough cold water to make a soft dough. Cover and let the

pastry cool for about 15 minutes.

3   Line a large flat baking sheet or roasting tin (12x8x1½ in / 30.5x20x4 cm) with foil. Roll out the pastry to a large square to fit in the tin, taking it up the sides a little. Prick the pastry all over to stop it rising.

4   Set on the hot baking sheet in the oven and bake for about 20 minutes in all. If during the baking any surface bubbles appear, just pat them down again. Remove the pastry square tin and allow to cool.

5   To prepare the filling: fry the onions in the oil for about 8 minutes until soft. Add the mushrooms and cook for a further minute.

6   Drain off as much liquid as possible, then spread the mixture over the pastry base. Sprinkle over the cheese.

7   Blend the anchovies, eggs, cream, milk and pepper in a liquidizer or processor. Pour this mixture over the filling.

8   Bake for 30–40 minutes or until set. Leave to cool in the tin.

9   To turn out the quiche, run a knife around the edge of the tin to loosen the square. Cut into neat squares.

SMOKED SALMON QUICHE WITH LEMON PASTRY

Serves 6–9

This is a large flattish oblong quiche, to cut into squares or fingers. Look out for smoked salmon trimmings which are ideal for this recipe – cheaper too.

Lemon Pastry
6 oz (175 g) plain white flour
3 oz (75 g) margarine or butter, plus more
    for greasing
finely grated rind from 1 lemon

Filling
3 size-1 eggs, beaten
¼ pt (150 ml) sour cream
¼ pt (150 ml) milk

¼ pt (150 ml) **whipping cream**
2 tablespoons **chopped fresh parsley**
8 oz (225 g) **smoked salmon trimmings**
4 oz (125 g) **peeled cooked prawns**
    (defrosted and drained if frozen)
salt and pepper

1   Preheat the oven to gas6/400°F/200°C. Put a baking sheet in the oven to get hot. Grease a roasting tin or baking tin with sides measuring about 12x8x1½ in (30.5 x 20x4 cm) and line it with greased foil.

2   Make the pastry: sift the flour into a bowl, rub in the margarine or butter until the mixture looks like breadcrumbs. Stir in the lemon rind and enough cold water to make a softish dough. Set the pastry aside in a cool place covered.

3   Roll out the pastry and use to line the prepared tin, taking the pastry up the sides. Prick the pastry base all over with a sharp fork or a skewer.

4   Stand the tin on the hot baking sheet and bake the pastry blind for 10 minutes. Take the pastry tin out and brush a thin covering of beaten egg over the pastry. Return it to the oven for a further 10 minutes. Turn the oven temperature down to gas5/375°F/190°C.

5   Make the filling: whisk the eggs into the sour cream and then pour in the milk and whipping cream. Stir in the parsley and season with salt and pepper.

6   Cut the smoked salmon into pieces and arrange with the prawns on the pastry base (still in the tin). Pour over the milk and cream mixture.

7   Bake for 40–45 minutes, or until the savoury custard has set. Leave to cool in the tin.

8   When very cold, run a knife round the outside of the quiche to loosen it. Turn it out on a wooden board and cut into squares or fingers.

CAERPHILLY WHOLEMEAL QUICHE WITH SHALLOTS

Serves 6–9

This Welsh cheese is mild and creamy and a good partner for wholemeal pastry. Use a food processor for the pastry if you have one.

Pastry
4¹/₂ oz (135 ml) butter and solid vegetable fat mixed, plus more for greasing
8 oz (225 g) plain wholemeal flour, plus more for dusting
4 oz (125 g) self-raising white flour
³/₄ oz (20 g) soft brown sugar
pinch of salt
2 teaspoons oil

Filling
1 tablespoon oil
6 shallots, peeled and finely chopped
1 garlic clove, peeled and finely chopped
1 tablespoon chopped fresh parsley
1 tablespoon chopped fresh chives
10 oz (275 g) Caerphilly cheese, cubed
2 eggs, plus 2 extra yolks
1 pt (600 ml) milk
¹/₄ teaspoon grated nutmeg
salt and pepper

1   Preheat the oven to gas6/400°F/200°C. Grease a 10 in (25 cm) flan tin, about 2 in (5 cm) deep.
2   Make the pastry: rub the fats into the mixed flours or use a food processor. Stir in the sugar and salt. Add ¹/₄ pt (150 ml) water and the oil and mix to a fairly wet dough. If it looks just too sloppy, leave the dough aside for 10–20 minutes and it will soon absorb the water.
3   Roll out on a lightly floured board and use to line the flan tin. Trim away excess pastry. Prick the pastry all over with a skewer or a fork.
4   Set the flan tin on the hot baking sheet and bake for about 20 minutes. Keep a careful eye on the pastry and if any bubbles appear just pat them down again. Set aside to cool.

5   Make filling: heat the oil in a frying pan and fry the shallots and garlic very gently for 10–15 minutes, or until shallots are soft. Leave to cool.
6   Spread the cooled onions and garlic in the bottom of the pastry case, then top with half of the herbs and the Caerphilly cubes.
7   Whisk together the eggs, egg yolks, milk, nutmeg and seasoning. Pour into the pastry case, stopping short of brim. Sprinkle the rest of the herbs over and carry the flan to the oven. Set it on the hot baking sheet. Pour in the remaining custard.
8   Bake for about 20 minutes, or until set. Serve warm.

GRUYÈRE & SPINACH QUICHE WITH RICH BUTTER PASTRY

Serves 8

This quiche is based on a recipe by Mary Berry, which she made in her Aga cooker. It was delicious and colourful.

Rich Butter Pastry
4 oz (125 g) hard butter, cut into pieces, plus more for greasing
8 oz (225 g) plain white flour
1 egg yolk
3 tablespoons ice-cold water

Filling
12 oz (325 g) smoked bacon or bacon pieces
little oil
10 oz (275 g) onions, peeled and chopped
12 oz (325 g) fresh spinach (or a packet of frozen spinach leaves, defrosted and very well drained)
4 size-1 eggs plus white of 1 extra egg (left over from pastry)
1 pt (575 ml) milk and double cream, mixed
knob of butter
7 oz (200 g) Gruyère cheese, grated
salt and pepper

1   Preheat the oven to gas7/425°F/220°C and
put in a metal baking sheet. Grease an ovenproof
dish or a large flan ring approximately 13x10 in
(33x25 cm) and with sides at least 2 in (5 cm)
deep, set on a greased baking sheet.
2   Make the pastry: rub the butter into the flour
until the mixture looks like damp breadcrumbs.
Using a long-bladed knife, mix in the egg yolk
and the water. Stir and press the 'crumbs'
together, then gather the pastry in your hands
and work it around a few times to make it
smooth. A sprinkle of dry flour often helps at
this point. Set the pastry aside in a cool place.
3   Now cover a pastry board in flour and roll out
the pastry so it is big enough to fit the tin or
dish. Lift the pastry up on your rolling pin and
drop it into the centre of your dish or flan ring.
Ease it gently into the angle at the base of the
quiche and press the pastry carefully to the sides.
Set this in the fridge to chill.
4   Now prepare the filling: grill the bacon and
chop it into smallish pieces. Allow to cool. Pour
any bacon fat into a roomy pan, add a spot of oil
and fry the onion until soft and melting. Put all
the rinsed spinach in a steamer on top of the
onion in a steamer and steam it until it wilts
(this happens quite quickly). Take a large pair of
scissors and chop the spinach into pieces. Season
with pepper. Drain off as much liquid as
possible.
5   Whisk the eggs, egg white, cream and milk
mixture and a tablespoon of the Gruyère in a jug.
Spread the bacon over the pastry base and top
with the spinach and onion mixture. Level this
off. Pour the milk and egg mixture over, but stop
short of the brim.
6   Now return the dish to the oven and set it on
the hot baking sheet. Pour over the rest of the
milky mixture, add the butter and scatter the
grated cheese on top. Bake for 10–12 minutes at
the high temperature setting, then turn down
the heat a little to complete the cooking. The
pastry should look pale golden and the filling
just set and no more. Do not overcook.
7   Serve hot or cold.

Broccoli Florets in a Low-fat Pastry

Serves 6–9

Low-fat Pastry
4 oz (125 g) plain white flour, sieved
4 oz (125 g) fine plain wholemeal flour
2 oz (50 g) soft butter, plus more for
   greasing

Filling
8 oz (225 g) broccoli florets
3 size-1 eggs
just under ½ pt (300 ml) milk
1 tablespoon chopped chives
3 oz (75 g) Cheddar cheese, grated

1   Make the pastry: mix the flours in a bowl and
use a fork at the start to mix in the soft butter and
4 fl oz (100 ml) water to a soft dough. Put dough
in a plastic bag and set aside for 15 minutes.
2   Preheat the oven to gas4/350°F/180°C and
put a baking sheet in the oven to heat up. Grease
an 8–9 inch (20–23 cm) flan tin or flan ring set
on a greased baking sheet.
3   Roll out the pastry on a lightly floured board
until it is thin. Lift it on your rolling pin and
ease it into the flan tin, taking great care to avoid
stretching. Trim off surplus pastry. Press the
pastry firmly into the sides of the tin. Now prick
the pastry all over with a skewer or sharp fork
and set it in the fridge to firm up.
4   To bake, set the tin on top of the hot tray in
the oven and bake blind for about 10 minutes.
Remove the flan tin from the oven.
5   Make the filling: plunge the broccoli florets into
boiling salted water and simmer for 3 minutes.
Drain well. When cool set them in pastry case.
6   Whisk the eggs with the milk and stir in the
chives and almost all the grated cheese, save a
tablespoon. Pour this mixture over the broccoli
in the pastry case, stopping short at filling right
to the brim. Take the flan and set it again on the
hot baking sheet. Fill up to the brim and scatter
the reserved cheese over.
7   Bake for a further 30–35 minutes, or until
the custard has set. Serve warm.

SAVOURY MUFFINS

Muffins, especially savoury ones, are fairly new to this country. They come from America. They are quickly made and puff up well, due to a large proportion of raising agent in them.

ONION MUFFINS

Makes 12

1 medium onion, peeled and finely chopped
1 oz (25 g) butter, plus more for greasing
1 tablespoon oil
4 oz (125 g) white flour
5 oz (150 g) fine cornmeal
1 tablespoon baking powder
1/2 teaspoon salt
8 fl oz (250 ml) milk
1 size-2 egg, beaten
1 oz (25 g) melted butter

1   You will need a deep muffin tin with 12 indentations. Grease these thoroughly with butter and if you have muffin paper cases, which are very much deeper than normal bun tin papers, set one in each.
2   First cook the onion: melt the butter with the oil in a pan. Add the finely chopped onion and fry gently until the onion is cooked and soft, about 8-10 minutes. Drain and set aside.
3   Preheat the oven to gas7/425°F/225°C.
4   Sift into one bowl the white flour, cornmeal, baking powder and salt. Put the milk, egg and melted butter into another bowl. Using a large spatula, fold the two together, adding the onion as you go.
5   Spoon this mixture into the tins, until each indentation or cup is just over half full.
6   Bake in the oven for about 25 minutes. Eat as soon as possible.

SWEETCORN & BACON MUFFINS

Makes 12

These buns are good for breakfast and are excellent with soup.

4 oz (125 g) fine cornmeal
5 oz (150 g) plain flour
1 teaspoon sugar
1 tablespoon baking powder
1 size-1 egg, beaten
8 fl oz (250 ml) milk and water mixed
4 rashers of streaky smoked bacon, grilled
    and chopped very finely
1 1/2 oz (40 g) sweetcorn kernels, cooked and
    drained
salt and pepper
lard or butter, for greasing

1   Preheat the oven to gas7/425°F/220°C. You will need a muffin tray with about 12 holes to make the muffins. Grease each with lard or butter and set a muffin paper inside each indentation.
2   Stir together the cornmeal, flour, sugar, baking powder, salt and pepper. In a large bowl, whisk the egg into the milk or milk and water.
3   Using a spatula, fold the dry ingredients into the egg and milk mixture, adding the bacon and sweetcorn last.
4   Spoon this mixture into the muffin papers, filling them just over half full.
5   Bake for about 20 minutes. Put a metal skewer into a bun to check that they are fully cooked: the skewer should come out clean.

BAKED SAMOSAS

Samosas are traditionally deep-fried triangles of thin crisp pastry with a spicy filling, usually of potatoes and peas. However, we have fallen in love with these tasty morsels from India and fill them with all sorts of other modern mixtures. The most unusual samosa I ever had was in a wonderful Scottish butcher's shop in Dunfermline. This go-ahead chap employed a young Indian lady who made proper deep-fried samosas for him, stuffed with haggis! Honestly, they could not have been nicer. Crisply baked or fried samosas are usually served with a dip or a relish. These dips are always freshly made and not intended to be as long-keeping as our relishes and pickles. Recipes for several such relishes are given at the end of the section.

GREEN SAMOSAS

Makes about 25

I use only the broccoli florets for this recipe. Cut off the stems and use them in a vegetable stir-fry.

Pastry
1 lb (450 g) packet filo pastry, thawed
2–3 tablespoons vegetable oil
4 oz (100 g) butter, melted

Filling
½ pt (300 ml) milk
2 oz (50 g) plain flour
1 oz (25 g) butter
4 oz (125 g) frozen spinach, defrosted, lightly cooked in hot butter, drained and chopped
2 oz (50 g) broccoli florets, steamed and chopped
3 oz (75 g) cream cheese
3 oz (75 g) Cheddar cheese, grated
salt and pepper

1 Preheat the oven to gas5/375°F/190°C.
2 Make filling: put milk into a pan and whisk flour into it while it is still cold. When the flour has dispersed, turn on heat. Stir constantly with a wooden spoon until mixture thickens. Drop in the butter. Taste to see if the flour taste is no more, then take off heat. Stir in seasoning, vegetables and cheeses. Beat well then let cool.
3 Melt the 4 oz (125 g) butter in the microwave and stir in the oil.
4 Unwrap the filo pastry and immediately cover with a dampened tea towel. Separate the sheets and brush them one at a time with the butter and oil mixture, then cut it into 3-in (7.5-cm) wide strips. Put one fat teaspoon of mixture on a bottom corner then fold the strip over the mixture to form a triangle. Keep folding and you will reach the end of the strip. Repeat this over and over again until all the filling is used up.
5 Set on a greased baking tray. Brush all over again with the oil and butter. Bake for 8–9 minutes, or until the pastry has browned nicely.
6 Serve warm, with one or more dips.

SPICED POTATO & PEA SAMOSAS

Makes about 25

Pastry
4 sheets of filo pastry
2–3 tablespoons vegetable oil
4 oz (100 g) butter, melted

Filling
8 oz (225 g) freshly cooked and mashed potato
1 teaspoon mustard seed
1 teaspoon cumin seeds
2 oz (50 g) cooked green peas
1/4 green chilli, deseeded and finely chopped
1 tablespoon chopped fresh coriander
1 teaspoon brown sugar
1 tablespoon chopped cashew nuts

1   Preheat the oven to gas5/375°F/190°C.
2   Make the filling: heat a non-stick frying pan and roast the cumin and mustard seeds. Shake a lot and remove from the heat quickly. Let cool. Stir in the other ingredients.
3   Melt the butter for the pastry and stir in the oil. Make the pastry strips as in the previous recipe and brush all over with the butter and oil mixture.
4   Take a large teaspoon of the mixture and set it in one corner of the strip. Fold pastry over to form a triangle. Go on doing this, folding to the end of the strip. Repeat until all mixture is used.
5   Lay on greased baking sheet and brush with oil and butter. Bake for 8–10 minutes or until crisp.

CURRIED POTATO & CORIANDER SAMOSAS

Makes about 25

Pastry
4 sheets of filo pastry
2–3 tablespoons vegetable oil
4 oz (100 g) butter, melted

Filling
1 lb (450 g) waxy potatoes, boiled whole, peeled and chopped into 1/4 in (5 mm) cubes
2 level tablespoons mild curry paste
1 tablespoon chopped fresh or 1 teaspoon dried mint
1 tablespoon chopped coriander

1   Preheat the oven to gas5/375°F/190°C.
2   Mix all the filling ingredients together and set aside for an hour to allow the flavours to develop.
3   Melt the butter and stir in the oil.
4   Unwrap pastry and cover with a damp cloth. Separate 1 sheet at a time, brush with the oil and butter mixture then cut into 3 in (7.5 cm) strips.
5   Put one fat teaspoon of potato mixture on a bottom corner of one strip. Fold this over to form a triangle, enclosing the curried potato. Go on folding over and over until you reach the end of the strip. Repeat until all the filling is used up.
6   Set on a greased baking tray and brush them all over with the butter and oil. Bake for about 8–9 minutes or until the pastry is brown and crisp.

YOGHURT & MINT RELISH

Natural yoghurt is also nice with chopped chives.

3 tablespoons natural yoghurt
1 tablespoon chopped fresh mint

Stir together yoghurt and mint and let stand for 1 hour before use to allow the flavours to develop.

SAVOURY YOGHURT DIP

1 small garlic clove, peeled
1/4 pt (150 ml) natural yoghurt (a small carton)
2 tablespoons freshly chopped mint
1 tablespoon lemon juice
1 tablespoon olive oil
salt and white pepper

1   Using the flat side of a blade pressed down on the clove, crush the garlic with a sprinkling of salt on a wooden board. Press hard and pull aside.
2   Mix all the dressing ingredients together, then allow to stand and develop flavour.

RAITA (CUCUMBER AND YOGHURT RELISH)

$^1/_2$ small cucumber
1 garlic clove, crushed
$^1/_4$ pt (150 ml) natural yoghurt (a small carton)
2 fat spring onions
salt and pepper

1   Wipe and trim the cucumber and dice small. Sprinkle with salt and leave in a nylon strainer for 1 hour. Dry with kitchen paper.
2   Put cucumber in a bowl and stir in the garlic and yoghurt.
3   Slice the spring onions very, very thinly and add to the mixture with some pepper.

CUCUMBER CHUTNEY

$^1/_2$ small cucumber
$^1/_4$ pt (150 ml) natural yoghurt (a small carton)
1 tablespoon mango chutney preserve (without any lumps)
pinch of chilli powder (use the tip of a spoon handle, do not touch with your finger)
salt and pepper

1   Wipe and chop the cucumber and sprinkle with salt. Set it to drain in a nylon sieve for 1 hour. Dry off as much as you can with kitchen paper.
2   Stir all the ingredients together. Taste and add pepper if necessary.

CARROT & MANGO DIP

$^1/_4$ pt (150 ml) natural yoghurt (a small carton)
1 small fresh carrot
1 fresh mango
1 teaspoon mild curry paste
salt and pepper

1   Peel and grate the carrot and then chop even more finely (use scissors in a tall jug).
2   Cut the mango down its length on each side of the stone. Peel and finely dice enough to make about 2 tablespoons. (Use rest in a fruit salad.)
3   Combine all the ingredients, season and set aside for 1 hour to mellow.

CARROT & FRESH COCONUT RELISH

$^1/_4$ pt (150 ml) natural yoghurt (a small carton)
2 tablespoons freshly grated coconut
1 small fresh carrot, grated
$^1/_2$ small fresh green chilli (or less if you do not care for too much heat)
squeeze of lemon juice to taste

1   Peel and grate the fresh carrot and chop into fine shreds.
2   Grate the coconut on a metal grater.
3   Stir all the ingredients together.

COCONUT CHUTNEY

2 tablespoons freshly grated coconut
3 tablespoons apple purée
1 teaspoon sugar
2 in (5 cm) piece of cucumber, finely chopped
pepper

Mix all the ingredients together in a bowl and set them aside to mellow for 2 hours.

VOL-AU-VENTS

The French term vol-au-vent means something like 'light as air'. At their best they can be just that – with a hot savoury filling. At their worst, they can be heavy with a congealed filling sunk inside.

Vol-au-vents are always better filled at the last minute. I think it is easier to get a perfect result by reheating the pastry and the filling separately. I do not think it is worth making the traditionally oval-shaped vol-au-vents in the tiny sizes. They can be bought both cooked and raw in this size – usually referred to as cocktail size, which in my book is just one mouthful or, more politely, one bite. The next size up to that is big enough for 2 bites. If you are baking them from frozen, do pay particular attention to the oven temperature. Make sure it has got up to the temperature specified on the packet.

The following fillings are all based on a white sauce. The amount of sauce varies so always prepare the main ingredient after you make the sauce and pour in just enough to make a filling that is moist but certainly not sloppy.

BASIC WHITE SAUCE

This white sauce will have little or no flavour. It should certainly not taste of uncooked flour so try it to make sure. If you can still taste the flour cook it for a little longer.

10 fl oz (300 ml) milk (or milk and stock)
1 rounded dessertspoon plain flour
salt and pepper

1   Put the cold liquid into a pan.
2   Use a loop whisk to disperse the dry flour through the cold liquid. When not a trace of dry flour remains, change to a wooden spoon and then turn on the heat.
3   Stirring all the time, heat the flour and liquid mixture until it thickens (this should take about 5 minutes). Season to taste.

MICROWAVE WHITE SAUCE

10 fl oz (300 ml) milk (or milk and stock)
1 rounded dessertspoon plain flour
salt and pepper

1   Put the cold liquid into a large jug, preferably with a rounded inside base. I use a 3 pt (2 litre) plastic jug.
2   Use a loop whisk to disperse the dry flour through the cold liquid. Whisk hard and cook on full power for 3 minutes, stopping and whisking hard every minute.
3   It is important to make sure that no flour escapes this whisking treatment, otherwise the sauce will not be smooth. Season the sauce to taste.

'Strange to say how a good dinner and feasting reconciles everybody.'

Samuel Pepys

FILLINGS FOR HOT VOL-AU-VENTS

FOR ABOUT 12 COCKTAIL OR
8 LARGER VOL-AU-VENTS

MUSHROOMS WITH A BUTTER SAUCE

Mushrooms have an annoying habit of shrinking when cooked, so add the sauce very carefully.

8 oz (225 g) fresh mushrooms, wiped and
    finely chopped
1 oz (25 g) butter
2 teaspoons oil
salt and pepper

1   Melt half the butter in a pan, add the oil and fry the mushrooms gently for just 1–2 minutes.
2   Spoon off any free liquid and add a little of your white sauce to the mushrooms so that you have a thick but not stiff filling.
3   Lastly add the remaining butter. Taste and adjust the seasoning and reheat as needed.

PRAWN & EGG

Prawns do not always have a strong flavour so I suggest you make the sauce with a milk and water mixture in which you have dissolved about ½ of a fish stock cube.

4 oz (125 g) peeled cooked prawns
2 teaspoons chopped fresh parsley
1 size-1 egg, hard-boiled and chopped

1   Put prawns in a bowl and chop with scissors. Add the parsley, egg and enough sauce to make a soft thick filling. Season well and reheat as required.

DRIED MUSHROOMS & TARRAGON

Dried mushrooms have a more intense flavour than the fresh ones. Of course, you have to soak them to rehydrate them by pouring boiling water over and waiting for the time specified on the packet until they fill out.

4 oz (125 g) dried mushrooms, soaked in
    boiling water and drained
1 oz (25 g) butter
2 teaspoons of oil
2 teaspoons of chopped fresh tarragon leaves
salt and pepper

1   Pat the soaked mushrooms with kitchen paper and cut into small pieces with scissors.
2   Melt half the butter in a pan with the oil and fry the mushroom pieces gently for 1–2 minutes.
3   Spoon off any spare liquid and add the tarragon leaves. Pour in some of the white sauce and stir the mixture. It should be thick but not stiff.
4   Finally, stir in the rest of the butter. Taste and adjust the seasoning. Reheat as needed.

HAM & PARSLEY

4 oz (125 g) cooked ham, chopped small (a
    thick slice of ham will chop into small
    dice more readily)
1 tablespoon chopped fresh parsley
pepper

1   Stir the ham and parsley together and add enough sauce to make a thick filling.

CREAM CHEESE & CHIVES

4 oz (125 g) firm cream cheese, beaten smooth
2 tablespoons grated mature Cheddar cheese
1 tablespoon chopped fresh chives
salt and pepper

1   Beat a little of the white sauce into the cream cheese with the grated cheese and the chives.
2   Adjust the texture of the cheese filling with more sauce if necessary, until thick but not stiff.
3   Season to taste. Reheat as needed.

SMOKED BACON

6 oz (175 g) smoked streaky bacon
2 tablespoons cooked frozen peas
pepper

1   Grill the bacon until almost crisp. Drain and chop into small pieces.
2   Mix the bacon and peas with enough white sauce to make a thick filling.
3   Add a little of the bacon fat and some pepper. Reheat as required.

ROASTED TOMATO & BASIL

This is the filling to make in summer, when the tomatoes are full of flavour.

fat pinch of dried basil
4 medium-sized tomatoes (ripe but firm)
olive oil
4 large fresh basil leaves, chopped
1 dessertspoon tomato purée
1 teaspoon sugar

1   Flavour the white sauce with the dried basil. Stir it in and reheat.
2   Cut the tomatoes into quarters. Squeeze out the seeds and lay the quarters on a baking sheet brushed with olive oil. Season with salt and pepper. Dribble over a little more olive oil and roast either in a very hot oven or under a well-heated grill, until the tomatoes are just beginning to wilt. Remove from the heat and allow to cool, then transfer to a bowl.
3   Take a pair of scissors and chop the tomatoes into small pieces. Add the chopped basil, the tomato purée and sugar and stir well.
4   Reheat when required. Spoon a little of the basil flavoured-sauce into each vol-au-vent and top with the tomato mixture. You may have to drain off some tomato juice.

SMOKED MACKEREL & EGG

1 small (or ½ large) smoked mackerel
   (about 6 oz / 175 g)
2 teaspoons lemon juice
1 dessertspoon chopped fresh parsley
1 size-1 egg, hard-boiled and chopped
pepper

1   Flake the mackerel and remove all bones and also the dark flesh which runs down the back next to the skin. There is nothing wrong with this flesh but it is very dark.
2   Mix the mackerel, lemon juice, parsley and egg. Stir in enough white sauce to give a thick filling.
3   Season with pepper only, taste and adjust the seasoning. Reheat as required.

FILLINGS FOR COLD VOL-AU-VENTS

FOR ABOUT 12 COCKTAIL OR
8 LARGER VOL-AU-VENTS

HAM PÂTÉ

6 oz (175 g) cooked gammon in a piece
¼ teaspoon made-up mustard
2 oz (50 g) soft unsalted butter
2–6 tablespoons double cream to taste
pepper

1 Put the gammon in a food processor or a
mincer and reduce to a fine crumb.
2 Turn into a bowl and beat in the mustard and
the soft butter with a little pepper.
3 Now beat in the double cream a little at a time,
until the texture of the pâté is soft and smooth.
4 Pipe or spoon into the little vol-au-vents.

CHICKEN LIVER PÂTÉ

4 oz (125 g) chicken livers, trimmed
3 oz (75 g) butter, softened
2 teaspoons oil
1 small garlic clove, crushed
1 small level teaspoon dry mustard
2–6 tablespoons double cream to taste
salt and pepper

1 Take a knob of butter from the 3 oz (75 g)
and put it in a small frying pan with the oil. Put
the livers with the garlic in the frying pan and
cook gently for about 4 minutes on each side,
until lightly browned. Remove from heat.
2 Scrape the cooked livers, juices and all, into a
food processor. Add the mustard and whizz to a
fine crumb, then leave the pâté to go almost cold.
3 Add the butter and whizz again. Turn out
into a bowl. If it is cool, start to beat in the
double cream. Do this a little at a time until you
get it to the flavour you wish. Season well.

4 Pipe or spoon into the warm vol-au-vents. If
you are using a piping bag, use a plain nozzle,
just in case the pâté is not too smooth.
5 Pipe any spare pâté into shallow ramekins,
smooth over and cover with a thin layer of
melted butter. Eat with fingers of hot toast.

CHICKEN & CHILLI

6 oz (175 g) cooked chicken
2 oz (50 g) soft unsalted butter
knife tip of powdered chilli
2–6 tablespoons double cream to taste

1 In a food processor, reduce the cooked chicken
to a fine crumb and turn the crumbs into a bowl.
2 Beat in the unsalted butter and the chilli and
follow this with the double cream until you have
a smooth soft pâté. Add an extra knife tip of
chilli at this point if you like it.
3 Pipe or spoon into the vol-au-vent cases.

SIMPLE VOL-AU-VENT SQUARES AND ROUNDS

A less bothersome way of combining flaky
pastry with a saucy filling is to roll out puff
pastry extremely thinly and cut small squares or
rounds. Arrange on greased trays, brush with
beaten egg and bake in an oven preheated to
gas8/450°F/230°C for about 10 minutes, until
risen and brown. Remove and allow to cool
down. Cut each across the middle and spread
with some of the above fillings, but remember
the filling should be quite firm and generous.
Replace the lid and serve warm.

FILO PARCELS

These one-bite pre-dinner nibbles are a real fiddle to make, but people love them. The warm savoury filling and the crisp pastry make an irresistible combination. Buy a packet of filo pastry, defrost it, then unroll it and immediately cover it with a damp tea-towel. Work with one sheet at a time. It dries out very easily and once it starts to crack and the flexibility is lost, you might just as well give up. You will need melted butter to brush over the pastry.

I favour two different kinds of parcels: the 'Dick Whittington' bundle and the tiny envelope shape. Cut the pastry sheets into 4 in (10 cm) squares for the bundle shape. Brush the top of the one sheet with butter and lay another sheet diagonally across it.

The other shape is just a small flat envelope and the filling should be rather more finely chopped. I think it is worth making up a 'glue' to make sure the envelope stays closed. Just work a couple of teaspoons of flour into cold water to the consistency of a thick sauce. A dab of this will keep your 'envelopes' closed.

Sit the bundles or envelopes on a greased baking sheet and dab more melted butter on the outside. Bake in an oven preheated to gas4/350°F/180°C for about 10–12 minutes, or until the pastry is crisp and golden. Serve the filo parcels warm.

FILLING SUGGESTIONS

Each filling needs something moist to bind it together. The Basic White Sauce for vol-au-vents on page 46 would be suitable, or just a tiny spoonful of cream cheese, thick Greek yoghurt or whipped double cream. Season well.

MUSHROOM, PARMESAN & PESTO

4 oz (125 g) firm mushrooms
½ oz (15 g) butter
2 teaspoons oil
1 heaped teaspoon grated Parmesan cheese
1 teaspoon ready-made pesto sauce
little sauce or cream cheese, etc (see above)

1 Wipe the mushrooms and chop finely.
2 Melt the butter in a frying pan and stir in the oil. Fry the mushrooms briefly, stirring often.

3 Transfer mushrooms to a bowl and stir in the cheese and pesto.
4 Bind with a tiny amount of white sauce, cream cheese, Greek yoghurt or whipped double cream.

PRAWN & BEANSPROUT

4 oz (25 g) prawns
½ oz (15 g) butter
1 teaspoon oil
2 oz (50 g) beansprouts
¼ teaspoon chopped parsley
little Basic White Sauce (page 46), cream cheese, Greek yoghurt or whipped double cream

1 Chop the prawns into small pieces.
2 In a small pan, melt the butter and add the oil. Chop the beansprouts small and stir-fry them very briefly in the hot butter and oil mixture.
3 Mix in the prawns, beansprouts and parsley.
4 Bind with a tiny amount of white sauce, cream cheese, Greek yoghurt or whipped double cream.

MINCED SALMON & DILL

4 oz (125 g) fresh or tinned, cooked salmon
2 teaspoons of lemon juice
2 fat pinches of dry dill
little Basic White Sauce (page 46), cream
 cheese, Greek yoghurt or whipped
 double cream

1 Chop salmon, removing all bones and skin.
2 Stir in the lemon juice and dill.
3 Bind with a tiny amount of white sauce, cream
cheese, Greek yoghurt or whipped double cream.

CREAM CHEESE & YELLOW PEPPER

4 oz (125 g) firm cream cheese or cream
 cheese with herbs
½ small yellow pepper
1 teaspoon chopped chives

1 Allow the cheese to come to room temperature.
2 Deseed the pepper, then chop very finely.
3 Beat the cheese with chives and stir in pepper.

ROASTED RED PEPPER & TARRAGON

1 red pepper, quartered and deseeded
little olive oil
1 teaspoon fresh chopped tarragon leaves or
 2 pinches of dried tarragon
salt and pepper

1 Preheat the grill to its highest setting.
2 Brush the pepper with oil. Set the quarters
under the grill, not too near the heat, and roast
until the edges are just beginning singe.

3 When cool, chop the peppers into tiny pieces.
4 Season well and mix in the herbs. This filling
will probably be moist enough to use as it is.

TURKEY & CRANBERRY

4 oz (125 g) cooked turkey, minced or finely
 chopped
2 teaspoons cranberry sauce or jelly
½ teaspoon lemon juice
salt and pepper

Mix the ingredients together and season well.

SMOKY BACON & CHICKEN

5 strips of smoky bacon
3 oz (75 g) cooked chicken, finely chopped
little Basic White Sauce (page 46), cream
 cheese or whipped cream

1 Grill the bacon until crisp and chop finely.
2 Mix the bacon and chicken, together with a
tiny bit of white sauce, cheese or whipped cream.

CUCUMBER, SOUR CREAM & CHIVES

4 in (10 cm) piece of cucumber, chopped
 small
1 tablespoon thick sour cream
1 tablespoon chopped fresh chives
salt

1 First set the cucumber in a flat dish and
sprinkle lightly with salt. Leave it to drain.
2 Pat the cucumber dry with kitchen paper.
3 Stir in the sour cream and chives.

COUSCOUS WITH NUTS & HERBS

2 oz (50 g) couscous, rinsed
1 oz (25 g) walnuts, finely chopped
1 oz (25 g) almonds, finely chopped
1 tablespoon chopped mint, parsley and
    thyme leaves
little Basic White Sauce (page 46), cream
    cheese or whipped cream

1   Put the couscous in a small bowl, cover with
water and stand it in a pan of simmering water
for 5–6 minutes, or until the grains swell up.
2   Drain and mix in the nuts and herbs.
3   Stir in a tiny amount of Basic White Sauce,
cream cheese or whipped cream to bind lightly.

CHILLI & RED BEAN

1 tablespoon oil
½ small onion, chopped small
4 oz (125 g) minced beef
knife tip of ground chilli
1 tablespoon cooked or canned red kidney
    beans, rinsed if canned

1   Heat the oil in a frying pan and fry the onion
briskly. Toss in the minced beef. Break it up and
keep turning it over and over again to brown.
2   Stir in the knife tip of ground chilli and
enough water barely to cover. Reduce the heat
and simmer gently for about 15 minutes.
3   Pour off some liquid and reserve. Sprinkle the
flour over the mince. Stir, then return the gravy
and simmer until the mince thickens slightly.
4   Stir in the drained and rinsed red kidney beans.
5   Taste and adjust the seasoning.

LENTIL, PEPPER & SOFT CHEESE

2 tablespoons green lentils, soaked overnight
1½ oz (40 g) cream cheese with herbs
2 teaspoons lemon juice
pepper

1   Drain the lentils and cover again with fresh
water. Bring to the boil then simmer until the
lentils are soft, about 10 minutes.
2   Beat the soft cheese with the lemon juice. Stir
in the drained lentils and season with pepper.

MIXED VEGETABLES WITH CORIANDER SEEDS

4 oz (125 g) mixed vegetables, such as
    grated carrot, finely chopped raw onion,
    cooked sweetcorn, peas
½ teaspoon of coriander seeds, crushed to a
    powder in a mortar
1 heaped teaspoon cream cheese

1   Lightly steam each vegetable and allow to
cool down.
2   Mix the vegetables with the coriander and
cream cheese. Season with salt and pepper.

SAVOURY CHOUX PUFFS

Unlike any other type of pastry, choux starts off as a hot sauce. It is not at all difficult to make.

BASIC CHOUX PUFFS

2½ oz (65 g) strong plain (bread) flour
pinch of salt and pepper
2 oz (50 g) butter, cut into small pieces
2 size-3 eggs, well beaten

1 Preheat the oven to gas6/400°F/200°C.
2 Sift the flour on to a square of greaseproof paper and season.
3 Put the butter and 5 fl oz (125 ml) water in a roomy pan and bring to a boil. When all the butter has melted, 'shoot' the flour into the pan and immediately remove it from the heat.
4 With a wooden spoon, beat the flour, butter and water mixture until it is quite smooth. (At this point let the mixture cool a little, covered.)
5 Pour half of the egg mixture on to the paste and beat hard, adding the rest a little at a time.
6 At this point the mixture should be slack enough to pipe easily, but firm enough to retain its shape. Allow to cool slightly again.
7 Using 2 teaspoons, spoon out tiny rough balls on non-stick baking paper set on a greased baking sheet. Or, using a ½ in (1 cm) plain nozzle in a forcing bag, pipe small rounds.
8 Bake for 20–25 minutes, until crisp, golden and puffy.
9 As soon as the puffs are out of the oven, take a sharp knife and slit them down one side to let the steam escape. Cool on a wire rack.

Note
Bigger puffs are made in the same way, only it is a good plan when they have cooled to cut them fully through and scoop out the uncooked pastry.

VARIOUS FILLINGS FOR HOT OR COLD CHOUX PUFFS

The puffs must be crisp, so they should not be filled until just before serving.

CHEDDAR CHEESE & MUSTARD

4 oz (125 g) Cheddar cheese, grated
1 teaspoon of grainy mustard
enough soft cream cheese to bind

Mix the cheese with the mustard and enough soft cream cheese to bind.

APPLE & SMOKED CHEESE

1 Bramley apple
½ dessert apple, chopped into small dice
2 oz (50 g) smoked cheese, grated
2 teaspoons lemon juice

1 Peel, core and stew a small Bramley apple until it falls. Drain very thoroughly.
2 Put the chopped dessert apple into a cup and toss in the lemon juice.
3 Mix everything together.

GRUYÈRE & SPRING ONION

4 spring onions
3 oz (75 g) Gruyère cheese, grated
enough cream cheese to bind

1   Prepare spring onions by rinsing them and then topping and tailing. Finally, chop them very small.
2   Mix the cheese with the spring onions and enough soft cream cheese to bind.

SMOKED SALMON & HORSERADISH

4 oz (125 g) smoked salmon pieces
1 teaspoon horseradish sauce
enough soft cream cheese to bind the ingredients together

1   Chop the smoked salmon into very small pieces.
2   Stir in the horseradish and enough soft cream cheese to bind.

CREAM CHEESE & GARLIC CHIVES

Garlic chives grow very strongly in my garden. I think they need to be cut very finely.

2 oz (50 g) cream cheese
little double cream
2 teaspoons chopped garlic chives

1   Beat the cream cheese with enough double cream to make it soft.
2   Stir in the garlic chives.

MUSTARD, CREAM CHEESE & TONGUE

Tongue is a very undervalued meat. Its delicate texture is ideal for beating into a stuffing such as this or into a fine pâté.

1 teaspoon Dijon mustard
1½ oz (40 g) soft cream cheese
4 oz (125 g) finely chopped cooked tongue

Beat all the ingredients together adding more cream cheese if necessary.

CHICKEN, CHOPPED HERBS AND TABASCO

4 oz (125 g) cooked chicken, finely chopped or minced
1 tablespoon chopped parsley, thyme and chives
dash of Tabasco sauce
enough soft cream cheese to bind to a soft filling

Mix all the ingredients together and season with a dash or two of Tabasco to make a soft filling.

HAM & HOT CHUTNEY

2 oz (50 g) cooked ham, minced
1 teaspoon Indian hot sweet chutney (or mango chutney and a dash of mustard)
enough soft cream cheese to bind

Beat all the ingredients together adding just enough soft cheese to bind.

TUNA, ANCHOVY & CHOPPED FENNEL

½ small tin of tuna in oil
4 anchovy fillets, rinsed and dried
1 tablespoon chopped raw fennel

1   Finely chop the tuna and the rinsed anchovy fillets.
3   Mix all the ingredients together with enough soft cream cheese to bind.

CREAMED CRAB & LEMON

3 oz (75 g) crab meat (mixed brown and white)
grated rind of 1 lemon and 1 tablespoon of juice
little soft cream cheese
salt and pepper

1   Check the crab meat for bits of shell.
2   Mix the crab meat with the lemon rind and juice and just a little soft cream cheese.
3   Season with salt and pepper.

'In baiting a mouse-trap with cheese, always leave room for the mouse.'

The Infernal Parliament, Saki

INDIVIDUAL SUET PUDDINGS

Steak and kidney suet puddings – like treacle tart and spotted dick – are always fondly remembered. Suet crust has had a bit of a revival recently and, since it is the easiest pastry to make, I am not surprised. The 'fat' is suet, which you buy ready-prepared in packets. There is no tiresome rubbing in. The only thing you must remember is that suet crust, being made with self-raising flour, should be made and baked immediately. Other pastries, of course, benefit from a resting period between mixing and rolling.

The little flowerpot-shaped dariole moulds used in these recipes are also useful for individual sponge cakes, castle puddings, jellies, etc. The ones I have are very tiny, holding just 2 fl oz (60 ml) and that is filled to the brim. You can get little disposable aluminium moulds which are slightly bigger, holding 6 fl oz (175 ml), and are a good size for mini-Christmas puddings. This size is also easier for fitting the pastry. You do not need to fill them to the top.

TRADITIONAL SUET CRUST

This, of course, is suet pastry made with beef suet you buy at the butchers. Some people say that you can only get the true flavour this way. Also you must do the grating yourself. I think this is easier on an old-fashioned tin grater and it helps if the suet is really cold. There are transparent linking skins throughout suet, which get stuck on the grater and have to be discarded.

8 oz (225 g) butcher's suet
1 lb (45 g) self-raising white flour, sifted
about 8 fl oz (225 ml) cold water
salt and pepper

1   Prepare the suet by grating it on a metal grater. It helps if it is very cold. Discard any transparent linking skins. Handle the grated suet lightly.
2   Stir the suet into the sifted flour. Season, make a well in the centre and pour in almost all of the water. Use a fork to bring the flour and suet mixture into a ball. Add more water if necessary to get a smooth elastic dough.
3   Now use a hand to knead it gently in the bowl, then turn out on a lightly floured board, adding a little more flour if it is sticky. Use the pastry at once.

BUTTER & SUET CRUST

1 lb (450 g) self-raising white flour, sifted
4 oz (125 g) butter, hardened in the freezer
4 oz (125 g) packet suet
about 8 fl oz (225 ml) cold water
salt and pepper

1   Grate the butter on the big holes of a metal grater. It helps to wrap the end in foil.
2   Stir the suet and butter into the sifted flour.
3   Continue as in the previous recipe, from step 2.

VEGETARIAN SUET CRUST

It is possible to buy shredded vegetable suet made from vegetable oil. The recipe is the same for this as for the packet suet which most people use. In both cases the suet is shredded into tiny oblongs (looking like rice) and dressed with flour.

VARIOUS FILLINGS FOR INDIVIDUAL SUET PUDDINGS

CHICKEN, LIVER & GARLIC

Makes 4

8 oz (225 g) suet crust

Filling
8 oz (225 g) chicken livers (now mostly
    frozen)
1 oz (25 g) butter
2 teaspoons (or more) oil
1 small garlic clove, peeled and crushed
2 oz (50 g) mushrooms, chopped small
1 teaspoon flour
2 fl oz (50 ml) red wine or chicken stock
    (cube)
salt and pepper
melted vegetable fat or oil, for greasing

1   Prepare the filling: defrost the livers if
necessary and, using the back of a small knife,
scrape the flesh from the whitish sinews which
lead to the central core. If any part of the livers
look green, cut this away as well. (Chicken livers
can be very pale or very dark and sometimes
almost liquid, but they firm up on cooking.)
2   Melt the butter, add the oil, garlic and livers
and fry gently until light brown. Do not
overcook.
3   Stir in the mushrooms and fry briefly. Season
to taste.
4   Sprinkle the flour over the chicken liver
mixture and stir in. Pour a little of the wine or
stock in the pan at the same time. You are
aiming at a wet mixture, but not a sloppy one.
Continue to cook for another minute, then set it
aside to cool down.

To line the dariole moulds with the suet crust
1   Use melted vegetable fat or oil to grease the
moulds thoroughly.
2   Cut 4 little circles of greaseproof paper and
set one in the base of each mould.
3   Sprinkle a work surface with flour, make a
thick sausage of the suet crust and divide it into
4 equal pieces (you could weigh them if you
wish).
4   Roll out each piece to a rough circle about
$^1/_8$ in (3 mm) thick. Cut one-third of each circle
away in a wedge shape and set aside for the lids.
5   Now use the biggest pieces of crust to line
the little mould, wetting the cut edges so that
they will stick together. Take care to get the
dough right down into the bottom angle.

To fill and cook the puddings
1   Divide the filling between the moulds. Do
not fill the moulds more than two-thirds full.
Add a little of the gravy barely to cover the
mixture.
2   To make a lid for each mould, roll the
reserved pastry pieces and cut circles to fit inside
the mould at the top.
3   Place the circles over the filling. Run a wet
finger round the top outer edge and bring the
sides of the crust down and over the lid. Pinch
the pastry all round to make a seal. There should
still be a space at the top of the mould to allow
the puddings to rise.
4   Cover each bowl tightly with greased foil.
5   Set the puddings in the top half of a steamer
and cook for 1½ hours, or stand the puddings on
an old plate set in the bottom of a pan and pour
in boiling water to come halfway up the
puddings. The water should simmer gently, not
boil furiously.
6   Serve on a hot plate with some decorative
greenery, such as a few salad leaves or a sprig of
watercress.

SMALL-CUT STEAK & KIDNEY

Makes 4

8 oz (225 g) suet crust

Filling
5 oz (150 g) stewing steak, cut small
2 oz (50 g) lambs' kidneys, trimmed and
    diced
½ small onion, peeled and finely chopped
1 tablespoon oil
1 teaspoon flour
sprig of thyme
boiling water or stock

1   Cut way any fat or gristle from the meat.
2   Heat the oil in a pan and fry the meat until
well browned and almost beginning to singe.
Add the kidney and cook until brown.
3   Push the meat to one side, add a drop more
oil and fry the onions for 2–3 minutes. Stir all
the mixture together and add the thyme.
4   Sprinkle the white flour over the meat mixture
and stir this in. Follow this with boiling water or
stock barely to cover. Simmer until the meat is
really tender, about 1 hour. Set aside to cool.
5   Line 4 dariole moulds with the suet crust, fill
and cook the puddings as described on page 57.

CHICKEN IN LEMON SAUCE

Makes 4

To bring out the lemon flavour you could also
add the grated lemon rind to the suet crust.

8 oz (225 g) suet crust

Filling
1 chicken portion on the bone (about 8 oz/
    225 g)

2 oz (50 g) cooked peas
2 salad onions, chopped
1 tablespoon oil
about ½ pt (300 ml) hot water
½ chicken stock cube
1 teaspoon white flour
juice of 1 lemon (about 2 tablespoons)

1   In a small deep frying pan with a lid, heat the
oil and fry the salad onions lightly.
2   Dry the chicken portion with kitchen roll,
then brown the portion on both sides in the hot
oil.
3   Now poach the chicken: pour into the pan the
hot water along with the crumbled ½ stock cube.
Put the lid on and simmer gently until the chicken
is fully cooked, about 30 minutes. Check that the
chicken is not pink and uncooked by taking a pair
of scissors and cutting down to the bone. Twist the
blade slightly and you will be able to see. Let the
chicken cool in the poaching liquid.
4   Take the chicken out and discard the skin and
bone. Chop up the remaining chicken meat.
5   Boil the poaching liquid down by half, then
mix the flour with the lemon juice until smooth.
Pour a little of the hot liquid into the lemon and
flour mixture, stir and then pour the whole lot
back into the pan. Simmer until the mixture is
cooked, then return the chicken to the lemon
sauce along with the peas. Set aside to cool.
6   Line 4 dariole moulds with the suet crust and
fill and cook the puddings as described on page 57.

DUCK & ORANGE

Makes 4

8 oz (225 g) suet crust

Filling
1 duck portion (on the bone), weighing
    about 8 oz (225 g)
1 tablespoon oil
½ pt (300 ml) vegetable stock, made up
    with ½ vegetable stock cube and water
1 small orange
1 teaspoon flour

1   In a small deep frying pan with a lid, heat the oil and fry the duck portion hard on both sides.
2   Pour in the stock. Bring up to a boil then turn down the heat and simmer for about 45 minutes. Check that the duck is fully cooked, then remove it from the pan. Discard the skin and bone and chop the meat.
3   Grate some orange peel into the stock – about 1 level tablespoon will be enough. Then boil the stock down to about half. Moisten the flour with a little cold water and, when it is smooth, stir this into the stock. Simmer for a few minutes then return the duck meat and remove from the heat.
4   Cut the pith from the orange as if you were peeling an apple, then take out the orange segments from between the sections. Cut each segment in two and add to the duck in the sauce. Taste and adjust the seasoning.
5   Line 4 dariole moulds with the suet crust and fill and cook the puddings as described on page 57.

chunks.
2   Peel, core and chop the apple and put it in a small bowl. Pour over the lemon juice.
3   Now line the four dariole moulds with the suet crust as described on page 57.
4   Discard the lemon juice and mix only the sausage and the apple to fill the puddings. Put a small amount of cider in each pudding.
5   Seal and cook the puddings as described on page 57.
6   To make the sauce: whisk the flour into the stock. Bring this mixture to the boil and then lower the heat to a simmer until the flour taste has gone.
7   Stir in the mustard and the currants and season to taste.
8   Serve the puddings with the sauce separately.

POLISH SAUSAGE & APPLE WITH A MUSTARD & CURRANT SAUCE

Makes 4

8 oz (225 g) suet crust

Filling
8 oz (225 g) piece of Polish boiling sausage
4 fl oz (100 ml) cider
1 medium-size dessert apple
2 tablespoons lemon juice

Mustard & Currant Sauce
1 teaspoon flour
½ pt (300 ml) vegetable stock (made from ½ vegetable cube)
2 teaspoons grainy mustard
1 teaspoon currants

1   First skin the sausage and cut it into small

'A highbrow is the kind of person who looks at a sausage and thinks of Picasso.'

The Highbrow, Sir Alan Patrick Herbert

SMALL FLAT PORK PIES

You can cut these up and serve as a snack or nibble.

SAVOURY PORK PIE WITH SUET PASTRY

Makes 16 small portions

These flat pork pies are very rich and look attractive with the pastry in a lattice effect. There are two ways to do this, each with the aid of a gadget. The square hole effect is made by rolling the pastry lid down on to a shape which has square holes rising from the surface. The other effect is with the use of a roller which slices the pastry. You then stretch the pasty out to give a lattice effect on the lid. You will need two 7 in (18 cm) rings or flan tins for the pies.

12 oz (350 g) Suet Pastry (page 17)

Filling
1 lb (450 g) pork sausage meat
1 tablespoon finely chopped onion
4 oz (125 g) cooked ham, diced
2 tablespoons chopped fresh parsley
2 fat pinches of ground mace
2 size-1 eggs, beaten
little milk
salt and pepper
flour for dusting

1   Preheat the oven to gas5/375°F/190°C. Grease the rings or bases or flan tins with oil or vegetable fat.
2   On a floured board, roll out about two-thirds of the pastry and use to line the two rings or flan tins, taking great care to ease the pastry down into the lower angle. Set the rest of the pastry aside for the lids.
3   Make the filling: mash down the sausage meat with the onion (I usually use a mixer for this job). Stir in the ham, parsley and mace. Lastly, add the beaten eggs, saving a little for glazing the pie tops.
4   Divide the pork mixture between the two pies and smooth it down carefully.
5   Roll out the rest of the pastry and cut two lids. You might have a pan lid to act as a giant cutter. Moisten the edges of both lids and pies, secure the lids in place and pinch the edges to seal. Cut two or more slits in the lid. If you are using a lattice-effect lid, secure the edges well and cut a long narrow strip of pastry about ¼ in (5 mm) thick to press down over the edge. Use the reserved egg with a little added milk to brush over the surface of the pies.
6   Bake for 30 minutes, then reduce the heat to gas4/350°F/180°C for the last 15 minutes.

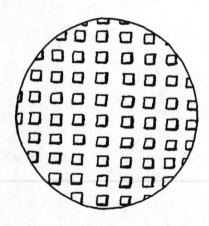

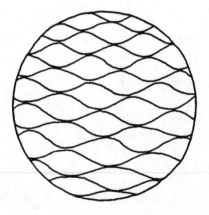

PORK SAUSAGEMEAT & SMOKY BACON PIE

Makes 16 small portions

If you like a really meaty filling, ask your butcher to mince pork for you on the coarse blade of his mincing machine. Smoked bacon is now available with a hint of garlic, if this takes your fancy. Again, this recipe makes two pies and you will need two 7 in (18 cm) flan tins or flan rings set on a baking sheet.

12 oz (350 g) Shortcrust Pastry (page 16)
1 lb (450 g) coarse-cut pork
4 oz (125 g) smoky bacon, cut into pieces
2 tablespoons cooked peas
2 size-1 eggs, beaten
little milk
salt and pepper
flour, for dusting

1   Preheat the oven to gas5/375°F/190°C. Grease the two 7 in (18 cm) flan tins or flan rings and the baking sheet.
2   On a lightly floured board, roll out about two-thirds of the pastry to line the two tins. Take care to push the pastry well down into the tin. Set the rest of the pastry aside for the lids.
3   To make the filling: break up the meat. Stir in the bacon and peas. Lastly add the beaten eggs, reserving about 1 tablespoon to glaze the finished pie. Season the meat well with more pepper than salt.
4   Divide the meat mixture between the two tins and level it out.
5   Roll out the remaining pastry and cut 2 lids. Moisten the outer edge of the pies. Position the lids, secure them in place by pinching the edge to seal. Make two or three slits in the pastry, then brush all over with the reserved egg (add a drop of milk to make it go further).
6   Bake for the first 30 minutes at the top of the oven, then reduce the heat to gas4/350°F/180°C for the last 15 minutes.

PORK & PIPPIN PIE

Makes 8–10 slices

Getting hold of apples with the old Pippin word in the name will be the hardest part of this recipe I think. Instead I use a dessert apple which will keep its shape. The rectangular flan frame measures 4x12 in (11x30 cm) and the finished shape is ideal for slicing.

10 oz (275 g) Shortcrust Pastry (page 16)

Filling
1 medium-size Granny Smith or dessert
     apple which does not 'fall'
1 lb (450 g) pork sausagemeat
4 oz (125 g) rindless streaky bacon, cut
     small
1 tablespoon fresh parsley
2 size-1 eggs, beaten
little milk
salt and pepper

1   Preheat the oven to gas5/375°F/190°C. Grease the inside of the flan frame and the baking sheet on which it sits.
2   Roll out two-thirds of the pastry to an oblong which will fit the tin and ease the pastry into it. Take great care about fitting the pastry into the corners. Trim off any surplus but leave the pastry standing just a little above the metal frame.
3   Make the filling: peel, core and chop the apple quite small. Work together the sausagemeat, apple, bacon pieces and parsley. Next add the beaten eggs, reserving 1 tablespoon, mix well and season to taste.
4   Spoon this mixture into the pastry case and smooth it out.
5   Roll the reserved pastry to an oblong to fit the pie. Moisten the top edge of the pie, lay the lid over and squeeze the edge together at regular intervals giving a good seal. Make two or three steam vents. Decorate with pastry leaves etc.
6   Mix the reserved egg with a spoonful of milk and brush all over the top. Bake for 30 minutes, then reduce the heat to gas4/350°F/180°C and cook for a further 15 minutes. Remove from the oven and allow to cool before removing frame.

PORK SAUSAGE PIE

Serves 8–10

There are many well-flavoured sausages about now, from an exotic tandoori to one of my favourites, leek and pork. Buy thick sausages to make this pie and have a look at some of the variations.

8 oz (225 g) Shortcrust Pastry (page 16), try
    using a mixture of white and
    wholewheat flour
butter or lard, for greasing

Filling
8 oz (225 g) sausages (about 5 thick ones)
2 tablespoons well-flavoured chutney
2 size-1 eggs, hard-boiled and sliced
2 large tomatoes, skinned and sliced thickly
1 teaspoon mixed herbs
little milk
salt and pepper

1   Preheat the oven to gas7/425°F/220°C. Grease an 8 in (23 cm) flan tin or pie plate really well.
2   Take a knife and make a slit down each sausage and peel away the skin.
3   Make the filling: in a roomy bowl, mix together the sausagemeat and chutney and set this aside while you roll out the pastry.
4   Using about two-thirds of the pastry, roll it out and line the base of the tin. Take up about half of the sausagemeat mixture and spread this in an even layer.
5   Then lay the hard-boiled egg slices in an even layer on top of the sausagemeat and a layer of sliced tomatoes on top of that. Season the tomatoes and sprinkle over the thyme leaves. Spread the remaining sausagemeat on top.
6   Roll out the reserved pastry and cut a circle to fit the tin. Lift the pastry up on your rolling pin and fit the lid, having first moistened the edge with water. Press the edges together firmly. Make 3 or 4 slits in the pastry lid and score the surface of the pie with the tip of a knife. A diagonal pattern always looks good. Brush the surface with milk.

7   Bake on a baking sheet for about 15 minutes. Reduce the heat to a moderate gas4/350°F/180°C and cook for a further 45 minutes. If the top of the pie starts to look too dark, cover it with foil (if using a fan oven, screw up the corners to prevent the fan blowing it away).

VEAL & HAM PIE

Serves 8–10

This famous combination is usually part of a stand or raised pie made with hot-water crust pastry. I sometimes use the ham from boiling a ham shank. If not, look out for the end pieces of cooked ham at the deli counter.

8 oz (225 g) Shortcrust Pastry (page 16)

Filling
8 oz (225 g) cooked ham pieces
1 tablespoon stock (if you have boiled a ham
    shank)
1 uncooked veal escalope or an escalope of
    pork
1/2 oz (15 g) butter, plus more for greasing
2 teaspoons grainy mustard
little milk
salt and pepper

1   Preheat the oven to gas4/350°F/180°C. Grease an 8 in (20 cm) flan tin or flan ring and a baking sheet.
2   Roll out two-thirds of the pastry and use to line the flan tin or flan ring. Set the other piece of pastry aside for a lid.
3   Make the filling: mince the ham or chop it very small. If there is any fat round the ham, chop a little of that in too.
4   Divide the ham in two and press one half into the base of the flan tin. Take the escalope and slice it horizontally if you can. Mix the butter and mustard and spread this roughly over the escalope then lay this on top of the ham. Now use the rest of the ham to cover the escalope. Press the mixture down well.
5   Roll out the remaining pastry and cut out a

lid. Moisten the pastry edges and press the lid down to seal well. Make a few slits in the pastry lid and brush with milk.

6 Bake for about 30 minutes, then turn the heat down to gas4/350°F/180°C and cook for another 10 minutes.

FRANKFURTER & FRENCH MUSTARD PIE

Serves 8–10

For this pie I use a shallow sponge cake tin which is 7 in (18 cm) square.

8 oz (225 g) Shortcrust Pastry (page 16), made using a mixture of brown and white flour
melted vegetable fat or oil, for greasing
flour, for dusting

Filling
2 oz (60 g) sun-dried tomatoes
8 oz (225 g) pork sausagemeat
8 long frankfurters
French mustard
little milk
salt and pepper

1 First soak the sun-dried tomatoes for the filling in boiling water for 10 minutes. Pat dry and cut small.

2 Preheat the oven to gas5/375°F/190°C. Grease the tin thoroughly with melted vegetable fat or oil.

3 On a lightly floured board, roll out two-thirds of the pastry big enough to cover the tin and go 1¼ in (3 cm) up the sides. Ease the pastry in position, taking care with the corners that they are not too thinly covered with pastry that they will split. Set aside the rest of the pastry for the lid.

4 Make the filling: in a bowl, mash together the sausagemeat and tomato bits, then season with salt and pepper. Divide the mixture in two and pat half in an even layer on the pastry bottom.

5 Run a sharp knife down one side of each frankfurter, trying to avoid cutting it right through. Spread the mustard down each slit, close the sausage up again and lay them in a row on top of the sausagemeat. Cover the sausages with the rest of the sausagemeat and press the filling quite firmly.

6 Roll out the pastry for the lid, wet the edges and secure by nipping the pastry together or pressing it hard with a fork all the way round. Cut a few slits on the lid and brush all over with milk.

7 Bake for about 30 minutes. Then turn down the heat to gas4/350°F/180°C and cook for a further 10 minutes.

Said to be the last words of William Pitt the Younger, 1759-1806:

'I think I could eat one of Bellamy's Veal Pies.'
(Bellamy was the first caterer to the Houses of Parliament.)

SAUSAGE ROLLS

Sausage rolls, like egg and cress sandwiches, are part of the British way of life and can be exceedingly good. Like all pastry-based items, they are at their best when freshly made. The pastry should be as thin as the filling will allow, and it should be crisp. They are better served warm, possibly with a dip of something spicy like thick yoghurt flavoured with mustard and apple chutney or mayonnaise tarted up with tomato purée and ginger preserve.

Both shortcrust and flaky pastry work well on sausage rolls. Fillings can be as adventurous as you like, but the filling should, I think, be fairly strongly flavoured. I think it is best to make a good batch at one go and bake only what you need, the rest is better frozen raw. I do not care for cooked pastry which has been frozen. There is a leaden quality about it which does not easily go away.

MINCED PORK & BACON SAUSAGE ROLLS

Makes about 24 medium-sized rolls

You can always substitute sausagemeat if you wish, but some time do try real minced pork. Your butcher will be happy to do this for you, but not on a busy day.

10 oz (275 g) New Flaky Pastry (page 19)
1 size-7 egg, beaten
little milk
oil or melted vegetable fat, for greasing
flour, for dusting

Filling
1 lb (450 g) finely minced fresh shoulder pork
3 oz (75 g) onion, grated or finely chopped
2 fat pinches of ground mace
2 fat pinches of thyme leaves
4 oz (125 g) fatty bacon, cut small

1   Preheat the oven to gas 7/425°F/220°C. Lightly grease 1 or 2 baking sheets with oil or melted vegetable fat.
2   In a bowl, mix together the filling ingredients. Season well with more pepper than salt. With floured hands, divide the filling into 3 and roll the meat into long fat sausage shapes about the thickness of a fat cigar.
3   Use a long rolling pin if you have one. Roll out the pastry as thinly as you can to make a large even rectangle. Cut off the ragged bits and square the edges.
4   Lay the first meat roll a little way in from the bottom edge of the pastry. Moisten the lower edge of the pastry and lift this up and over the roll to meet the pastry at the other side. Push the pastry up tight to the pork filling. Cut the long sausage roll from the main piece of pastry. Turn it over so that the join is underneath and press lightly to flatten. Set this aside and repeat until the meat filling is used up.
5   Now mix the beaten egg with a little milk and brush this mixture along the rolls. Cut the rolls to the size you wish and, with a pair of scissors, make 3 or 4 snips on the top of each roll.
6   Set the rolls on the baking sheets and bake for about 20–25 minutes, or until the pastry is well browned. Cool on wire baking trays.

MINCED PORK & LEEK SAUSAGE ROLLS

This recipe is similar to the one above. Instead of flaky pastry this time use the same weight of Shortcrust Pastry (page 16) and instead of the grated onion substitute 6 oz (175 g) chopped leek, pre-cooked as follows. Rinse well and chop finely. Melt ½ oz (15 g) butter and briefly fry the leeks in this. Cool before stirring into the pork mixture.

MINCED PORK/APPLE & BACON

Makes about 24 medium-sized rolls

This recipe is similar to Minced Pork and Bacon Sausage Rolls on page 64, but omit the onion and add 1 small eating apple, peeled, cored and chopped small.

GLAMORGAN SAUSAGE ROLLS

Makes about 18 medium-sized rolls

No one seems to know why this meatless 'sausage roll' got this name, but in this recipe the filling is based on cheese suitable for vegetarians. (The rennet used in vegetarian cheese is not from an animal.)

10 oz (275 g) Rich Cheese Pastry (page 17), made using vegetarian cheese

Filling
8 oz (225 g) grated vegetarian cheese
6 oz (225 g) fresh breadcrumbs
3 tablespoons finely chopped salad onions
2 size-1 eggs, beaten
1 large tablespoon chopped parsley
little milk
flour, for dusting

1   In a bowl, mix together the grated cheese, breadcrumbs, salad onion and parsley. Bind with the beaten eggs, reserving a little for glazing. If the cheese and breadcrumbs are dry use a little cold water as well to help bind the whole lot together.

2   Now, with floured hands, roll the filling into three long thin sausage shapes and proceed as in the main recipe on page 64.

BULGAR WHEAT & VEGETABLES

Makes about 18 medium-sized rolls

Bulgar wheat is a much under-used cereal in this country. It has several names, bulgur, burghul, cracked wheat and pourgouri. Much used in Greek-Cypriot and Lebanese cooking, it makes a good base for a vegetarian filling. Prepare it by covering the grains with boiling water, then steam over a pan of water or boil in the microwave until the grains have softened and swelled. It has a nutty flavour.

10 oz (275 g) Shortcrust Pastry (page 16)

Filling
2 oz (50 g) bulgar wheat
8 oz (225 g) cooked carrot, peas and potato, chopped small
2 large teaspoons hot curry paste
1 size-1 egg, beaten
1 tablespoon chopped fresh coriander
flour

1   Prepare the bulgar wheat by covering with boiling water. Steam or boil or cook in the microwave until the grains have swollen and softened. Drain and dry in kitchen roll.

2   In a bowl, mix the cooked vegetables which have been chopped small, the curry paste and coriander. Add the egg, now stir in as much bulgar as it takes to get the mixture to stick together.

3   Flour you hands well and roll the mixture together into three long thin sausage shapes.

4   Proceed as in the main recipe opposite.

SPINACH & CELERY ROLLS

Makes about 24 medium-sized rolls

10 oz (275 g) Rich Cheese Pastry (page 17)

Filling
1½ lb (675 g) fresh spinach or 1 lb (450 g)
    frozen, defrosted
knob of butter
6 oz (175 g) celery, cut finely and cooked
1 small teaspoon caraway seeds, bruised
4 oz (125 g) wholemeal breadcrumbs
2 size-1 eggs, beaten
salt and pepper

1   First prepare the spinach: cut out any tough
stems and rinse the leaves in cold water. Shake
well and stuff into a pan which looks too small to
hold it all. Add a knob of butter and some salt.
Hold the lid on and cook until the spinach wilts
and the stems are soft. Shake often. Drain well and
chop the leaves quite finely with scissors. Drain
again. If you are using frozen spinach, look for
frozen whole leaves rather than chopped. Drain it
thoroughly and cook quickly. Drain again.
2   Prepare the celery: rinse and chop into small
dice, cover with salted water and cook gently
until the celery is soft. Drain.
3   In a bowl, mix the cooked spinach, the
cooked celery, caraway seeds and breadcrumbs.
Bind with the eggs, reserving a little to glaze the
finished rolls.
4   Follow the instructions for rolling out the
pastry and assembling the rolls as in the main
recipe on page 64.

PEANUT & PORK SAUSAGEMEAT ROLLS

Makes about 18 medium-sized rolls

10 oz (275 g) Shortcrust Pastry (page 16)

Filling
1 lb (450 g) good-quality pork sausagemeat
2 large tablespoons chopped parsley
2 tablespoons finely chopped roasted
    peanuts
2 size-1 eggs, beaten
little milk
flour, for dusting

1   Prepare the filling by mashing together the
sausagemeat, parsley and peanuts.
2   Bind the mixture with enough of the egg mix
to make a soft filling. Reserve a little of the egg
to mix with milk and brush over the rolls.
3   Flour your hands to roll the sausagemeat into
three long thin rolls and proceed as in the main
recipe on page 64.

SAUSAGE SPIRALS

Makes about 6

5 oz (150 g) Shortcrust Pastry (page 16)
6 thin good-quality sausages
1 size-7 egg, beaten
butter or lard, for greasing
flour, for dusting

1   Preheat the oven to gas4/350°F/180°C. Grease
a baking tray.
2   Roll out the pastry on a floured board and cut
narrow strips about ½ in (1cm) wide.
3   Wind strips of pastry round each sausage.
4   Lay the sausages spirals on the greased baking
tray and brush them with the beaten egg.
5   Bake for 20–25 minutes, or until the sausages
are cooked and the pastry crisp and brown.

No-pastry Sausage Rolls

Makes about 6

1 lb (450 g) cooked thin sausages (about 6)
about 6 thin-cut brown or white sliced
    bread
little tomato sauce or made-up mustard
knob of salty butter
oil for greasing

1   Preheat the oven to gas4/350°F/180°C and
brush a baking sheet with oil.
2   Cook the sausages either by frying them
gently in a little oil, turning them often, or by
grilling them gently or baking in the oven on a
baking sheet brushed with oil. Allow the
sausages to cool down.
3   For children, remove the crusts from a square
of the bread and spread a little tomato sauce on
it, then wrap this around a sausage.
4   For adults, spread made-up mustard thinly on
the square of bread and wrap round a sausage.
5   When all the sausages are wrapped, place
them with the join underneath on the greased
baking tray. Melt the butter and brush this over
each 'roll'.
6   Bake for just 10–12 minutes or until the
bread is crunchy on top and lightly coloured.
Serve hot.

*'Oxford gave the world marmalade and a
manner, Cambridge science and a sausage.'*

Anon

Homemade Pork Sausages

Makes about 5 lb (2.3 kg)

These sausages do taste of pork and are really
special.
    Your butcher will mince the two lots of
meat for you. Some big mixers have a sausage-
making attachment which attaches to the
electric mincer, which in turn is fastened to the
mixer itself.
    The wholewheat flour does hold the sausages
together very well.

4½ lb (2 kg) pork shoulder
1½ lb (675 g) fat belly pork
¼ oz (6 g) ground sage
pinch of marjoram
1 oz (25 g) white pepper
1 oz (25 g) salt
4 oz (125 g) soft white breadcrumbs
wholewheat flour, for rolling the sausage
oil, for greasing

1   Preheat the oven to gas5/375°F/190°C.
2   Mix all the ingredients together in a
machine. To test the flavouring and seasoning of
your mixture, take a teaspoon of the mixture and
fry it quickly in a little oil. Adjust the flavouring
and seasoning if necessary.
3   Shape the mixture into long thin rolls, then
roll these in the flour. Cut the rolls into sausage-
sized pieces and chill for an hour or so.
4   Brush a baking tin with oil and arrange the
sausages on it. Bake for about 10–15 minutes
until well browned, moving them about from
time to time to prevent them sticking.

Talking about the ability to make a pie:
'Few moments in a cook's life can be more
agreeable than cutting the first wedge from a
beefsteak and kidney pie. The wonderful smell,
the looks of anticipation around the table, the air
of restlessness until the eating may begin, are the
rewards of this skill.'

Jane Grigson, *Good Things, 1971*

3

MAIN COURSE FAVOURITES

SHEPHERD'S & COTTAGE PIES

In days gone by these potato-topped pies were put together with the remains of the Sunday joint. Made with fresh meat, however, they make uncomplicated good standby fare, liked by young and old alike

SIMPLE SHEPHERD'S PIE

Serves 4

Make sure you fry the lamb hard in the first place in order to get a strong flavour. Mash the potatoes until they are quite fluffy and soft. There are many variations of this pie in different districts, such as a layer of cooked vegetables between the meat and the mashed potato and even chopped pickle in with the meat.

1 tablespoon oil
1 lb (450 g) minced lamb
1 medium onion, peeled and finely chopped
1 level tablespoon white flour
1/2 pt (300 ml) lamb stock (made from a cube)
dash of Worcestershire sauce
1 dessertspoon chopped fresh parsley
fat pinch of dried marjoram
knife tip of gravy browning
1 lb (450 g) floury potatoes
knob of butter
little milk
salt and pepper

1   Heat the oil in a frying pan and fry the lamb hard on a high heat. Break up all the lumps and do not worry if the meat sticks and starts to scorch. This will help to flavour the stock.
2   Push the mince to one side of the pan and add the chopped onion. Fry briefly, then mix in with the minced lamb.
3   Sprinkle over the flour. Stir in briefly and add the stock. Reduce the heat to a simmer and stir in the Worcestershire sauce, parsley and marjoram. Simmer for 20–25 minutes, when the mince will be cooked. Season to taste. Add a knife tip of gravy browning to darken the meat.
4   Use a slotted spoon to put the cooked mince in

an ovenproof dish. Traditionally this would be about 3 in (8 cm) deep. You may not need all the gravy, but do not allow the mince to be too dry (serve the extra gravy separately). Allow to go cold.
5   Meanwhile, peel the potatoes and boil in salted water. When tender, drain and return the to the hob to dry off slightly. Mash the potatoes well while hot. Change to a wooden spoon, add a knob of butter and a little milk to beat to a fluffy texture. Taste and add pepper.
6   Preheat the oven to gas4/350°F/180°C and a hot grill.
7   Spread the potato over the lamb, taking care to cover and seal the meat in. Smooth the potato and criss-cross with a fork. To get a browned top, quickly flash under the hot grill and then put in the oven to reheat for about 20 minutes.

Note
A good tip for checking if something like this is hot all the way through is to plunge a knife into the centre, then test the blade on your hand. This is particularly useful if you are using a microwave to reheat something.

INDIVIDUAL SHEPHERDS' PIES

Use the same recipe as above, but spoon into individual dishes or foil containers. When the pies are cold, cover with foil and store in a fridge or freezer. The recipe makes about 6 modest pies.

SHEPHERD'S PIE ITALIANO

This is a variation on the Simple Shepherd's Pie above. At step 3, add a large can of chopped Italian tomatoes with herbs and 1 dessertspoon of tomato purée with the other flavourings. Tomatoes in cans are cheap and will make the mince go further. Another addition which would also extend the mince is a large tablespoon of cooked pasta. If you add either of these, remember to cook 2 or 3 more potatoes.

LUXURY SHEPHERD'S PIE

Serves 6–8

2 lb (1 kg) neck of lamb or leg of lamb
2 tablespoons oil
1 large onion, peeled and chopped finely
1 garlic clove, peeled and crushed
2 teaspoons finely chopped rosemary
1 tablespoon plain flour
1 pt (600 ml) lamb stock (made from a cube)
pinch of marjoram
1 tablespoon chopped parsley
2 tablespoons Worcestershire sauce
4 oz (125 g) mushrooms, sliced
knife tip of gravy browning (optional)
2 lb (900 g) floury potatoes
2 or 3 knobs of butter
little cream
salt and pepper

1 Ask your butcher to mince the lamb for you on the coarse blade of his machine and to cut out some of the fat. Heat the oil in a frying pan and fry the meat really hard, breaking up any lumps which stick together. Do not worry if the meat sticks and appears to scorch, this will add to the flavour.
2 Push the meat to one side of the pan and fry the onion for a few minutes. Turn the heat down and mix the onion into the meat, stir in the garlic, rosemary and the flour. Mix this in well and stir in the stock, marjoram, parsley and Worcestershire sauce. Stir well, cover the pan and simmer for about 20–25 minutes or until the meat is cooked. Add the sliced mushrooms and cook for just 1 or 2 minutes more. Spoon into a flattish heatproof dish and allow to go cold. Season to taste. Add a knife tip of gravy browning to darken the meat if you wish.
3 Meanwhile, peel the potatoes and boil in salted water. When cooked, drain off the hot water and return the pan to the warm hob with the heat switched off.
4 Preheat the oven to gas4/350F/180C and a hot grill.
5 Using a traditional masher, reduce the potatoes to a cream with the addition of a knob of butter, a little cream, salt and pepper. Cover the meat and smooth the surface with a flat blade. Mark the potatoes in a pattern with a fork. Dot the surface with flakes of butter.
6 Flash under a hot grill to brown evenly then put in the oven for about 20 minutes to heat through.

VARIATIONS FOR SHEPHERD'S PIES & COTTAGE PIES

Cooked vegetables like chopped carrots, swedes, peas and sweetcorn can all be added to the basic mince recipe.

For toppings instead of potato you might like to try:

Mashed swede: boil in salted water until soft. Mash and drain again in a nylon sieve. Beat in butter and freshly grated nutmeg. Season to taste.

Mashed carrots: boil in salted water until cooked. Mash well and beat in a large tablespoon of chopped parsley and a knob of butter. Season to taste.

Winter turnips: these make a lovely topping mixed with mashed potato and a crushed garlic clove.

Celeriac and orange: celeriac root looks like a pale turnip with knobs on. Peel it hard, chop and cook in a mixture of orange juice and water. Drain when soft and then mash, adding some grated orange rind which goes well with the strong celery taste.

Mashed potato is good with finely chopped cooked cauliflower stirred into it, plus a tablespoon of chopped chives and a little milk and butter.

COTTAGE PIE

Serves 4

Cottage pie is traditionally made with beef, usually the remains of the Sunday roast. It is much better with fresh beef mince, flavoured with horseradish cream.

1 tablespoon oil
1 lb (450 g) fresh minced beef
1 medium onion, peeled and chopped
1 level tablespoon white flour

½ pt (300 ml) beef stock
1 dessertspoon horseradish cream
1 dessertspoon chopped parsley
knife tip of gravy browning (optional)
1 lb (450 g) floury potatoes
knob of butter
little milk
salt and pepper

1   Heat the oil in a frying pan and brown the beef mince really hard. Even if the meat catches slightly over the high heat it does not matter. Push the meat aside and fry the onion for a couple of minutes, then mix in with the meat.
2   Sprinkle the flour over the mixture. Stir this in, then slowly add the stock. Turn the heat down and add the horseradish cream and parsley. Stir well and simmer for 20–25 minutes or until the meat is cooked. Season to taste and stir in a knife tip of gravy browning if the meat looks pale.
3   Spoon the mince into an ovenproof pie dish which is about 3 in (7.5 cm) deep. Do not add too much gravy but, on the other hand, the meat should not be dry. Allow to cool down.
4   Peel the potatoes and boil in salted water. When soft, drain off the water and return the pan to the warm hob to dry the potatoes. Mash the potatoes thoroughly, change to a wooden spoon and beat in a knob of butter and enough milk to make the potatoes soft and fluffy.
5   Preheat the oven to gas4/250°F/180°C and a hot grill.
6   Spread the potato evenly over the pie. Smooth the surface, then drag a fork across to make a pattern. Brown the topping under the hot grill, then reheat in the oven for about 20 minutes.

LUXURY COTTAGE PIE

Serves 6–8

2 lb (1 kg) good-quality beef (skirt has a lovely flavour if you can get it)
4 oz (125 g) ox kidney, cored and chopped
1 large onion, peeled and chopped
1 garlic clove, peeled and crushed
1 tablespoon plain flour

1 pt (600 ml) meat stock (made from a cube)
2 tablespoons of Worcestershire sauce
6 oz (175 g) mushrooms, sliced
knife tip of gravy browning (optional)
2 lb (900 g) floury potatoes
2 or 3 knobs of butter
4 tablespoons cream
salt and pepper

1   Ask your butcher to mince your meat on the coarse blade of his machine and to remove some of the fat.
2   Heat the oil in a frying pan and fry the meat really hard so that it browns well and is even slightly scorched, to give the gravy more flavour. Stir in the kidney and brown this briefly. Push the meat to one side and fry the onion and the garlic for a couple of minutes. Turn the heat down and sprinkle over the flour. Stir this in and follow it with the meat stock and Worcestershire sauce. Stir well, cover and simmer for 25–30 minutes or until the mince is cooked through.
3   Stir in the mushrooms and simmer for just a minute or two more. Colour with a knife tip of gravy browning if necessary. Spoon into the dish and let cool. Reserve any extra gravy.
4   Peel the potatoes and boil in salted water. When they are soft, drain and return the pan to the warm hob to allow the potatoes to dry off a bit. Mash the potatoes thoroughly. Change to a wooden spoon and beat in some butter and cream to make a really fluffy potato. Season to taste.
5   Preheat the oven to gas4/350°F/180°C and a hot grill.
6   Spread the mashed potato over the meat, smooth it down and drag a fork across to form a pattern. Scatter a few flakes of butter here and there. Brown the top under the hot grill then put in the oven for 20 minutes to heat through.

VARIATIONS ON COTTAGE PIE TOPPING

On the surface of the mashed potato add a layer of crushed potato crisps and serve at once before the crisps go soggy.

Another tasty variation is to add a layer of creamy onion sauce on top of the potato as follows:

Onion Sauce
1 tablespoon oil
1 medium onion, peeled and finely chopped
1 level tablespoon white flour
1/2 pt (300 ml) mixed vegetable stock and milk
1 dessertspoon parsley
knob of butter
salt and pepper

1   Heat the oil in a frying pan and fry the onion carefully until very soft.
2   Sprinkle over the flour, stir this round a bit and follow up with almost all of the milk and stock. Cook gently stirring all the time until thick.
3   Stir in the parsley and the knob of butter. Season to taste and pour over the potato topping. The sauce should be quite thick.

Wartime Poster:

'Better pot luck
With Churchill today
Than humble pie
With Hitler tomorrow.
Don't waste food.'

PIE WITH LAMB & ROSEMARY

Serves 6

Mutton – that is, lamb from older sheep – is difficult to get hold of today. I for one miss that rich rounded flavour. Instead use the herb rosemary with your lamb. This herb has a very powerful flavour so use it with discretion.

2½ lb (1.2 kg) leg of lamb, cut into 1 in (2.5 cm) pieces
8 oz (225 g) belly pork, skinned and chopped into 1 in (2.5 cm) pieces
3 tablespoons oil
2 large onions, peeled and chopped
2 tablespoons plain white flour
2 pt (1.2 litres) lamb stock (made from 2 cubes)
2 teaspoons very finely scissored rosemary needles
2 lb (900 g) waxy potatoes, cut in slices and simmered in salted water until done
1 oz (50 g) butter, melted

1   In a large pan, heat the oil and brown the lamb and pork over a high heat until very brown. Push the meat to one side and lower the heat. Now fry the onions for about 4 minutes, stirring frequently.
2   Stir the onions and meat together, sprinkle the flour over and stir that in followed by the stock and the rosemary. Bring to the boil, then turn the heat down and simmer for about 2 hours, or until the meats are both cooked. Taste and season, adding more rosemary if you wish.
3   Preheat the oven to gas6/400°F/200°C. Spoon the meat and pork into a flattish heatproof dish or pie dish. Barely cover with gravy and reserve the rest to serve separately. Lay the cooked potato slices in rows overlapping each other.
4   Brush with the melted butter, set the dish on a baking sheet and bake for about 25 minutes, or until the potatoes are tinged with brown. Serve with a green vegetable and some mint jelly.

PORK, APPLE & BLACK PUDDING PIE

Serves 6–8

1½ lb (675 g) shoulder pork, cubed
1 tablespoon cornflour
1 tablespoon oil
1 large onion, peeled and chopped
½ pt (300 ml) dry cider
½ pt (300 ml) chicken stock (made from a cube)
1 small garlic clove, peeled and crushed
4 cloves
2 pinches of marjoram
1 Granny Smith apple, peeled, cored and chopped
4 oz (125 g) black pudding, skinned and cubed
1½ lb (675 g) waxy potatoes, sliced and cooked
1 oz (25 g) butter, melted
salt and pepper

1   Season the cornflour with salt and pepper and dry the cubed pork with paper towel. Stir the pork cubes into the cornflour. Shake off any loose flour.
2   Heat the oil in a roomy pan and gently cook the onions for 4–5 minutes. Push the onions aside and, adding extra oil if you need it, fry the pork. Turn the cubes over and over until they are nicely browned.
3   Add the cider, stock, garlic, cloves, marjoram, salt and pepper. Bring to the boil, then turn down the heat and simmer for about 1½ hours with the lid on.
4   Just before the end of cooking time, stir in the apples and the black pudding. Season with salt and pepper. Do not stir vigorously or the black pudding will break up.
5   Preheat the oven to gas4/350°F/180°C.
6   Put the pork mixture in a flattish ovenproof dish or a pie dish and lay the potato slices on the meat, overlapping them neatly. The first slices should rest on the pie rim. Pack as many slices as you can, then brush the melted butter over the slices. Reheat carefully.

PORK & GARLIC SAUSAGE PIE

Serves 4 generously

4 pork escalopes (from the leg), each about
    4–5 oz (125–150 g)
2 oz (50 g) butter
2 medium-size onions, peeled and sliced
little brown sugar
1 tablespoon flour
½ pt (300 ml) dry cider
1 tablespoon tomato purée
4 oz (125 g) piece of chorizo sausage (spicy
    Spanish pork sausage)

Potato and Onion Bunches
3 medium-sized potatoes, baked in the oven
    until done but firm
1 medium onion, peeled, chopped and
    boiled in salted water until soft
1½ oz (40 g) butter

1   Preheat the oven to gas4/350°F/180°C.
2   Melt half butter in a roomy pan and fry the onions until brown. Transfer to a large casserole.
3   Brown both sides of the escalopes in the remaining butter. Set them on top of the onions in a single layer. Sprinkle the brown sugar over.
4   In a jug, whisk the flour into the cider. Whisk in the tomato purée. Pour over the chops.
5   Bake covered for about 1 hour, or until the meat is tender. About 15 minutes before the end of cooking time, slice the sausage and lay the slices on top of the sauce. Remove from the oven.
6   To make the potato and onion bunches you will need a greased baking sheet. Peel and grate the potatoes coarsely into a bowl. Drain the onions very well. In fact, it is easier to do this by putting them in a nylon sieve and applying a kitchen paper towel. Mix into the potato. Stir the melted butter in gently. Using your hands, grab a bundle and sit it on the greased baking sheet. This does not need to be a tidy bundle, just a good mound. Bake for 20–30 minutes until brown and crispy.
7   Transfer the bunches to the top of the pork. Reheat for just 10–15 minutes.

FISH PIES

SEA FISH PIE

Serves 4

12 oz (325 g) white fish
½ pt (300 ml) milk
1 level tablespoon flour
knife tip of made-up mustard
knob of butter, plus 1 oz (25 g) melted butter
2 size-1 eggs, hard-boiled
12 oz (325 g) waxy potatoes, peeled
3 oz (75 g) grated cheese

1   Cut the fish up into chunks and seek out any bones. Put in a heatproof dish and barely cover with a mixture of half the milk and water.
2   Cover with cling-film and microwave for just 2–3 minutes or until fish is done. Otherwise poach gently for 5 about minutes.

3   Drain off the fish stock and mix with the remaining milk and more cold water to make up to ½ pt (300 ml). Whisk in the flour then put the jug back in the microwave. Cook for about 4 minutes on full power, whisking hard every minute, or in a pan over a low heat. Once thickened, add the mustard and butter. Season.
4   Quarter the eggs and add to the fish in an ovenproof dish. Pour over enough sauce to moisten. Stir and reserve the rest of the sauce (add a little more milk to thin for pouring).
5   Cut potatoes into slices about ¼ in (5 mm) thick. Cover with salted water and boil gently until soft. Drain carefully and allow to cool a bit.
6   Preheat oven to gas4/350°F/180°C and a hot grill. Lay the potato slices over the fish, overlapping as neatly as possible. Brush melted butter over them, then scatter over grated cheese. Flash under grill to melt cheese and toast edges of the potatoes. Reheat in oven for about 20 minutes.

KITCHEN SUPPER FISH PIE

Serves 6–8

Looking for a cheaper fish to go round a lot of people, I suggest you try coley. Its dark colour is not very appealing on the slab, but it lightens considerably when it is cooked and when very fresh its flavour is excellent. I have used a rich parsley sauce to partner coley and the pie is topped with a layer of creamy mashed potato with a crunchy layer of butter-fried crumbs (see the recipe below) on top of that.

1 lb (450 g) fresh coley, skin on
about ¼ pt (150 ml) milk
3 hard-boiled eggs
½ fish stock cube (optional)
1 level tablespoon white flour
2 tablespoons chopped parsley
knob of butter
12 oz (325 g) creamy mashed potatoes
    (beaten with milk and a knob of butter)
3 oz (75 g) Butter-fried Crumbs (see below)
salt and pepper

1   Put the coley in a flattish ovenproof dish and pour over a mixture of milk and water to cover.
2   Poach the fish either in the microwave or in the oven. For the microwave: cover the dish with cling-film and puncture a few holes in it. Cook on high for about 3 minutes, or until the fish is done. For cooking in the oven preheated to gas4/350°F/180°C, cover with foil and cook for about 10–15 minutes. An alternative way, of course, is to cook it in a lidded frying pan on top of the stove. When the fish is cooked it will look opaque. Drain off the poaching liquid into a jug. Strip the skin off the fish and cut the flesh up into pieces. Set these back in the flattish dish. Cut each egg into quarters and add these to the fish.
3   Now make the parsley sauce: top up the milk and water mixture in the jug to ½ pt (300 ml). At this point you could dissolve ½ a fish stock cube in a little boiling water to add to the fish stock and milk if you felt the fish taste was rather weak. Pour this mixture into a pan and whisk the flour into it. When the flour has dispersed, take a wooden spoon and stir over a low heat until the liquid thickens. Cook for a couple of minutes. Then stir in the parsley and butter. Season with pepper. Pour this sauce over the fish and egg mixture (you may not need all of it). Stir it round a bit and leave the mixture to cool and firm up.
4   Preheat the oven to gas4/350°F/180°C.
5   Spread the mashed potato over the fish and smooth down the surface. Top with the butter-fried breadcrumbs and reheat uncovered in the oven.

Note
This pie is very suitable for dividing up into separate one-portion containers and storing wrapped in foil in a freezer.

BUTTER-FRIED CRUMBS

These are quite easy to do, but the drawback is that you must not leave them. They must be turned over constantly.

2 oz (50 g) butter
1 teaspoon oil
4 oz (125 g) fresh white breadcrumbs
salt and pepper

1   Melt the butter and oil in a non-stick pan. Add the crumbs.
2   Over a moderate heat, fry the crumbs, turning them over and over all the time. Remove the crumbs from the pan when they are a good gold colour.
3   When cold, season with salt and pepper, then store in a tin.

LUXURY FISH PIE

Serves 6–8

1½ lb (675 g) best-quality haddock and
  halibut mixed
about ¼ pt (150 ml) milk
6 oz (175 g) fresh or defrosted frozen
  prawns
½ fish stock cube (optional)
1 tablespoon flour
grated rind and juice of 1 lemon
1 tablespoon chopped tarragon leaves plus
  extra whole tarragon leaves
½ head of fennel
1 lb (450 g) floury potatoes
knob of butter
salt and pepper

1   Poach the haddock and halibut in a mixture
of milk and water until cooked. This can be done
either in the microwave, on the stove or in the
oven. Season with salt and pepper. Drain off the
poaching liquid into a measuring jug.
2   Break up the fish and set it in a flattish
ovenproof dish. Add the prawns to the fish in the
dish. (If the prawns were frozen, save the liquid
which drained off them and add this to the milk
and water mixture already in the measuring jug.)
3   Make the mixture in the jug up to ½ pt
(300 ml) with more milk. Taste the liquid and if
it is not fishy enough you could add ½ a fish
stock cube dissolved in a small amount of hot
water. Now thicken this sauce. Whisk the flour
into the milk and fish stock mixture. Do this in a
pan on the stove or in the microwave for 4
minutes (beating hard every minute). In the pan,
keep stirring until the mixture thickens. At this
point stir in the lemon rind and the chopped
tarragon. Remove from the heat and pour the
fish sauce into the flat dish with the cooked fish
and prawns. You may not need all of the sauce
but be generous, because the cooked fennel is
going to make another layer.
4   To cook the fennel: chop off any bruised bits
along with any green fronds which could be used
for decoration. Chop the fennel into small pieces
and simmer in salted water until done. Drain
and lay the chopped pieces on top of the sauce.

5   Peel the potatoes and cook in salted water.
When soft, drain off the water and return the
pan to the warm hob to allow the potatoes to dry
off a bit.
6   Preheat the oven to gas4/350°F/180°C.
7   Now put the potatoes, 2 at a time, through a
ricer – this is a gadget which forces the potatoes
through little holes and the potato arrives like
white rice, hence the name. The potatoes are very
airy and look pretty. (This is also a means of
making extremely smooth creamy potatoes,
because once they have been riced the potato is
then beaten up to a smooth cream with milk,
butter or cream.) Arrange the riced potatoes on
top of the fennel and reheat the pie in the oven
for 20 minutes.

Alternative fillings for fish pies:
Use 1 lb (450 g) cod or haddock with 4 hard-
boiled eggs, quartered, for a simple tasty pie.

Alternative sauce:
Add a knob of butter to the liquid and a small
carton (¼ pt / 150 ml) of single cream to the
sauce. What is not used inside the pie can be
served separately.

Mashed potato:
Arrive at an extremely smooth and creamy
mixture by using a ricer as described above. Put
the creamy potato in a large piping bag fitted
with a giant star tube. Pipe large rosettes all over
the top of the pie. Toast under a hot grill to
brown the rosettes, then return the pie to an
oven preheated to gas4/350°F/180°C to heat it
through.

STARGAZEY PIE

Serves 6–8

You can use either herrings or pilchards for this fish pie. This delightfully named and famous dish from Cornwall is quoted in all the traditional cookery books. I suspect, however, that it is not made all that often, except for exhibitions, visitors and the like. I once saw it featured in a cookery book, where the photograph was of the pie before it was cooked. The pie was immensely attractive, with a plaited trim of finely cut pastry decorating the border and the top covered with flowers and leaves. The fish heads are set above the pastry.

8 medium herrings, gutted, cleaned and
    boned but heads left on
2 hard-boiled eggs, chopped
4 rashers of rindless bacon, chopped small
2 oz (50 g) onion, peeled and finely chopped
¼ pt (150 ml) cider
10 oz (275 g) Shortcrust Pastry (see page 16)
1 size-7 egg, beaten with a little milk
salt and pepper

Stuffing
4 oz (125 g) white breadcrumbs
2 fl oz (50 ml) milk
1 tablespoon fresh parsley
juice and grated rind of 1 lemon
2 oz (50 g) onions, chopped small

First make the stuffing
1   Soak the breadcrumbs briefly in the milk.
2   Squeeze the crumbs and put in a small bowl with the parsley, lemon rind and juice and the onion. Mix together.
3   Divide this into 8 and stuff into the herring.

To assemble the pie
1   Preheat the oven to gas6/400°F/200°C.
2   Use a deepish pie plate with a rim. Arrange the herring with their heads just resting on the pie plate rim and all the tails meeting in the centre. In between the fish, arrange the chopped eggs, bacon and the onions. Season with salt and pepper and pour over the cider.

3   Roll the pastry out into a circle big enough to accommodate the herring heads. Cut a very narrow strip of pastry and fix this with water all round the edge of the pie dish. Dampen the edge first, then press down the strip. Now dampen the top of the strip and fit the pastry across but leaving the herring heads exposed. Press the lid down firmly and brush the pastry with the beaten egg and milk. Use the pastry trimmings to decorate the top of the pie and around the steam hole in the middle. Leaves and flowers would look good, as would a finely made plait of pastry to fit round the edge. Re-brush the pie lid with the egg and milk mixture.
4   Bake the pie on a baking sheet in the oven for about 50 minutes.

STARGAZEY PIE – A MODERN VERSION

Serves 6–8

You can buy cans of pilchards in tomato sauce for this recipe, but fresh pilchards do come on the market every now and then. They look just like overgrown sardines.

First make a stuffing in exactly the same way as for the last recipe. Top, tail, gut and bone each pilchard (the fish merchant will do this for you), divide the stuffing into 8 and stuff this into the body cavity of each pilchard. Preheat the oven to gas6/400°F/200°C.

stuffing as in the last recipe
8 prepared pilchards
½ jar (8 fl oz / 250 ml) of passata (sieved
    tomatoes)
1 teaspoon flour
knob of butter
1 teaspoon sugar
4 oz (125 g) mushrooms
little oil
8 oz (225 g) Shortcrust Pastry (see page 16)
little milk
salt and pepper
flour, for dusting

1   Grease well a deepish pie plate about 9 in (23 cm) across.
2   Divide the stuffing into 8 and roll each piece into a sausage shape. Put one in each fish. Set the fish down side by side in the pie dish bottom.
3   Put the passata in a pan and sprinkle the flour in. Stirring all the time, heat the sauce until it thickens. Stir in the butter and sugar. Season to taste.
4   Chop the mushrooms and lightly fry them in a little oil.
5   Scatter the mushrooms over the stuffed pilchards, then pour over the tomato sauce.
6   On a floured board, roll out the pastry slightly larger than the pie dish. Cut a narrow strip of pastry off and fix this on the pie dish rim, running a wet finger round it first. Press on the strip. Wet that and then lay the pastry lid on and press it down firmly on the rim of the dish. Brush over with milk and bake for about 40 minutes.

TROUT, OYSTER & EEL PIE

Serves 4–6

This recipe is based on one which was unearthed by the late Michael Smith, dated 1738. The eels, oysters and artichokes would have been fresh, but the smoked version here is very tasty.

4 small skinned trout fillets (total weight about 12 oz / 325 g)
1 tablespoon pickled capers
8 oz (225 g) tin of smoked eel fillets
4 oz (125 g) tin of smoked oysters in brine, drained, rinsed and chopped
4 oz (125 g) mushrooms, wiped and sliced
8 oz (225 g) jar of artichoke bottoms, drained
2 tablespoons chopped parsley
1 tablespoon chopped chives
juice of 1 lemon (about 2 tablespoons)
8 oz (225 g) Shortcrust Pastry (see page 16)
1 size-7 egg, beaten
salt and pepper
butter, for greasing

1   Preheat the oven to gas6/400°F/200°C and liberally butter a 2 pt (1.2 litre) pie dish.
2   Lay the trout fillets on the bottom, followed by the capers, then the eel fillets, then the oysters, then the mushrooms and lastly the artichokes. Sprinkle the parsley, chives and a little salt between each layer, and squeeze the lemon juice over everything. Dot the last of the butter here and there.
3   'Close the pye' as it says in the original recipe. On a floured board, roll out the pastry slightly larger than the pie dish. Cut a narrow strip of pastry just wide enough to fit round the lip of the dish. Wet the rim first, press the pastry down and wet the top of that. Lift the pastry over the pie and press down the edges either with a fork or your fingers. Trim off the excess pastry and make a few slits in the top of the pastry. Brush over with beaten egg.
4   Set on a baking sheet and bake in the oven for 45–50 minutes.

'Promises and pie-crust are made to be broken.'

Polite Conversation, Jonathan Swift

EEL PIE

Serves 6

East Anglia has always been associated with eels. Living in the North East, I knew nothing of them until I took a trip to London's East End to try their famous jellied eels. The flesh is sweet and dense and I liked it. My friend John tells me that, when he was in his teens working on a barge, the old bargemen caught and boiled eels with onions and vegetables. The tough job was skinning them.

2 lb (900 g) eel, skinned and cut into ½ in (5 cm) slices
2 tablespoons oil
2 oz (50 g) butter
2 medium onions, peeled and finely chopped
2 oz (50 g) plain flour, seasoned
grated rind and juice of 1 large lemon
1 glass of white wine
1 teaspoon chopped fennel
1 teaspoon chopped tarragon leaves
1 oz (25 g) currants
½ level teaspoon ground ginger
¼ pt (5 fl oz) single cream
1 size-1 egg, hard-boiled and thinly sliced
8 oz (225 g) New Flaky Pastry (see page 19)
1 size-7 egg, beaten
salt and pepper

1   Preheat the oven to gas7/425°F/220°C.
2   Roll the eel pieces in the seasoned flour. Heat the oil and butter in a frying pan and fry the eel pieces until they turn golden. Remove and transfer the eel pieces to a 2 pt (1.2 litre) pie dish.
3   Next fry the onions in the same pan. Turn down the heat and sprinkle about 2 teaspoons of the seasoned flour over the onion. Stir this in and gradually add the lemon juice and white wine, followed by the herbs, lemon rind, currants, ginger and the cream. Simmer for a minute, season, then pour over the eel pieces. Top with the sliced hard-boiled egg.
4   Roll out the pastry on a floured board to a round rather larger than the pie dish and cut a narrow band of pastry to fit the rim of the dish. Wet the rim, then secure the strip of pastry. Wet

the top of that, then cover the pie with the piece of pastry. Seal the edges carefully. Make one or two steam vents and decorate with pastry leaves and flowers. Brush over with the beaten egg.
5   Set the pie on a baking sheet and bake for 20 minutes or so at the high heat, then turn the oven down to gas4/350°F/180°C and cook for a further 40 minutes or so.

COCKLE PIE

Serves 4

A viewer from Gwent gave us a recipe for cockle cakes (*teisen gocos*) and we made them on one of my programmes. The cockles were mixed with batter and dropped by the spoonful into hot oil. They were very good eaten with lemon juice sprinkled over and with brown bread and butter. This cockle pie recipe comes from the Gower Peninsula, where the harvesting of cockles from the muddy sand was women's work in days gone by.

8 oz (225 g) Shortcrust Pastry (see page 16)
8 oz (225 g) prepared fresh cockles
3 tablespoons chopped spring onions
8 strips of streaky bacon, chopped small
little single cream or fish stock (from cube)
pepper
little milk, for glazing
butter or lard, for greasing

1   Preheat the oven gas6/400°F/200°C and grease well a deepish pie plate about 8 in (20 cm) across with butter or lard.
2   Roll out the pastry thinly and use to line the pie plate. Trim off the excess pastry.
3   Layer the cockles, spring onions and bacon, seasoning each layer with pepper as you go. Lastly, dribble over a little cream or fish stock, just enough to moisten the mixture.
4   Roll out the pastry trimmings and cut narrow strips of pastry to make a lattice-effect lid for the pie. Fix the strips securely at each side by pressing down firmly on the border.
5   Brush with milk and bake for 30 minutes.

SUET PUDDINGS

TRADITIONAL STEAK & KIDNEY PUDDING

Serves 6–8

This is steak and kidney pudding made in the traditional way. The suet crust is made with butcher's suet and the meat goes in raw. Because of this, the pudding has to be steamed for at least 4 hours – 5 if the meat is chunky.

Buy your lump of beef suet from the butcher. Have it really cold and grate it on the largest holes of a metal grater. There are transparent linking skins throughout the suet which have to be discarded. Weigh it out and handle it gently.

Suet Crust
10 oz (275 g) self-raising flour, plus more
    for dusting
1 level teaspoon baking powder
¼ teaspoon dried thyme
5 oz (150 g) grated suet
salt and pepper

Filling
2 lb (900 g) best stewing steak or rump
    steak
¾ lb (325 g) ox kidney
2 tablespoons plain flour
1 large onion, peeled and chopped
1 pt (575 ml) beef stock (or half stock and
    half red wine)
8 oz (225 g) firm small mushrooms, sliced
bay leaf

Make the suet crust
1 Sieve the flour and baking powder into a bowl, adding some salt and pepper and the thyme. Stir in the grated suet and then add as little cold water as possible to make the dough. This should be softish but not sticky.
2 On a floured board, roll the dough out to a large circle. Cut away about one-quarter of this circle and set aside for the lid. Butter a 3 pt (1.75 litre) pudding basin generously and drop the three-quarters circle of pastry into it. Press this gently all round to fit the basin, paying particular attention to the join and allow the pastry to overhang the top of the basin slightly.

Prepare the filling
1 Cut the steak into neat 1 in (2.5 cm) pieces and cut the kidney slightly smaller. Discard all fat and skin from both meats and pay particular attention to removing the core from the kidneys. Put the flour into a plastic bag. Season it well and toss in the meat and kidneys to coat them well too.
2 Spoon the meats into the lined basin, alternating with layers of the mushrooms and seasoning. Pour over the stock or half stock and half red wine barely to cover the meat. Push the bay leaf down into the filling.
3 Now roll out the remaining pastry to form a circle which will drop neatly on top of the meat. Run a wet finger round the outer rim of the circle and bring the two edges together.
4 Firmly cover the bowl first with a circle of greaseproof paper and then with a circle of foil, allowing this to balloon up slightly but fit the foil really securely under the rim.
5 Now stand the basin on an old plate in a saucepan and pour boiling water in to come two-thirds of the way up the basin. Put the lid on and simmer gently for at least 4 hours, checking from time to time and adding more boiling water to the saucepan as necessary.

'England is merely an island of beef flesh swimming in a warm gulf stream of gravy.'

The Modern Soul, Katherine Mansfield

STEAK & KIDNEY PUDDING – A MODERN VERSION

Serves 6–8

It is more common now to cook the filling in advance. This has the added advantage that more fat can be skimmed off and the steaming time can be reduced to 2 hours. The suet crust also stays slightly crisp on the outside. The crust itself can be made with half suet and half butter and this does enhance the flavour. Instead of butcher's suet, this time I am using ready-prepared packet suet.

Suet Crust
10 oz (275 g) self-raising flour
2¹/₂ oz (65 g) butter, frozen and grated
2¹/₂ oz (65 g) packet suet
¹/₄ teaspoon dried thyme
salt and pepper

Filling
2 lb (900 g) best stewing steak or rump
    steak
³/₄ lb (325 g) ox kidney
2 tablespoons plain flour seasoned with salt
    and pepper
2 tablespoons oil
1 large onion, peeled and chopped
1 pt (575 ml) beef stock (made from a cube)
    or half stock and half red wine
1 bay leaf
8 oz (225 g) firm small mushrooms, sliced

The day before: make filling
1   Prepare the meats by cutting the steak into neat 1 in (2.5 cm) pieces. Cut the kidney pieces slightly smaller. Discard all fat skin and gristle and pay particular attention to removing the core from the kidneys.
2   Heat the oil in a roomy pan. Toss the meat and kidneys in the seasoned flour in a plastic bag. Shake off the loose flour and fry the meat and kidney in the hot oil, keeping the meats moving, until quite brown. Push the meat to one side and

add the onions. Fry them for just a couple of minutes, then stir the two together.
3   Pour in the stock or the stock mixed with red wine together with the bay leaf. Stir with a wooden spoon and loosen any stuck-on bits of meat and flour on the bottom of the pan. Put the lid on and simmer for about 1¹/₂ hours. The meat will not be fully cooked, but remember it is going to have another 2 hours in the pudding.
4   Stir in the sliced mushrooms and remove from the heat. Leave to cool down and next day you will be able to lift off and discard any solidified fat.

Make suet crust
1   Sift the flour into a bowl, stir in the suet and grate the butter directly into the bowl. Use the biggest holes on a metal grater and wrap the butter in a piece of foil until you get down to the last bit. Add the dried thyme and mix the flour, suet and butter around a bit. Season with salt and pepper, then use a little cold water to make a soft but not sticky dough. I use a long-bladed knife to stir and press the dough into a mass, which I can then gather up with my hand and I knead it lightly first in the bowl and then on a floured board.
2   Roll the pastry out to a large circle and cut out a triangular piece, about one-quarter of the pastry, and set this aside for the lid. Grease a 3 pt (1.75 litre) basin, drop the pastry into this and ease it round to fit, paying particular attention to the join. Allow the pastry to overhang the basin slightly.
3   Spoon the steak and kidney mixture in and pour in about ¹/₄ pt (150 ml) gravy. Cover with the pastry lid (having re-rolled it out to a circle) and seal the lid carefully by nipping the pastry together. Cover the pudding first with a circle of greaseproof paper and then foil, allowing the foil to balloon up slightly but tucking it tightly under the rim.

Cooking pudding
1   Stand the basin on an old plate and sit it inside a large pan. Pour in enough boiling water to come two-thirds of the way up the basin.
2   Turn the heat down to a simmer, put the lid on and cook for 2 hours (it does not matter if this goes up to 3 hours, the pudding will be fine). Do

keep an eagle eye on the water level and see that it does not run dry.

Variations
The addition of oysters to the filling is said to be delicious. Reduce the amount of gravy you put in with the meat for the fresh oysters will certainly add a great deal more. I did see a suggestion that a can of smoked oysters, drained and added to the filling is equally delicious. It sounds a good idea to me.

QUORN BACON ROLL

Serves 6–8

Quorn country is hunting country and this hearty dish would be a welcome meal after a cold day in the field.

A boiled pudding like this would have been cooked in a cloth. It is, however, much easier to manage with the use of greaseproof paper and foil.

Suet Crust
4 oz (125 g) packet suet
12 oz (325 g) self-raising flour
3 oz (75 g) block of butter from the freezer
2 fat pinches of dried thyme
salt and pepper

Filling
8–10 rashers of rindless bacon
1 tablespoon chopped chives
2 teaspoons fresh sage (cut into small pieces)
1 large Spanish onion, peeled and cut fairly small

1 First make the suet pastry: stir the suet into the flour in a roomy bowl. Next grate the hard butter into the flour through the holes on a grater. Use a fork to stir the butter through the flour. Season and add the thyme.
2 Then add about 6 fl oz (175 ml) of cold water, using a long knife to stir the mixture and press it together as you go along. When it is just beginning to hold together, use your hand to gather it together and knead gently first in the bowl and then on a floured board.
3 Roll the pastry out to a large square about 1/4 in (5 mm) thick. Lay the bacon pieces all over it, leaving a narrow border. Sprinkle over the chives and sage, and then the onion. Roll up to a big sausage and squeeze the ends together.
4 Grease a square of greaseproof paper, lay the 'sausage' on that and roll it up loosely. Cut a piece of foil a little larger than the paper and wrap the sausage up in that. Nip the ends very tightly – a paper-covered wire strip helps.
5 Lower the parcel into gently boiling water and cook for 2 hours.
6 Some sort of a sauce or gravy is needed, or you could serve a vegetable with a sauce, such as cauliflower cheese or leeks with a white sauce.

BACON ROLY-POLY

This is an oven-baked version of the boiled bacon roll above. The only variation is that the suet crust should be rolled out very thinly and the finished roll brushed with beaten egg to give it some colour.

Bake on a greased baking sheet in an oven preheated to gas6/400°F/200°C for 40–50 minutes, when it should be golden and crusty.

STEAK & KIDNEY PIE

Serves 6–8

Whenever I casserole meat I like to mix shin beef with stewing beef. The reason for this is that while shin beef has the best flavour it does tend to disintegrate into shreds with long cooking and the stewing beef does not.

1½ lb (675 g) stewing steak, cut into 1 in (2.5 cm) cubes
8 oz (225 g) shin beef, cut small
5 oz (150 g) ox kidneys
1½ oz (40 g) dripping or 2 tablespoons of oil
1 large onion, peeled and finely chopped
2 generous pinches of dried thyme
dash of Worcestershire sauce
1 heaped tablespoon plain flour
1 pt (600 ml) beef stock (from a cube)
6 oz (175 g) open-cap mushrooms, sliced
salt and pepper

Extra Gravy
½ pt (300 ml) cold beef stock (made from a cube)
1 heaped dessertspoon plain flour
gravy browning or gravy salt (optional)

Suet Pastry
12 oz (325 g) self-raising flour, sifted
6 oz (175 g) packet suet
2 generous pinches of dried thyme
2 teaspoons finely chopped parsley
1 size-7 egg, beaten
little milk

1 Check the meat carefully and cut away any skin and some of the fat. Skin the kidney and chop quite small. Cut away the core.
2 In a large pan, put the dripping or oil over a fairly high heat. Fry the meat and kidneys until brown, turning often. Push the meat to one side and fry the onions briefly. Stir them together.

3 Add the dried thyme and Worcestershire sauce. Season with salt and pepper and sprinkle the flour over. Stir this round a bit and then pour in the beef stock. Bring to a boil, then reduce the heat and simmer for about 2 hours. Watch that it does not boil dry.
4 Just before the end of the cooking time, stir in the mushrooms. Set aside to go cold.
5 Make up the extra gravy: dissolve the stock cube in a little hot water then top with some cold water to take it up to the ½ pt (300 ml) mark. Whisk the flour into the water. When the flour has dispersed, use a wooden spoon to stir the gravy over a medium heat until it has thickened.
6 Spoon the meat mixture into a 1½ – 2 pt (850 ml–1.1 litre) pie dish. Add some of the gravy. Set a pie funnel in the centre or pile the meat up there in the middle to support the pastry until it sets.
7 Preheat the oven to gas7/425°F/220°C.
8 Make the pastry: sift the flour into a bowl. Stir in the suet, salt, pepper and thyme and parsley. Mix in just enough cold water to give a soft but not sticky dough. Draw the pastry together and use your hand to knead it gently in the bowl and then on a floured board.
9 Roll out the pastry to the shape of the pie, but slightly larger. It should be about ½ in (1 cm) thick. From the outside edge, cut a narrow strip about ½ in (1 cm) wide to place round the rim. Wet the rim with water and press the strip down on to it. Wet the top of the strip and lift the pastry lid over and set it evenly over the meat. Press the edges firmly and slice off the extra pastry. Brush over the egg and milk mixture glaze. Add leaves and flowers if you wish and brush over them as well. Make one or two steam holes.
10 Set the pie on a baking sheet and bake for about 40 minutes. If there is any gravy left from the stew, add that to the thickened stock you made earlier. A touch of gravy browning or gravy salt will help the colour of your gravy. You can always extend the gravy with more beef stock.

BAKED MEAT ROLL

Serves 4–5

This is a variation on the bacon roly-poly.

Suet Pastry
12 oz (325 g) self-raising flour
6 oz (175 g) packet suet
2 fat pinches of dried thyme
salt and pepper
1 size-7 egg, beaten
little milk

Filling
1 lb (450 g) minced beef
1 tablespoon oil
1 medium-size onion, peeled and chopped
2 medium carrots, scraped and chopped
2 heaped teaspoons plain flour
½ pt (300 ml) meat stock (made from a cube)
knife point of gravy browning (optional)

1   First cook the minced beef: in a roomy pan, heat the oil and add the mince. Fry it hard over a high heat. It will probably stick a bit but use your wooden spoon to keep it moving.
2   Push the meat over to one side and fry the onions for 2–3 minutes, then add the carrots. Stir all three together over a lower heat.
3   Sprinkle the flour over and stir in really well. Stir in the meat stock and cook gently for about 20–25 minutes. Add a knife point of gravy browning if you wish. Set aside to cool.
4   Preheat the oven to gas6/400°F/200°C.
5   Make up the pastry: stir the suet into the flour along with the salt, ground pepper and thyme. Stir in enough cold water to make a soft but not sticky dough. As soon as it comes together in the bowl use your hand to knead it gently.
6   On a floured board, roll the pastry out fairly thinly to a square about ¼ in (5 mm) thick. Now use a slotted spoon to cover the pastry with the mince mixture. Leave a border all round.
7   Roll the suet pastry up like a Swiss roll. Place it on a greased baking sheet with the join underneath. Brush over the egg and milk glaze.
8   Bake for about 40–50 minutes.

VARIATIONS FOR A BAKED ROLL

CHEESE & ONION

8 oz (225 g) mature Cheddar cheese, grated
1 large Spanish onion, peeled and finely
   chopped
1 tablespoon chopped parsley

Use the same suet pastry recipe as for the baked meat roll. Scatter the cheese over the rolled-out pastry. Follow that with the onion and parsley. Roll up, glaze and bake for 40–50 minutes.

MUSHROOM & BACON

8 oz (225 g) streaky bacon, grilled and
   chopped
6 oz (175 g) mushrooms, sliced and lightly
   fried in butter

Use the same suet pastry recipe as for the baked meat roll. Scatter over the bacon and the mushrooms. Roll up, glaze and bake for about 40–50 minutes.

SMOKY BACON BADGER

Serves 4–6

This is another of those recipes which can be boiled or steamed. To be contrary I baked mine.

Suet Crust
5 oz (150 g) packet suet
3 oz (75 g) hard butter, grated
10 oz (275 g) self-raising flour
1 level teaspoon dried mixed herbs
1 size-7 egg
little milk

Filling
10 slices of smoked streaky bacon
1 medium-size onion, peeled and chopped
10 oz (275 g) waxy potatoes, peeled and
   cubed
1 teaspoon chopped sage leaves or 2 pinches
   of dried sage
2 oz (50 g) butter
oil, for frying
salt and pepper

1   Start making the filling: cook the bacon. Grill until well done and then chop it up.
2   Heat the oil and fry the onions slowly until soft and golden.
3   Boil the potato cubes in salted water. Remove from the water when they are almost done.
4   Pour some oil into a large frying pan to a depth of about ⅛ in (3 mm). Fry the potato cubes until they are brown and crusty. Drain on kitchen paper.
5   Preheat the oven to gas6/400°F/200°C.
6   Make up the pastry: stir the suet and butter into the flour along with the dried herbs.
7   Use just enough cold water to mix the flour into a soft but not sticky dough. Start with a knife pressing the pastry together, then use your hand to knead the pastry gently, first in the bowl and then on a floured board.
8   When it is relatively smooth, roll it out to a square about ¼ in (5 mm) thick. Spread the bacon all over the pastry and put the potatoes on top. Sprinkle with the sage, then cut the butter into little bits and scatter these about too. Roll

the badger up like a Swiss roll and lay the roll on a greased baking sheet with the join underneath. Beat the egg and milk together and brush this glaze over the top.
9   Bake for about 40–50 minutes.

PARTRIDGE PUDDING

Serves 4–6

Not long ago I was given a brace of partridge and I found this recipe to use them. As in a lot of very early recipes, the partridges were supposed to go into the suet crust raw, bones and all. I have altered that bit.

1 brace of partridge
4 oz (125 g) rump steak, cut thin
1 medium onion
2 tablespoons oil
1 pt (575 ml) meat stock
1 heaped tablespoon white flour
4 oz (125 g) mushrooms sliced
10 oz (275 g) Suet Pastry (see page 17)
1 teaspoon finely chopped fresh parsley
salt and pepper

1   Wipe the birds and joint them. Heat the oil and turn the pieces of partridge in it to brown. Turn them over and over. Add the rump steak to brown as well. Push the meat to one side and then fry the chopped onion. Mix together and season with salt and pepper.
2   Pour over the meat stock. Bring to a boil, then reduce the heat and simmer for about 2 hours or until the meat is falling off the bones. Fish out all the bones and skin.
3   Now sprinkle the flour over and stir this in a over a gentle heat. Continue to cook the stew for a few minutes more. Stir in the sliced mushrooms.
4   Roll out the pastry to a large circle about ½ in (1 cm) thick. Cut away one-quarter of the pastry and reserve this for the lid. Ease the rest of the pastry into a 3 pt (1.75 litre) basin, paying particular attention to the join.
5   Strain off the stew and reserve the gravy.

Arrange the meats in the pudding basin. Sprinkle in the parsley and just enough gravy to make the filling moist. Reserve the rest of the gravy to serve with the pudding.

6   Roll out the reserved piece of pastry to a circle which will fit the top of the pudding. Wet the edges and squeeze these two edges together all round.

7   Cover the top with greaseproof paper and foil and set the pudding basin on an old plate inside a large pan. Pour in boiling water to come two-thirds of the way up the basin, put the lid on and steam for about 2 hours.

LIKKY PIE

Serves 4

This recipe name must have come from the word leek.

1½ lb (700 g) young leeks
¾ lb (350 g) smoked streaky bacon, cut small
about ½ pt (300 ml) milk
6 oz (175 g) Suet Pastry (see page 17)
2 size-3 eggs, beaten
1 tablespoon double cream
salt and pepper

1   First cook the filling: clean the leeks, then chop them into ½ in (1 cm) slices. In a casserole, cover them with boiling water and cook for 5 minutes. Drain off the water and stir in the chopped bacon and just enough milk to cover. Simmer for about 30 minutes. Allow to go cold.

2   Preheat the oven to gas6/400°F/200°C and roll out the pastry. The pastry should just fit inside the casserole.

3   Just before you cover the casserole with the pastry, beat the eggs with the cream and pour this over the leek and bacon mixture. Season well, then fit the pastry over.

4   Bake for about 30 minutes or until the pastry is cooked and crisp.

ORIGINAL HARVEST PUDDING

Serves 6–8

16 oz (450 g) Suet Pastry (see page 17)
1 large or 2 small rabbit(s), jointed
6 oz (175 g) chopped onions
8 oz (225 g) chopped mushrooms
8 oz (225 g) streaky bacon, cut small
1 teaspoon fresh chopped sage
¼ pt (150 ml) vegetable stock (made from a cube)
salt and pepper

1   Make the pastry and use three-quarters of it to line a very large pudding basin, 3½–4 pts (2–2.25 litres). Layer the rabbit pieces, onions, mushrooms and bacon in the basin, seasoning as you go with salt, pepper and sage.

2   Pour over the stock and cover with a lid made from the remaining pastry rolled out to fit. Seal the edges firmly and trim away the excess pastry. Cover the pudding top with greaseproof paper and then foil.

3   Place in a roomy pan sitting on an old plate. Pour in boiling water to reach two-thirds of the way up the side of the basin. Steam for 2–2½ hours, keeping an eye on the water level.

4   When you turn the pudding out, do so into a dish with a deep side since the filling is so heavy that it may break the crust.

HARVEST PUDDING – A MODERN VARIATION

Serves 6–8

I prefer to cook the rabbit in advance, stripping all the meat from the bones. You will need a 3 pt (1.75 litre) basin.

1 large rabbit, jointed, or eight small rabbit
    joints
2 tablespoons oil
6 oz (175 g) chopped onions
1 small carrot, peeled and chopped
2 celery stalks, chopped
1 pt (575 ml) vegetable stock (from a cube)
16 oz (450 g) Suet Pastry (see page 17)
8 oz (225 g) mushrooms, sliced
8 oz (225 g) bacon, diced
1 teaspoon chopped fresh sage
salt and pepper

1   First cook the filling: heat the oil in a roomy pan or casserole and fry the onions for 4–5 minutes. Add the carrot and celery and continue cooking for another 2 minutes. Push the vegetables aside and fry the rabbit joints until they are browned on both sides.
2   Now pour in the stock and simmer for about 1½ hours or until the meat is falling off the bones. Set aside to go cold, when you can also skim off the fat.
3   Remove the meat from the rabbit and discard the bones.
4   On a floured board, roll out the suet crust to a large circle about ¼ in (5 mm) thick. Cut out one-quarter of this circle and set aside for a lid.
5   Ease the larger piece of pastry into the pudding basin, paying particular attention to the join. Allow the pastry to overhang the top edge. Now spoon the cooked rabbit, carrot and onion and celery into the basin and gently stir in the sliced mushrooms, bacon and sage. Season well then pour in just ¼ pt (150 ml) of the gravy and reserve the rest to serve separately.
6   Roll out the reserved pastry. Wet the crust round the edge and press the lid into position, squeezing the sides and the lid together. Trim off any excess pastry. Cover the pudding with some greaseproof paper and then with foil.
7   Steam for about 1½ hours (see notes on steaming, page 10).

CROCKY PIE OR POT PIE

Serves 4–6

This old idea seems to me to be worth reviving. The suet pastry is dropped on the contents of the casserole and it goes back into the oven lidless until the pastry is cooked.

1 lb (450 g) lamb (shoulder has a good
    flavour but cut into ¼ in / 5 mm pieces
    and you must trim it carefully, or use leg)
2 oz (50 g) flour
2 tablespoons oil
2 large onions, peeled and chopped
¼ lb (350 g) carrots, scraped and chopped
    into 1 in (2.5 cm) chunks
8 oz (225 g) turnip, chopped into 1 in
    (2.5 cm) chunks
¾ pt (425 ml) lamb stock (from a cube)
1 bay leaf
small bunch of parsley, chopped
6 oz (175 g) Suet Pastry (see page 17)
salt and pepper

1   Toss the meat pieces in seasoned flour. Remove the meat, shake off any loose flour and fry in the oil, turning the meat often. When brown all over, push the meat to one side of the casserole and fry the onions, carrots and turnips.
2   Preheat the oven to gas4/350°F/180°C and pour the stock into the casserole, along with the bay leaf and the parsley. Put on the lid and return the casserole to the oven for 1¾ hours, or until the lamb is tender.
3   Remove the casserole lid and roll out the suet crust to fit in inside the casserole. Drop it on the meat and vegetables and return the casserole immediately to the oven, but turn up the temperature to gas6/400°F/200°C. Bake for 25–30 minutes or until the crust is golden brown and cooked through.

COBBLERS

CHEESE, HAM & CELERY COBBLER

Serves 6

Cobblers are casseroles topped with a layer made up of rounds of scone dough. Here the topping consists of cheesy scones.

Filling
1 large onion, peeled and chopped
4 large celery stalks, chopped
1 tablespoon oil
5 level tablespoons flour
3 level teaspoons mustard powder
¾ pt (450 ml) milk
½ chicken stock cube
1 teaspoon dried oregano
8 oz (225 g) cooked ham, chopped

Cobbler Topping
3 oz (75 g) butter or margarine
9 oz (250 g) self-raising flour
pinch of salt
pinch of cayenne pepper
4 oz (125 g) grated Cheddar cheese
little milk, for glazing

1   Preheat the oven to gas6/400°F/200°C.
2   Make the filling: fry the onion and celery in the oil for 3–4 minutes. Stir in the flour and mustard for half a minute, then take the pan off the heat.
3   Stir in the milk a little at a time, adding the crumbled stock cube and the oregano. Return to the heat and simmer for 3–4 minutes to thicken. Stir in the ham and turn the mixture into an oval ovenproof dish, about 12 in (30 cm) long.
4   Make the cobbler topping: rub the fat into the flour, add seasoning, cayenne and half the cheese. Use about 6 tablespoons of cold water to mix to a soft dough.
5   Scatter the rest of the cheese over a pastry board and roll the scone dough out on it to a

thickness of 1 in (2.5 cm). Using a 2 in (5 cm) biscuit cutter, cut as many circles as you can, gathering up the trimmings and re-rolling them to make more.
6   Set cheese side up in an overlapping circle round the dish and resting partially on the outside rim. Brush the cheese scones all over with milk.
7   Bake in the oven for about 25 minutes.

GOULASH COBBLER

Serves 6

Goulash
1½ lb (675 g) braising steak, cubed
2 tablespoon oil
2 medium onions, peeled and sliced
2 teaspoons paprika
knife tip of chilli powder
1 teaspoon caraway seeds
2 teaspoons plain flour
¼ pt (150 ml) beef stock (made from a cube)
14 oz (400 g) can of chopped tomatoes
1 tablespoon chopped fresh parsley
¼ pt (150 ml) red wine
sour cream, to serve

Cobbler
pinch of salt
pinch of cayenne pepper
½ teaspoon caraway seeds, plus extra
9 oz (250 g) self-raising flour
3 oz (75 g) butter or margarine
little milk

1   Preheat the oven to gas4/350°F/180°C.
2   Heat half the oil in a large casserole, add the meat and fry hard, turning. When well browned, push to one side. Add remaining oil and fry onions, sprinkle over paprika and chilli, caraway and flour. Stir well and remove from heat.
3   Slowly add the stock. Return to the heat and bring to a boil, reduce to a simmer and add the tomatoes, wine, parsley and seasoning. Mix well.
4   Cook in the oven for about 1½ hours.
5   Raise oven setting to gas6/400°F/200°C.
6   To make the cobbler: stir the seasoning, pepper and caraway seeds into the flour. Rub the butter in until the mixture looks like breadcrumbs. Stir in 6 tablespoons of cold water to make a soft dough.
7   On a floured board, roll out the dough to a thickness of about 1 in (2.5 cm). Using a 2 in (5 cm) cutter, cut out as many circles as you can, re-rolling trimmings to make more.
8   Set circles overlapping round the edge. Brush with milk and sprinkle a few caraway seeds over.
9   Bake for 25 minutes and serve with a spoonful of sour cream on each plate.

DUMPLINGS

Yet another traditional old-fashioned favourite to help to stretch the meat. The most usual way to make dumplings, or dough boys, is with suet and they are cooked on top of a casserole or stew. You can also simmer the dough boys in a pan of stock and add them to the meat when cooked. Another way is to oven-bake them so that they become crisp on the outside. Suet dumplings are also excellent in soup.

PARSLEY DUMPLINGS

Makes 8

4 oz (125 g) self-raising flour, plus more for rolling
2 pinches of salt
2 oz (50 g) shredded suet
1 tablespoon freshly chopped parsley

1   Mix the flour with the salt, suet and parsley. Mix to a softish dough with 3–4 tablespoons water.
2   Turn out on a well-floured board and divide into 8 pieces. Roll into neat balls.
3   Simmer the dumplings for 20 minutes in a closed pan or about the same in a closed casserole.

SMOKY BACON AND THYME DUMPLINGS

Makes 8

3 rashers of smoky bacon, cut small
1 tiny onion, peeled and finely chopped
1 level teaspoon fresh thyme

1   Fry the bacon until it is almost done, add the onion and thyme and continue until the onion is golden. Allow to cool down.
2   Add to the basic mixture, omitting parsley.

CRUSTY DOUGH BOYS

Makes 8

Make up the dumplings as in the basic recipe above, or just rolled out to a circle and marked off in wedges. Bake on a well-greased baking sheet at gas6/400°F/200°C for about 15 minutes, or until crisp on the outside but still soft within.

SUET-FREE DUMPLINGS

Makes 6–8

4 oz (125 g) plain flour
1 teaspoon baking powder
¼ teaspoon salt
1 tablespoon finely chopped and cooked onions
2 tablespoons mixed herbs (parsley and chives)
1 size-3 egg
2 fl oz (50 ml) milk

1   Sieve flour, baking powder and salt into a bowl.
2   Stir in the onion and herbs.
3   Beat the egg with a little milk and mix this into the flour, adding more milk to get a soft but not sticky dough.
4   Handle lightly and roll into a sausage. Divide this sausage into dumplings the size of golf balls.
5   Use in the usual way on top of a stew or casserole with the lid on and bake for about 12 minutes.

BROWN ALE VEGETABLE STEW WITH DUMPLINGS

Serves 6–8

2 tablespoons olive oil
12 oz (325 g) small onions (large pickling onions)
2 garlic cloves, peeled and finely chopped
2 celery stalks, finely chopped
8 oz (225 g) carrots, scraped and cut into chunks
1 small swede, peeled and cut into cubes
2 small white and purple turnips, peeled and cubed
1 lb (450 g) brown mushrooms, wiped and cut into thick slices
2 tablespoons plain flour
1¼ pts (750 ml) vegetable stock
½ pt (300 ml) brown ale
2 tablespoons tomato purée
1 heaped tablespoon thyme leaves or 1 teaspoon dried thyme
salt and pepper

Dumplings
4 oz (125 g) plain flour, plus more for rolling
1 teaspoon baking powder
½ teaspoon salt
2 tablespoons grated Parmesan cheese
2 tablespoons freshly chopped parsley
1 size-3 egg
2 tablespoons milk

1   In a large casserole, heat half the oil and fry the onions, garlic, celery, carrots, swede and turnips for 3 minutes, until they all turn light brown. Push the vegetables to one side, add the remaining oil and fry the mushrooms for about 4 minutes. Now mix them thoroughly.
2   Sprinkle the flour over the vegetables, stir it in well and cook for a minute. Pour in the stock, ale, purée and thyme. Season and bring to the boil, then turn down the heat and simmer for about 30 minutes.
3   Now make the dumplings: sieve the flour, baking powder and salt into a bowl. Stir in the Parmesan and parsley well.
4   Beat the egg with the milk and mix in to make a soft dough. On a floured board, roll the dough into a sausage, divide into pieces and roll these into balls. Add some dry flour to your hands. The dumplings should be about the size of golf balls.
5   Slip the dumplings into the stew, put the lid back on and cook for a further 15 minutes.

Note
If the gravy is rather low, add a little more vegetable stock.

Casseroled Beef & Horseradish Dumplings

Serves 6–8

1½ lb (675 g) best stewing beef
½ lb (225 g) shin beef
3 tablespoons oil
1 large onion, peeled and chopped
4 small carrots, scraped and chopped
2 garlic cloves, peeled and crushed
   (optional)
3 level tablespoons flour
¼ pt (150 ml) red wine
¾ pt (450 ml) beef stock
6 oz (175 g) mushrooms
large knob of butter
salt and pepper

Horseradish Dumplings
7 oz (200 g) plain flour
2 teaspoon baking powder
½ teaspoon salt
2 tablespoons chopped fresh parsley
1 size-1 egg, beaten
4 fl oz (125 g) milk
1 tablespoon horseradish cream sauce

1   Preheat the oven to gas4/350°F/180°C. Prepare the beef and shin beef: trim away any skin, sinew and most of the fat. Chop into cubes about 1 in (2.5 cm) in size.

2   In a large casserole, heat the oil and brown the meat cubes. Keep stirring so that they do not stick. When well-coloured, push the meat aside and fry the onions, carrots and garlic, if you are using it, for a further 2–3 minutes.

3   Now sprinkle the flour over the meat and vegetables and stir it in. Follow up with the red wine and the beef stock. Bring to a boil, then reduce to a simmer and cover.

4   Set in the oven for 1½–2 hours, or until the meat is tender.

5   Prepare the dumplings towards the end of cooking time: sift the flour, baking powder and salt into a bowl. In a jug, beat the egg into half of the milk, add the horseradish cream sauce and beat again. Use this mixture to make a soft dough, adding more milk if needed.

6   Turn the dough out on a floured board and shape into a long sausage. Divide this into 8 or 10 pieces and shape these pieces into balls.

7   Turn up the oven to gas6/400°F/200°C. Lightly turn the mushrooms in a little melted butter, stir into the casserole and check that it is bubbling. Then slip the dumplings into the casserole, replace the lid and cook for a further 25 minutes, when the dumplings should be light and fluffy.

'Now, good digestion wait upon appetite,
And health on both!'

Macbeth, William Shakespeare

SAVOURY ROULADES

Perhaps the idea of a savoury Swiss roll does not at once catch the imagination. Give it its French title of *roulade,* however, and it is altogether a different matter. These popular – usually cold – mixtures are more often than not based on spinach with seafood like prawns and smoked salmon. Cream cheese, mayonnaise and yoghurt are often used as binding agents.

SPINACH ROULADE WITH PRAWNS & SMOKED SALMON

Serves 4–6

Serve a slice with a few salad leaves as a starter or as part of a seafood hors d'oeuvres, with two or three smoked oysters or mussels.

½ oz (15 g) butter, plus more for greasing
6 oz (170 g) frozen chopped spinach
   defrosted and drained
½ oz (15 g) plain flour
4 size-3 eggs, separated
3 tablespoons freshly grated Parmesan
   cheese, plus extra for sprinkling
salt and pepper

Filling
5 tablespoons soft cream cheese or
   2 tablespoons mayonnaise mixed with
   3 tablespoons of Greek yoghurt
2 oz (50 g) peeled prawns (defrosted frozen
   will do), chopped
2 oz (50 g) smoked salmon trimmings,
   chopped
1 tablespoon lemon juice
1 tablespoon of fresh dill, chopped
little milk

1   Preheat the oven to gas5/375°F/190°C. Grease a Swiss roll tin about 12x8 in (30.5x 20.5 cm) well with butter and line the base with non-stick baking paper.

2   Melt the butter in a large pan and cook the spinach for 2 or 3 minutes over a low heat. If the liquid does not all evaporate, just pour it away. Stir in the plain flour and cook for just 1 minute. Remove the pan from the heat and beat in the 4 egg yolks and Parmesan. Season with salt and pepper.
3   In a perfectly dry bowl, whisk the egg whites until fairly stiff and fold these into the spinach mixture.
4   Pour into the prepared tin, smooth it over and sprinkle a little extra Parmesan all over.
5   Bake for not more than 15 minutes, or until firm to the touch. Do not overcook as the spinach goes brown.
6   Take the roulade out of the oven and let it rest for 3–4 minutes. Turn it out on a sheet of greaseproof paper, dusted over with finely grated Parmesan. Remove the non-stick paper and trim the long edges slightly since they often crisp. Leave to cool while you put together the filling.
7   Put the cream cheese or the mayonnaise and yoghurt in a bowl and mix in the prawns, smoked salmon, lemon juice and fresh dill. Season with salt and pepper and spread over the roulade to ½ in (1 cm) of the edge.
8   Finally, using the foil or greaseproof paper, lift up the roulade and gently roll it up. Transfer carefully to a long serving plate with the join underneath.

A SIMPLE FILLING

5 tablespoons cream cheese, beaten into
2 oz (50 g) toasted walnuts, chopped

FILLING VARIATIONS:

VEGETARIAN FILLING:

6 tablespoons garlic mayonnaise
1 tablespoon chopped chives
1½ oz (40 g) chopped walnuts

THIN FILLINGS FOR PRE-DRINK NIBBLES

Cut the cooked roulade in two. Lay smoked salmon all over the roulade halves. Spread cream cheese over the salmon in a thin layer (about 1 tablespoon on each). Dot with coloured dice cut from a red or green pepper. Roll up as tightly as possible. Chill and cut small to serve.

POTATO MEAT ROLL

Serves 6

The idea for using a potato mixture like a Swiss roll came originally from Josceline Dimbleby. It makes 1 lb (450 g) of beef mince look quite partyish and go round a large number of people. The garlic-flavoured mashed potato is quite addictive.

1½ lb (675 g) floury potatoes
1 lb (450 g) broccoli (stalks only, use the florets as a vegetable accompaniment)
1 tablespoon oil
1 lb (450 g) minced beef
1 large onion, peeled and chopped
1 tablespoon plain flour, plus extra for dusting

1 pt (575 ml) meat stock (made from a cube)
knife tip of gravy salt or gravy browning (optional)
3 oz (75 g) butter or margarine
3 fat garlic cloves, peeled and crushed
1 size-3 egg, beaten

1   You will need 3 saucepans. In the first, cook the peeled and halved potatoes in salted water until soft.
2   In the second pan, put the broccoli stalks cut into little log shapes in some salted water. Cook until softish, drain and set aside.
3   In the third pan, heat the oil and fry the beef mince hard so that it gets really brown. Push the mince to one side, then fry the onion, adding another drop of oil if you have to. After just 2–3 minutes, stir together and sprinkle over the flour then stir again. Now slowly add the stock, stirring all the time.
4   Simmer for about 20–25 minutes or until the meat is cooked. Darken the mince if you wish with a knife tip of gravy salt or gravy browning. Set aside to go cold.
5   Once the potatoes have cooked, drain off the water and mash as smoothly as possible with some butter or margarine and the crushed garlic. Taste and season further if necessary. Preheat the oven to gas6/400°F/200°C.
6   To assemble the roll: sprinkle a sheet of foil or greaseproof paper very generously with flour and, using well-floured hands, shape the potato into a rectangle about the size of a Swiss roll tin. Drain the mince and spread it over the potato. Cover the mince with the broccoli stalks. Dot a few flakes of butter or margarine all over. Then, with the help of the foil, roll the potato up from the short end. Slip it carefully on to a well-greased rectangular ovenproof dish.
7   Mark the top of the roll with criss-cross lines, dot it all over with flakes of butter or margarine and bake in the oven for about 20–30 minutes, or until the roll is good and brown.
8   Serve with the reserved gravy and the steamed broccoli florets.

MEAT, POULTRY & GAME PIES

MEAT & POTATO PIE

Serves 6–8

Or, as they would say in some parts, 'meat & tattie pie'.

1½ lb (675 g) braising steak or good-quality stewing steak, cut into cubes
1 large onion, peeled and chopped
2 tablespoons oil
2 large carrots, scraped and chopped chunkily
3 thin leeks, washed and sliced
2 tablespoons flour
¾ pt (450 ml) meat stock (made from a cube)
½ pt (300 ml) ale or cider
1 large fresh bay leaf
few parsley stalks
1 large thyme sprig
salt and pepper
2 tablespoons parsley
knife tip of gravy browning
2 lb (900 g) waxy potatoes, par-boiled for 10 minutes with their skins on
8 oz (225 g) Herby Suet Crust Pastry (see page 84)
little milk

1 Heat the oil and brown the meat first, turning it over and over on a high heat. Turn the heat down, push the meat to one side and fry the onions, carrots and leeks for 4–5 minutes.
2 Stir the meat and vegetables together and sprinkle over the flour. Stir this in, then follow up with the stock and other liquids.
3 Take the large bay leaf and fold around some parsley stalks and a large sprig of thyme. Tie up and put into the meat. Bring to a boil, then reduce the heat and simmer for an hour.
4 At this point, peel the potatoes and chop into large cubes (1 in / 2.5 cm square). Stir these into the meat along with the knife tip of gravy colouring. Season to taste.
5 Simmer for a further 30–40 minutes, or until meat and potatoes are fully cooked. Stir in the parsley and set filling aside to let it cool down.
6 Preheat the oven to gas6/400°F/200°C.
7 To assemble pie: retrieve the bay leaf bundle and discard it. Spoon the meat and potatoes into a 2 pt (1.1 litre) pie dish. Put just enough of the gravy barely to cover the meat. Save the rest to serve separately. Pile the meat up in the middle of the pie or set a pie funnel in place.
8 Roll out the pastry slightly larger than the pie dish. Cut a narrow strip from the outside to fit the rim of the pie dish. Wet the rim first and press it down. Then lift the pastry over the pie and press it down all round the rim. Trim off the excess pastry, cut two slits on the top and brush over with milk. Cut leaves or flowers from the trimmings and use to decorate the top. Paint over again with milk.
9 Set pie on a baking sheet and bake for about 40 minutes or until pastry is brown and crisp.

VARIATIONS ON A TRADITIONAL MEAT AND POTATO PIE

- For extra flavour, mix shin beef with stewing beef.
- Flavour the pie filling with a tin of chopped tomatoes.
- Use other pastries, such as plain shortcrust or shortcrust with some dried chives stirred in, flaky pastry or rough puff.
- Add garlic if you like it. A small clove, peeled and crushed would be enough.
- If you absolutely have to, a tin of top-quality cooked beef could be tarted up with herbs, garlic and parsley.

LAMB & PIPPIN PIE

Serves 4–6

Cox's orange pippin apples go well with all kinds of meat and they do stay in shape and do not collapse into a purée. I first added the chopped prunes at the end of cooking because the stew looked so pale, then I found I liked the flavour so I include them as well.

1½ lb (675 g) cubed leg of lamb, trimmed of skin and some of the fat
3 tablespoons oil
1 medium onion, peeled and chopped
1 tablespoon plain white flour
¾ pt (450 ml) lamb stock (made from a cube)
2 fl oz (5 ml) apple juice
1 oz (25 g) butter
2 small Cox's Orange Pippin apples
2 large ready-to-eat prunes
8 oz (225 g) Herby Shortcrust Pastry (see page 22)
little milk

1   First cook the lamb: heat 2 tablespoons of the oil and fry the lamb cubes really hard, almost to the point of burning.
2   Push the lamb to one side of the pan and fry the onion over a moderate heat for just 3–4 minutes.
3   Stir the meat and onion together and sprinkle the flour all over. Stir this in well, then gradually pour in the lamb stock, stirring all the time. Simmer for about 1½–1¾ hours, or until the meat is tender. Stir in the apple juice and allow to go cold.
4   In a small pan, heat the butter and the remaining oil. Peel, core and slice the apples into rings and fry in the butter mixture just long enough to soften slightly.
5   Preheat the oven to gas6/400°F/200°C. Take the lamb and onion out of the pan and put in a 2 pt (1.2 litre) pie dish or tin. Add just enough gravy to moisten, then layer the buttery apples on top.
6   Snip the prunes with scissors and put them on top of the apples.

7   On a floured board, roll out the pastry rather larger than the pie dish. Cut a narrow strip of pastry from the outside edge. Moisten the rim of the dish with water and press this strip of pastry down firmly on the pie dish rim, making a neat join. Moisten the top of the strip, then lift the pastry up on your rolling pin and drop it over the pie. Press firmly all round the outer edge of the pie. Trim away the excess pastry. Brush the top of the pastry with milk, then decorate with pastry leaves if you wish. Brush all over with milk.
8   Set the pie on a baking sheet and place in the oven for about 30–40 minutes, or until the pastry is brown and crisp.

SPICED LAMB PIE

Serves 4–6

Lamb lends itself to spicing as no other meat does. Here is a Moroccan-type stew, given the pie treatment.

1½ lb (675 g) boneless lamb fillet, cut into cubes
2 tablespoons oil
1 medium onion, finely chopped
1 heaped teaspoon freshly grated root ginger
2 small garlic cloves, peeled and crushed
½ teaspoon ground cumin
½ teaspoon ground cinnamon
½ pt (300 ml) vegetable stock
3 oz (75 g) no-soak dried apricots
1 tablespoon fresh chopped coriander
2 oz (50 g) almonds, chopped
1 heaped tablespoon couscous
8 oz (225 g) frozen puff pastry, defrosted
flour, for dusting
1 size-7 egg, beaten, to glaze

Cook the filling

1   Fry the lamb in the oil until well browned. Add the onion and cook for 3–4 minutes. Stir in the ginger, garlic, cumin and cinnamon.
2   Stir in the vegetable stock. Bring to the boil,

reduce the heat and simmer for about 1¾ hours or until the lamb is tender. A few minutes before you take the lamb off the heat, cut up the apricots and stir them in with the chopped coriander, chopped almonds and the couscous (see note below). Set aside to keep hot.

Prepare and cook the couscous

1   Pour boiling water over the dry couscous and allow it to swell up slightly.
2   Then drain the couscous and return it to the bowl. At this point, sit the bowl in a steamer above simmering water for just 10 minutes and it is ready.

Pastry squares topping

1   Preheat the oven to gas7/425°F/220°C.
2   Roll out the pastry on a floured board. It should be quite thin. Square off the ragged edges and trim to a large square. Divide the pastry into squares about 2 in (5 cm). Take the point of a knife and score the pastry, but do not cut through to the board. Brush the beaten egg all over and bake for 10–15 minutes or until the squares are brown and crisp.

Assemble the pie

1   Use a slotted spoon to transfer the lamb to a flattish heatproof dish. Spoon in just a little of the gravy. Save the rest to serve separately. Break up the pastry into squares and lay the squares overlapping one another and resting on the rim all round the dish.
2   Reheat briefly and serve.

CASSEROLE PIE OF LAMB

Serves 4–6

The idea of partnering fennel and lamb is a little different. The fat white bulbs of fennel are not cheap but in a casserole a little goes a long way. Shoulder lamb has a lovely flavour, but you do need to be ruthless in cutting away a lot of fat.

1½ lb (675 g) shoulder lamb (or leg), cubed
1 large onion, peeled and chopped
1 large carrot, peeled and grated
1 small fennel bulb or ½ a large one, chopped in strips
1 small garlic clove, peeled and crushed
1 tablespoon flour
1 pt (575 ml) lamb stock (made from a cube)
knife point of gravy browning or gravy salt (optional)
salt and pepper
1 small uncut loaf
2 oz (50 g) butter
1 tablespoon oil
little milk
1 teaspoon sesame seeds

1   First cook the lamb: in a large pan, heat the oil and brown the lamb thoroughly. Push the meat to one side and fry the onion, carrot, chopped fennel and the garlic on a lower heat for a few minutes.
2   Stir the meat and vegetables together, sprinkle over the flour and give this a good stir. Pour in the stock, slowly at first and stirring all the time. Bring to the boil and reduce the heat to a simmer.
3   Cook with the lid on for about 1¾ hours, or until the lamb is really tender. Stir in the gravy browning or gravy salt if you wish. Taste and season if necessary. Spoon the meat and vegetables into an ovenproof dish.
4   Break loaf into chunks and crumb in the food processor. Stir the butter and oil into the crumbs and scatter over the top, followed by the sesame seeds. Reheat briefly at gas4/350°F/180°C, until the crumbs are crisp and the filling piping hot.

PORK & PRUNES

Serves 4–6

1½ lb (675 g) shoulder pork, cut in small
    cubes
1 tablespoon cornflour
1 tablespoon oil
1 large onion, peeled and chopped
½ pt (300 ml) dry cider
½ pt (300 ml) chicken stock
1 small garlic clove, peeled and crushed
4 cloves
2 pinches of marjoram
8 small soft prunes
8 oz (225 g) Suet Crust Pastry with Herbs
    (see page 84)
salt and pepper
little milk, for glazing

1   Season the cornflour with salt and pepper and
dry the cubed pork with paper towel. Stir the
pork cubes into the cornflour. Shake off any loose
flour.
2   Heat the oil in a roomy pan and gently cook
the onions for 4–5 minutes. Push the onions
aside and, adding extra oil if you need it, fry the
pork. Turn the cubes over and over until they are
nicely browned.
3   Add the cider, stock, garlic, cloves, marjoram,
salt and pepper. Bring to the boil, then turn
down the heat and simmer for about 1½ hours
with the lid on.
4   Stir in the prunes and continue cooking for
just 2–3 minutes more, then season to taste and
allow to cool down.
5   Preheat the oven to gas6/400°F/200°C. Roll
out the pastry on a floured board to a size just
bigger than the pie dish. Wet the rim of the dish
and cut a very narrow strip from the outside
edge. Press this down very firmly and wet the
top surface of the strip. Lift the pastry and lay it
on top of the meat and press heavily all the way
round the pie dish. Trim off excess pastry. Make a
steam hole, then cut out fancy leaves and flowers
to decorate if you wish.
6   Brush the milk all over the surface and bake
for about 30–40 minutes or until the pastry is
brown and crisp.

EARLS BARTON LEEK PIE

Serves 4–6

I have seen this recipe in two different old
cookery books and neither says who or what
Earls Barton is. I am told it is a place. Chuck
steak is a very high-quality steak from near the
blade bone. The recipe is also unusual in that
beef and pork are mixed. Here is my version.

¾ lb (225 g) belly pork
¾ lb (225 g) chuck steak, cut into 1 in
    (2.5 cm) pieces
1 small onion, peeled and chopped
15 fl oz (425 ml) beef stock (made from a
    cube)
1½ lb (675 g) young leeks
1 oz (25 g) butter
8 oz (225 g) shortcrust pasty
little milk
salt and pepper

1   Belly pork is almost always sold with the
skin, so cut this off and chop the meat into small
strips. This is not the easiest meat to cut with a
knife, so use scissors.
2   In a large roomy pan, fry the belly pork pieces
until they are brown. They usually have plenty of
fat. Stir them round and round as they have a
tendency to stick. Push the pork to one side and
fry the chuck steak until it is brown too. Push
that to one side and fry the onion for just a few
minutes. Now stir them all together and season
with salt and pepper.
3   Pour over the stock and simmer on top of the
stove for about 1½ hours or cook in the oven
preheated to gas4/350°F/180°C for about the
same time.
4   Check that the two meats are tender before
setting aside and allowing the dish to go cold. It
is then far easier to lift off the fat and this will
improve the quality of the dish.
5   Now wash and chop the leeks and cut into
chunks. Steam or boil until tender, season to
taste and stir in the butter. Set aside to cool.
6   Layer the meat mixture and the leeks to fill

an 8 in (20 cm) pie dish. Pour in the gravy.

7 Preheat the oven to gas6/400°F/200°C.

8 Roll out the pastry rather larger than the dish. Wet the rim of the pie dish and cut a narrow strip of pastry in order to press this down and then fit the pie lid on top. Wet the top part of the strip and press the edges together. Trim off the excess. Mark all the pastry around with a fork. Brush the pastry with milk and make one or two steam holes. Decorate with leaves and flowers if you wish and brush them over with milk too.

9 Bake for about 25 minutes, or until the pastry is cooked and brown.

CHICKEN WITH FORCEMEAT BALLS

4 chicken joints
1 tablespoon flour
2 tablespoons oil
4 oz (125 g) pork sausagemeat
1 level tablespoon fine fresh breadcrumbs
1 teaspoon chopped parsley
6 strips of smoked streaky bacon
1 medium-sized onion, peeled and sliced
8 oz (225 g) can of chopped tomatoes
1/4 pt (150 ml) chicken stock (made from a
  cube)
1 teaspoon sugar
1 tablespoon chopped mixed herbs or
  1/2 teaspoon mixed dried herbs
pinch of mace
6 oz (175 g) Shortcrust Pastry (see page 16)
little milk
pepper

1 Preheat the oven to gas4/350°F/180°C.

2 Take the skin off the chicken joints and pat them dry with kitchen paper. Use a teaspoon of the flour to dust them back and front.

3 Heat the oil in a casserole and fry the joints on both sides until they are well coloured. Set the joints aside.

4 Mix the sausage meat with the breadcrumbs and parsley and, with damp hands, roll into 8 firm balls. Brown in the casserole and set them aside too.

5 In the remaining oil, cook the bacon until lightly browned, followed by the onion and cook until translucent. Pour in the small tin of chopped tomatoes over a low heat. Stir well and scrape up any residue from the chicken, sausagemeat, etc stuck on the bottom of the casserole.

6 In another bowl, whisk the remaining flour into the cold chicken stock using a loop whisk. When the flour has dispersed, pour into the casserole. Add the sugar and herbs and stir over a moderate heat until the sauce thickens. Taste and adjust the seasoning.

7 Return the chicken and meat balls to the casserole, together with the mace. Season with pepper, put the lid on and bake for about 1 hour, or until the chicken is cooked through. Allow to go cold.

8 Preheat the oven to gas6/400°F/200°C. Lift off any fat which is visible, remove any bones and put the chicken, etc. into a 2 pt / 1.2 litre pie dish with enough gravy barely to cover.

9 Roll out the pastry just a bit larger than the pie dish itself. Cut a narrow strip from the outside edge and press this down on to the rim of the dish. It helps if you run a wet finger over the rim first. Make a neat joint, then lift the remaining pastry on a rolling pin and cover the pie dish. Press the pastry down on top of the narrow strip. You can damp this surface too to make it stick. Press with a fork all round and trim away the excess pastry. Use this to make decorative leaves. Brush the pie all over with milk and make a couple of slits in the top.

10 Bake for about 25 minutes or until the pastry is brown and crisp.

CHICKEN & LEEK PIE

Serves 4

This pie is different because the bottom of the pie is shortcrust pastry and the top is flaky. I often use this idea for mince pies. They are much easier to handle this way. You will need a loose-bottomed flan or cake tin about 9 in (23 cm) across and at least 1½ in (4 cm) deep.

4 oz (125 g) Shortcrust Pastry (see page 16)
4 oz (125 g) New Flaky Pastry (see page 19)
1 size-7 egg, beaten

Sauce
small piece of onion
small piece of carrot
1 bay leaf
sprig of thyme
½ pt (300 ml) milk
1 oz (25 g) plain white flour
1 oz (25 g) butter or margarine

Filling
2 chicken breasts, about 12 oz (325 g) in
    total
2 fat pinches of ground mace
1 oz (25 g) butter
1 tablespoon oil
8 thin leeks
1 tablespoon chopped parsley
salt and pepper

1 First start the sauce: put the onion, carrot, bay leaf and sprig of thyme into the milk. Bring to the boil either in a jug in the microwave or in a pan. Set it aside to go cold.
2 Prepare the filing: dry the chicken breast off and cut into thick strips or small chunks. Sprinkle salt and mace all over the pieces.
3 Heat the butter and oil in a small frying pan and, when it is hot, fry the chicken pieces just to brown lightly, turning over and over. It is probably easier to do this in two batches. Set aside.
4 Now prepare the leeks: slit each one down the middle but hold on to the bundles and rinse well. Top and tail them, then chop the leeks quite small. Cook them lightly in the frying pan

adding just a little oil and set them aside too.
5 To finish the sauce: fish out the onion, bay leaf and thyme. Whisk the flour into the milk and, when it has dispersed, cook gently in a small pan and stir all the time. When the milk starts to thicken, drop the butter or margarine in and allow that to melt. Taste and add salt and pepper. Stir the leeks and chicken into this sauce, plus the parsley and allow to cool down.
6 To assemble and cook the pie: preheat the oven to gas7/425°F/220°C and put a baking sheet in the oven. On a floured board, roll the shortcrust pastry out at least 3 in (7.5 cm) more than the width of your tin (see above). Grease the tin with melted vegetable fat or oil. Lift the pastry on your rolling pin and fit it into the tin, taking care not to stretch it. Allow the pastry to cool down a bit if the kitchen is hot.
7 Using a slotted spoon, transfer the chicken and leek mixture to the tin and pile it up a bit in the centre. Roll out the flaky pastry just slightly bigger than your tin. Moisten the top edge of the shortcrust. Cover the pie and press the pastry down to meet the shortcrust. Press the edges well together and slice off the extra pastry, use these trimmings to make decorative leaves or spirals. Brush the pie with egg and knock up the edges, that is with a knife make horizontal marks in the pastry all round. This helps to make the pie rise.
8 Set the tin on the hot baking sheet in the oven and bake for 25–30 minutes, or until the pastry is puffed up and crisp and brown.

SMOKY BACON & CHICKEN PIECES PIE

This is a good highly flavoured recipe for using up the last of the cooked chicken from a roast.

4 full rashers of smoky bacon, rind on
½ pt (300 ml) chicken stock (fresh or made
    using a cube)
1 small onion, peeled and grated
12 oz (325 g) cooked chicken pieces
2 tablespoons chopped parsley
1 small teaspoon brown sugar

2 fat pinches of ground mace
1 level teaspoon sesame seeds
6 oz (175 g) Wholewheat Pastry (see page
   16)
little milk

1   First trim the rind off the bacon and drop it
into the stock. Bring that to a boil and simmer
for a few minutes. Set it aside to cool down. This
should give the stock a slight smoky taste.
2   You will need a pie dish with a capacity of
about 1½ pts (1 litre). Preheat the oven to
gas6/400°F/200°C.
3   First cut the bacon into tiny pieces and put
that in the pie dish with the chopped parsley.
Follow that with the grated onion and the cooked
chicken. Mix the brown sugar and the mace and
sprinkle that over. Strain the chicken stock over
the pie filling, just covering it and no more.
4   Sprinkle the sesame seeds over your board and
roll out the wholewheat pastry rather bigger than
you need. Cut a narrow strip from the outer edge
to set on the pie rim. Wet the rim first and the
strip will stick more easily. Press it in position
and make a neat join. Now cover the pie with
the pastry, seed side up. Wet the top of the
narrow strip and press the pie lid down on top of
that. Slice off the spare pastry and make
decorative leaves and flowers with that if you
wish. Press the rim all round for a good seal.
Make one or two slits in the top of the pie.
5   Brush over with milk and bake for about 40
minutes or until the pastry is crisp and firm.

PLATE PIE OF CHICKEN, LEEK & TONGUE

Serves 4–6

You will need a pie plate with a shallow bowl.
They are usually made of metal, either
aluminium or enamel.

3 thin leeks, trimmed and chopped small
2 large chicken joints
1 small onion, peeled and chopped

1 heaped tablespoon chopped celery
some parsley stalks
sprig of thyme
1 bay leaf
8 oz (225 g) Shortcrust Pastry (see page 16)
2 oz (50 g) cooked sliced tongue, chopped
2 teaspoons plain white flour
1 tablespoon chopped parsley
1 size-7 egg, beaten
salt and pepper
butter or lard, for greasing

1   Cook the leeks in boiling salted water for 2
minutes. Drain well and set aside. Preheat the oven
to gas7/425°F/220°C and put a baking sheet in it.
2   First poach the chicken: put the two joints in
a pan with the onion and celery. Tie the parsley
stalks and thyme inside a folded bay leaf, put this
bouquet garni in the pan and barely cover with
water. Bring to the boil, then reduce the heat and
simmer until the chicken is cooked through,
about 30–40 minutes. Set this aside to become
cool enough to handle. Separate the chicken
pieces and set them aside. Discard the bones and
skin.
3   Roll out the pastry and cut 2 circles large
enough to cover the pie plate with one circle
slightly smaller than the other. Grease the pie
plate and fit the smaller circle on it, then set the
chicken pieces on the pastry. Use a slotted spoon
to lift out some of the celery and onion and
spread this over the chicken. On top of that
scatter the bits of tongue. Spread the drained
leeks on top of the tongue.
4   Now to make a little thickened stock: put
½ pt (300 ml) of the cooking liquid in a pan and
whisk the flour into that. Change to a wooden
spoon and stir the stock over a low heat until it
thickens. Add half of the parsley, then dribble this
thickened stock over the filling, just enough to
make it moist. Scatter over the rest of the parsley.
5   Moisten the outer rim of the bottom pastry
and cover the pie with the second circle. Press the
edges really firmly and slice off the excess pastry
and use this to make trimmings if you wish.
Brush the surface with the beaten egg and place
on the hot baking sheet for 20 minutes. Then
lower the temperature to gas4/350°F/180°C and
cook for another 20 minutes or until the pastry is
set, golden and crisp.

CHICKEN, HAM & MUSHROOM PIE

Serves 6

1½ lb (675 g) boneless chicken thighs
few parsley stalks
2 teaspoons fresh thyme leaves
1 large bay leaf
1½ oz (40 g) butter
2 tablespoons oil
4 thin leeks, trimmed, washed and chopped
½ lb (225 g) chestnut (brown) mushrooms
¼ pt (150 ml) single cream or milk
1 chicken stock cube
3 level tablespoons plain white flour
6 oz (175 g) cooked ham, diced
2 fat pinches of dried oregano
1 lb (450 g) frozen puff pastry, defrosted or
    New Flaky Pastry (see page 19)
1 size-7 egg, beaten

1   Preheat the oven to gas6/400°F/200°C. First
poach the chicken: take the skin off the thighs
and discard it. Put the pieces in a pan with a
bouquet garni (wrap a few parsley stalks and a
sprig of thyme in a large bay leaf and tie up), salt
and pepper and enough cold water barely to
cover. Bring to the boil, reduce the heat and
simmer for about 20 minutes.
2   Heat the butter and oil in a frying pan and
fry the leeks briefly. Use a slotted spoon to
remove them. Now chop the mushrooms into
quarters and fry in the oil and butter mixture.
3   Drain the chicken and put ¾ pt (450 ml) of
the stock in a pan. Chop up the chicken, not too
finely, and spoon into a 2 pt (1.2 litre) pie dish.
4   Pour the milk or cream into a pan with the
stock and crumble the stock cube into it. Using a
small whisk, put the flour into the cold stock and
whisk hard over a moderate heat to disperse it. Stir
until the stock thickens (about 2 minutes). Stir in
the leeks, mushrooms, ham and oregano. Pour
over the chopped chicken and leave to go cold.
5   Set a pie funnel in the centre of the pie and
roll out the pastry on a floured board so that it is
about 1½ in (3.5 cm) bigger than the pie dish.
Trim a narrow strip about 1 in (2.5 cm) wide

from around the pastry, dampen this and press it
round the rim. Dampen the pastry strip and lay
the lid over the pie, pressing the edges together.
Trim carefully, angling the knife outwards and
the handle underneath the pastry. Knock up the
edges of the pastry (see page 105) to help it rise.
Traditionally the edge of a flaky pastry pie is
scalloped (see page 105). Re-roll the trimmings
for leaves and brush the beaten egg all over the
top of the pie.
6   Bake for about 30 minutes, until the pastry is
brown and crisp.

CHARTER PIE FROM CORNWALL

Serves 8

This rich and tasty recipe dating from 1883 was
originally unearthed by Jane Grigson. This is
my version. I like it better cold than hot, when
the stock has set to a rich jelly with the cream.
You will need a dish large enough to hold 8
chicken joints lying side by side.

8 chicken joints
2 oz (50 g) butter
2 tablespoons oil
1 very large onion, peeled and chopped
2 tablespoons plain flour
3 oz (75 g) parsley
¼ pt (150 ml) milk
¼ pt (150 ml) single cream
6 spring onions, chopped small
½ pt (300 ml) double cream
12 oz (325 g) Shortcrust Pastry (see page 16)
1 size-7 egg, beaten
salt and pepper

1   Preheat the oven to gas7/425°F/220°C. Heat
1 oz (25 g) butter and 1 tablespoon oil in a
frying pan and cook the chopped onion in that
for about 5 minutes. Use a slotted spoon to
transfer the onion to a large shallow dish.
2   Dry the chicken joints and roll them in the
seasoned flour. Shake off any loose flour. Add the

rest of the butter to the frying pan and brown the chicken pieces lightly.

3 Now pack the chicken tightly on top of the onion in the dish in a single layer.

4 Using a pair of scissors, hold the bunch of rinsed parsley very tightly and snip it finely into a pan containing the milk and single cream. Add the finely chopped spring onions. Bring this pan to a boil and simmer for just 2–3 minutes. Pour about one-third of the double cream over the chicken followed by the hot parsley, spring onions and cream and milk mixture. Season well.

5 Now roll out the pastry on a floured board and make it big enough to cover the pie. Settle a pie funnel as near the centre of the pie as you can get. Cut a narrow strip of pastry to go along round the dish (if there is a rim), moisten it and press it down on the rim. Lift the big piece of pastry on your rolling pin and lower it over the pie, making a hole over the top of the funnel. Make a pastry tassel and put this into the funnel. Decorate the pie with leaves, veined with the tip of a knife. Press the outer rim of the pie together with the narrow pastry strip and either flute the edge or press all round with a fork.

6 Brush all over the surface of the pie with beaten egg and bake for 20 minutes, until the pastry sets. Then lower the heat to gas6/400°F/200°C for another 1 hour.

7 Just before serving, ease the tassel out of the steam vent, bring the rest of the double cream to boiling point and pour it down into the pie. Replace the tassel and serve.

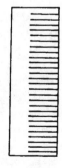

SPICY SAUSAGE & CHICKEN CRUMBLE

Serves 4-6

A pie does not always mean pastry. This one has a savoury crumble topping made from that popular Italian bread, ciabatta.

8 oz (225 g) cooked chicken
4 oz (225 g) garlic sausage in a piece
6 tiny tomatoes
½ pt (300 ml) chicken stock (from a cube)
2 heaped teaspoons plain flour
2 fresh celery stalks
4 oz (100 g) butter
1 tablespoon oil
8 oz (225 g) coarse crumbs from a ciabatta loaf
2 fat pinches of marjoram
pepper

1 Preheat the oven to gas4/350°F/180°C. Put the chicken in the bottom of a 3 pt (1.75 litres pie dish or a straight-sided heatproof soufflé dish. Peel off any skin from the garlic slicing sausage, cut the sausage into small ½ in (1 cm) cubes and scatter these over. Pierce each tomato once or twice and add these to the dish.

2 Put the stock into a pan and whisk the dry flour into it. When the flour is all dispersed, put the pan over a moderate heat and stir constantly until the stock thickens. Remove from the heat.

3 Now chop up the celery into smallish slices. Heat one-quarter of the butter with the oil in a small pan and fry the celery in that until almost cooked. Turn into the dish as well. Pour in enough of the thickened stock barely to cover the contents of the dish. Mix the filling really well and leave to cool down a bit.

4 Rub the remaining butter into the breadcrumbs as if making pastry and stir in the marjoram. Season with pepper. Sprinkle over the filling and spread it evenly with a spoon.

5 Bake for about 30 minutes but keep an eye on the crumble topping, it may singe very quickly.

DESPERATE DAN'S COW PEH (PIE)

I come from the East Coast city of Dundee, in the old county of Angus in Scotland. Not only is it a beautiful city, perched on the River Tay, it is the home of Scott's ship 'Discovery', which you can see as you come across the Tay from Fife. It is also the birthplace of Desperate Dan, the famous character featured in the children's comic The Dandy, which is published there.

Steak pies, as they are called, were traditionally made by butchers in oblong pie dishes of white enamel with a narrow blue border. Such pies were often served for Sunday dinner – a simple stew with puff pastry top.

1½ lb (675 g) stewing beef
4 oz (125 g) shin beef
2 tablespoons oil
1 large onion, peeled and chopped
2 small carrots, scraped and chopped
2 tablespoons plain white flour
1 pt (600 ml) beef stock (made from a cube)
spot of gravy salt
8 oz (225 g) frozen puff pastry, defrosted
1 size-7 egg, beaten
salt and pepper

1   Check over the meats and remove all the skin and some of the fat.
2   In a roomy pan, brown the meat in the oil over a fairly high heat, stirring all the time. Push to one side and fry the onions and carrots for a few minutes (you may need a little more oil).
3   Stir the meat and vegetables together, sprinkle the flour on top and stir this through. Pour in just enough stock a little at a time, stirring all the time, barely to cover the beef and vegetables. Season and stew for about 2 hours, or until the meat is really tender. Stir with care to avoid breaking up the meat. Add just a spot of gravy salt for colour. Set aside to go cold.
4   Preheat the oven to gas6/400°F/200°C. Roll out the pastry on a floured board to a thickness of about ½ in (1 cm) and about 1 in (2.5 cm) bigger than you need it.
5   Remove any solidified fat on the steak.

Transfer the meat and vegetables to the pie dish. Add just enough gravy to keep the meat moist. Position the pie funnel in the middle of the pie to hold up the pastry as it cooks.
6   Now cut a narrow strip from the outside of the rolled out pastry, long enough to fit round the pie dish. Wet the rim of the pie dish lightly with water and press the strip all round it. Press the edges very firmly to get a good seal. Lift the pie carefully in your left hand and trim off the excess pastry. You should try to do this at an angle in the hope that the top of the pie will not sink into the filling. Knock up the outside edge with horizontal knife strokes and use your finger and thumb to make a scalloped edge (see opposite). Make a neat steam hole over the pie funnel.
7   Brush the pastry with beaten egg and set the pie on a baking sheet. Bake for 30–40 minutes, or until the pastry is crisp and brown. Reheat the leftover gravy and add to this the leftover stock.

TRADITIONAL STEAK & KIDNEY PIE

Serves 6–8

1½ lb (675 g) stewing steak, cut into 1 in (2.5 cm) cubes
8 oz (225 g) shin beef, cut small
5 oz (150 g) ox kidney
2 tablespoons oil or 1 oz (25 g) dripping
1 large onion, peeled and finely chopped
2 fat pinches of dried thyme
dash of Worcestershire sauce
1 heaped tablespoon white flour
1 pt (600 ml) beef stock (made from a cube)
6 oz (175 g) dark mushrooms, sliced
12 oz (325 g) frozen puff pastry, defrosted
1 size-7 egg, beaten with a little milk
salt and pepper

1   First check the meat and cut away any skin and some of the fat. Peel any membrane off the kidney and cut across the middle. Use scissors to snip out the whitish core. Then chop quite small.

2 In a roomy pan, heat the oil or dripping and fry the chopped onion for a couple of minutes, then add the stewing steak, shin and kidney. Stir well until the meats are nicely browned.

3 Turn the heat down and add the thyme and Worcestershire sauce. Season with and sprinkle the flour over. Stir this in and follow it with the stock. Bring to the boil, reduce the heat to a steady simmer and cook either on the hob or in the oven for at least 2 hours. Half an hour before the end of cooking, stir in the mushrooms. When cooked, set aside to go cold.

4 Using a slotted spoon, transfer the cold cooked steak and kidney into a 2 pt (1.2 litre) pie dish. Fill up the dish to within 1 in (2.5 cm) of the rim. Spoon in just enough gravy to keep the meat moist and pile the meat up high in the centre of the dish to support the pastry or set a pie funnel in the middle.

5 Preheat the oven to gas7/425°F/220°C. Roll out the pastry on a floured board to the shape of the pie dish but slightly larger. From the outside of the pastry, cut a narrow strip about ½ in (1 cm) wide to place round the rim of the pie dish to ensure a good seal. Wet the rim with water and press the strip down on it making a neat join. Wet the top of the strip, lift the pastry over the dish and set it evenly over the meat, trying not to stretch it. Press it down firmly all the way round. Slice off the excess pastry and use for decorative leaves and flowers if you wish. Nip and squeeze the pastry all round to give a fluted effect. Brush all over with the egg and milk mixture. Set on any decorative leaves and brush over again with the glaze.

6 Set on a baking sheet and bake for about 40 minutes, or until the pastry is nicely coloured.

LUXURY STEAK & KIDNEY PIE WITH OYSTERS & PUFF PASTRY

Serves 6–8

There is a tradition of putting oysters into a steak and kidney pie. About 1 dozen would be about right, to go in just at the end of the first cooking. They do exude a lot of juice, so allow for that and not put so much stock into the pie.

While fresh oysters are pretty scarce in some parts, I think a much nicer idea is to add a can of smoked oysters to the pie filling with just a little of their brine to flavour the stock. As for the puff pastry, you can make your own version like the New Flaky Pastry on page 19 or you can buy the frozen which has to be defrosted.

It is traditional to 'knock up' flaky pastry. This means that once you have got the lid on the pie you should use a knife to 'knock up' the outside edge of the pastry. Just take a knife and make horizontal knife marks all round. This is said to help the air to get into the pastry. Following that, a scalloped effect can be achieved by pressing your thumb firmly at regular intervals while pushing the pastry outwards in a scallop and dragging the pastry at intervals back to shape the scallop (often using the back of a knife).

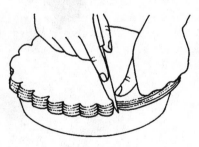

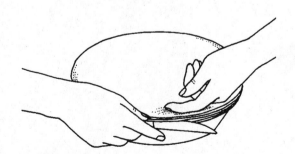

BEEF OLIVE PIE

Serves 4

Old recipes for beef olives used to tell you to 'beat the beef out until it is very thin'. This was a slow business involving a rolling pin and plastic sheeting. Nowadays I just ask my butcher to cut me 4 thin slices on one of his slicing machines. My own butcher told me that if he had a lot to do he would freeze the meat for a while and slice before it got too hard.

4 thin slices of topside
3 tablespoons oil
1 medium onion, peeled and very finely chopped
1 large celery stalk, finely chopped
2 oz (50 g) fresh fine breadcrumbs
1 tablespoon chopped parsley
2 oz (50 g) sliced cooked ham
1/2 teaspoon made-up mustard
1 size-3 egg, beaten
1/4 pt (150 ml) beef stock (made from a cube)
1/4 pt (150 ml) cider
1 tablespoon plain white flour, plus more for dusting
6 oz (175 g) Shortcrust Pastry (see page 16)
little milk
salt and pepper

1   Preheat the oven to gas4/350°F/180°C. Trim the meat into neat squares about 4 in (10 cm). Season with salt and black pepper.
2   To make the stuffing: heat 1 tablespoon of the oil and fry the onion until soft. Add the celery and continue cooking until it is lightly coloured. Allow to cool slightly, then turn the onion and celery out into a bowl.

3   Stir in the breadcrumbs, parsley, cooked ham, mustard and a little of the beaten egg to bind (you may not need all the egg).
4   Divide the stuffing between the 4 slices of beef. Roll up neatly. If you are nervous about the rolls coming undone, secure each roll with a bit of fine white string or a cocktail stick. I usually do not bother and just handle them carefully.
5   Heat the rest of the oil and fry the beef olives to a good brown. I put the olives in the pan with the join down. Once fried, they usually stay closed.
6   Transfer the beef olives to a 2 pt (1.2 litre) pie dish.
7   Put the stock and cider in a pan, whisk in the dry flour and cook over a moderate heat until thickened. Pour over the beef olives. Cover tightly with foil and bake for 1¼ hours, or until the meat is fully cooked.
8   When the olives are cooked and cooled down, preheat the oven to gas6/400°F/200°C and prepare the pastry topping: roll the pastry out on a floured board to rather larger than the pie dish. Wet the pie dish rim, cut a very narrow strip off the outside of the pastry and press it down on the rim. Make a neat join, then lift the pastry up and over the meat and set it evenly over the pie dish. Moisten the top of the pastry strip and press the lid down on to that. Trim off the excess pastry and brush the pie top all over with milk. Make a slit in the centre and decorate with leaves and flowers made from the trimmings if you wish. Brush over again with milk,
9   Place on a baking sheet and cook for about 40 minutes, or until the pastry is brown and set.

HAM OLIVE PIE

Serves 4

This turned out to be a nicely flavoured lighter pie and quicker to do, since the ham olives do not need to be cooked in advance.

4 slices of thin cooked ham
dash of oil
1 tablespoon finely chopped onion
1 large celery stalk, finely chopped
2 oz (50 g) walnuts, finely chopped
2 oz (50 g) fresh white breadcrumbs
1 tablespoon chopped fresh parsley
1 size-7 egg, beaten
1/2 pt (300 ml) vegetable stock
1 level tablespoon plain flour
1 heaped teaspoon tomato purée
6 oz (175 g) Shortcrust Pastry (see page 16)

1   First lay out the ham and trim to even squares about 4 in (10 cm).
2   To make the stuffing: put a dash of oil in a frying pan. Cook the onion on a low heat until soft, stir in the celery and cook that until it is just beginning to colour. Make up the stuffing by mixing together the walnuts, breadcrumbs, celery, onion and parsley. Use a little of the beaten egg to bind the stuffing together. You probably will not need all of it.
3   Divide the stuffing between the 4 ham slices and roll up neatly. Set the rolls side by side in a 2 pt (1.2 litre) pie dish.
4   Make up a little sauce: put the vegetable stock into a pan and whisk the flour into it. When all the flour is dispersed, change to a wooden spoon and cook and stir until the liquid thickens. Stir in the tomato purée. Pour this sauce over the olives.
5   Now follow the instructions as in the previous recipe, from step 8.

POACHER'S PIE

Serves 4

Rabbits must have been the most poached animal in the countryside and there are a wonderful array of recipes for rabbit pie. This one has a crumb topping not unlike a crumble.

1 wild rabbit or 4 rabbit joints
2 tablespoons oil or 1 oz (25 g) dripping
1 oz (25 g) plain flour
1/2 pt (300 ml) ale
1 medium onion, peeled and sliced
1 carrot, scraped and chopped
2 oz (50 g) mushrooms, wiped and sliced
2 dessert apples, peeled, cored and sliced
2 sprigs of thyme
1 bay leaf
4 oz (125 g) wholewheat flour
4 oz (50 g) plain white flour
1 level teaspoon baking powder
3 oz (75 g) softish butter
2 size-1 eggs, hard-boiled
salt and pepper

1   If using wild rabbit, soak it in cold salty water and set aside for 1 hour.
2   Preheat the oven to gas4/350°F/180°C.
3   Drain the rabbit, cut into pieces and pat dry. Heat the oil or dripping in a frying pan and fry the rabbit until golden. Put in a casserole.
4   Whisk the flour into the cold ale and pour this into the frying pan. Over a moderate heat, stir until thickened. Scrape up any residue from frying the joints. Now pour this mixture over the rabbit. Stir in the onion, carrot, mushrooms, apples, thyme and bay leaf. Cover and cook for almost 2 hours, until the rabbit is cooked. Set aside to cool. Fish out any bones, the thyme and bay.
5   Prepare the savoury crumble: stir together the flours with the baking powder. Rub the softish butter into this mixture and mix or run it through the food processor. Season highly.
6   To finish off the pie: slice the hard-boiled eggs thinly and lay the slices in a single layer on top of the rabbit. Sprinkle the 'crumble' mixture over.
7   Bake for about 40 minutes or until the pie top looks brown enough.

OLD-STYLE RABBIT PIE

Serves 5

This pie is done the old way, with the raw meat under the pastry. It has a definite gamy flavour – liked by some and hated by others. The liver and kidneys are used to make the forcemeat balls which go into the pie.

1 rabbit, weighing about 2½ lb (1.1 kg)
1 oz (25 g) fine white breadcrumbs
1 small apple, peeled, cored and chopped very finely
1 size-7 egg, separated
8 oz (225 g) fatty bacon, cut small
1 tablespoon parsley and chives or 1 teaspoon dried mixed herbs
8 oz (225 g) small onions, peeled and quartered
8 oz (225 g) cider or chicken stock (made from a cube)
1 lb (450 g) frozen flaky pastry, defrosted
little milk

1   Preheat the oven to gas6/400°F/200°C. Joint the rabbit and put the pieces in a large pie dish with a 3 pt (1.75 litre) capacity.
2   Make up the forcemeat balls: prepare the rabbit kidney by removing the outer membrane and chop up finely, removing the pale core. Do the same with the liver. Alternatively, you can pass both through a processor which will whizz the liver and kidney to a fine paste. Add the breadcrumbs, apple, salt and pepper and just a tiny bit of the egg yolk to bind this all together. With damp hands, roll into small balls (smaller than a golf ball). Set these in your pie dish along with the bacon, herbs and onions.
3   Season the rabbit well and pour over the cider or stock. Set a pie funnel in the middle of the pie dish.
4   Roll out the flaky pastry on a floured board to a thickness of about ¼ in (5 mm) and rather larger than the size of your pie dish. Cut a narrow strip of pastry from the outside edge, wet the rim of the pie dish and press the strip down firmly on that and make a neat join. Brush some water on the top of the narrow pastry strip. Lift the pie top on your rolling pin and position it on the pie. Press the outside edges together and slice off the extra pastry. 'Knock up' the cut edges with horizontal strokes to help the pastry to rise. Puff pastry pies are usually scalloped (see page 105); press the edge of the pastry with the thumb of one hand and with a knife in the other hand, drag the pastry back towards the middle to shape a scallop.
5   Brush over the surface with the milk and egg white mixed. Cut one or two slits for steam to escape, set the pie on a baking sheet and bake for 1½–2 hours. When the pastry is well browned, cover it with a sheet of foil screwed up at the corner to keep it on.

SHROPSHIRE PIE

Serves 6

I spent the early part of my married life in Shropshire and I think my neighbour must have been a poacher. He used to leave me 'presents' at the door and many a morning I would come down and find a rabbit hanging on the door handle, or a box of mushrooms, or a pheasant.

This recipe uses red wine with the stock and whole onions. It is not all that easy to get small onions or shallots which are the perfect size to go with this dish. I look for pickling onions and pick only the biggest of these.

Again, this pie is baked the old way, with the rabbit joints raw under the pastry. You can buy 'loose' rabbit joints in some fishmongers. Buy bacon chops to cut into nice chunky pieces.

6 rabbit joints, about 2½ lb (1.1 kg) in total
1 tablespoon flour
8 oz (225 g) small onions, peeled
½ teaspoon grated nutmeg
2 bacon chops, cut very small
6 small no-soak prunes
8 fl oz (225 ml) red wine and chicken stock mixed
1 tablespoon parsley
sprig of thyme
1 lb (450 g) Shortcrust Pastry (see page 16)
1 size-7 egg, beaten

1   Preheat the oven to gas6/400°F/200°C. Rinse the rabbit joints, pat dry and roll them in the flour. Set them in a 3 pt (1.75 litre) capacity pie dish with a pie funnel placed in the centre.

2   Place the peeled onions between the joints, sprinkle the ground nutmeg over. Scatter over the chopped bacon and whole prunes. Season thoroughly and pour over the red wine and stock. Stir in the parsley and thyme.

3   Since this is quite a large pie, roll out the pastry rather thicker than you normally would for shortcrust. Cut a narrow strip from the outside and fit this on the pie rim, having first brushed the rim with a wet brush.

4   Now brush the top of the rim with water and, using your rolling pin, lift the pastry. Position it over the pie and press the two edges together. Trim off the spare pastry and use a fork to mark the rim of the pie all round. A lightly marked diagonal pattern scored on the pastry top always looks good. Finally, brush the beaten egg all over and make a steam hole over the funnel.

5   Place the pie on a baking sheet and bake in the oven for 2 hours. When the pastry is well-coloured, fasten a foil lid over the top and screw up the corners. This will stop the pastry getting any darker.

BUCKINGHAMSHIRE RABBIT PIE

Serves 3-4

I was very intrigued by this recipe which I found in an old WI county cookery book so I tried it out and it is very good. I do not know why, but it seemed rather incongruous to use macaroni and double cream with rabbit and cheese! The rabbit is pre-cooked.

1 small rabbit or 2 lb (900 g) rabbit joints
1 medium-size onion
4 cloves
1 bay leaf
some parsley stalks
3 sprigs of fresh thyme

1 small piece of carrot
1 small celery stalk
4 black peppercorns
2 oz (50 g) short-cut macaroni
2 oz (50 g) Cheddar cheese, grated
2 oz (50 g) onion, peeled and finely chopped
½ pt (300 ml) double cream
8 oz (225 g) New Flaky Pastry (see page 19)
1 size-7 egg, beaten
salt and pepper

1   Soak the rabbit in cold water for 1 hour.

2   Drain the rabbit and cover again with fresh water. Bring to the boil and skim carefully. Turn down the heat to a simmer and add the onion stuck with the cloves, the bay leaf, parsley stalks, and 1 of the sprigs of thyme, the carrot, celery, peppercorns and salt. Cover and simmer for about 1½ hours, or until the rabbit is cooked.

3   Remove the joints and strain the stock into a clean saucepan. Take all the meat off the bones and try to keep the big pieces intact.

4   Preheat the oven to gas7/425°F/220°C. Bring the stock up to the boil and cook the macaroni in it until it is tender. Take the macaroni out and save the stock for soup.

5   Mix the macaroni with the rabbit meat, chopped onion, cheese and remaining thyme chopped. Season well, pack into the pie dish and set a pie funnel in position. Pour the cream over the filling.

6   Roll out the pastry on a floured board until it is rather larger than the pie. Cut a narrow strip of pastry for the rim. Wet the surface of the rim and fix a strip of pastry on to it, making a neat join. Lift the rest of the pastry on to the pie and press the edges together to make a good seal. Slice off the spare pastry. 'Knock up' the edges with horizontal strokes to help the pastry to rise. Cut a hole over the funnel and brush the pie all over with beaten egg.

7   Set the pie on a baking sheet and bake for about 35–40 minutes.

PIGEON PIE

Serves 4

Young tender pigeons are much more readily available than they used to be. In the past, the great houses bred pigeons for the table.

2 medium-size pigeons
12 oz (350 g) stewing beef, chopped small
1 medium-size onion, peeled and chopped
2 small carrots, cut in chunks
2 rashers of streaky bacon, chopped small
6 oz (175 g) Shortcrust Pastry (see page 16)
little milk
salt and pepper

1   Preheat the oven to gas4/350°F/180°C. Rinse the pigeons and joint them. Put them to stew in a pan with the stewing beef, onion and carrot. Barely cover with water and cook for 2½ hours, or longer if the birds are not young.
2   Take the pigeon meat off the bones and set in a 1½ pt (1 litre) pie dish. Add the vegetables and steak and just a little of the cooking liquid to moisten. Scatter the chopped bacon over the top and season.
3   Roll the pastry out rather larger than the pie dish. Cut a narrow strip of pastry from the outer edge and fix it on the dampened rim of the dish. Now wet the top of this pastry rim and fit the pastry over the pie, making a good seal all round the pie. Trim off the extra pastry. Brush the pie with milk and make a steam hole in the top.
4   Bake for about 30-40 minutes.

SQUAB PIE

Serves 4–6

Squabs were very young pigeons bred on squab farms for the table. I am told there used to be such farms in England before the last war.

4 small pigeons, each cut in half
2 oz (50 g) butter
6 strips of smoked streaky bacon, chopped
1 medium onion, peeled and chopped small
2 oz (50 g) currants
2 oz (50 g) dates, chopped
2 dessert apples, cored and sliced
grated rind of ½ orange
4 cloves
½ pt (300 ml) dry cider
8 oz (225 g) Herby Shortcrust Pastry (see page 16)
little milk
salt and pepper
oil, for frying

1   Preheat the oven to gas4/350°F/180°C.
2   In a large frying pan, heat the oil and fry the pigeons back and front to brown them. Transfer them to a large pie dish with a capacity of 2-3 pts (1.2–1.75 litres).
3   Add the butter and fry the bacon pieces and the onion until browned. Sprinkle all these over as well. Pack all the fruits in and around the joints, adding the orange rind, cloves and seasoning. Pour in the cider to cover.
4   Roll out the pastry on a floured board so that you can cut a narrow strip from the outside. Fit this narrow strip on the pie rim which has been brushed with water. Press it down, making a neat join. Lift the pastry lid over and fit. Brush the top of the narrow pastry rim with water and press the edges together. Trim off the excess pastry. Press a fork all round to ensure a good seal. Make a steam hole on top and brush all over with milk.
5   Set the pie on a baking sheet and bake for about 1½–2 hours. If the pastry is starting to get very brown, fit a cover of foil and screw up the corners to hold it in place.

RAISED PIES

Raised pies, or 'stand pies' as they used to be called, are among the glories of British cooking. Traditionally eaten cold with pickles, the fillings for such pies are many and varied. It is common to have two or three different kinds of meat or game. Texture is important too, with perhaps one of the meats minced, another chopped and another in flat slices. The pastry was always a hot-water-crust made with lard. Nowadays the pastry is often less rich and with an egg in the mixture to give a crisp finish. Stand pies were, and are still, made by hand with the help of a wooden mould. The pastry is moulded from the bottom up. A substitute for a wooden mould is a jam jar. Once the pastry has been gently coaxed to the right depth, the mould is removed. Support for the sides is just strips of brown paper, well greased with lard and fastened in place for the baking. There are very elaborate hinged moulds made of tin, but these are very expensive. Good strong cake tins make a good substitute for pork pie tins. If they are loose-bottomed, this is an advantage.

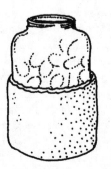

HELEN'S EXTRA-SPECIAL PARTY PIE

Serves about 12

My friend Helen is Yorkshire through and
through and a keen and interested cook. The
big pork pie which follows is her own recipe,
developed over the years. I have tasted many
versions, since she changes the meats according
to what she has in her freezer or sees in the
butcher's. An old bit of advice about a pork pie:
'for best flavour leave it for 24 hours before
eating' (in a fridge of course).

Helen uses a round loose-bottomed spring-
form cake tin which is 9 in (23 cm) round and
2 in (5 cm) deep.

Unminced Meats
1 large pheasant (uncooked)
2 chicken breasts, boned and skinned
1 lb (450 g) thick raw ham, cut into ½ in
    (1 cm) wide strips

Marinade
4 tablespoons brandy
4 tablespoons port or good-quality red wine
1 bay leaf

Stuffing
1¼ lb (550 g) minced belly pork or half lean
    pork and half pork fat
3 tablespoons fresh chopped herbs (parsley,
    thyme, marjoram, basil, etc) or
    1 teaspoon of dried mixed herbs
¼ teaspoon ground allspice
¼ teaspoon salt
2 shallots or 1 medium onion, peeled and
    chopped finely

Pastry
1 lb (450 g) plain white flour
½ teaspoon salt
8 oz (225 g) butter, plus more for greasing
1 size-3 egg

Glaze
1 size-7 egg
little milk

Savoury Jelly
1 small onion
2 teaspoons gelatine

1   Start the day before you wish to bake the pie.
With a very sharp knife, cut all the meat off the
pheasant, slicing the two breasts horizontally
into 4 or more flat pieces. Slice the chicken
breasts horizontally into flat pieces too.
2   Place all the pheasant, ham and chicken meat
in a china or glass dish. Mix the marinade
ingredients and pour over. Cover the dish with a
lid or plate and leave in the fridge for at least 6
hours or overnight if possible. Turn the meat
over a couple of times.
3   Preheat the oven to gas6/400°F/200°C. Mix all
the ingredients for the stuffing together. Do this
in a mixing machine if you have one. Make sure
that the herbs and spices are well distributed.
4   To make the pastry: sift the flour and salt into
a bowl. Cut the butter into small pieces and rub
into the flour mixture by hand or in a food
processor. Beat the egg with 4 tablespoons of
water and use this to mix into the flour and
butter to make a pastry of a not too soft
consistency.
5   To line the tin: first grease it well with
butter. Take about two-thirds of the pastry and
roll it out on a floured board. Line the tin with
it, making sure that the pastry is even and not
too thick at the bottom. Reserve the other piece
of pastry for the lid.
6   To fill the pie: take up half of the stuffing and
press it evenly in the bottom of the pie. Take care
to make it as even as possible. Use your hand to
do this, since a spoon or knife could easily split
the pastry. Next take some of the ham strips out
of the marinade and push them into the stuffing
in two rings (see the diagram opposite).
7   Next fit the chicken breast slices as evenly as
possible in a flat layer. Follow the chicken with
the pheasant, also in a flat layer. Fill up any
spaces between the chicken and pheasant with
what is left of the meats. Finish off with the rest
of the stuffing. Level this off carefully. This
should bring the filling up to within ¼ in

(5 mm) of the pie tin rim. Dribble about
1 tablespoon of the marinade over the filling.
8   On a floured board, roll out the remaining
pastry. You may find a pan lid which will act as a
giant cutter about the same size as your tin.
Failing that, stand the pie on a piece of paper and
cut a pattern. The lid should be a little larger
than the diameter of the tin. Dampen the edges
of the lid and the top of the pastry with egg or
water. Fit the lid, making a good seal. Nip the
pastry together to make a fluted rim.
9   Make 4 neat holes in the lid (I use an apple
corer). Beat the egg with some milk and brush
this all over the lid. Roll out the pastry
trimmings, cut some decorative leaves and
arrange on top. Make 4 extra leaves to cover up
the holes after the pie is baked. These need to be
glazed and baked separately.

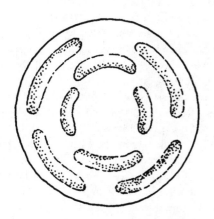

10 Make four 'funnels' with non-stick or
greaseproof paper and insert them into the holes.
These will help to stop the juices bubbling up
and out all over the pastry during cooking.
Remove them very carefully afterwards.
11 Set the pie on a baking sheet and bake for 20
minutes. Then reduce the temperature to
gas3/325°F/170°C and cook for a further 30
minutes. Reduce the temperature to
gas2/300°F/150°C and cook for a further 30
minutes. Finally, reduce the temperature to
gas1/275°F/140°C and cook for 40–70 minutes
more. The total baking time is between 2 and
2½ hours depending on the oven. If it is getting
too brown at any point, make a foil 'hat' for it
(screwing up the corners to hold it in place).
12 When the pie is cooked, allow it to cool and
then place in the fridge for a few hours or
overnight. Do remember to allow the pie to come
back to room temperature before you serve it.
13 The jelly Helen makes is a well-flavoured one
made with the pheasant bones. Barely cover
them with water and boil for about 1 hour along
with a small chopped onion. Strain this liquid
into a pan and discard the bones. Reduce the
liquid – that is, boil fairly hard without a lid –
until you have about ½ pt (300 ml). Sprinkle
2 level teaspoons of gelatine over the surface. Set
the pan aside for a couple of minutes, then whisk
the gelatine until it dissolves. Pour a tiny bit of
this liquid into a saucer, put this in the fridge to
check that it is going to set to a firm jelly. If by
any chance it does not set on the saucer add a
little more gelatine to the stock.
14 To add the jelly to the pie, wait until the pie
is cold and the jelly cool. It must, however, still
be liquid to trickle into the pie through a small
funnel. It may not all go in at once, but leave
time for it to settle then put some more in until
it comes up to the holes on top of the pie.
15 When the jelly has set, cover the pastry holes
with the extra leaves. They will stick on with a
little egg white. If, by any bad luck, the jelly
starts to leak out of a crack, plaster the crack up
with hard butter from the fridge, it can hardly be
seen. Finis! (And the best of luck!! says Helen).

British Traditional Pork Pie

Serves 4–6

Long ago, butchers protected the kind and variety of spices or herbs they used in their pork pies and often advertised a 'secret ingredient'. One of the main flavourings was mace – that lacy-looking outer coating of a nutmeg. Salt and pepper were rather more lavish than we like today and saltpetre was often used to keep the meat looking pink. Commercial manufacturers are still able to use this ploy, but it is not available to the public. So a home-made pork pie will not have that pink hue, but will score handsomely when it comes to flavour. You will need a tin about 6 in (15 cm) round and 3 in (8 cm) deep.

Savoury Jelly
1 pig's trotter
6 black peppercorns
1 bay leaf
sprig of thyme

Filling
1 lb (450 g) shoulder pork
¼ level teaspoon ground mace
3 strips of streaky bacon, cut small
salt and pepper

Traditional Hot-water-crust Pastry
4 oz (125 g) lard
10 oz (275 g) strong plain flour
½ level teaspoon salt
1 size-7 egg, beaten

1   The savoury jelly must be made the day before you make your pie. Ask your butcher to cut the pig's trotter in two for you. Boil the trotter with the peppercorns, bay leaf and thyme in 1 pt (600 ml) water, until the trotter is very soft (about 3 hours). Strain the liquid into a bowl and leave to set in the fridge overnight.
2   Next day, preheat the oven to gas6/400°F/200°C. Remove any fat from the surface of the jelly. If the jelly is still wobbly (it

should be fairly firm), melt it down again and reduce some more. Discard the trotter.
3   To prepare the filling: trim away any gristle from the pork and cut it into small pieces (about the size of a pea). Mix in the seasoning. Alternatively, using the coarse cutter, you can put the pork through a mincer or use a food processor, but stop the blades before the pork is reduced to a paste. Stir in the bacon.
4   Make the pastry: boil 4 fl oz (125 ml) water, add the lard and when it has melted and heated up again, pour all into a bowl with the flour and salt. Using a long-bladed knife with a round end, mix the flour into the liquid. As soon as you can, use your hand to knead the pastry until quite smooth. Allow to cool slightly before rolling out.
5   Roll out three-quarters of the pastry to fit a loose-bottomed tin. Press the pastry into position to make an even thickness all round. Pack the filling in, but not too tightly.
6   Roll out the pastry for the lid. Brush the edges of both the lid and the top of the pie with egg, nip the two pastry edges together and cut away any surplus pastry with a pair of scissors. Roll the trimmings out and cut some decorative leaves. Brush these with beaten egg and position on the pie, then brush all over the lid to give a good glaze. Make a hole in the centre of the lid and enlarge it slightly.
7   Set the pie on a baking sheet and bake for 30 minutes. Reduce the heat to gas5/375°F/190°C and cook for a further 1 hour.
8   Allow the pie to cool, boil up the jelly again and allow that to cool also. Use a small funnel to pour the still liquid jelly into the pie. When it has settled, pour in a little more – about ¼ pt (150 ml) altogether. If it leaks through a crack, you can plug the crack with cold butter.

PORK PIE WITH EGGS IN A LOAF SHAPE

Serves 6–8

Sage is another well-liked flavouring for a pork pie. This one is in the shape of a loaf and, because of that, is very easy to cut. The appearance of a slice of egg in the middle of each piece of pie is also very attractive. Tiny eggs are available from specialist egg producers. My local market always has them – size 6 or 7. You will need a long loaf tin, about 11 x 4½ x 3 in (28 x 11.5 x 7.5 cm).

Filling

1½ lb (675 g) lean pork
8 oz (225 g) fatty bacon
1 large tablespoon of chopped fresh sage
¼ teaspoon black pepper
5 size-6 or size-7 eggs, hard-boiled and shelled

Hot-water-crust Pastry

5 oz (150 g) lard or white cooking fat
4 fl oz (150 ml) milk and water mixed
1 lb (450 g) plain white strong flour
1 teaspoon of salt

Savoury Jelly

¼ pt (150 ml) strongly flavoured stock
1 teaspoon gelatine

1   Preheat the oven to gas6/400°F/200°C.
2   To prepare the filling: put the pork and bacon in a food processor, aim for a coarse cut rather than a paste. Stir in the sage and black pepper.
3   To make the pastry: melt the lard or white cooking fat in the milk and water mixture. When the liquid is boiling, pour into a bowl into which the flour and salt have been sifted. Mix quickly to a soft dough adding a drop more water if it is needed. As soon as the dough is cool enough to handle, turn it out and knead with your hands until it is smooth.

4   To line the loaf tin: roll out three-quarters of the pastry and use this to shape the bottom and sides. Press and pull the pastry into shape. Unlike other pastries, this rough treatment will not affect the end result. Aim to have an even thickness all over with the pastry, reaching the top of the tin.
5   Make up half of the pork and bacon mixture and set it in the pie tin bottom in an even layer. Now lay the shelled hard-boiled eggs in, end to end. Take the rest of the pork mixture and press it down to cover the eggs. Level the surface (a narrow slice off each end of each egg will mean that they fit better in a row).
6   Make a lid by rolling out the reserved pastry to an oblong shape. Brush the top edge of the pie pastry and the outer edge of the lid. Lay the lid on top of the filling and fasten the lid to the pie by pressing and squeezing the two pastries together. Trim off the excess pastry and use the trimmings to make leaves or tassels or anything decorative. Brush the decorations with egg and stick them to the pie surface, then brush all over the top of the lid.
7   Set the pie on a tin and bake for 30 minutes. Reduce the temperature to gas4/350°F/180°C and cook for another 1½ hours. If the pie is getting too brown, fix a foil lid over the top, screwing up the corners to stop it blowing away. Remove from the oven and allow to cool down.
8   To make the savoury jelly you need a generous ¼ pt (150 ml) strongly flavoured stock (use a cube if you have no fresh stock.) Put 2 tablespoons of stock into a small bowl and sprinkle over the gelatine. Allow to swell up for about 3 minutes, then stand the bowl in a pan of hot water and stir until the gelatine melts. Stir the gelatine mixture into the stock. Allow the gelatine mixture to cool but not set. Pour slowly into the pie just a bit at a time (a small funnel helps). Allow to settle, then pour in some more. Cool down then chill.
9   Eat within 4 days. If there is a leak, plug up the crack with cold butter.

HAM, EGG & VEAL STAND PIE

Serves 4

A stand pie is made without a tin. If you do not own a wooden pork pie mould, and very few people do, an empty 2 lb (900 g) jam jar makes a good substitute. The pastry for the pie is moulded by hand up the sides of the jar, the jar is removed and the pastry stands up by itself. For baking, however, you have to grease a strip of brown paper with lard or white fat. This is wound round the pie twice and fastened to support the sides of the pie.

Veal was popular for pork pies, as its pale colour looked good against the pink colour of the pork meat.

12 oz (325 g) Hot-water-crust Pastry (see page 18)
1 egg size-7, beaten
lard, for greasing
flour, for dusting

Filling
³/₄ lb (325 g) fillet or shoulder of veal (if using shoulder, get a little extra to allow for trimming of fat)
¹/₄ lb (150 g) raw ham (buy a thick slice, pour boiling water over it and drain)
1 teaspoon salt
¹/₂ teaspoon pepper
¹/₂ teaspoon ground mace
1 size-1 egg, hard-boiled and sliced (on a wire cutter if possible)
1 bay leaf

Savoury Jelly
¹/₄ pt (150 ml) strongly flavoured stock
1 teaspoon gelatine

1   Preheat the oven to gas5/375°F/190°C.
2   Have ready a long piece of brown paper which is about 3 in (7.5 cm) wide, heavily greased with lard and long enough to go round the pie twice.
3   Make the pastry and remove a piece weighing

about 2 oz (50 g) for the lid.
4   Knead the rest of the pastry into a thick pancake about 4 in (10 cm) across. Take the empty jam jar (see above), dust it with flour and press it down centrally on this pancake. Make one or two twisting actions to squeeze the pastry out and up. Now lift the jam jar and gently ease the pastry up the sides of the jar while twisting the jar round and round. I find this easier if the jar is horizontal with the base nearest to me. Aim for the pie to be about 3 in (7.5 cm) deep. Stand the jar upright and give the jar a slight twist to move it and lift it away. Allow the pastry to stand while your prepare the filling.
5   Remove one-quarter of veal and cut it into small chunks. Put the rest of the veal, ham, salt, pepper and mace into a food processor and whizz to a coarse crumb.
6   Pack half of the mixture gently into the pie, pushing it well into the corners. Press half of the veal chunks into the minced meat. Smooth the surface and place the thinly sliced egg in a packed layer. Pack the rest of the minced meat on top. Press in the rest of the veal and smooth it over. Lay a bay leaf on top.
7   Make the jelly by placing 2 tablespoons of stock in a small cup, sprinkle over the gelatine and leave for 3 minutes to swell. Then stand the cup in a pan of gently simmering water and stir until the gelatine dissolves. Take 1 tablespoon of the liquid jelly and dribble it over the pie filling.
8   Roll out the reserved pastry to make the lid. If it has gone hard, a few seconds in the microwave works.
9   Paint the edge of the round of pastry with some of the egg and do the same to the top of the pie. Put the lid on and squeeze the pastry join together. Trim off the excess with scissors. Wind the paper round the pie twice and brush the top with the egg. Make a hole in the pastry.
10   Bake for 1 hour. Reduce to gas3/325°F/160°C and cook for another 45–50 minutes. Remove the paper and brush the egg all over the pie top and sides. Return the pie to the oven for a few minutes or until the egg dries. Allow the pie to cool down. Boil up the jelly again and allow that to cool down.
11   Use a small funnel to pour the cool but still liquid jellied stock into the pie, a bit at a time. Cool down and chill.

PICNIC PORK PIE

Serves 6

I think it was Marks & Spencer who first introduced flat pork pies with lattice tops. About 2 in (5 cm) deep, they are certainly easier to handle and are particularly good for picnics. The addition of an egg to the pastry makes the finished pie quite crusty. This pastry recipe was first given in a TV programme by Anne Wallace of Ayrshire.

10 oz (275 g) plain white flour (or half white and half wholewheat)
$\frac{1}{2}$ teaspoon salt
$4\frac{1}{2}$ oz (140 g) lard
1 size-3 egg, beaten
little milk

Filling
$\frac{3}{4}$ lb (325 g) good-quality sausagemeat or the meat from some good sausages
3 oz (75 g) streaky bacon, rinded and chopped small
1 large teaspoon chopped fresh parsley
2 fat pinches of dried marjoram
$\frac{1}{2}$ large dessert apple, peeled, cored and finely chopped
1 size-1 egg, beaten
salt and pepper

1   Mix the flour and salt in a bowl. Rub in the lard (or, for speed, whizz in a food processor). Holding back about 1 teaspoon to glaze the pie, beat the beaten egg into $2\frac{1}{2}$ fl oz (65 ml) cold water. Use this egg and water mixture to make a fairly soft elastic dough. (Be ready to add a little extra water if necessary.) Set the dough aside for at least 1 hour before rolling out.

2   Preheat the oven to gas5/375°F/190°C. Now mix the pie filling. I nearly always use my mixer for this but, of course, the old way and probably the best was to use your hand. Put the sausagemeat and everything else in a bowl and mix thoroughly.
3   Take up about two-thirds of the pastry and roll it out thinly on a floured board. Grease an 8 or 9 in (20 or 23 cm) loose-bottomed flat tin or flan ring set on a greased baking sheet and line with the pastry. Always ease pastry into a tin – that is, do not stretch it across from rim to rim but ease it gently and press to fit, starting at the middle. This is when I wish I could show you exactly what I mean. The whole idea is to prevent the pastry shrinking during cooking. Push the side of the pastry down, then roll the excess pastry over the top. Take your rolling pin and roll it across hard. You can then lift the pastry away easily.
4   Pack the filling in, pushing it well down and into the side. Level it off. If you have any filling left over, roll it into tiny balls, brush with oil and bake with the pie. Remove when brown and serve with drinks.
5   To make the lattice top: cut strips $\frac{1}{2}$ in (1 cm) wide from the rest of the pastry. If you have an old-fashioned roller to make a crimped edge to your lattice strips, it looks attractive. Criss-cross the strips over your pie, laying the strips one way and then the other. If you have the patience you can basket-weave the strips. Trim off the edges, moisten the end of each strip and press it down to make a firm join.
6   Lastly, mix your reserved egg with a tiny bit of milk and brush this all over your lattice top.
7   Bake for about 30 minutes, then turn oven down to gas4/350°F/180°C for the last 10–15 minutes of cooking. As always, if the pie top is browning too fast, cover it with a 'hat' of foil, screwing up the corners to stop it blowing away.

FAT-BELLIED PORK PIE

Serves 6

Melton Mowbray was described as the great pie centre of England and in the past it was notable for the unusual addition to the pork meat filling of anchovy essence. The other very obvious characteristic of a Melton Mowbray pie, which survives to this day, is its shape – fat-bellied is the only way to describe it.

I cannot believe that there are pie tins shaped like that, but I did manage a sort of fat belly by putting a metal flan ring a little bigger than the pie round the bottom of the pie. Sadly the pie did sink a bit too much and, yes, the bottom was wider than the top, but the shape was not too smooth. Perhaps someone will write and tell me how to do it. It tasted very good indeed and the mixture of smoothly minced pork contrasted well with the chopped chunks.

Traditionally, the savoury jelly would have been made with a pig's trotter, flavourings and a lot of cooking time. An easier savoury jelly can be made as here.

Crust

12 oz (350 g) Hot-water-crust Pastry (see
    page 18), slightly warm
1 size-3 egg, beaten
melted vegetable fat, for greasing
flour, for dusting

Filling

2 lb (900 g) pork spare ribs, trimmed of
    some fat
8 oz (225 g) thin-cut rindless streaky bacon,
    cut small
1 teaspoon fresh chopped sage leaves
1 teaspoon liquid anchovy essence
$\frac{1}{2}$ teaspoon ground nutmeg
$\frac{1}{2}$ teaspoon ground allspice
salt and pepper

Jelly

$\frac{1}{4}$ pt (150 ml) strongly flavoured chicken or
    beef stock (made from a cube, if
    necessary)
1 teaspoon gelatine powder

1   Preheat the oven to gas5/375°F/190°C (unless leaving the uncooked pie overnight to mature as described below). Using melted vegetable fat, grease a cake tin (with a loose bottom if possible) 7 in (18 cm) across and $3\frac{1}{2}$ in (8.5 cm) deep.

2   Set aside about one-quarter of the pastry for the lid. Roll out the rest on a floured board to a thickness of about $\frac{1}{3}$ in (8 mm) and ease this into the pie tin. Press the pastry flat at the bottom of the tin and smoothly work the rest of the pastry up to fit the tin and drop over the top edge slightly.

3   Make the filling: take about 6 oz (175 g) of the pork and chop into small pieces about the size of peas. This is easier with scissors. Set aside.

4   Put the rest of the pork and half of the bacon through the mincer. For a fine texture, mince the pork and bacon again. Now add the flavourings to the minced pork and mix this well. I use a mixer for this job and add 1 or 2 tablespoons of water to make the filling less stiff.

5   To fill the pie: take half of the minced mixture and push this into the base of the pie tin. Next make a layer of the chopped pieces of pork. Top with the rest of the minced pork and level it off. Do not fill the pie right to the top – about $\frac{1}{2}$ in (1 cm) down is about enough.

6   On a floured board, roll out the reserved pastry for a lid. Cut a circle slightly larger than needed. Moisten the top of the pastry round the tin and round the outside edge of the lid. Set the lid on the pie and make a good seal by nipping the two pastry edges together. Trim off the spare pastry with scissors. Make a steam hole in the centre and nip the pastry into a fluted edge. Brush the beaten egg over the lid. Make any decorations with the trimmings if you wish. A very easy form of decoration is to roll out a strip of pastry about $1\frac{1}{2}$ in (3.5 cm) wide and 7 in (18 cm) long. Cut a tassel effect at each end. Twist the strip and set it across the lid. Brush this all over with egg too.

7   Pie makers often say to leave the pie uncooked overnight to 'mature' before you bake it.

8   Set the pie on a baking sheet and bake for 1 hour. Turn the heat down to gas3/325°F/160°C and cook for another 50 minutes. You can brush the egg mixture over the lid again during cooking for an even glossier finish.

9   To make the jelly: put 2 tablespoons of the

stock in a cup or small bowl. Sprinkle the gelatine over the surface and leave it for 2–3 minutes to swell up. Now stand the cup or bowl in a pan of simmering water until the gelatine has melted. Stir well to make sure that it is smooth. Now stir the gelatine mixture into the stock. This has to be poured into the pie after it has cooled down. A small funnel makes it easier. The jelly itself should be cool too. The jelly may not all go in at once, you may have to allow it to trickle down for a bit then pour in some more.
10 The pie will keep in the fridge for up to 4 days, but the pastry looses its crispiness.

CHRISTMAS PORK PIE WITH CHESTNUTS & CRANBERRIES

Serves 6

This is a very attractive and festive-looking pie. Instead of a pastry lid, the pie is cooked with just foil covering the pie filling. After the pie has cooled, a thick layer of jellied spiced cranberries are set in the space left for it at the top of the pie. The brilliant colour make this pie ideal for Christmas.

Cranberries are very tart and you may be surprised that I have only added 1 oz (25 g) of sugar, but the lemon jelly is quite sweet. Wait until the topping is complete and taste again.

Crust
9 oz (250 g) Hot-water-crust Pastry (see page 18), slightly warm
1 size-3 egg, beaten
melted vegetable fat, for greasing
flour, for dusting

Filling
1¾ lb (800 g) pork spare ribs, trimmed of some fat
8 oz (225 g) thin-cut rindless streaky bacon, cut small
1 teaspoon fresh chopped sage leaves

1 teaspoon liquid anchovy essence
½ teaspoon ground nutmeg
½ teaspoon ground allspice
4 oz (125 g) drained canned chestnuts
salt and pepper

Topping
8 oz (225 g) fresh or frozen cranberries
1 oz (25 g) caster sugar
1 pinch of cinnamon
1 level teaspoon made-up mustard
2–3 drops of Tabasco sauce
½ packet of lemon jelly, melted

1   Make the pie using the recipe for the previous pie, but use all the pastry to line the tin and just before you put in the layer of chopped pork in the middle cut the drained canned chestnuts into small pieces (picking out any brown skin still sticking to the chestnuts). Push half of the chestnuts down into the filling and cover the holes up again. Set the chunky pieces of raw pork in a layer, then top with the rest of the minced pork. Push the remaining chestnuts into the soft stuffing. Smooth over the holes.
2   Now scrunch a good big sheet of greaseproof paper into a thick pad to put on top of the pork pie filling instead of a pastry lid. The aim is to hold up the 'walls' of the pie. Cook as in the previous recipe and allow to cool.
3   Melt the lemon jelly in ¼ pt (150 ml) water. Put the cranberries, sugar, cinnamon, mustard and Tabasco in a pan and barely cover with water. Stew gently until very soft. Before the final cooking stage, take a teaspoon and remove 6–7 whole cranberries before they collapse. This is purely for decorative reasons. Allow the rest to go very soft indeed. Strain off the pulp and stir it into the lemon jelly. Wait until the jellied cranberries are just on the point of setting and pour them into the top of the pork pie. Set the whole cranberries here and there and allow to go cold.

PICNIC PLATE PIE

Serves 4–6

It is always said that pork finely chopped by hand gives a much better flavour for a pork pie. Cutting pork by hand is a very tedious job as it is very wobbly. My own solution is to freeze the pork, but not quite to the solid-hard stage before chopping.

10 oz (275 g) Shortcrust Pastry (see page 16)
1 size-7 egg
little milk
butter or lard, for greasing

Filling
10 oz (275 g) chopped pork or sausagemeat
  or 6 thin sausages
1 oz (50 g) fine fresh breadcrumbs
1 tablespoon chopped parsley
4 oz (125 g) smoked streaky bacon, chopped
  small
dash of Worcestershire sauce

1   Preheat the oven to gas5/375°F/190°C and set a baking sheet in the oven. Using butter or lard, grease an aluminium or enamel pie plate with a deepish bowl about 8–9 inches (20–23 cm) across.
2   Mix together the filling ingredients very thoroughly, adding 1–2 tablespoons of water just to slacken the mixture slightly.
3   Roll out just under half of the pastry fairly thinly and use to line the pie plate, taking care not to stretch it. Trim off the surplus. Spread the filling over the pastry and leave a narrow border round the outside.
4   Roll out the remaining pastry for the lid. Moisten the outer edge of the bottom pastry and set the rest of the pastry over. Seal the edges and trim off the excess. Press a fork all round the join and cut a steam hole in the centre. Brush over the pastry with the beaten egg mixed with a little milk.
5   Set the pie on the hot baking sheet and bake for 30 minutes. Reduce the oven to gas4/350°F/180°C and cook for another 30 minutes. If the top is getting too brown, make a hat of foil and screw up the corners to keep it in position.

CHESHIRE PORK & APPLE PIE

Serves 6–8

10 oz (285 g) Shortcrust Pastry (see page 16)
1 size-7 egg, beaten

Filling
1 oz (25 g) butter
1 tablespoon oil
1½ lb (675 g) pork fillet, chopped into
  small chunks
12 oz (325 g) onions, peeled and chopped
1 oz (25 g) plain flour
½ pt (300 ml) chicken stock
½ pt (300 ml) dry cider
6 oz (175 g) button mushrooms, sliced
2 hard dessert apples, peeled, cored and cut
  into wedges
1 level teaspoon marjoram
salt and pepper

1   First cook filling: heat the butter and oil in a roomy pan and fry pork hard until brown. Push to one side and fry onion (you may need a little more oil) on a lower heat for about 5 minutes.
2   Stir the meat and onions together and sprinkle the flour over. Stir this in and gradually pour in the stock and cider. Stir until thickened. Add the mushrooms, apples, marjoram and seasoning. Cook gently for about 40–60 minutes. Check meat is cooked through. Set aside.
3   Spoon the mixture into a 3 pt (1.75 litre) pie dish and pile it in the centre or use a pie funnel.
4   Roll out the pastry rather larger than the pie dish and cut a narrow strip of pastry to fit round the rim. Dampen the rim of the pie dish, set the pastry on this and press it down. Cover the pie with the rest of the pastry having moistened the upper surface of the pastry rim. Set the pastry lid over, cut a steam hole in the centre and press the two pastry edges together. Trim off the surplus pastry, brush over with beaten egg and use the trimmings to make decorative leaves and flowers for the lid. Brush over again with beaten egg.
5   Set pie on a baking sheet and bake for 30 minutes, or until the pastry is brown and crisp.

SPECIAL LARGE GAME PIE

Serves 10

This pie is cooked in a large but shallow loaf tin, measuring about 11 in (28 cm) by 4½ in (11.5 cm) and 3 in (7.5 cm) deep. It is very easy to slice thinly when it is cold and looks magnificent at a buffet.

1 lb (450 g) Hot-water-crust Pastry (see page 18)
1 size-7 egg, beaten
butter or lard, for greasing

Filling
1 large pheasant
8 oz (225 g) smoked bacon
4 oz (125 g) pork fat (ask your butcher)
8 oz (225 g) cubed venison
4 oz (125 g) sausagemeat
1 medium onion, peeled and chopped
2 teaspoons fresh thyme leaves or
    ½ teaspoon dried thyme
1 large tablespoon drained green peppercorns
    in brine (sold in delicatessens)
salt and pepper

Savoury Jelly
1 onion
1 carrot
sprig of thyme
1 teaspoon gelatine powder

1   Prepare the filling. Remove the two breasts from the pheasant and set them aside. Pull the rest of the meat off the bones. This is usually easy to do with your fingers. Reserve the bones for the jelly stock. Put this meat, the bacon, the pork fat, cubed venison, sausagemeat, onion, thyme, 2 tablespoons water and salt and pepper in a food processor. Whizz until roughly blended. Stir the peppercorns into this mixture.

2   Preheat the oven to gas6/400°F/200°C and set a baking sheet in the oven. Grease the tin (see above).
3   Roll out two-thirds of the pastry thinly and use to line the tin. You will have to ease the pastry into the corners and check that the pastry is not too thin. Allow the pastry to drape over the top of the tin.
4   Divide the processed meat in two, press one lot into the bottom of the tin and level it off carefully. Now slice the pheasant breasts very thinly horizontally and arrange a layer of pieces packed together. Top with the rest of the minced meat and level that off.
5   Roll out an oblong of pastry to fit the top of the tin. Moisten the pastry casing where it is likely that the joins will be. Set the pastry over and press the pastry at the rim of the tin. Trim away any excess. Press the pie all round the edge with a fork or tweak the pastry up in flutes all round, then brush the pie with the beaten egg. Make a steam hole.
6   Set the pie on the hot baking sheet in the oven for 30 minutes or until the pastry is set. Reduce the temperature to gas4/350°F/180°C and cook for about 1½ hours more. Set aside to go cold.
7   Make the savoury jelly: first make a well-flavoured stock with the carcass of the pheasant. Break up the bones and put them in a pan with an onion, carrot and sprig of thyme. Barely cover with water. Bring to a boil, skim then reduce to a simmer for 2 hours with a lid on. Drain off the liquid, then reduce it by boiling in an open pan. Taste and reduce some more if the flavour is weak.
8   To make the jelly, put 2 tablespoons of the stock in a small bowl or cup, sprinkle the gelatine over and set it aside to swell up for 2–3 minutes. Now stand the bowl or cup in a pan of hot water and stir until the gelatine melts completely. Pour the gelatine mixture into the remaining stock.
9   Allow the jelly to go almost cold. While still pourable, trickle it through the steam hole in the lid of the pie.

VENISON PIE

Serves at least 12

Venison meat is increasingly available now in the form of steaks, joints, sausages and mince. Its low-fat content appeals. The meat should be dark and finely grained. You will need a very large pie dish or an ovenproof roasting dish.

1 lb (450 g) frozen puff pastry, defrosted or
    New Flaky Pastry (see page 19)
flour, for dusting
1 size-7 egg

Filling
3 lb (1.3 kg) venison, cut into large chunks
1 lb (450 g) belly pork, rinded and cut small
2 oz (50 g) butter
1 bay leaf
2 sprigs of thyme
1 tablespoon oil
1 garlic clove, crushed
about 2 dozen small onions (pickling onions
    are about the right size)
4 medium sized carrots, cleaned and
    chopped
about 2 dozen button mushrooms
2 tablespoons chopped parsley

Marinade
6 black peppercorns
6 juniper berries
2 bay leaves
1 pt (575 ml) red wine
1 large garlic clove, peeled and crushed
1/4 pt (150 ml) red wine vinegar
2 tablespoons oil
1 large onion, peeled and coarsely chopped
2 carrots, peeled and chopped
2 celery stalks, chopped

1   First marinate the venison: put it in a large glass, china or stainless steel bowl. Crush the peppercorns and juniper berries in a mortar with a pestle and add these with the bay leaves, red wine, garlic and wine vinegar.
2   In a roomy pan, heat the oil and fry the onion, carrot and celery until beginning to go brown. Allow these vegetables to go cold, then stir them into the marinade. Give the whole lot a good stir and leave for about 4 hours.
3   Preheat the oven to gas3/325°F/170°C. Make up a bouquet garni with 2 pieces of celery from the root end of the stalks. Sandwich between them several parsley stalks, another bay leaf and 2 sprigs of thyme. Tie this bundle with string. Pick out the venison from the marinade and dry the pieces on kitchen paper.
4   Heat some oil in a large casserole and fry the venison, a few pieces at a time, until they are all browned. Add another peeled and crushed garlic clove plus the drained liquid from the marinade and the bouquet garni. Pour in just enough water to just cover the meat and no more. Bring to the boil, then reduce to a simmer. Cover and cook in the oven for 2 hours.
5   While the venison is cooking, put the belly pork in a pan and barely cover with water. Bring to a boil and remove any scum which rises. Reduce the heat and simmer for about 20–30 minutes. Drain off the water, then dry the pieces of pork over the warm hob or pat dry.
6   In a large pan, heat the butter and the oil and fry the pork until quite brown round the edges. Push to one side and fry the onions and carrots for a further 5 minutes. Lastly add the mushrooms and give them a quick fry in the hot pan. Stir the contents of this pan and the parsley into the casserole with the venison and continue cooking for another 30–40 minutes. Let cool.
7   To assemble the pie: first preheat the oven to gas6/400°F/200°C. Spoon the venison filling into the pie dish and mound it up in the centre or set a pie funnel in the centre. Add just enough gravy to keep the meat moist and reserve any surplus.
8   On a floured board, roll the pastry out rather larger than the size of the pie dish and slightly thicker than you would shortcrust pastry. Cut off a narrow strip from around the pastry, dampen and press around the rim of the dish. Now dampen the pastry rim and lay the lid over the pie. Press the pastry together. Trim away any excess. Knock up and scallop the edge (see page 105). Re-roll the trimmings for decoration such as leaves. Brush with beaten egg first, then set the decorations in place and brush over again.
9   Set the pie on a baking sheet and bake for about 30 minutes until risen and golden.

BOSTON ROYAL SWAN PIE

Serves 6

When I read this recipe, found and revised by Michael Smith, it sounded to me a recipe for the filling in a stand pie rather than baked under a crust. Michael Smith says that it is not known for certain if the title refers to the flesh of a swan, but he rather thought it must have been after a local inn and perhaps was the speciality of the house. So, with apologies to Boston and Michael, here's my version in a stand pie. It works well.

10 oz (275 g) strong plain white flour
4 oz (125 g) lard
½ level teaspoon salt
1 size-7 egg

Filling
2 oz (50 g) pig's liver, blanched
8 oz (225 g) uncooked chicken meat
8 oz (225 g) belly pork
4 oz (125 g) piece of cooked gammon
    (1 thick slice will do)
1½ oz (40 g) fine white breadcrumbs
2 teaspoons anchovy essence (either liquid
    or from a tube)
fat pinch each of thyme, rosemary, ground
    ginger and allspice
salt and pepper

Savoury Jelly
¼ pt (150 ml) strongly flavoured stock
    (fresh or made from a cube)
1 heaped teaspoon gelatine powder

1   Preheat the oven to gas6/400°F/200°C and set a baking sheet in the oven. Thoroughly grease a loose-bottomed tin measuring 6 in (15 cm) across and 3 in (8 cm) deep.
2   To make the pastry: sift the flour and salt into a bowl. Bring the lard and 4 fl oz (330 ml) cold water to a boil and, when the lard has melted,

pour this into the flour. Using a knife, draw the flour and water together. Once the pastry has cooled sufficiently, use your hand to knead it until smooth and free from cracks.
3   Roll about two-thirds of the pastry out on a floured board. Ease the pastry into the greased tin, paying particular attention to the join. Use your fingers to pat and work the pastry into the base and up the sides. Allow the pastry to drop over the top slightly.
4   Prepare the filling: to blanch the liver, just pour boiling water over it to start the cooking process. Peel off any skin you can see, chop coarsely and put in a large bowl. Chop the chicken meat and belly pork coarsely, leaving most of the pork fat in. Put all of these through a mincer or whizz in a food processor. Once minced, add the breadcrumbs, anchovy essence and herbs. Season well with salt and pepper and whizz again. Add 1 or 2 tablespoons of water to slacken the mixture. Cut the cooked gammon by hand into small dice or batons.
5   Now pack the minced mixture into the tin in three lots, with a layer of gammon pieces in between each layer. Level the surface.
6   Take up the remaining piece of pastry and roll it out to a circle to fit. Moisten the edge of the lid and the pastry in the tin. Lay the lid over and press the lid on the pastry bottom. Trim off the extra pastry and nip the border all round in a fluted design. Use the pastry trimmings to make decorations like tassels, scrolls, leaves or flowers. Make a steam hole in the middle and paint the pie top all over with beaten egg. Set the decorations and paint all over the top again.
7   Set the pie on a baking sheet and bake for 30 minutes, then reduce oven to gas5/375°F/190°C and cook for a further 1 hour. Allow to go cold.
8   Make the jelly: put 2 tablespoon of water in a cup or small bowl, sprinkle the gelatine powder over and leave for 3 minutes to swell a bit. Now set the cup or bowl in a pan of simmering water and stir gently until all the gelatine has melted. Stir this gelatine mixture into the stock.
9   Allow this liquid jelly to cool down and, when it is on the point of setting, pour into the pie a little at a time. This lets the jelly trickle down to the bottom of the pie.

CELEBRATION PIES

A really big pie, say with 3 lb (1 kg) of filling and smooth shortcrust always looks impressive on the table, but write a message on it and it becomes a real centrepiece – even if it just says 'chicken pie'. For obvious reasons it is easier to put a message on a rectangular or square pie. To write a message on pastry you can cut out pastry letters: children's alphabet plastic letters are easy to lay on raw pastry, press down and you have then just got to cut the letters out with a small knife. I have found that the shop-bought shortcrust pastry makes the best lettering; it is fairly firm and you can roll it out quite thinly. I have two sets of these plastic letters kept from the days when my children used them. They have also come in handy for writing posters and notices, but that is another story. Once the pastry letters are cut out, brush the top of the pie with egg, fasten on the letters and paint the egg all over the top again. Another way of doing a message is with joined-up writing using a paste made up of just white flour and water. If you are not used to making up icing paper cones you can manage with a plastic freezer bag. (It must be freezer-quality, food bags are not strong enough.) Just sift some white flour into a small bowl, add cold water until you have a fairly smooth paste – not too runny but soft enough to flow easily. As in decorative sweet icing, if you are using paper bags just put enough paste in the bag to allow you to fasten over the opening (not more than about one-third full). Make up several paper bags ready for filling. Once you have got the paste in and the opening secure, you then snip off a tiny bit of paper at the point. Test it to see if the hole is big enough and away you go. Unlike the pastry lettering which you put on before the pie is cooked, for the joined-up writing I think it is better to wait until the pie is fully cooked. Write the message, then pop it back in the oven again to dry off. It is slightly awkward in that you cannot rest your wrist whilst doing the writing because the pie is hot. If you cannot make up a paper cone, you can use a small freezer-quality plastic bag. Scoop the paste into the bag and screw it up into a corner.

Again, do not overfill the bag. Hold the bag with the point upwards and snip a tiny piece off the end and away you go.

Another possibility: if you are a dab hand at the icing you will probably have a biggish nylon icing bag into which you can put a metal or plastic nozzle with about 1/8 in (3 mm) round opening. If the bag is big enough you can put all the paste in at once.

This is also the way that I use to put the crosses on my hot cross buns before they go into the oven. First I score the cross with a pin or the point of a knife on the risen buns then pipe on the cross with the paste.

VEGETABLE PIES & MIXED PIES

PARSLEY PLATE PIE

Serves 4

With pastry top and bottom, this is a typically economical dish. You will need a metal pie plate with a deepish bowl, about 8–9 in (20–23 cm) across.

8 oz (225 g) Shortcrust Pastry (see page 16)
little milk
butter or lard, for greasing

Filling
1 bunch of spring onions
4 strips of smoked streaky bacon
3 tablespoons fresh parsley
4 size-6 eggs
little milk
salt and pepper

1   Preheat the oven to gas6/400°F/200°C and put a metal baking sheet inside the oven.
2   First trim the spring onions and chop into 1/2 in (1 cm) lengths. Fry the bacon gently until

the fat runs. Stir in the onions and cook for just 2–3 minutes.

3   Grease the pie plate and then roll out enough of the pastry to cover it. Trim off the excess. Sprinkle half the parsley on the bottom of the pie. Cover with the bacon mixture. Make 4 small spaces and break an egg into each. Season. Finally, cover with the rest of the parsley.

4   Roll out the remaining pastry to make a lid. Moisten the outer edge of the bottom pie and fix the lid evenly over the pie. Press the two pastry edges together and trim off the spare pastry. Use a fork or a handle to press the pastry together. Brush all over the top of the pie with milk. Make a steam hole in the middle.

5   Set the pie on the hot baking sheet in the oven and bake for about 30 minutes, or until the pastry is well browned.

FARMHOUSE CHEESE, APPLE & ONION PIE

Serves 4

Another plate pie with a traditional filling for eating hot or cold. A good 'pack-up pie', you will need an aluminium or enamel pie plate about 8–9 in (20–23 cm) across.

8 oz (225 g) Shortcrust Pastry (see page 16)
2 small dessert apples, peeled, cored and
     cut in dice
1 tablespoon oil
10 oz (275 g) onion, peeled and chopped small
1 size-7 egg, beaten
4 oz (125 g) farmhouse Cheddar cheese (or
     other strongly flavoured cheese), grated
1 tablespoon fine breadcrumbs
little milk
pepper
butter or lard for greasing

1   Preheat the oven to gas6/400°F/200°C and put a metal baking sheet in the oven.
2   First toss the chopped apple in the hot oil for just a minute, then drain the apple on a double

sheet of greaseproof paper and set aside. In the same pan-fry the onion gently until soft. This means you have to keep turning the mixture often. Set aside to cool.

3   Roll out half of the pastry, grease the pie plate and cover with pastry. Trim away the excess pastry. Put the chopped apple on the bottom of the pie. Whisk the egg with a fork and stir it into the onion along with the grated cheese and the breadcrumbs. Spoon this mixture into the pie plate. Do not overfill.

4   Follow the instructions from step 4 of the previous recipe.

WATERCRESS & EGG PIE

Serves 4

This traditional sandwich filling makes a lovely green filling for a plate pie. Try to roll the pastry really thinly. You will need a pie plate about 8–9 in (20–23 cm) across.

8 oz (225 g) Shortcrust Pastry (see page 16)
2 large bunches of very fresh watercress
4 oz (125 g) soft butter, plus more for greasing
1/4 nutmeg
4 size-6 eggs

1   Preheat the oven to gas6/400°F/200°C and put a metal baking sheet inside. Grease the pie plate.
2   Rinse the watercress in cold water. Pick over carefully and remove any yellow leaves. Pat as dry as possible and chop fairly finely (you can do it in the food processor but it tends to fly up and stick to the sides). Divide between two bowls and put half the soft butter in each bowl. Use a fork to mix the butter with the watercress quite roughly.
3   Roll out about half of the pastry quite thinly on a floured board and use to line the pie plate. Trim off the excess. Spread one bowlful of watercress over the pie and grate the nutmeg lightly over. Make 4 hollows in the watercress and break an egg into each. Season, then lightly sprinkle the remaining watercress over the eggs.
4   Now follow instructions as in Parsley Plate Pie recipe on pages 124–5, starting at step 4.

SAVOY PIE

Serves 4–6

The idea for using a Savoy cabbage came from an article by Anton Edelmann, the famous chef at the Savoy Hotel, London. I had been looking for a meatless pie which was moist and tasty.

Puy lentils from France are small and grey-green and are not so easy to find. They are popular because of their distinctive taste and because they keep their shape and colour after cooking. Try a wholefood shop for them.

You will need a flan ring about 7 in (18 cm) across and 1½ in (4 cm) deep. Set it on a flat heatproof plate.

1 small Savoy cabbage with the outer leaves
    removed
2 tablespoons oil
1 oz (25 g) butter
1 oz (25 g) onion, very finely chopped
1 garlic clove, peeled and crushed
1 oz (25 g) carrots, peeled and very finely
    chopped
1 oz (25 g) leek, washed and cut small (use a
    little green and white)
1 oz (25 g) celeriac (or white turnip or white
    radish), peeled and cut into small dice
4 oz (125 g) puy lentils, washed
1 pt (600 ml) vegetable stock
¼ pt (150 ml) double cream
1 teaspoon made-up or grain mustard
3 egg yolks
salt and pepper

1   Preheat the oven to gas6/400°F/200°C. Choose 10 unblemished cabbage leaves and blanch them in salted water for 1 minute. Have ready a basin full of icy water. Dunk the cabbage leaves in the hot water for 1 minute. Time it, lift them out with a fish slice and dunk into the cold water. Try not to tear them. Remove from the cold water, drain and squeeze out as much water as possible. Slice the rest of the cabbage.
2   Heat the oil and butter over a low heat in a big pan and sweat the onions until they are translucent. Add the garlic, sliced cabbage and other vegetables and sweat for 3–4 minutes.

3   In an other pan, put the washed lentils and the stock. Cover and simmer until the lentils are done and almost all the liquid has been absorbed (about 30 minutes). Set aside to cool.
4   Line the flan ring with some of the large cabbage leaves, overlapping them carefully. I found this a little difficult until I cut out 2 or 3 tough stalks which would not bend. Season well.
5   Mix the cream, mustard and the egg yolks. Stir into the lentil mixture, taste and adjust the seasoning. Pour into the flan ring, pushing the cabbage leaves down so that they do not split. Smooth the filling and cover with the remaining leaves.
6   Enclose the pie with foil and bake for about 30–40 minutes. Set the pie to rest for at least 10 minutes before slicing into wedges.

SKINNY & LONG VEGETABLE PIE

Serves 6

A pie can be made without a pie dish or flan tin. The only thing you must be careful about is to see that the filling is not too soft and runny. You will need a large well-greased baking sheet.

1 lb (450 g) frozen puff pastry, defrosted
    and ready to roll
1 size-7 egg, beaten, to glaze
butter or lard, for greasing

Filling
1 large or two small carrots
8 oz (225 g) firm button mushrooms, sliced
1 small red or yellow pepper
4 thin leeks, cleaned and chopped into
    small pieces
1–2 tablespoons oil
2 teaspoons fresh thyme leaves or
    ½ teaspoon dried thyme
3 teaspoons of spicy chutney or sauce
6 oz (175 g) red Leicester cheese, grated
6 oz (175 g) grated vegetarian cheese
salt and pepper

1 Preheat the oven to gas6/400°F/200°C.
Prepare the vegetables: peel the carrots and use a
swivel peeler to shred them into long wafer-thin
strips. Put the strips into a narrow mug and use
your scissors to chop them up a bit. Wipe and
slice the mushrooms. Remove the core and seeds
from the pepper and chop into small dice (I find
it easier with scissors, but wear a long apron as
the juice jumps).
2 Heat the oil over a high heat and fry the
carrots, mushrooms, pepper and leeks for just 3
minutes. Season and set aside.
3 On a floured board, cut the puff pastry in
two. Roll out one piece into a long oblong about
15 in (38 cm) by 6 in (15 cm). Trim to neaten
the edges.
4 Mix the thyme leaves into the chutney and
spread this over the rolled-out pastry. Put the
cooked vegetables in a sieve and drain off any
liquid, then transfer the vegetables to the pastry.
Spread it out neatly and top with the grated
cheese.
5 Roll out the second piece of pastry to make a
lid. Dampen the upper edge of the bottom
pastry, fit the top over and press the edges
together to seal all the way round. Brush the
beaten egg all over the pie. Make two steam
holes in the lid and decorate with any pastry
trimmings shaped into flowers or leaves. Brush
over again with the beaten egg. Check again that
the pastry is well sealed all round.
6 Bake for about 20–25 minutes or until the
pastry is risen and brown.

CROCKY VEGETABLE CASSEROLE

Serves 6

Start making this the night before by cooking
the beans.

6 oz (175 g) Suet Pastry (see page 17)
little milk

Filling
2 tablespoons oil (a nut oil would be nice,
  but use just one tablespoon mixed with
  one of sunflower oil)
2 large onions, peeled and sliced
1 lb (450 g) turnip, peeled and cut into 1 in
  (2.5 cm) chunks
12 oz (325 g) carrots, peeled and cut into
  1 in (2.5 cm) chunks
1 garlic clove, peeled and crushed
2 oz (50 g) dried butter beans (soaked
  overnight and boiled until cooked, but
  still crisp)
1 tablespoon white wine vinegar
$3/4$ pt (425 ml) vegetable stock (made from a
  cube)
few parsley stalks
2 sprigs of thyme
1 bay leaf
salt and pepper

1 Heat the oil and fry the onions, turnip,
carrots and garlic fairly briskly until the edges
are just turning brown.
2 Transfer the vegetables to a large casserole
which will go in the oven. Add the beans,
vinegar and stock. Bring to the boil and reduce
to a simmer.
3 Make up a bouquet garni: take 2 tough bits
of leek and enclose the parsley stalks, thyme
sprigs and bay leaf. Tie up this little bundle and
drop into the casserole. Cover the pot and put it
into the oven for about 1 hour, or until the
vegetables are done. Try to avoid getting the
vegetables too mushy. Retrieve the bouquet
garni and discard it. If there is any excess liquid
in the casserole, spoon it into a jug and reserve
for gravy.
4 Roll out the pastry to a circle and fit it inside
the casserole, resting on the vegetables. Brush
over the top with milk and bake uncovered for
about 20–25 minutes.

SKINNY LEEK & MUSHROOM PIE

Serves 4

This is another flattish pie baked on a greased baking sheet – a round one this time.

9 oz (250 g) Herby Suet Pastry (see page 84)
1 size-7 egg
butter or lard, for greasing

Filling
4 oz (125 g) dried mushrooms
6 thin leeks (white and green parts)
2 tablespoons oil
2 teaspoons flour
$\frac{1}{2}$ teaspoon crushed fennel seeds
2 oz (50 g) baby sweetcorn, cut into pieces
2 oz (50 g) sugar snap peas, cut into small
    pieces

1   First put the mushrooms to soak in about $\frac{1}{4}$ pt (150 ml) of hot water until they swell (about 30 minutes).
2   Cook the leeks: having cleaned them, cut into smallish pieces. Heat 1 tablespoon oil and fry them briefly in the oil. Sprinkle the flour over, stir that in then gradually add the mushroom soaking liquid. Bring to the boil and allow to thicken. Stir in the fennel seeds.
3   Using the other tablespoon of oil, fry the baby sweetcorn and sugar snap peas briefly. Set aside to cool. Finally, fry the drained and dried mushrooms.
4   Roll out half of the pastry into a large circle about 9 in (23 cm) across. Lay the pastry on a greased baking sheet. Set all the vegetables on the middle of the pie and make a neat circle of the filling adding the mushrooms last. Mop up any juices running out.
5   Roll out the rest of the pastry and use to cover the pie. Press the edges to seal. Thoroughly beat the egg and brush it carefully over the top.
6   Bake for about 25 minutes or until the pastry is set and golden.

FENNEL & GREEN PEPPERCORN POTATO PIE

Serves 4

4 small heads of fennel
1 tablespoon lemon juice
2 teaspoons drained green peppercorns
$\frac{1}{2}$ pt (300 ml) vegetable or chicken stock
1 tablespoon white flour
$1\frac{1}{2}$ oz (40 g) butter
1 lb (450 g) floury potatoes
1 small garlic clove, peeled and crushed
little milk

1   Cut away any bruised outer leaves from the fennel and chop off any green fronds and reserve. Cut each fennel bulb in 4, so that a piece of solid root holds the layers together on each quarter. Drop these pieces into boiling water with a little lemon juice in it (fennel discolours quickly, hence the lemon juice). Bring to the boil, then reduce the heat to a simmer and cook until the fennel is soft – root and all. Reserve the fennel cooking water for the sauce.
2   Set the pieces of cooked fennel in a heatproof shallow dish. Cut each quarter in 2 and sprinkle over the peppercorns.
3   Put the stock in a pan and whisk in the tablespoon of flour. Once the flour has dispersed, take up a wooden spoon and stir over a low heat until the sauce thickens. Add two-thirds of the butter and enough of the fennel cooking water to make a thin sauce. Season to taste. Pour just enough of this sauce over the fennel to keep it moist. Keep any extra to serve separately.
4   Boil the peeled and sliced potatoes and the garlic until they are soft. Drain off the water and mash the potatoes and garlic over the heat. Add milk and remaining butter and beat until really creamy. Taste and adjust the seasoning. Spread the mashed potato evenly over the fennel. Smooth the surface and mark with a fork.
5   Slide the pie under a hot grill to brown the surface. Reheat in a moderate oven preheated to gas4/350°F/180°C for about 30 minutes.

SALMON IN A PUFF

Serves 4

Fennel used to be the preferred herb to go with salmon, especially fresh Scottish salmon. My own favourite is tarragon.

1–1½ lb (450–675 g) fresh tail fillet of
    salmon
14 oz (400 g) frozen puff pastry, defrosted
2 teaspoons chopped fresh tarragon
1 oz (25 g) cream cheese with chives
little soft butter
½ lemon
1 size-7 egg, beaten
salt and pepper

1 Preheat the oven to gas7/425°F/220°C and grease a baking sheet with a little of the butter.
2 Cut the puff pastry in two. Roll the first piece out really thinly into an oblong shape big enough to put the salmon down flat and have a border all round.
3 Beat the tarragon into the cream cheese and add enough butter to make the mixture spreadable. Spread this roughly all over the salmon. Squeeze the lemon up and down the salmon as well. Season with salt and pepper.
4 Roll out the other piece of pastry big enough to encompass the piece of salmon. Wet the bottom pastry about ½ in (1 cm) away from the salmon all round. Lift the pastry over and lay it gently on top of the salmon. Press and seal the edges and trim off the excess pastry. You can flute the pastry edges if you wish. Brush all over with beaten egg. To simulate scales, take a pair of scissors and snip the pastry with the end of the blades all over the back of the pastry fish. Slide the 'fish' on to the baking sheet.
5 Bake for 15 minutes, then reduce the temperature to gas4/350°F/180°C and cook for another 30 minutes, or until the pastry is risen and brown.

AUBERGINE PIE WITH ALMONDS

Serves 3–4

Filling
1 lb (450 g) aubergine, topped and tailed
    and cut into chunky cubes
2 tablespoons good olive oil
1 tablespoon grated Gruyère cheese
1 oz (25 g) whole almonds chopped

Topping
1 large potato or 2 smaller ones (about 1½lb /
    675 g), baked with skins on (they need to
    be cooked but still firm)
1 large onion, peeled and coarsely chopped
1½ oz (40 g) butter, softened
salt and pepper

1 Preheat the oven to gas6/400°F/200°C.
2 For the topping: bake the potatoes. Put the onion in salted water and boil until soft, then drain very well. Now grate the potatoes, skins and all, on the big holes of the grater. Mix the drained onion with the soft butter and the grated potato. Season well and set aside.
3 Heat the oil and fry the aubergine until brown on all sides and softish. Season well and set the cubes in a pie dish or a shallow heatproof dish. Scatter the cheese and almonds over.
4 Now use the potato mixture to cover the aubergine in rough bundles. It is easier to do this with your hands.
5 Bake for 20 minutes, then reduce the heat to gas4/350°F/180°C and cook for another 10 minutes. Serve hot.

BANGERS IN A FILO CRUST

Serves 4

Try using a flavoured sausage, like pork and leek or pork and apple.

2 oz (50 g) melted butter
10 oz (275 g) filo pastry
1 large onion, peeled and finely chopped
1 oz (25 g) butter
dash of oil
1 lb (450 g) top-quality sausages, grilled and sliced into diagonal chunks
3 tablespoons apple purée
1 tablespoon Dijon mustard
1 tablespoon grain mustard
2 oz (50 g) dried apples, cut small
1 tablespoon chopped fresh parsley

1   Preheat the oven to gas6/400°F/200°C. Use the melted butter first to brush an 8 in (20 cm) flan tin or a flan ring set on a baking sheet, then to brush between each sheet of pastry.
2   Lay the filo sheets in layers to cover the tin and its sides and allow the pastry to come up and over the sides of the tin. Reserve 3 sheets for the lid.
3   Make up the filling: fry the onions in the oil and butter mixture until they are soft. Stir in the sausages, apple purée, mustards, dried apple and parsley. Spoon into pastry shell and smooth over.
4   Cover the top of the pie with the remaining pastry sheets, buttering each layer. Turn the pastry edges up over the pie and brush butter over the surface.
5   Bake for 20 minutes until good and brown.

PORK FILLET STRUDEL

Serves 6

2 lb (900 g) pork fillet, cut into 1 in (2.5 cm) cubes
2 oz (50 g) butter
2 tablespoons finely chopped onion
1 tablespoon flour
1/4 pt (150 ml) chicken stock
1/2 pt (300 ml) milk
2 tablespoons orange juice and 1 tablespoon of grated rind
8 oz (225 g) chopped frozen spinach, defrosted and drained
1 large packet of filo pastry sheets
2 oz (50 g) melted butter
1 tablespoon grated Parmesan cheese
salt and pepper

1   First cook the pork filling: season the pork cubes with salt and pepper. Melt the butter and fry the pork until well browned. Transfer the pork to a casserole. Fry the onion in the same pan until soft, then sprinkle over the tablespoon of flour and stir this in. Follow with the chicken stock and milk and bring to a boil. Add the orange juice and rind and pour over the pork.
2   Cover the casserole and bake for about 50 minutes or until the pork is tender.
3   Preheat the oven to gas5/375°F/190°C. Stir the chopped spinach into the pork filling. Taste and adjust the seasoning. Strain off most of the gravy to serve in a jug.
4   Assemble 2 strudels and adjust the size and thickness to whatever you wish. I think 2 sheets of filo for 1 strudel. Brush melted butter in between each sheet, then roll up with a thick sausage of pork inside. Brush the pastry with butter and dust with cheese.
5   Bake the strudels for about 20–25 minutes, until brown and crisp.

WONTON PORK ROLLS

Makes about 6 medium-size rolls

You can buy wonton 'skins', as they are called, at a Chinese supermarket or you can use filo pastry to roll up the filling. These wonton rolls are usually deep-fried.

1 bunch of spring onions
1 tablespoon oil
8 oz (225 g) minced pork
6 cubes of canned water chestnuts, drained and cut into tiny dice
2 fat pinches of Chinese five-spice powder
2 teaspoons cornflour
1/4 pt (150 ml) meat stock
about 6 wonton skins or packet of filo pastry, defrosted
2 oz (50 g) melted butter

1   First cut the spring onions very finely and stir-fry in the oil until soft.
2   Dry-fry the pork in a non-stick pan until well browned. Stir into the spring onions, add the water chestnuts and the five-spice powder.
3   Sprinkle the cornflour over and stir this in over a low heat. Slowly add a little stock at a time until all of it has gone in. This can now be simmered for 20 minutes or so until the mince is cooked. Add a little water if it is too thick. Taste and adjust the seasoning and allow to go cold.
4   Preheat the oven to gas6/400°F/200°C. Make up the rolls using wonton skins or filo pastry. Brush over each roll with melted butter.
5   Bake for 15 minutes, or until the pastry is brown and crisp.

MERLAN STEAMED PUDDING

Serves 2

Merlan and merling are other names for whiting. This pudding is tasty and would be welcome by someone eating a fairly light diet.

4 oz (125 g) whiting (cooked in a little milk in the microwave or lightly poached)
2 oz (50 g) fresh breadcrumbs
1 teaspoon grated lemon rind
1/4 pt (150 ml) milk
2 oz (50 g) butter
1 size-3 egg, beaten
2 oz (50 g) finely chopped mushrooms
1 teaspoon chopped parsley
salt and pepper

1   First drain the fish and flake it into a bowl. Mix in the breadcrumbs, salt, pepper and lemon rind.
2   Warm the milk in the microwave or in a small pan and stir in two-thirds of the butter to melt. Pour this mixture over the fish. Stir in the beaten egg and mushrooms and mix well.
3   Use the last of the butter to grease a 1 pt (575 ml) pudding basin or dish. Sprinkle the parsley into the base of the pudding basin. Spoon in the fish mixture. Cover the bowl with a piece of foil tucked in all round.
4   Set the basin in a steamer and steam for about 45–60 minutes. Turn the pudding out by running a flat knife blade round the outside of the pudding to release it.

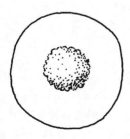
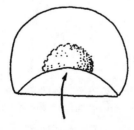

MIXED MUSHROOM & GREEN PEA ROLY-POLY

Serves 4–6

This is a real mixture of old and new. Suet pastry roly-poly and a mixture of dried mushrooms and green peas. Dried ceps, morels and chanterelles can all be bought in packets. To reconstitute them, just steep in hot water for about half an hour, then use normally. Strain and reserve the liquid as it makes excellent stock.

Suet Pastry
8 oz (225 g) self-raising flour
1 tablespoon chopped parsley
1 teaspoon grated lemon rind and
    1 tablespoon lemon juice
2 oz (50 g) packet suet
3 oz (75 g) hard butter (put it in the fridge)
1 size-3 egg, beaten
little milk

Filling
8 oz (225 g) firm small mushrooms, sliced
2 oz (50 g) dried mushrooms (rehydrated as
    above)
2 oz (50 g) butter
4 oz (125 g) frozen peas, cooked

1   Preheat the oven to gas6/400°F/200°C and put in a baking sheet.
2   Cook the filling first: melt the butter and fry the mushrooms briskly for just a few minutes, then remove from the heat.
3   Make the pastry: sieve the flour into a bowl, add the parsley and lemon rind. Lightly toss in the suet and then grate in the butter on the biggest holes of a grater (dip in flour if it starts to stick). Use a fork to stir it round loosely. Now put the beaten egg in a measuring jug (setting aside 1 teaspoon for glazing) with the lemon juice and make up to 6 fl oz (175 ml) with cold water. Make a well in the centre of the flour and stir in the mixture to make a soft dough.
4   Roll this pastry into a square about ¼ in (5 mm) thick. Lay it on a floured sheet of greaseproof paper.
5   Spread the mushrooms all over the square and cover with the cooked peas. Use the greaseproof paper to roll up the suet pastry. Mix the reserved egg with a little milk and brush this all over the roll.
6   Transfer the roll to the hot baking sheet in the oven and bake for about 1¼ hours, when the roll should be crisp and brown on the outside.

'Parboil some cocks combs, lamb stones and veal sweetbreads, blanch ox-palates and cut them in slices. Add to them a pint of oysters, slices of interlarded bacon, some blanched in chestnuts, a handful of pine kernels, and some dates, sliced. Season them with salt, nutmeg and mace and fill your pie with them, lay slices of butter over them and close it up. When baked, take veal gravy, a handful of white wine, a little butter rolled in flour, made hot and pour it in. So serve it up.

To make a Bride Pye by Ann Peckham, Leeds 1773

4

Afternoon Tea

TEA-TIME SAVOURIES

INDIVIDUAL SAVOURY TARTS

These tiny tartlets are a joy to eat, especially if the pastry is thin and crisp and the fillings are freshly made. They should be filled not more than 4 hours before they are needed. Nowadays they are often sent out by a restaurant chef with his compliments to eat with pre-dinner drinks.

Pastry
Savoury Shortcrust Pastry (see page 16) made with butter. An egg yolk used with a little water to mix the pastry will give a crisp finish. Grease the tiny shallow pattie tins (not more than 2 in / 5 cm across) well. If you have a scalloped cutter to stamp out the pastry circles so much the better. Set each circle of pastry in a pattie tin and weight it down with a tiny piece of greaseproof paper and a few baking beans. Bake in a hot (about gas6/400°F/200°C) oven for 10–15 minutes. Allow to cool in the tins and, when cold, store in an airtight tin until needed.

Filling
For the base filling use something like cream cheese or pâté. Beat either with soft butter or cream to achieve a soft fluffy texture. Chicken liver pâté and soft butter would give a nice creamy pale brown base or double cream beaten into a softened cream cheese would look snowy white. These base creams do look nice piped into pastry cases in a whirl but you can do it just as easily with a small spoon.

Toppings
Toppings set over the base fillings can be as simple as just a sprinkling of chopped chives or a few chopped walnut pieces.

For Serving Cold:
CAMEMBERT, CREAM CHEESE AND GHERKINS. Put a few finely chopped gherkin pieces on top of the cream cheese and a wafer-thin slice of Camembert cheese stuck upright into it.

WALNUTS & CREAM CHEESE
Beat finely chopped walnuts into the cream cheese base and top each tart with no more than one-quarter of a whole walnut.

CHICKEN AND TARRAGON
Beat some finely chopped fresh tarragon into a cream cheese base and flavour further with lemon juice. Top with a tiny bundle of finely chopped cooked chicken. You might also try a filling of chopped chicken, soft butter and lemon juice whizzed to a soft paste in a food processor.

TONGUE AND REDCURRANT JELLY
Tongue looks very pretty in a tiny roll sitting on a cream cheese base with a spot of redcurrant jelly. Tongue also makes a good creamy savoury filling. In a food processor, whizz together some cooked tongue, an equal quantity of soft butter, salt and pepper and a touch of made-up mustard. Fill the pattie cases and top each with a sprinkling of finely chopped orange rind.

LEMON-FLAVOURED AND POUNDED SARDINES
This old favourite is delicious. Bone and skin each sardine very carefully. Whizz them in a food processor with double cream, finely chopped lemon rind, lemon juice and a touch of Worcestershire sauce. Taste before you add salt and pepper. Top with thread-fine squiggles of lemon rind.

CREAM CHEESE, CHOPPED PEPPERS AND OLIVES
Add soft butter or cream to cream cheese, together with some very finely chopped green pepper and stoned green olives. Top the filling with a strip of finely cut red pepper.

CUCUMBER, CELERY AND CREAM CHEESE
Fill the tarts with soft cream cheese and top with a half slice of cucumber and a thin slice of canned celery heart. Sprinkle with finely chopped chives.

FILO PASTRY TARTLETS

Thin and crisp filo pastry lends itself to these savoury morsels. Two layers of pastry with a brush of melted butter in between will be enough. Just cut small squares of pastry and fold the edges in once in the tins. Weigh down each tartlet with a scrap of greaseproof paper and a few beans. Bake for just 10 minutes at gas4/350°F/180°C. Do not over-bake.

Suggestions for Fillings:

TOMATO AND BLACK OLIVE
Beat some tomato purée into a little cream cheese. Fill the filo tartlets with a spoonful and top with a slice of the tiny tomato like Gardener's delight and top that with a slice of olive.

GARLIC AND PARMESAN
Beat a small amount of crushed garlic into cream cheese softened with butter. Add freshly grated Parmesan cheese. Spoon into the tartlets and decorate the top with some chopped parsley.

INDIVIDUAL SAVOURY FLANS

These flans may be served hot or cold and need to be baked in individual flan tins with straight sides, using 2 or 3 different flavourings in the pastries, like cheese or herb. See Basic Shortcrust Pastry on page 16 for recipes.

Grease the tins well and roll out the pastry thinly. Stamp out the pastry circles and fit them into the tins. Bake blind with a greaseproof paper circle in each tartlet weighted down with a few pastry beans. (These used to be old dried up haricot beans or peas until you could buy ceramic and washable 'beans'.) I think a diameter of about 3 in (7.5 cm) is a good size.

All the savoury tarts and flans that follow will be enhanced by displaying them on a large tray set in rows or scattered. Other additions which might add to their appeal include: chopped parsley or chives, chopped nuts, tiny sprigs of perfect watercress, fronds of fennel or dill, small pieces of tomato, cucumber and pepper. In fact, anything fresh and colourful.

'There are few hours in life more agreeable than the hour dedicated to the ceremony known as Afternoon Tea.'

Henry James

BÉCHAMEL SAUCE

A simple béchamel or white sauce is a useful base for hot tartlet fillings.

¼ pt (150 ml) milk
1 slice of onion
1 blade of mace
3 black peppercorns
½ oz (15 g) plain white flour
½ oz (15 g) butter
1 teaspoon grated Parmesan cheese
   (optional)

1   Whisk the flour into the cold milk in a small pan. When the flour has dispersed, change to a wooden spoon. Add the onion, mace, butter and peppercorns. Cook over a gentle heat until the milk thickens.
2   Then, using a perforated spoon, scoop out and discard the onion, mace and peppercorns. Stir in the cheese until it melts and set aside.

Suggestions for Fillings:

PRAWNY SEAFOOD
This is probably the most popular of all tartlet fillings. When I am using prawns in a sauce I usually buy prawns in their shells so that I can make a tiny amount of stock by cooking the shells (having first removed the prawns) in a small amount of water. Simmer gently, pressing and stirring hard to extract as much flavour as possible. Strain off the liquid after 7–8 minutes. Then reduce this by boiling hard to strengthen the flavour. Use this mixed with milk as part of the ¼ pt (150 ml) liquid for the béchamel sauce. Chop into the cold sauce the prawns, some little bits of cooked salmon or just chopped hard-boiled eggs to make the expensive prawns go further. Chop some fresh parsley into the mixture too.

MUSHROOM
Mushrooms give out a lot of juice, so it is important to get rid of this by either draining the mushrooms or cooking them long enough to evaporate off the liquid. Fry the chopped mushrooms in a little butter, then add just enough of the béchamel sauce to make the filling

moist. Top the tartlet with a tiny dollop of cream cheese.

SCRAMBLED EGG AND ASPARAGUS
You do not need a sauce for this one, just lightly scramble your eggs and stir in some finely sliced cooked asparagus. Season well. Heat the tartlets and spoon the filling into them. Top with chopped mustard and cress and serve at once. They will go soggy if they have to sit about.

BREAD SAUCE AND STEAMED VEGETABLES
This idea is not mine. Richard Cawley wrote about it in an article I read recently. He took great care with the steamed vegetables, cut flower shapes in carrot and used baby sweetcorn, green peas and chopped chives. Warm the pastry cases first, fill them and reheat briefly. Steam and chop your vegetables in advance. These tartlets would also have to be eaten fairly quickly after preparation.

BREAD SAUCE
Strictly speaking, this sauce should not be made in a hurry. Time must be allowed for the onion and other flavourings to infuse the milk.

½ small onion, peeled
2 cloves
¼ pt (150 ml) milk
½ oz (15 g) butter
about 4 oz (125 g) fresh white breadcrumbs

1   Put the onion stuck with the cloves in a pan with the milk and bring slowly to a boil. Now set the pan aside for as long as you can.
2   Then strain off the milk, add the butter and reheat. Stir in as many breadcrumbs as will give a soft but not sloppy texture.
3   Season well. Spoon into the tartlet cases and top with lightly cooked vegetables. I think I would also like to dribble some melted butter over the vegetables before serving.

CHICKEN & LEMON PARFAIT
Chicken liver pâté beaten with soft butter, a little crushed garlic, finely chopped lemon zest and a dash of lemon juice, gives a tasty tartlet, but is best only just warm. I like this filling with chopped walnuts as well.

HAM AND PARSLEY IN A SAVOURY ASPIC

This is nothing like as difficult as it sounds. Buy a packet of savoury aspic jelly crystals and make it up following the instructions on the packet – half the quantity will be enough. To give added flavour, make up the jelly with dry white wine and water mixed.

When the jelly is cool but not set, stir in chopped cooked ham and lots of chopped fresh parsley. I suggest you heat up the tartlet cases on their own and fill with the coarsely chopped jellied ham.

TOMATO SALSA AND MIREPOIX OF VEGETABLES

A mirepoix of vegetables is a mixture of cooked vegetables cut into small dice. When cold, they are usually tossed in a little French dressing. Suitable vegetables include: carrots, turnip, peas, artichokes, sweetcorn and salad onions. The tomato base could also be used with other toppings.

1 small tin of tomatoes
1 dessertspoon tomato purée
1 tablespoon finely chopped onion
1 dessertspoon oil
1 fat pinch of sugar
1 fat pinch of fennel seeds
salt and pepper

1   Drain the tomatoes in a nylon sieve for a while and leave while you fry the onion in the oil until soft.
2   Put the drained tomatoes, tomato purée, cooked onion, sugar and fennel in a small pan. Cook gently until the mixture is almost like jam. Taste and season with salt and pepper.
3   Fill the tartlets with the tomato mixture and top with a spoonful of mixed vegetables. Reheat with care.

WALNUT AND CHEESE SABLÉS

These two last recipes in this section are not based on tartlets at all, but are more like savoury biscuits.

3 oz (75 g) butter, cut into small pieces
3 oz (75 g) plain white flour, plus more for dusting
2 oz (50 g) finely grated Parmesan cheese
1 size-6 egg, beaten
3 oz (75 g) walnuts, coarsely chopped
salt and pepper

1   Preheat the oven to gas4/350°F/180°C.
2   Rub the butter into the flour or whizz in a food processor. Add the cheese and work together to a paste. You may need just a bit of the beaten egg to get the right consistency.
3   Turn out on a floured board and roll out very thinly indeed. Cut into strips about 2 in (5 cm) wide. Re-roll the trimmings to get more strips. Brush these strips with the beaten egg and cover with the chopped walnuts. Grind some sea salt over the walnuts and cut into neat triangles with a very sharp knife.
4   Bake on a tin lined with non-stick baking paper for about 10 minutes. Allow to go cold and crisp up. Reheat briefly before serving.

TOASTED AND CHOPPED ALMOND SABLÉS

Make up the basic biscuit mixture as in the above recipe. Bake the plain triangles at the same temperature for about 10 minutes. Top the cooled biscuits with a small spoonful of cream cheese beaten with a little soft butter. Toast the chopped almonds until lightly brown and add these on top of the cream cheese. Reheat briefly.

SAVOURY BREADCUPS WITH FILLINGS

These savoury cases are an alternative to pastry. They are quite easy to do, but I think that non-stick pattie tins are an advantage. You can make them in two sizes – tiny cocktail and medium. Use differently coloured breads to make the fillings, thinly cut white, brown and saffron.

To make them: grease the pattie tins thoroughly, cut the bread into squares big enough to fill indentations in the tin and stick up slightly above it. Melt butter and brush the bread squares with the butter on both sides. Sprinkle lightly with salt, then press each square into a tin, using a rounded knife handle to push it down. You can put a square of greaseproof in each cup and weight it down with a few ceramic beans. I manage quite well without doing this, but I keep opening the oven to press down any cups which have sprung up.

Bake in a preheated moderate oven (gas4/350°F/180°C) for 10 minutes until crisp but not brittle. They also get more crisp as they cool.

The texture of these cups is very light and crisp, so the fillings should also be delicate. Fill them about 2 hours before you intend to use them. You will need light savoury sauces with small-cut additions:

- Seafood sauce and finely chopped cooked scallops and cucumber.
- Mayonnaise with whipped seasoned cream, topped with fresh tomato.
- Creamed avocado, seasoned and piped into the cups and topped with chopped nuts (remember that avocado loses its lovely green colour within 2 hours so leave this one to make last).
- Creamed horseradish with whipped mayonnaise, topped with a few flakes of cooked smoked trout.
- Seasoned whipped cream mixed with mayonnaise and topped with shredded vegetables.
- Crab meat beaten into mayonnaise and topped with chopped green salad onion.

- Finely chopped hard-boiled egg mixed with mayonnaise and topped with crumbled bacon.

ANCHOVY AND CHEESE STRAWS

Based on puff or shortcrust pastry, these savoury stick shapes are cheap and easy to do. The pastry itself can be flavoured with different types of cheese, such as finely grated farmhouse Cheddar, apple-smoked Cheddar, Parmesan or Stilton. Herbs can also be added. In this case it is better to use dried herbs, like tarragon or freeze-dried chives. Different finishes look and taste good; try sesame seeds, poppy seeds or dill seeds.

ANCHOVY STRAWS
Anchovies are the tiny fish sold in small oblong tins and have a powerful flavour. Rinse each one carefully, pat dry on kitchen paper. Then cut in two lengthwise with scissors, if big enough.

- **with frozen puff pastry**
  Preheat the oven to gas6/400°F/200°C. Roll out the defrosted pastry very thinly and cut into strips about ½ in (1 cm) wide and about 7 in (18 cm) long. Put the strip of anchovy on top and twist 2 or 3 times to hold the anchovy in place. Set on a baking sheet covered with non-stick paper and bake for about 10 minutes, or until the pastry is puffed up and crisp.

- **with shortcrust pastry**
  You can get a similar effect with a tube of anchovy paste. Roll the pastry out very thinly and trim the edges square. Spread the anchovy paste over the pastry thinly with a knife. Cut into narrow strips, twist and bake as above.

ANCHOVY ROLLS
Use thinly cut bread with the crusts removed. Lay the strips of anchovy across the bread and roll up like a sausage roll (1 slice should make 2

good-size rolls). Set the rolls well spaced out on a baking sheet covered with a sheet of non-stick paper, brush them all over with some melted salty butter and bake in a moderate oven until they are nice and crisp.

ANCHOVY ALLUMETTES

This is the same idea as anchovy rolls above, but instead of bread use thinly rolled pastry – either puff or shortcrust. Beaten egg or melted butter brushed over before baking gives a good finish.

PLATE TARTS

Plate tarts were, I suspect, originally baked on old plates, just as in some old recipes they talk about 'saucer tarts'. Nowadays we have metal plates, mostly about 8 or 9 in (20 or 23 cm) across with a shallow dip in the centre. Plate tarts with fruit fillings have pastry on both top and bottom. They can be eaten cold in wedges for tea or served hot with custard or cream as a pudding.

About 8 oz (225 g) of pastry is sufficient for a plate tart measuring about 8 or 9 in (20 or 23 cm) across. The lid is usually brushed with milk or a beaten egg and a little sugar scattered over gives a nice crunchy finish. Do not forget to cut one or two steam holes in the lid and bake the tart sitting on a baking sheet which you have already heated in the moderately hot oven (preheated to gas5/375°F/190°C). Bake for about 35-40 minutes.

Rhubarb Plate Tart

Pre-cook the rhubarb. Having first wiped and topped and tailed the stalks first, cut them into 1 in (2.5 cm) pieces. The best way is to bake them gently in a covered dish in the oven until almost soft. I put in just a couple of spoonfuls of water because lots of juice will come out of the fruit. The amount of sugar needed is very much a personal thing. I like the fruit quite sharp, so I would add just 1½ tablespoons. You will need about 1½ lb (675 g) rhubarb to fill your tart. Drain the fruit really well. You could use the drained juice as a sauce, thickening it with cornflour (1 dessertspoon to 10 fl oz / 300 ml). **Note:** forced rhubarb (in January and February) falls when cooked as it is so tender, so you would need to buy 2 lb (900 g). Rhubarb later in the year is much firmer. Other flavourings could include: a dash of lemon juice or a spoonful of chopped preserved ginger.

Apple Plate Tart

For me there is only one apple and that is the old favourite, Bramley seedling. There are other cooking apples, too, and many people prefer a sweeter dessert apple which does not 'fall' or go into a purée as easily as a Bramley does.

Pre-cook peeled and cored apples, but do not cut too small. Again use very little water – about ½ in (1 cm) – in pan with about 1½ tablespoons of sugar. Cook gently until juice begins to run. Let cool and drain well before filling tart. Use about 1 lb (450 g) of cooked apple.

Other flavourings might include: 2 or 3 cloves cooked with the apple and then removed; ½ teaspoon ground cinnamon; dash of lemon juice; chopped preserved ginger.

Apricot Plate Tart

Canned, fresh or dried apricots are all good in plate tarts. I have found that very cheap canned apricots make good tarts since they are not mushy. Fresh fruit need just a little heat to soften the skins. The easiest way to cut open an apricot is to take a knife right round the fruit, cutting through to the stone. A slight twist, one half one way and one half the other, should separate the two halves. Sometimes the fruit is very ripe and you have to cook the apricots first and then fish out the stones. Again, use just about ½ in (1 cm) of water. Take care with the sugar since apricots are fairly sweet to start with. Dried apricots need to be soaked to allow them to swell up before being stewed to soften them. Drain them well before filling the tart. You will need 1 lb (450 g) fresh fruit and about 8-10 oz (225-275 g) dried fruit.

Other suggested flavourings: chopped blanched almonds are often added to apricots or a few apricot kernels are nice too, but you do need a fairly strong set of nut crackers.

Blackcurrant Plate Tart

Fresh or canned blackcurrants make a mouth-tuckering filling. I prefer to mix them with apples. You will need a lot of sugar, but the intense flavour is superb. Again, stew them gently in a little water then drain thoroughly before adding them to your tart. For 1 tart you will need about ¾ lb (325 g) blackcurrants and 6 oz (175 g) apples.

Marrow and Ginger Plate Tart

This is a classic mixture for a tart. Stew about 1¼ lb (550 g) peeled marrow until soft. Drain and add 1 tablespoon of chopped preserved ginger with just 1 teaspoon of the ginger syrup. Add sugar to taste. Again, drain the fruit well before adding to your tart.

Apple and Blackberry Plate Tart

The pink colour of this mixture is lovely. Stew about 1¼ lb (550 g) of apple and stir in just 4 oz (125 g) of blackberries. Strain well and sweeten to taste.

Apple and Redcurrant Plate Tart

Again, this pretty pink mixture is excellent. Stew about 1¼ lb (550 g) of apple and stir in just 2 oz (50 g) of redcurrants. Strain well and sweeten to taste. Redcurrants are very tart so you will need just a bit more sugar.

Plum Plate Tart

Plums of all kinds make excellent tart fillings, with the Victoria among the best. Stew gently and remove as many stones as possible. Drain well and do not over-sweeten.

Plated Jam Tarts

You do not see this type of tart so often now, but they are a cheap and easy afternoon-tea tart. There is only one bottom layer of pastry and on top are placed narrow strips of pastry twisted slightly to give a lattice effect. Differently coloured jams are spooned into the sections.

It is easy to burn this sort of tart as you need quite a high temperature for the pastry, so take care. You can also bake the tart without the jams, then spoon the warmed jams into the sections afterwards. They look very pretty, especially if you put lemon curd in one or two of the sections.

Plated Curd Tarts

This is exactly the same idea as the above jam tarts, except that you spoon differently coloured curd into each section. This is better done after the pastry is cooked as the curd dries up rather in the hot oven. You can make a curd with almost any fruit: say lemon, gooseberry or cranberry.

It is quite common to add one or two drops of green food colouring to gooseberries as they tend to lose their green colour on cooking.

BISCUIT-BASED INDIVIDUAL FRUIT AND CREAM TARTLETS

You can make these quickly on small sweet round biscuits, but you must make the cream fairly stiff so that it does not fall off. I used to make these with Barmouth biscuits, but I have not seen them for ages. They are very thin and have a texture like that of a langue-de-chat.

Another way is to make a crushed biscuit base like that for an unbaked cheesecake. You will need some thin card to make rings about 2 in (5 cm) across. They are quite easy to make: cut the card in strips about 1 in (2.5 cm) wide, twist them round into a circle and staple or fasten with tape. Line the inside of each card ring with foil. Set the circles on a flat greased tray. Make up the biscuit base and spoon it into the rings. Press the biscuit mixture down firmly. The biscuit base needs to be just under ½ in (1 cm) deep. I realize you need to be fairly nimble-fingered, but I use a coffee spoon to fill the rings and press the biscuit mixture down. Leave in a cold place to firm up. Serve soon after they are made. They look pretty set in little paper muffin cases.

Base

6 oz (175 g) biscuits, crushed (use a food
   processor or a rolling pin in a deep tin)
3 oz (75 g) melted butter

Try:

- crumbled ginger-snap biscuits, spread with a whirl of whipped cream and topped with fresh pineapple.
- crumbled ginger-snap biscuits, spread with whipped cream flavoured with vanilla and topped with 2 slices of fresh nectarine.
- crumbled Marie biscuits, spread with whipped double cream and topped with strawberry slices.
- crumbled wheatmeal or digestive biscuits, spread with firm crème fraîche and topped with fresh grapes.
- crumbled Marie biscuits, spread with double cream flavoured with almond and topped with a slice of kiwi fruit and crushed toffee.
- crumbled chocolate biscuits, spread with whipped cream and crushed praline.

For crushed toffee: use peanut brittle from a sweet shop, put in a heavy plastic bag and bang with your rolling pin.

For crushed praline: in a very heavy-based metal pan, melt 4 oz (125 g) of granulated sugar. Do not stir, just shake the pan back and forth, taking it off the heat to do so. The sugar will dissolve into a brown liquid. Allow this liquid to boil to a dark brown liquid. To check if the toffee is ready, take a teaspoon and dribble some into a jug of ice-cold water: this should set to a crisp if the toffee is ready.

Pour this on to a sheet of oiled foil and allow it to set in quite a thin layer. When hard, crush in the same way as the peanut brittle. Break it up, put the pieces in a heavy plastic bag and bang the bag with a rolling pin. It is a messy business, but it tastes lovely. You can also use a food processor, if you can stand the noise.

'Instead of by battles and Ecumenical Councils the rival portions of humanity will one day dispute each other's excellence in the manufacture of little cakes.'

Lectures and Biographical Sketches, Emerson

PUDDINGS WHICH CAN BE BAKED AND EATEN COLD, CUT INTO FINGERS

BREAD AND BUTTER PUDDING FINGERS

Makes about 12

I think this is a fairly recent idea. I do not remember any bakery selling these bread and butter pudding slices until just a couple of years ago. However, it is a rather pleasant flavour and damp texture. The pudding is made fairly shallow and is then cut into fingers.

Since the pudding is to be cut into fingers it is best baked in a 7 in (18 cm) square (but shallow) sponge tin. The one I have is about 1½ in (3.5 cm) deep.

5 slices of brown bread
about 1½ oz (35 g) soft butter
2 tablespoons sugar
2 oz (50 g) raisins
1 teaspoon chopped candied peel
ground cinnamon
1 size-1 egg, beaten
¼ pt (150 ml) milk

1   Preheat the oven to a moderate gas4/350°F/180°C. Grease the tin with some butter and line the base with non-stick baking paper.
2   Cut the crusts from the slices of bread and butter each one liberally. Lay a layer of bread in the tin, cutting the bread to fit.
3   Sprinkle over one-third of the sugar, half the raisins, half the peel and a sprinkling of ground cinnamon.
4   Lay another layer of bread and repeat the sugar, raisins, candied peel and cinnamon.
5   Lay on the top layer of bread and sprinkle over the last of the sugar and a little more cinnamon.
6   Whisk the egg into the milk and pour this over the pudding. Leave it to one side for the milk to soak in. Press the pudding down with

the back of a fork to help this.
7   Cover the tin with foil and bake for about 30–40 minutes, or until the custard has set. Leave to cool.
8   Turn out, peel away the baking paper and cut into neat fingers when cool.

CINNAMON AND APPLE CRUNCH

Makes 6

6 oz (175 g) plain white flour
3 oz (75 g) block margarine
3 oz (75 g) soft brown sugar
1 oz (25 g) very finely chopped walnuts

Apple Topping
1 large cooking apple
1 oz (25 g) soft brown sugar
1 level teaspoon ground cinnamon
1 oz (25 g) butter

1   Preheat the oven to gas6/400°F/200°C. Carefully grease a tin measuring about 7 in (18 cm) square and 1½ in (3.5 cm) deep.
2   Rub the margarine into the flour as if you were going to make pastry. When it looks like damp breadcrumbs, stir in the sugar and the walnuts.
3   Spread this mixture evenly in the bottom of the tin, pressing slightly.
4   Peel, core and slice the apple. Press the slices in overlapping rows on top of the crumble mixture. Press the apple layer down carefully.
5   Mix the sugar and cinnamon and sprinkle this evenly over the apples. Finally, cut the butter into tiny pieces and dot all over the apple topping.
6   Bake uncovered for about 35–40 minutes. Leave to cool in the tin, but remove before it gets stone cold. Cut into 6 neat bars.

DERBYSHIRE ALMOND TART

Makes 6-8

4 oz (125 g) Shortcrust Pastry (see page 16)

Filling
2 oz (50 g) soft butter
2 oz (50 g) caster sugar
2 size-3 eggs, beaten
1 oz (25 g) ground almonds
2-3 drops of real almond essence
about 2 tablespoons raspberry jam

1   Grease an 8 in (20 cm) flan tin or flan ring sitting on a greased baking sheet. Preheat the oven to gas5/375°F/190°C. If you are using a flan tin, place a baking sheet in the oven to get hot.
2   Roll out the pastry on a floured board and use to line the flan tin or ring, bringing the pastry up the sides. Trim off any excess pastry.
3   To make the filling: cream the butter and sugar together until soft. Beat the eggs into the mixture, gradually adding the ground almonds and essence and beat well.
4   Spread a thin layer of raspberry jam on the base of the flan tin or ring. Pour in the filling, making sure it covers all the jam and bake for about 30 minutes, until the filling is set. Allow to cool in the tin. Turn out and slice into wedges.

GOLDEN SYRUP TART

Makes about 12

6 oz (175 g) Shortcrust Pastry (see page 16)
1 tablespoon fresh lemon juice
2 large tablespoons golden syrup, warmed
4 oz (125 g) wholewheat breadcrumbs
butter, for greasing

1   Grease well a 7 in (18 cm) square tin about 1½ in (3.5 cm) deep or an 8 in (20 cm) pie plate. Preheat the oven to gas6/400°F/200°C and put a baking sheet in the oven to heat up.
2   Roll out three-quarters of the pastry and use to line the tin, bringing the pastry halfway up the sides only.
3   Add the lemon juice to the golden syrup and mix in the breadcrumbs. Pour this into the pastry case.
4   Roll out the rest of the pastry and cut it into narrow strips about ¼ in (5 mm) wide. Dampen the edge of the pastry and lay the strips criss-cross over the tart. Press the ends of the strips to join the tart sides.
5   Set the tin on the hot baking sheet and bake for about 25–30 minutes.
6   Leave the tart to cool in the tin, then run a knife along each edge to release it. When cold cut into narrow bars or wedges.

CURD TART

Makes 8-12

6 oz (175 g) Shortcrust Pastry (see page 16)
8 oz (225 g) curd or cottage cheese
½ oz (15 g) soft butter, plus more for
   greasing
generous 1 oz (25 g) currants
1 size-1 egg, beaten
1 tablespoon golden syrup

1   Grease an 8 in (20 cm) flan tin or flan ring set on a greased baking sheet. Preheat the oven to gas6/400°F/200°C and put in a baking sheet to heat up if you are using a flan tin.
2   Roll out the pastry and use to line the tin or ring. Trim off the excess pastry.
3   If you are using cottage cheese, mash it down with a potato masher. Mix all the ingredients, reserving a few currants. Stir well and pour into the flan tin. Sprinkle over the reserved currants.
4   Set the tin on the hot baking sheet and bake for about 30 minutes, or until the filling has set.
5   Allow to cool in the tin, then cut into small wedges to serve.

SPONGE FLANS

PLAIN SPONGE FLAN

This simple fatless sponge recipe is used for all
the flans. You will need a flan tin 8–9 in (20–
23 cm) across with a rounded base and a raised
middle. This flan tin needs to be very well
greased. A non-stick one is a big help but you
can also set a circle of greaseproof paper on the
raised circle in the middle. Another thing you
can do is cut a narrow strip of paper in a circle
just ½ in (1 cm) wide and set in the sides.

3 size-1 eggs
3 oz (75 g) caster sugar
3 oz (75 g) plain white flour
butter, for greasing

1   You will need an 8-9 in (20–23 cm) flan tin
with a raised middle as described above. Preheat
the oven to gas3/325°F/160°C.
2   In a very clean bowl and using an electric
mixer or a hand-held electric mixer, whisk the
eggs and the sugar. Do this until you have a large
volume of cream-coloured fluff. Go on beating
until this fluff gets quite firm and thick.
3   Do the next bit by hand. Put about one-third
of the flour through a nylon sieve and sprinkle it
over the surface of the egg and sugar mixture.
Using a flexible rubber spatula and in big wide
movements, fold this flour in lightly but not
completely. Repeat this procedure twice and,
when all the flour is incorporated, scoop the
mixture – which should still be fluffy – into the
flan tin. It should fill the tin right to the top.
4   Bake for about 40 minutes, until the sponge
is firmish and golden.
5   Allow to cool in the tin and press down all
the way round the edge to loosen it. Slide a
flexible knife down the side, but take care not to
slice into the sponge. Lift the tin up on its side
and bang it down to loosen the whole thing.
Turn the tin and bang it down again. Set the
sponge flan on a wire tray to go cold.

CHOCOLATE SPONGE FLAN

This recipe is exactly the same as the one above,
except that you add 2 large teaspoons of cocoa
to the flour. Sift the cocoa and flour through the
sieve as described above. (Note: use cocoa not
drinking chocolate.)

VANILLA SPONGE

Makes about 8

Add 2–3 drops of vanilla essence while mixing
in the flour. Set the sponge on a flat plate.
Whip and sweeten ¼ pt (150 ml) double cream
to the floppy stage and spread it in the centre of
the flan. Top with circles of fresh fruit – halved
grapes, slices of peach, kiwi fruit, strawberries
or raspberries (fresh fruit looks best). Just before
serving, dribble a glass of sherry mixed with a
little water over the dry sponge 'walls'.
Alternatively, diluted orange juice is nice too.
Then cut into wedges.

CITRUS SPONGE FLAN WITH CREAM AND STUFFED APRICOTS

Makes about 8

1 Plain Sponge Flan (as above)
¼ pt (150 ml) double cream, whipped to
    soft peaks
1 small can of apricots

Stuffing
1 oz (25 g) ground almonds
1 oz (25 g) finely chopped almonds
1 tablespoon cake crumbs

Citrus Syrup
4 oz (125 g) granulated sugar
2 tablespoons orange juice
2 tablespoons lemon juice

1   First make the citrus syrup: in a small heavy
pan, dissolve the sugar in 8 fl oz (225 ml) water.
Then boil gently until the mixture reduces and
becomes golden and syrupy. Allow to cool.
2   When cold, stir in the orange and lemon
juices. Set aside.
3   To make the stuffing: mix the crumbs,
ground almonds and chopped almonds together
with a little of the citrus syrup.
4   Fill the drained apricots with a tiny spoonful
each of the nutty mixture.
5   Whip the cream to the floppy stage.
6   Set the sponge on a flat plate and dribble the
citrus syrup all over it. Stop when the syrup
starts to run out of the bottom of the sponge.
7   Spread the whipped cream in the middle and
set the stuffed apricots, cut side up, in circles.
Serve cut into wedges.

PLAIN SPONGE FLAN WITH RUM AND PEANUT BRITTLE

Makes about 8

1 Plain Sponge Flan (as above)
about 4 oz (100 g) crushed peanut brittle
    (from a sweet shop)
¼ pt (150 ml) double cream

Rum Syrup
4 oz (125 g) granulated sugar
3–4 tablespoons rum

1   First make the rum syrup: boil the sugar and
8 fl oz (225 ml) water together until very well
reduced and syrupy. Allow to cool, then stir in
the rum.
2   To crush the peanut brittle: put the large
pieces in a heavy plastic bag and then bash with
a rolling pin.
3   Set the flan on a flat plate and dribble the
rum syrup all over the dry sponge.
4   Whip the cream to the soft floppy stage and
spread it in the middle of the sponge.
5   Top with crushed peanut brittle and cut into
wedges to serve.

'Stands the Church clock at ten-to-three?
And is there honey still for tea?'

Rupert Brooke

CHOCOLATE SPONGE FLAN WITH CHOCOLATE AND ORANGE MOUSSE

Makes about 8

You can buy a ready-made chocolate mousse and stir in a dessertspoon of grated orange rind, but this recipe is easy and you get much more for your money.

1 Chocolate Sponge Flan (see page 144)

Chocolate and Orange Mousse
6 oz (175 g) plain chocolate
1 small orange
3 size-1 eggs, separated
½ oz (15 g) butter
1 teaspoon caster sugar

1   Make the mousse: break up the chocolate and place it in a heatproof bowl suspended over a pan of simmering water. Stir lightly but not vigorously.
2   Grate the zest from the orange and squeeze the juice.
3   When the chocolate is almost all melted, remove from the pan and stir in the zest (reserving a small spoonful), the orange juice and the butter. Stir and allow to cool a little.
4   Beat in the egg yolks, one at a time.
5   In another bowl, whip the egg whites until stiff. Sprinkle over the teaspoon of sugar and whisk again.
6   Now fold the egg whites into the chocolate mixture.
7   Set the chocolate sponge flan on a flat plate.
8   Spoon in the chocolate orange mousse. Level the surface and sprinkle over the reserved grated orange zest.
9   Cut into wedges.

CHOCOLATE SPONGE FLAN FILLED WITH MERINGUE AND CREAM

Makes about 8

1 Chocolate Sponge Flan (see page 144)

Filling
½ dozen broken meringues
¼ pt (150 ml) double cream, whipped
½ oz (15 g) plain chocolate, grated

1   When the flan is cold, set it on a flat plate.
2   Stir the meringues into the whipped cream and spread this mixture roughly into the flan.
3   Decorate with the grated plain chocolate.

PLAIN SPONGE FLAN WITH LOW-FAT CREAM AND PEACHES

Makes about 8

1 plain sponge flan (see page 144)
1 carton of low-fat whipping cream substitute
1 teaspoon powdered low-calorie sugar substitute
1 can of sliced peaches in juice or 2 fresh peaches, peeled and sliced

1   Set the sponge on a flat plate.
2   Whip the cream substitute and stir in the sugar substitute.
3   Drain the peaches if canned and reserve the juice.
4   Fill the flan with the cream and top with the sliced peaches.
5   Dribble a little fruit juice over the sides.

PLAIN SPONGE WITH FRUIT SET IN JELLY

1 Plain Sponge Flan (see page 144)
½ packet lemon jelly
4 oz (125 g) fresh grapes, halved
½ small can of tangerines, drained and
   juice reserved

1 Set the flan on a flat plate.
2 Make up the jelly, using slightly less water
than suggested.
3 Set the fruit in the flan and, when the jelly is
cool but still pourable, cover the fruit with it.
Allow to go cold and set.
4 Dribble some of the tangerine juice over the
dry sponge all round the flan.

*'When I makes tea I makes tea, as old mother
Grogan said. And when I makes water I makes
water... Begob, ma'am, says Mrs Cahill, God
send you don't make them in the one pot.'*

James Joyce

LEMON FLAN WITH FRESH ORANGES & GRAND MARNIER

1 Plain Sponge Flan (see page 144)
2-3 large oranges
cream or crème fraîche, to serve

Orange and Lemon Syrup
6 oz (175 g) demerara sugar
¼ pt (150 ml) fresh orange juice (or from a
   carton)
4-5 tablespoons fresh lemon juice
1 tablespoon Grand Marnier (or other
   orange liqueur)

1 First prepare the oranges: first peel off the
outer zest and the pith as if you were peeling an
apple. Then, using a sharp knife and holding the
orange in your hand and over a bowl to catch all
the juice, dislodge each of the sections of orange
from between the white pith.
2 Make the syrup: in a heavy pan, dissolve the
sugar in the strained orange and lemon juice.
(Use as much of the juice from the freshly
segmented oranges as you can.)
3 Once the sugar has dissolved completely,
bring to the boil and boil for 2 minutes. Take off
the heat and leave to cool.
4 When cool, stir in the Grand Marnier.
5 Set the sponge on a flat plate and pour the
syrup over it until the sponge is just moist.
Allow to go cold.
6 Set the drained orange pieces in the syrup-
soaked sponge. Serve with cream or crème fraîche.

PARCELS & TARTS

SWEET FILO PARCELS

Filo pastry can be used to make neat little oblong packets filled with different kinds of fruit. You can make these up well in advance and then just brush over with melted butter and bake them at the last minute.

Brush melted butter over one half of a sheet and fold this in two. I think it is easier to make a 'parcel' if the filling is set at an angle and just in from one corner. Wrap up and brush again with melted butter.

Set the filled parcels seam down on non-stick baking paper on a baking sheet and bake at gas7/425°F/220°C for just 8 minutes. Serve warm or cold.

MINCEMEAT AND APPLE FILLING
Peel, core and chop a very small cooking apple and mix into 2 oz (50 g) mincemeat.

SOFT APRICOT AND CHOPPED PISTACHIO NUT FILLING
Canned, freshly stewed or soaked and stewed dried apricots all are suitable for this filling, but they must be very well drained in a sieve. Stir in the chopped pistachio nuts.

DATE AND WALNUT FILLING
This old favourite mixture is easy: finely chop some stoned dates, pour just a tiny bit of water over and stew briefly. You are aiming for a very, very thick purée so be careful with the water. Stir in the chopped walnuts.

RASPBERRY FILLING
These are very delicious, but again stew briefly and drain very well in a sieve before you spoon them into the pastry. Sweeten with a tiny amount of sugar.

CHOCOLATE AND ALMOND FILLING
This is a good way to use up that brick-hard almond paste in your cupboard. First chop it roughly into your food processor and then whizz to a crumb. Use a commercial chocolate spread to bind it together to a thick paste. You may need a little added sugar, but I doubt it.

RHUBARB AND ORANGE FILLING
Grate the zest off a small orange, then squeeze the juice. Stew the chopped rhubarb in the orange juice.

When the rhubarb is soft, drain it very, very well indeed. Sweeten it with caster sugar and stir in the orange zest.

SWEET PUFF PASTRY OPEN TARTS

These tarts are very quickly made with defrosted frozen puff pastry. When cooked, they should be eaten swiftly. They do look nice cut in large circles about the size of a saucer, but work just as well in squares – which are probably more economical.

Roll out the pastry very thinly and cut out circles or squares. Dab water round the outer edge of the tarts and turn in the outside edge to make a little border. Preheat the oven to gas6/400°F/200°C and put in a baking sheet.

CHEESE AND APPLE PUFFS
Peel, core and slice either a cooking or a sweet dessert apple. Lay the slices round the pastry. Sprinkle a little sugar and top with grated mild cheese like Wensleydale. Bake for 15 minutes.

SWEET PUFF CHEESE AND PEAR TART
Peel, core and slice fairly ripe Comice pears and set these over the pastry, sprinkle first with sugar then with grated Wensleydale. Bake for 15 minutes.

PLUM PUFFS
Barely cooked plums are nice like this. Drain them well and remove all stones. Set the plums cut side up on the pastry, dot with little bits of butter and sprinkle with just a little sugar.

FLAKY BAKEWELL TART

Makes 6–10

8 oz (200 g) frozen puff pastry, defrosted

Filling
2 oz (50 g) butter, softened, plus more for
  greasing
2 oz (50 g) caster sugar
2 size-3 eggs, beaten
2-3 drops almond essence
1½ oz (40 g) ground almonds
about 2 tablespoons raspberry jam

1   Preheat the oven to gas6/400°F/200°C and
grease an 8 in (20 cm) tart tin. Roll the pastry
out and use to line the tart tin.
2   Make the filling: cream the butter and sugar.
Beat in the eggs gradually. Add the almond
essence and the ground almonds. Beat well.
3   Spread just a little raspberry jam over the
centre of the tart.
4   Spoon the almond mixture over the jam (you
will have enough for two tarts).
5   Bake at once for about 15 minutes, until
golden.

RASPBERRY MACAROON TART

Stewed, sweetened and well-drained fresh or
frozen raspberries go well with crushed
macaroons. Put the broken macaroons on the
pastry and cover with the raspberries. Bake
without delay.

MANGO AND MASCARPONE TART

Mascarpone cheese is a thick rich cream from
Italy. Set slices of drained canned mango over the
pastry and dollop a little Mascarpone cheese on
top. Bake quickly.

SOUR CREAM AND PEACH TART

Spread fresh or canned and drained peaches on
the pastry. Top with dollops of whipped sour
cream here and there. Bake quickly.

ROUGH PUFF GOOSEGOGS

Stew some gooseberries with sugar and drain
very carefully. Spread the gooseberry paste over
the pastry and dot with some flakes of butter.
Bake quickly.

'The kitchen table looks quite smart,
O'erspread with many a tempting tart,
And one enormous custard,
And other essential things,
Such as befit the board of Kings,
As pepper, salt and mustard.'

Holbeck Feast by Richard Spencer

INDIVIDUAL FRUIT PIES

These are made the Scottish way, with hot-water crust pastry rolled very thinly. Hot-water crust does not absorb juice quickly and is therefore very suitable for fruit tarts. Scottish ones are always made in straight-sided rings, like the ones some people use to fry eggs. Failing that you could use some of the new deep non-stick muffin tins. Grease the rings and tins really well. Make up the hot-water crust pastry (see page 18). Roll it out very thinly and use to line the rings or tins. You will need to use your fingers to work the pastry in. Leave enough pastry to make lids.

To identify each tart with its filling it is the custom in Scotland to make a syrup of the fruit juice and dribble it over the lid at the end of baking time.

The tarts should be baked in a hot oven, preheated to gas6/400°F/200°C, for about 15–20 minutes. If you are using rings, then these should be set on a greased baking sheet. If you are using individual deep muffin tins, these should be set on a baking sheet which has been preheated in the oven.

The syrup which is often used as a glaze on these tarts is just the sweetened juice drained from the fruit and boiled down in an open pan until it is thick. Do not boil fiercely – a steady boil will do. About 1/4 pt (150 ml) of juice boiled down to 1 or 2 tablespoons will be sufficient. Just dribble a little over each pie as it comes out of the oven – a splash will do.

FRUIT FILLINGS FOR INDIVIDUAL FRUIT PIES

The same rules apply when cooking fruit for any pie or tart. Stew briefly and drain well. Do not over-sweeten. Half the pleasure of a fruit pie is a nice tartness.

Rhubarb
Early rhubarb (January, February and March) is bright pink and soft. It needs to be carefully drained. Later rhubarb is thicker and usually more tart.

Rhubarb and Ginger
Preserved ginger added to the drained cooked rhubarb adds sweetness as well as the ginger flavour. Chop it finely and add 1 or 2 teaspoons of the ginger syrup as well.

Bramley Apple
Stew the peeled, cored and thickly sliced apple in a minimum of water, with a little sugar and a slight flavouring of fresh lemon juice. Drain well before filling the pastry shells. For maximum flavour you can cook the apples in just a knob of butter, but you do need to do this over a low heat, turning often.

Sweet Apple and Custard
This is a fruit filling made with peeled, cored and chopped dessert apples. You will get a much more mellow flavour and will not need as much sugar. Again, be sure to drain the fruit thoroughly. Bake the tarts without a pastry lid. Instead scrunch up a little foil and place directly over the fruit in each tart. Bake as usual.

When the pies are cold, make some custard, remove the foil and fill the top of each pie with about 1/2 in (1 cm) of cooked and slightly warm custard.

Microwave Vanilla Custard
10 fl oz (300 ml) milk
1½ heaped dessertspoons custard powder
1 level dessertspoon caster sugar
2–3 drops of vanilla essence

1 Put all the ingredients in a large plastic jug or bowl and whisk hard.
2 Cook on full power for a total of 4 minutes, whisking every minute.

Blackcurrant
Stew in a little water until the fruit is soft. Sweeten to taste and drain well. Many people find blackcurrant alone rather strong. It mixes well with stewed and drained apples. Of all fruit for pies, blackcurrant is probably the most tart of all, needing more sugar than most.

CHEESECAKES

INDIVIDUAL CHEESECAKES

Makes about 6

These cheesecakes are not baked, they are set in the fridge and can be made in small cardboard rings covered on the inside with foil. Cut narrow strips of card about 2 in (5 cm) deep and tape or staple into rings about 3 in (7.5 cm) across. Cover the inside of the rings only with foil and bend it over the card top and bottom, then press into shape. Set these rings on a greased flat plastic tray or plate.

Biscuit bases can be made with plain digestives, wholemeal and plain chocolate biscuits, and ginger biscuits. This quantity would also be sufficient for an 8 in (20 cm) flan.

Biscuit Base
6 oz (175 g) biscuits (see above)
3 oz (75 g) butter, melted

1 Crush the biscuits either in a food processor or put them in a freezer bag and hammer with a rolling pin.
2 Add to the melted butter and stir thoroughly.
3 Spoon the damp crumbs into the rings to a depth of about ½ in (1 cm). Press down lightly and level the surface. Set aside to firm up, preferably in the fridge.

Various other possible added flavourings for biscuit base:
*   1 oz (25 g) walnuts, finely chopped
*   2 fat pinches of ground cinnamon
*   2 fat pinches of ground cloves (particularly nice in an apple cheesecake)
*   1 teaspoon grated lemon or orange peel (good in a chocolate cheesecake)

Cheesecake Fillings:

CRUSHED PINEAPPLE AND CHOCOLATE
5 oz (150 g) dark chocolate
1½ oz (40 g) caster sugar
8 oz (225 g) block cream cheese
2 tablespoons brandy
about ½ small carton of double cream
1 small can crushed pineapple, drained well

1 Break the chocolate into small pieces and melt in a heatproof bowl suspended over a pan of simmering water or covered in a microwave for about 1½ minutes on full power.
2 Blend all the other ingredients except the pineapple into the melted chocolate by hand, or use a stick blender or processor. Mixture should be thick but not stiff. Add extra cream if needed. Stir in pineapple, reserving 2 tablespoons.
3 Spoon the chocolate mixture into the individual cheesecake shapes and level the surface. Set in the fridge to firm up.
4 To release: run a sharp knife round the outside edge and underneath. Serve with a tiny spoonful of pineapple on top of each cheesecake.

LIGHT RUM AND RAISIN CHEESECAKE

2 tablespoons rum
2 oz (50 g) fat dark raisins
1 packet of lemon jelly
about 4 fl oz (125 ml) ice-cold water
¼ pt (150 ml) double cream
8 oz (225 g) block cream cheese

1 Soak the raisins in the rum overnight (warming slightly in the microwave helps).
2 Drain the raisins and put the rum in a large bowl with the double cream and cream cheese.
3 Melt the jelly in 4 fl oz (125 ml) of water in the microwave. Stir until the jelly dissolves. Top up with ice-cold water to 8 fl oz (225 ml).
4 Stir this cooled jelly into the bowl with the rum, cream and cream cheese. Whisk together.
5 Set a few raisins in the bottom of each cheesecake and reserve some for the top. Spoon the cream cheese mixture on top and level the surface. Set the cheesecakes aside to firm up.
6 Release each cheesecake gently and serve each one with a small bundle of raisins on top.

ORANGE AND CHOCOLATE CHIP CHEESECAKE

1 small orange
just under 5 tablespoons concentrated orange juice (the stronger the flavour the better – I like the frozen kind)
2½ oz (65 g) sugar
10 oz (275 g) block cream cheese
2 oz (50 g) chocolate chips

1 Grate the rind from the orange and squeeze the juice. Set the rind aside, covered, and put the juice in a measuring jug. Top up with some of the strongly flavoured concentrated orange juice to make 3 fl oz (75 ml).

2 Put the orange juice, sugar and cream cheese in a bowl and blend together using a stick blender or food processor. Stir in about half of the chocolate chips.
3 Spoon the orange mixture into the biscuit base rings and smooth the surface.
4 Release by running a knife carefully round the outside edge and also under the base. Use the thinnest knife you have got for this.
5 Serve sprinkled with chocolate chips and the grated orange rind.

BLACKCURRANT AND VANILLA CHEESECAKE

3 oz (75 g) blackcurrants
2½–3 oz (65-75 g) sugar
10 oz (275 g) block cream cheese
1 teaspoon Cassis blackcurrant liqueur (optional)
¼ pt (150 ml) double cream
3-4 drops of vanilla essence

1 Stew the blackcurrants in 5 tablespoons of water until very soft. (If you are using frozen blackcurrants you may not need the water.)
2 Put the blackcurrant mixture in a bowl, add the sugar, cream cheese, and Cassis if you have it. Blend until smooth, using a food processor or blender.
3 Spoon the mixture into the biscuit base rings, smooth over the surface and set aside to firm up.
4 To serve: whip the double cream with the vanilla essence until thick. Spoon a little on top of each cheesecake and smooth over.
Alternatively, put the whipped cream in a piping bag with a star nozzle (½ in / 1 cm) and pipe a large whirl of on top of each cheesecake.

RICH VELVET CHEESECAKE WITH FROSTED GRAPES

5 oz (150 g) white chocolate
8 oz (225 g) block cream cheese
about 5 tablespoons double cream (plus a
    little extra if needed)
2 tablespoons dry sherry
whites of 1 size-6 egg
1/4 lb (100 g) seedless grapes
about 1 tablespoon caster sugar

1   Break the chocolate into squares and melt in
a heatproof bowl set over a pan of simmering
water, or in the microwave covered and on full
power for 1 1/2 minutes, stirring gently halfway.
2   Add the cream cheese, double cream and
sherry. Blend with a stick blender or a food
processor. Add extra cream if the mixture is stiff.
Taste at this point and add sugar to taste.
3   Spoon the mixture into the biscuit base rings.
4   Meanwhile, whisk the egg white lightly and
break the grapes into small bunches of 2 or 3.
Dunk these into the egg white to moisten all
over, shake off the spare liquid and then dip into
the caster sugar. Set aside to crisp up.
5   Release the cheesecakes by running a thin
knife round the inside and across the base. Set a
small group of frosted grapes on each cheesecake.

LIME, LEMON AND GINGER CHEESECAKE

Makes about 6

Ginger Base
6 oz (175 g) ginger snaps
3 oz (75 g) melted butter

Filling
1 packet of lemon jelly
about 5 tablespoons ice-cold water
grated rind and juice from 1 lime
grated rind and juice from 1 lemon
1/4 pt (150 ml) double cream
8 oz (225 g) cream cheese
1 large chunk of preserved ginger

1   Make up the biscuit base in the usual way:
crush the biscuits, melt the butter and stir into
the biscuits.
2   Spoon the buttery crumbs into the individual
rings as described on page 151. Press the crumbs
down and level the surface.
3   To make up the filling: first cut the jelly into
pieces and melt in about 5 tablespoons of hot
water. Use a measuring jug and stir until the
jelly is dissolved. Top up with ice-cold water to
the 6 fl oz (150 ml) mark.
4   Blend together the jelly, the rind and juice
from both the lemon and the lime, the double
cream and cream cheese. When smooth, spoon
into the biscuit bases to set.
5   To serve: run a thin knife round the inside of
each ring and under the biscuit base. Slice the
ginger into square or rectangle pieces. Slice these
into wafer-thin slices and set around the border
of each cheesecake.

TRAY BAKES

This is an easy way to make small pastry-based cakes. A Swiss roll tin measuring about 11½ x7½ in (29x19 cm) is lined with thinly rolled pastry, then this is filled and baked. When cold it is cut up into fingers or squares. Shortcrust pastry is the usual base (filo or puff pastry is not suitable), but not all the recipes are based on pastry.

CONFETTI BARS

Makes about 12

6 oz (175 g) Shortcrust Pastry (see page 16)

Filling
3 oz (75 g) soft margarine
2 oz (50 g) caster sugar
1 size-6 egg, beaten
2 oz (50 g) currants
1 oz (25 g) red glacé cherries, chopped small
1 oz (25 g) green glacé cherries, chopped small
1 oz (25 g) dried sour cherries, cut small
2½ oz (65 g) ground rice
2 oz (50 g) ground almonds

1 Preheat the oven to gas4/350°F/180°C
2 Roll the pastry out thinly and use to line the Swiss roll tin.
3 Make the filling: cream the margarine and sugar and beat in the egg a little at a time. Fold in the other ingredients and mix well.
4 Spread this mixture evenly over the pastry. Bake at a moderate temperature for 45 minutes, or until the filling no longer wobbles.

DATE AND WALNUT TEA-TIME TREATS

Makes about 16 squares

This is a famous combination. For the dates, I prefer to use the stoned type pressed into a solid block. There are lots of other types of dried dates, but if you buy ready-sugared dates you should then reduce the sugar to compensate.

8 oz (225 g) block dates
1 small orange
2 oz (50 g) walnuts finely chopped
6 oz (175 g) butter, melted, plus more for greasing
4 oz (125 g) plain flour
6 oz (175 g) rolled oats
4 oz (125 g) soft brown sugar

1 Preheat the oven to gas4/350°F/180°C and grease a shallow 7 in (18 cm) square tin.
2 Cut up the dates into small pieces and put in a small pan. Grate the orange rind on the big holes of a metal grater and add to the dates. Squeeze the juice from the orange and put that into a measuring jug. Top this up with water to the ¼ pt (150 ml) mark and pour over the dates. Cook over a gentle heat until thick and very soft, stir in the walnuts, set aside to cool.
3 Put the melted butter in a bowl with the flour, rolled oats and sugar. Use a fork to stir it all together so that it has a crumbly texture.
4 Take half of this mixture and press it evenly into the tin. Top with the date and walnut mixture and spread evenly. Finish with the rest of the crumb mix and press this down evenly.
5 Bake for about 25–30 minutes until golden. Leave to cool in the tin, then cut into 16 squares.

APPLE AMBER SQUARES

Makes about 10

This mixture has a sponge base with apples on top.

4 oz (125 g) butter or margarine, softened
4 oz (125 g) caster sugar
2 size-6 eggs, beaten
2–3 drops of almond essence
4 oz (125 g) self-raising flour, sifted
3–4 eating apples
1 oz (25 g) demerara sugar
white vegetable fat, for greasing

1   First grease a large Swiss roll tin measuring about 13x9 in (33x23 cm) and base-line with a piece of greaseproof paper.
2   Cream the butter or margarine with the caster sugar until pale and fluffy. Add the eggs bit by bit, beating well between each addition. Add the almond essence, then fold in the flour.
3   Spread this mixture evenly on the greaseproof paper in the tin.
4   Peel, quarter and core the apples, then slice thinly. Set them on top of the sponge mixture in a neat pattern. Sprinkle over the demerara sugar.
5   Bake for about 40 minutes. Allow to cool in the tin, then cut into neat squares.

NO-COOK TROPICAL LOGS

Makes about 16

6 oz (175 g) butter, softened
6 oz (175 g) icing sugar, sifted
1 teaspoon vanilla essence
8 oz (225 g) desiccated coconut
8 oz (225 g) best-quality cooking chocolate, melted

1   Cream the butter and sugar, then add the vanilla and coconut. Mix well and leave to stiffen up a bit.

2   Roll into tiny smooth neat logs and dip in the melted chocolate to cover (use sugar tongs). Leave to set on non-stick baking paper. When cold store in a tin.

REAL ALMOND SLICE

Makes about 12

6 oz (175 g) Shortcrust Pastry (see page 16)
butter or white vegetable fat, for greasing

Filling
2 size-6 eggs, beaten
4 oz (125 g) ground almonds
2 oz (50 g) ground rice
2-3 drops of almond essence
6 oz (175 g) caster sugar
2 tablespoons raspberry jam
1½ oz (40 g) flaked almonds

1   Preheat the oven to gas5/375°F/190°C and grease a Swiss roll tin measuring about 11½ x7½ in (29x19 cm).
2   Roll out the pastry and use to line the tin.
3   Put the eggs, ground almonds, ground rice, almond essence and caster sugar in a bowl. Mix well – the mixture should be quite soft.
4   Spread raspberry jam very thinly on the pastry and spoon the almond mixture on top of the jam as evenly as possible. Scatter the flaked almonds on top.
5   Bake for about 30–35 minutes. Do not let the tray bake get too brown. Leave in tin to set.
6   When cool, turn out in one piece on a wooden board and cut into neat squares.

HIGHLAND SQUARES

Makes about 16 pieces

9 oz (250 g) plain white flour
3 oz (75 g) cornflour
1 teaspoon baking powder
3 oz (75 g) caster sugar, plus more to
    decorate
8 oz (225 g) butter, melted, plus more for
    greasing

1   Preheat the oven to gas3/325°F/160°C and
grease well a Swiss roll tin measuring about
13 x9 in (33x23 cm).
2   Sift the flour, cornflour and baking powder
into a bowl and add the caster sugar. Stir well.
3   Pour in the melted butter and mix to a paste.
Press evenly into the tin and smooth well.
4   Bake for 45–60 minutes or until golden all
over.
5   Remove from the oven and, while still warm,
mark into squares. Do not cut right through to
the tin. Sprinkle over some more caster sugar and
leave to go cold.
6   When cold, break into pieces. Store in a tin
until needed.

JOAN'S BOSTON
BROWNIES

Makes about 16

This recipe comes from my friend Joan who is a
keen cook.

6 oz (175 g) butter, plus more for greasing
2 level tablespoons cocoa
5 oz (150 g) caster sugar
2 size-3 eggs
2 oz (50 g) self-raising flour
2 oz (50 g) chopped pecans

1   Preheat the oven to gas3/325°F/160°C. Grease
well a shallow cake tin about 7 in (18 cm) square.

2   Melt one-third of the butter in a small bowl
and sieve the cocoa into it. Mix to a smooth
paste. Set this aside.
3   Cream the remaining butter with the caster
sugar until very light. Gradually beat in the
lightly whisked eggs. Fold in the sieved flour,
cocoa mixture and pecans.
4   Smooth the mixture into the tin.
5   Bake for about 45 minutes. Leave in the tin
until cool.
6   When cool, run a knife round the outside of
the slab and turn it out. Cut into very small
squares. This is a very rich mixture and the
squares should be very dainty.

1,000-CALORIE SLICE

Makes 16

8 oz (225 g) good-quality plain cooking
    chocolate
2 oz (50 g) green glacé cherries, chopped
    small
2 oz (50 g) red glacé cherries, chopped small
3 oz (75 g) caster sugar
4 oz (125 g) desiccated coconut
2 oz (50 g) walnuts, chopped
1 size-3 egg, beaten

1   Preheat the oven to gas5/375°F/190°C. Line a
11½ x7½ in (29x19 cm) Swiss roll tin with foil,
bringing it up the sides.
2   Melt the chocolate and pour it into the foil-
lined tin. Tip the tin left and right so that the
chocolate runs to the sides. Use a knife to smooth
the chocolate if it does not run. Set aside to go
cold.
3   In a large bowl, mix the cherries, sugar,
coconut and walnuts with the beaten egg.
4   Spoon this mixture into the chocolate-lined
tin. Do not press down too much, but spread it
out evenly.
5   Bake for just 10 minutes or even less. Do not
allow the coconut to brown.
6   Allow to go cold, turn out upside down and
peel off the foil with care. Turn the slab over
again and cut into neat slices.

NO-COOK CRUNCH

Makes about 12

1½ oz (40 g) sour cherries (dried and stoned cherries with a sharp flavour)
about 6 oz (175 g) digestive biscuits
2 oz (50 g) butter, plus more for greasing
1 oz (25 g) caster sugar
2 tablespoons golden syrup
4 tablespoons crunchy peanut butter
2 oz (50 g) plain chocolate, melted in a small jug

1   Grease well a shallow 7 in (18 cm) square tin and base-line with a square of greaseproof paper.
2   First cut the sour cherries into tiny pieces with a pair of scissors. Next break 3 biscuits by hand into small bits. Put the rest of the biscuits into a food processor and reduce to crumbs.
3   In a large pan, melt the butter and add the sugar, syrup and peanut butter. Take the pan off the heat and stir in all the biscuits and the cherries. If the mixture is too damp (it should be crumbly), add more crushed biscuits.
4   Spread the mixture in the tin and level it off, but do not press down too hard. Allow to cool a little.
5   Dribble the melted chocolate over the biscuit mixture in a zig-zag fashion. Cut into small bars when quite cold.

FLAPJACKS

Makes about 12

An ever-popular slice.

4 oz (125 g) margarine, plus more for greasing
4 level tablespoons golden syrup
3 oz (75 g) demerara sugar
8 oz (225 g) rolled oats
large pinch of salt

1   Preheat the oven to gas3/325°F/160°C and grease well a shallow 7½ in (20 cm) square tin.
2   Melt the margarine with the syrup and sugar in a large pan over a low heat. Remove from the heat.
3   Stir in the rolled oats and salt. Mix well, press into the tin and level the surface.
4   Bake for about 30–40 minutes until golden. Remove from the oven, leave for 5 minutes then cut into neat bars. Leave to cool in the tin and then allow to get quite cold on a wire tray.

Variation
For Raisin Flapjack: stir in 1½ oz (40 g) dark raisins, cut small with scissors.

'Kissing don't last: cookery do!'

George Meredith

SWISS SLICE

Makes about 16

Condensed milk was always called Swiss milk in our house – I do not know why. This slice needs to be cut into very small pieces as it is very rich indeed.

Pastry Base
4 oz (125 g) block margarine or butter, softened, plus more for greasing
2 oz (50 g) caster sugar
5 oz (150 g) self-raising flour

Swiss Milk Filling
4 oz (125 g) margarine
4 oz (125 g) sugar
2 tablespoons golden syrup
1 small tin of condensed milk

Topping
4 oz (125 g) good-quality cooking chocolate

1   Preheat the oven to gas4/350°F/180°C and grease well a Swiss roll tin measuring about 11½ x7½ in (29x19 cm).
2   First make the base: cream the margarine or butter with the sugar. Sift the flour into the mixture and mix well. Spread this paste into the tin in an even layer and smooth down.
3   Bake for about 20 minutes, or until the base is golden brown. Allow to cool.
4   Make the filling: put the margarine, sugar and syrup into a heavy-based pan. Heat slowly to melt the margarine and the syrup. Stir in the condensed milk and bring to a gentle boil. Stir gently until a good toffee-brown. Dribble some toffee mixture into a jug of ice-cold water. The toffee should be able to be picked up and it should be soft but holding together. If you are in doubt, boil for a few more minutes. The mixture should be really toffee-coloured now. Pour this on top of the base and allow to go cold.
5   Melt the chocolate in a small jug and pour this over the toffee. Mark wavy lines with a fork and leave to set.
6   To release: run a knife round the inside of the tin, lift the slab out and cut into tiny pieces.

HONEY JACKS

Makes about 12

6 oz (175 g) rolled porridge oats
3 oz (75 g) margarine or white vegetable fat
1 level tablespoon honey
2 oz (50 g) soft brown sugar

1   Preheat the oven to gas3/325°F/160°C.
2   Melt the margarine or fat with the honey and sugar gently in a roomy pan.
3   Stir in the porridge oats and mix well.
4   Spread this mixture into a shallow 7½ in (20 cm) square tin and level it well.
5   Bake for about 30 minutes until golden. Watch carefully as anything with honey burns easily.
6   Leave for 5 minutes, then cut into bars. Allow to go cold in the tin.

YORKSHIRE MINT PASTIES

Makes about 16

The best time to make these very nice pasties is when there is plenty of young mint leaves about.

Pastry base
3 oz (75 g) block margarine
8 oz (225 g) plain white flour
1 level teaspoon salt
1 size-1 egg, separated

Filling
3 large tablespoons finely chopped mint
3 oz (75 g) currants
2 oz (50 g) butter, softened
2 oz (50 g) caster sugar

1   Preheat the oven to gas7/425°F/220°C.
2   Make the base: rub the margarine into the flour and salt. Stir in the egg yolk with just enough cold water to make a firm dough.

3 Roll out half of the pastry to an 8 in (20 cm) square.
4 Make the filling: mix the chopped mint, currants, butter and half the sugar. Spread this evenly over the pastry square, leaving a narrow border. Moisten this border with water.
5 Roll out the other piece of pastry and cover the pastie. Seal the edges and trim off any spare pastry. Mark all round with a fork and make two steam holes. Brush over with the egg white and sprinkle with the remaining sugar.
6 Bake for about 15–20 minutes or until brown and crisp.
7 Cool on a wire tray, then cut into neat pieces.

NO-COOK SNAP, CRACKLE AND POP CRUNCH

Makes about 16

Do not be tempted to use more than the amount of Rice Krispies specified.

4 oz (125 g) block margarine, plus more for
    greasing
4 oz (125 g) marshmallows
3½ oz (90 g) or 4 oz (125 g) block of plain
    toffee
8 oz (225 g) Rice Krispies

1 Grease well an oblong baking tin about 11½ x7½ in (29x19 cm) and about 1½ in (3.5 cm) deep.
2 Melt the margarine with the marshmallow and toffee in a large heavy-based pan, stirring often.
3 When it is all more or less blended, take off the heat and pour in the Rice Krispies. Stir well so that the toffee mixture coats every Krispie.
4 Spoon into the tin and press down with a large flexible metal spatula. Allow to cool and cut into neat fingers.

SESAME CRUNCH

Makes about 16

3 oz (75 g) sesame seeds
3 teaspoons runny honey
6 oz (175 g) butter or margarine
3 oz (75 g) dark muscovado sugar
3 oz (75 g) desiccated coconut
3 tablespoons sunflower seeds
6 oz (175 g) rolled porridge oats

1 Preheat the oven to gas3/325°F/160°C.
2 Put the sesame seeds on a baking tray and slip this under a hot grill. Watch carefully until the seeds change colour. Remove at once.
3 In a roomy pan, melt the honey and butter or margarine with the sugar. Off the heat, stir in everything else and mix well. Spoon this mixture into a shallow 7x11 in (18x27 cm) tin and level it off.
4 Bake for 20–30 minutes, or until golden brown.
5 Cool, then cut into neat squares.

SWEET TARTS & FLANS

PUMPKIN PIE

Serves 10

Unless you put strong flavours with pumpkin you will find its taste very delicate – its great glory is its wonderful orange colour and it is a shame to cover this up so, this is more of a Pumpkin Pie Flan!

To get the flesh from the pumpkin I find it easier to use a large spoon. Take off a 'lid' first, then scoop out the flesh.

12 oz (325 g) Shortcrust Pastry (see page 16)
1½ lb (675 g) fresh pumpkin chunks
1 oz (25 g) cornflour
10 fl oz (300 ml) milk
2 size-1 eggs
3 tablespoons maple syrup
2 tablespoons golden syrup
½ level teaspoon ground cinnamon
½ level teaspoon ground cloves
½ level teaspoon ground ginger
1 size-6 egg, for glazing
butter, for greasing
sieved icing sugar, for dusting

1   Preheat the oven to gas6/400°F/200°C and grease well a 9 in (23 cm) flan tin with a loose bottom if possible. A flan ring would be fine if you have one about 2 in (5 cm) deep. This would have to be set on a greased baking sheet. Set a baking sheet inside the oven to heat up if using a flan tin.
2   Roll out the pastry on a floured board and use to line the flan tin or ring. Trim off the excess pastry and reserve it.
3   Put the chunks of pumpkin in a steamer and cook for about 20 minutes, until tender. Remove from the pan and use a stick blender or a food processor to reduce the chunks to a purée. If the purée is very sloppy, put it to drain for about 10 minutes in a nylon sieve, then put it into a bowl.
4   Take a little of the milk and blend it with the cornflour. Stir this into the pumpkin purée along with the large eggs, syrups, spices and the remaining milk. Turn this mixture into the pastry case.
5   Use the pastry trimmings to make long strips about ½ in (1 cm) wide and use to make a lattice pattern over the pumpkin. If you have a pastry roller to give the edges a crimped look, so much the better. Brush both the lattice-work pastry and the pastry edges with the beaten small egg to glaze.
6   Slide into the oven on the hot baking sheet and cook for about 40 minutes, when the filling should be set.
7   To serve, sprinkle some icing sugar through a sieve to give the pie a light dusting.

RASPBERRY TART

Serves 8

Raspberries do collapse dramatically when cooked. One thing you can do to bulk up the filling before you bake the pie is to strain off the juice and thicken it with cornflour. Use about 2 level tablespoons per 10 fl oz (300 ml) of juice. Whisk the dry cornflour into the cold juice, then simmer on a low heat until thick, stirring all the time. Stir enough of the thickened juice into the berries to give a dense filling. Alternatively, mix the fresh or frozen raspberries with raspberry jam. It will be even better if the jam is home-made.

To make an attractive lattice-look top you will need one of those plastic plates with raised-up squares. The raspberries are such a lively colour it is a shame not to see it.

9 oz (250 g) Shortcrust Pastry (see page 16)
10 oz (275 g) fresh or frozen raspberries
2 teaspoons of fresh lemon juice
about 1–2 tablespoons raspberry jam
butter, for greasing
icing sugar, for dusting

1 Preheat the oven to gas5/375°F/190°C and set a baking sheet inside to heat up. Grease a loose-bottomed flan tin about 9 in (23 cm) across or a flan ring deep enough to take 2 layers of pastry and the filling set on a greased baking sheet.

2 Roll out about half of the pastry and use to line the flan tin or ring. Trim off the excess pastry and add it to the reserved pastry.

3 Gently mix the fresh raspberries, lemon juice and the jam together. Spoon into the pastry case and level it off.

4 Roll out the remaining pastry to a round as big as the plastic shape, lift it on your rolling pin and lay it on top of the protruding squares. Take the rolling pin over the pastry on the mould, trim round the circle and push through the tiny pastry squares (see page 117).

5 Wet the bottom pastry rim, then lift this pastry lattice over to cover the fruit. Seal the edges and trim off the extra pastry again. You can, if you wish, make a decorative edge to the pie by attaching the little squares, overlapping them as you go. Brush the edges of the pie with milk or water to help the squares to stick.

6 Bake for 40 minutes and dredge with icing sugar to serve.

ORANGE AND LEMON TART

Serves 6–8

6 oz (175 g) Rich Ground Almond Pastry (see page 204)

Filling
about 4 tablespoons Seville orange marmalade
3 thin-skinned lemons
2 thin-skinned oranges
2½ oz (65 g) softened butter, plus more for greasing
3 oz (75 g) caster sugar
2 size-1 or size-2 eggs, beaten
chopped nuts, for decorating
icing sugar, for dusting

1 Preheat the oven to gas5/375°F/190°C and put a baking sheet in the oven. Grease a loose-bottomed flan tin about 8 in (20 cm) across.

2 Roll out the pastry to a circle about 2 in (5 cm) wider than your tin. Line the flan tin with the pastry, avoiding stretching it if you can. Press the pastry carefully into the tin. Take a rolling pin across the top to slice off the excess pastry. Prick the base of the shell with a fork, then set it in the fridge for about 30 minutes.

3 Take the raw pastry case out of the fridge and line it with a sheet of foil, scrunching it up to fit. Pour baking beans into the foil. Put the flan tin in the oven on the hot baking sheet and cook for about 15 minutes. Remove the foil and the beans and bake for just 5 minutes more, then set the flan tin aside to cool down.

4 Before you start to make the filling, remove the lid from the jar of marmalade. Soften the marmalade by standing the jar in a pan of hot water on a low heat or heat it up in the microwave for 1 or 2 minutes. Check that it is not getting too hot. Now strain the marmalade through a nylon sieve to remove the peel. You need about 4 tablespoons.

5 Grate the peel from 1 lemon and 1 orange. You need 1 tablespoon of lemon peel and 1 level tablespoon of orange peel. Squeeze 2 lemons – you need 4–5 tablespoons of juice.

6 In another bowl, cream the butter and sugar. Then beat in the lemon and orange rind. Beat the eggs into this mixture, a little at a time.

7 Next is a messy job. With a sharp knife, peel both the oranges and the lemons as if you were peeling apples. Do this over a bowl to catch any juice. Peel right down to the fruit so that no pith remains. Now hold each fruit in your left hand, still over the bowl, and cut down in between the pith and membranes to lift out the segments.

8 Mix the fruit juices into the butter mixture and spread this in the pastry case. Press the orange and lemon segments into the filling.

9 Warm the marmalade if it has stiffened up again and paint generously over the tart filling.

10 Set the tart on the hot baking sheet in the oven again and bake for about 15 minutes. It is better to leave the tart in the tin to cool down for 15 minutes or so, before trying to move it. Scatter some nuts over the tart followed by a light sprinkling of icing sugar.

TREACLE AND WALNUT TART

Serves 6–8

Golden syrup is the basis of this delicious tart. Lemon juice and rind help to cut the sweetness and the addition of walnuts makes it a winner.

8 oz (225 g) Rich Sweet Shortcrust Pastry (see page 17)

Filling
4 oz (125 g) butter, softened, plus more for greasing
4 oz (125 g) soft brown sugar
3 size-1 or size-2 eggs, beaten
juice and grated rind from 1 lemon
6 oz (175 g) golden syrup
6 large tablespoons white breadcrumbs
4 oz (125 g) pale good-quality walnuts

1 Preheat the oven to gas4/350°F/180°C and put in a baking sheet to heat up. Grease an 8 in (20 cm) flan tin.
2 Roll out the pastry and use to line the tin. Trim off excess pastry.
3 Bake it blind: line the tin with foil and pour in some baking beans. Put the tin on the hot baking sheet in the oven and bake for just 10 minutes.
4 To make the filling: cream together the butter and sugar until pale and soft. Gradually beat in the eggs, a little at a time. Stir in the lemon juice and rind.
5 Weigh the syrup: put a pan on your scales and pour the syrup in slowly (it does help to warm the syrup up in its tin before you start). Watch the dial carefully until it registers 6 oz (175 g). Take the pan off the scales and stir in the breadcrumbs, walnuts and the creamed mixture.
6 Pour into the part-baked pastry case. Return the tart to the baking sheet in the oven and bake for a further 40–45 minutes, when it should be set and golden. It can be served hot or cold.

BLUEBERRY PIE

Serves 8

It is much easier to get blueberries now. They are a delicious fruit and are often paired with oranges. The only drawback is that the fruit does stain badly. The addition of cornflour helps to thicken the juices. An American friend of mine tells me that blueberry pie is always served with ice-cream.

8 oz (225 g) Shortcrust Pastry (see page 16)

Filling
1½ lb (675 g) fresh blueberries
4 oz (125 g) caster sugar, plus more for sprinkling
3 tablespoons orange juice
2 oz (50 g) cornflour
knob of butter, plus more for greasing

1 Preheat the oven to gas6/400°F/200°C and put a baking sheet in to heat up. Grease a pie plate about 8 in (20 cm) across.
2 Put the blueberries in a bowl and stir in the sugar. Use the orange juice to slake the cornflour and stir this mixture into the blueberries. Let this stand until you roll out the pastry.
3 Roll out half of the pastry on a floured board and use to line the pie plate. Trim off excess pastry.
4 Spoon the blueberry mixture into the pie. Moisten the outer edge of the pie with water and flake the butter all over the fruit.
5 Roll out the rest of the pastry and use to cover the pie. Press the edges down carefully and trim off the excess. Take a fork and press the back of the prongs down all round the edge. This will help to keep the juice in. Cut 2 steam holes in the lid, then brush all over with water and sprinkle over extra caster sugar.
6 Set the pie on the hot baking sheet in the oven and bake for 30–40 minutes.

MUD PIE FROM MISSISSIPPI

Serves 8–10

Base
10 oz (275 g) plain chocolate digestive biscuits
3 oz (75 g) butter, melted

Filling
4 tablespoons milk
9 oz (250 g) marshmallows
12 oz (325 g) good-quality plain chocolate
2 teaspoons instant coffee
2 tablespoons of boiling water
3/4 pt (450 ml) double cream

Decoration
2 oz (50 g) good-quality white chocolate

1 Make the base: first generously grease a spring-form cake tin about 8½ in (21.5 cm) across and put a circle of greaseproof paper in the bottom. Crush the biscuits finely in a food processor. Stir into the melted butter and mix well. Now carefully line the bottom and sides of the cake tin with the buttery crumbs. The difficult bit is putting the crumbs up the sides of the tin. Try to get this depth to about 2 in (5 cm). Press the crumbs down carefully with the back of a spoon on the base and the flat blade of a knife up the sides. Put in the fridge to set.

2 Make the filling: put the milk and the marshmallows in a heavy pan over a gentle heat. Stir gently and, when the marshmallows have all melted, remove from the heat and set aside to cool.
3 Break up the chocolate and put to melt in a heatproof bowl set over a pan of simmering water.
4 In a small bowl, dissolve the coffee in 2 tablespoons of boiling water. Set this aside to cool.
5 In yet another bowl, whip the cream to the soft peaks. Fold the cooled chocolate and coffee into the marshmallow mixture and stir in the whipped cream. Pour into the prepared crumb case.
6 Decorate before the chocolate sets: melt the white chocolate inside a paper icing bag in the microwave. Watch carefully and give the chocolate just 30 second bursts. When it is soft, fold up the opening, snip off a tiny bit from the point of the paper cone and pipe 3 circles on top of the chocolate. Take a skewer and make a spider's web by dragging a skewer across the circles of chocolate from the centre to the outer edge.
7 Allow to go cold and set. Remove the clip and slide the pie out on a flat serving dish. Use the circle of greaseproof to pull it over.

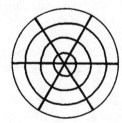

TARTE TATIN

Serves 6–8

This famous French apple pudding is like an upside-down tart. For once I recommend using a non-stick sandwich tin, about 8 in (20 cm) across.

2 oz (50 g) butter, plus more for greasing
2 oz (50 g) soft brown sugar
grated zest and juice of 1 lemon
1¾ lb (800 g) dessert apples (peeled and cored weight)

Pastry
4 oz (125 g) plain flour
½ oz (15 g) icing sugar
3 oz (75 g) butter, cut into tiny pieces
1 egg yolk

1   Preheat the oven to gas6/400°F/200°C and put a baking sheet in the oven to heat up. Grease the tin (see above) well.
2   Put the butter and sugar in a roomy pan and melt gently over a low heat. When the sugar has dissolved add the lemon rind and juice. Slice the apples fairly thickly and add them as well. Stir the apples round until they are well coated. Now use a skewer to lift the apples out and set them neatly on the base of the tin. Pour the juice over the fruit and set this aside to cool down.
3   Make the pastry: sift the flour and icing sugar together. Rub the butter lightly into the flour. Use the egg yolk mixed with a splash of water to make a firm dough. Set the dough aside, covered.
4   After 20 minutes, roll the pastry out to a circle. Use the pie tin to mark a circle big enough to cover the apples, yet small enough to fit inside the tin (you may have a pan lid just the right size to act as a giant cutter). Set the pastry over the apples and press down gently.
5   Place the tart on the hot baking sheet in the oven and bake for about 30 minutes. Keep an eye on the pastry and do not let it get too brown.
6   Remove the tart from the oven and pour off any excess juice into a small pan. Turn the pie out on to a flat plate, with the apples on top. Reduce the liquid in the pan until it is dark, then dribble it over the apples.

Note
To get the tart out of the tin, pour off the juices first then put a large serving plate over the tin and hold it firmly in place. Now swiftly turn the tin over. You may have to retrieve some of the apples.

MINCEMEAT STRUDEL

Serves 6–8

Filo pastry makes this famous pudding easy and very quick to do.

6 sheets of filo pastry, defrosted
2 oz (50 g) butter, melted, plus more for greasing
12 oz (325 g) mincemeat
5 oz (150 g) marzipan, grated or chopped small
2 hard dessert apples, peeled, cored and finely chopped

1   Preheat the oven to gas6/400°F/200°C and grease a large baking sheet.
2   Lay 2 sheets of filo pastry side by side but overlapping by about 2 in (5 cm). Brush over with melted butter. Lay another 2 sheets over the top and brush over with butter. Lay the last 2 sheets over in the same way.
3   Put the mincemeat in a bowl with the marzipan and the apples and mix well.
4   Spread the mincemeat mixture along the long pastry edge, stopping about 1 in (2.5 cm) from the edge.
5   Roll the strudel over a couple of times loosely, then turn the ends towards the centre and continue rolling.
6   Brush the roll with more melted butter, then slash the pastry 2 or 3 times diagonally.
7   Bake for 35 minutes, or until the pastry is golden. Do not over-bake.
8   Sprinkle icing sugar through a sieve over it just before you serve the strudel.

APPLE & ORANGE OPEN TART

Serves 8

1 lb (450 g) frozen puff pastry, defrosted
6 Granny Smith apples
3 oz (75 g) caster sugar
1 large orange
½ teaspoon ground cinnamon
1 oz (25 g) butter, plus more for greasing
3 tablespoons orange jelly marmalade, melted

1   Preheat the oven to gas7/425°F/220°C and grease well a large baking sheet about 13 in (32.5 cm) long.
2   Roll out the pastry to a rectangle with a thickness of about ⅛ in (3 mm) and about 10 in (25 cm) across. Set it on the baking sheet and put in the fridge or a cold place.
3   Peel, core and finely slice 3 apples. Stew the sliced apples in a little water with the two-thirds of the sugar. When soft, drain and mash to a purée.
4   Grate about 1 level tablespoon of zest from the orange. Now peel the orange as if you were peeling an apple. Take a sharp knife and remove the orange segments by slicing down on each side between the pith.
5   To assemble the tart: take the baking sheet out of the fridge and turn a narrow edge of pastry over all round. Spread the apple purée over the base, then scatter over the grated orange zest.
6   Peel, core and finely slice the remaining apples and lay the slices in neat rows, overlapping slightly. Cut the oranges into smaller pieces and tuck these between the apples. Sprinkle the remaining sugar all over and scatter over the cinnamon. Dot with tiny bits of butter.
7   Bake for 20 minutes until the pastry is crisp.
8   Remove from the oven and dab the melted orange jelly all over the fruit. Serve as soon as possible.

APPLE & PECAN FILO FLAN

Serves 8

2 oz (50 g) raisins
1 tablespoon rum
4 tablespoons apricot jam, sieved
8 sheets of filo pastry
2 oz (50 g) butter, melted, plus more for greasing
½ teaspoon ground cinnamon
6 eating apples, such as Cox's
juice of 1 lemon
1 oz (25 g) caster sugar
2 oz (50 g) shelled pecan nuts, chopped
icing sugar, to dust

1   Preheat the oven to gas5/375°F/190°C. Grease well an 8 in (30 cm) flan tin, with a loose bottom if possible.
2   First put the raisins in a small bowl with the rum and warm slightly in the microwave (10 seconds) to help plump them up.
3   Make the apricot glaze: warm the jam, again in the microwave (30 seconds at a time), but do not boil. Strain the liquid jam through a nylon sieve so that the large pieces of fruit are held back.
4   Cut the Filo sheets into squares, reserving the bits you have cut off. Place 1 square in the greased flan tin. Mix the cinnamon into the melted butter and use this to brush lightly over the first sheet. Layer the pastry sheets and spare bits on top of each other with a brush of melted butter and cinnamon in between. Set the squares at a different angle each time so that triangles of pastry sit up around the edge. Turn the edges down like a hem to form a border.
5   Peel, core and slice the apples. Toss the slices in the lemon juice and sugar and spoon into the pastry case.
6   Set the flan tin on the hot baking sheet in the oven and bake for 20–25 minutes, or until the pastry is brown and the apples soft.
7   Sprinkle with the nuts and raisins. Warm the strained apricot and brush this fairly generously all over the top of the apples, raisins and nuts. Serve warm.

LIME & CHOCOLATE TART

Serves 8–10

Pâte sucré is a French pastry which is made directly on the work surface. It is not difficult once you know how, but I have to admit it is very messy when you first start.

Pâte Sucré
6 oz (175 g) plain white flour, sieved
2½ oz (65 g) caster sugar
3 oz (75 g) butter, cut into small pieces and
    softened
2 small (size-6 or size-7) egg yolks

Filling
5 size-1 or size-2 eggs
6 oz (175 g) caster sugar
grated zest from 3 limes and about 4 fl oz
    (100 ml) juice
¼ pt (150 ml) double cream
5 oz (150 g) plain chocolate

1   Make the pâte sucré: put the sieved white flour in a heap on your pastry board or work surface. Push the flour so that there is a well in the centre. In this well, put the sugar, butter and egg yolks. Start by dabbing the white flour into the centre to break up the yolks, working round the heap in an orderly way. Keep doing this and break into the butter cubes as well. Sometimes I have to add just 1 or 2 teaspoons of water. Eventually you will see the pastry beginning to form. Once you have gathered the pastry into a rough ball and picked up all the bits of flour and butter, wrap it in a plastic bag and chill it for 30 minutes.

2   Remove the chilled pastry from the bag (you may have to wait for the pastry to return to room temperature) and roll it out on a floured board. Use to line a greased 8 in (20 cm) spring-form cake tin, lifting the pastry over on the rolling pin and press it into position and part way up the sides of the tin. Set in the fridge again for a further 30 minutes.

3   Preheat the oven to gas6/400°F/200°C and put in a baking sheet to heat up.

4   To bake the pastry case blind: scrunch up a large piece of foil and fit this inside the pastry case, pour in baking beans or ceramic beans and set the cake tin on the hot baking sheet to bake for 15 minutes. Remove the beans and foil and return the pastry case to the oven for a further 5 minutes, or until the pastry is brown all over. Remove from the oven and leave to cool down.

5   Make the filling: reduce the oven to gas2/300°F/130°C. Beat the eggs together, stir in the sugar and whisk until soft and fluffy. Add the grated zest of the limes plus the lime juice. Stir in the double cream. Now taste the mixture and sharpen with a little more lime juice if needed. Pour the mixture into the cooked pastry case.

6   Bake gently at this low temperature for about 60 minutes. Test with the tip of your finger to check that the whole pie is set. You will soon detect a wobble if not. Leave the tart in the tin to set for a little while.

7   To serve: use a swivel-bladed vegetable peeler to make short chocolate curls from the bar of chocolate. Scatter these in a thick border round the tart and serve.

STRAWBERRY TART

Serves 6–8

I got the idea for this recipe from another TV Cook, Josceline Dimbleby. Her biscuit pastry case is superb and I was amazed that it was so easy.

Pastry
6 oz (175 g) plain flour
2 tablespoons icing sugar
salt
2 oz (50 g) semolina
juice and grated zest of 1 orange
2 oz (50 g) butter, plus more for greasing

Creamed Custard
½ small (¼ pt / 150 ml) carton of double cream
1 single-portion carton (5½ oz/150 g) made custard
2 drops of vanilla essence

Topping
8 oz (225 g) orange jelly marmalade
1½ lb (675 g) perfect ripe strawberries, wiped and halved

1 Preheat the oven to gas6/400°F/200°C and grease a 9–10 in (23–25 cm) fluted loose-bottomed flan tin.
2 Make the pastry: sieve the flour, icing sugar, salt and semolina into a mixing bowl.
3 Heat the orange juice and rind and the butter in a small pan until it bubbles. Remove from the heat and leave to cool down for 3–4 minutes.
4 Now slowly stir the butter mixture into the flour to make a pastry dough.
5 Roll the dough out and use to line the flan tin. Ease the pastry down into the angle and try to allow the pastry to stick above the rim of the flan tin by about ¼ in (5 mm). Chill in the fridge for 30 minutes.
6 Line the pastry case with foil and fill with baking beans. Bake blind for about 20–25 minutes. Remove the baking beans and foil and set the pastry aside to go cold.
7 Leave the filling of the pastry case until about 2 hours before you need it. This ensures that the pastry stays crunchy.
8 In a small bowl, whip the cream and add the carton of custard. Whip them together, adding just 1 or 2 drops of vanilla essence.
9 Set the tart case on a serving dish. Pour in the creamed custard and level it off.
10 Prepare the glaze before you put the strawberries into the tart: melt the marmalade and then allow it to cool down again.
11 Set the strawberries in the creamed custard then spoon the marmalade over the top – just enough to make a glossy layer.

'The Queen of Hearts, she made some tarts,
All on a summer day:
The Knave of Hearts, he stole those tarts,
And took them quite away!'

Alice in Wonderland, Lewis Carroll

SECTION 2

PUDDINGS & DESSERT CAKES

'Sing a song of sixpence,
A Pocket full of rye;
Four-and-twenty blackbirds,
Baked in a pie.'

1

Nursery Classics

BOILED AND STEAMED PUDDINGS

WHITE LADIES PUDDING

Serves 3–4

This recipe was sent to the TV programme I used to do by a lady in Worcestershire, along with this nice story. The recipe is named after a village near Worcester called White Ladies Aston, where a convent of Cistercian nuns who wore white habits lived in the twelfth century. I have changed the recipe slightly, but you can bake the pudding as I describe or you can steam it by cutting the bread to fit a 2 pt (1.2 litre) basin rather than a pie dish. Cover the basin with foil and steam for 1½ hours.

3 medium-thick slices of white bread
1½ oz (40 g) butter, softened
2 oz (50 g) desiccated coconut
10 fl oz (300 ml) milk
pinch of salt
2–3 drops of vanilla essence
2 size-3 eggs
1½ oz (40 g) sugar

1 Preheat the oven to gas3/325°F/160°C.
2 Cut the crusts from the bread and butter the slices generously. Leave enough butter to grease a 2 pt (1.2 litre) pie dish. Sprinkle half of the coconut over the inside of the greased dish.
3 Lay the bread in the dish in layers, sprinkling coconut on each layer.
4 Warm the milk slightly, adding the salt and 2–3 drops of vanilla essence. Beat the eggs and sugar together in a jug. Pour in the milk and stir until the sugar has melted.
5 Pour the custard over the pudding and use a fork to press the bread down to help it absorb the milk. Set aside for at least 30 minutes.
6 Bake the pudding in a bain-marie, that is a water bath. Stand it in a roasting tin and pour boiling water into the tin to come halfway up the sides of the dish. Bake for 1½ hours until set.

MARBLE PUDDING

Serves 4–6

I remember this steamed pudding well from school. There were no worries then about vicious colouring – the pink was a real Technicolor job.

4 oz (125 g) soft margarine, plus more for greasing
3 oz (75 g) caster sugar
2 size-1 or 2 eggs, beaten
2 tablespoons of milk, plus extra if necessary
6 oz (175 g) self-raising flour, sieved
pinch of salt
2–3 drops of pink food colouring
2 teaspoons cocoa
2–3 teaspoons boiling water

Vanilla Sauce
(Makes ½ pt / 300 ml)
10 fl oz (300 ml) milk
2 dessertspoons vanilla sugar
2 size-3 eggs, beaten

1 Grease well a 2 pt (1.2 litre) pudding basin and put a small circle of greaseproof paper in the bottom.
2 In a large bowl, cream the margarine and sugar until pale and fluffy.
3 Mix the beaten eggs with the milk in a second bowl and, in a third, stir the salt into the flour. Then stir alternating spoonfuls of the flour and the milk and egg mixture into the creamed margarine. Add 2 or more tablespoons of milk to achieve a soft consistency.
4 Spoon about one-third of this mixture into one bowl and another one-third into another. Colour one of these portions a pale pink with just 2–3 drops of food colour and beat it well. To achieve a chocolate colour, mix the cocoa with 2–3 teaspoons of boiling water. Stir this paste into the second bowl and beat well.

5   Spoon into the basin alternating spoonfuls of the plain, pink and chocolate mixtures. Smooth over the top. Cover with greaseproof paper then with foil and tuck the edges under carefully.
6   Steam in a steamer set over a pan of water or stand on an old saucer in a large pan. Pour in boiling water to come halfway up the basin. Steam for 1½ hours and always watch the water level carefully in case it needs to be replenished (see Notes on Steaming, page 10).
7   While the pudding is cooking, make the vanilla sauce: heat the milk and the vanilla sugar, but do not boil. Pour the milk over the eggs, beating all the time. Stir this around, then pass it through a strainer into a heatproof bowl. Set this bowl over a pan of simmering water. Stir from time to time for about 10 minutes, until the sauce will coat the back of a wooden spoon.
8   Serve with the vanilla sauce.

Note
To make vanilla sugar: store a vanilla pod in a jar of caster sugar. Keep tightly closed and within 2 weeks the sugar will have taken up the aroma and flavour of the pod. To flavour a sauce, you can put the vanilla pod directly into the milk (it can be washed and dried for further use).

CHILTERN HILLS PUDDING

Serves 4–5

Even people who swear they hate tapioca (because of childhood names like 'frog's spawn' which tilt the strongest stomach) will enjoy this. It is totally out of fashion but I like it.

4 level tablespoons seed tapioca
7½ fl oz (210 ml) milk
4 oz (125 g) black raisins
1 oz (25 g) shredded suet
3 oz (75 g) sugar
4 oz (125 g) fresh white breadcrumbs
1 level teaspoon bicarbonate of soda
butter or margarine, for greasing

1   In a mixing bowl, soak the tapioca in the milk for 2 hours.
2   Strain off the milk and reserve it. Add the raisins, suet, sugar and crumbs to the tapioca.
3   Dissolve the bicarbonate of soda in the milk and then stir that into the mixture in the bowl.
4   Spoon the mixture into a greased 2 pt (1.2 litre) basin, cover with greaseproof paper and then foil, folding it neatly over and under the rim.
5   Steam for 3 hours (see notes on steaming, page 10).

STEAMED LEXIA RAISIN SPONGE

Serves 4–6

Lexia raisins are the big sticky ones you see at Christmas. You can chop them up if you wish, but I think they are better left whole.

4 oz (125 g) butter, softened, plus more for greasing
3 oz (75 g) soft brown sugar
pinch of salt
6 oz (175 g) self-raising flour, sieved
2 size-1 or size-2 eggs, beaten
4 oz (125 g) lexia raisins
about 2 tablespoons milk

1   Cream the butter and sugar in a large bowl until light and fluffy.
2   Stir the salt into the flour, then fold alternating spoonfuls of the flour and the beaten egg into the butter mixture. Add the raisins and about 2 tablespoons of milk to get a softish consistency.
3   Grease a 2 pt (1.2 litre) basin well and put a circle of greaseproof paper in the base. Spoon the pudding into the basin and smooth over the top. Cover the top with first greaseproof paper and then foil.
4   Steam for 1½ hours (see notes on steaming, page 10).
5   Serve with Vanilla Custard Sauce (see page 172).

TOASTED ALMOND SPONGE WITH BUTTERSCOTCH SAUCE

Serves 4–6

2 oz (50 g) flaked almonds, toasted briefly
  under a grill
4 oz (120 g) butter, softened, plus more for
  greasing
2 oz (50 g) sugar
2 size-1 or size-2 eggs, beaten
2-3 drops of almond essence
1 oz (25 g) ground almonds
5 oz (150 g) self-raising flour, sifted
2–3 tablespoons milk

Butterscotch Sauce
5 oz (150 g) golden syrup, warmed (stand
  tin in a pan of hot water)
2 oz (50 g) butter
3 oz (75 g) soft brown sugar
2 oz (50 g) white sugar
1/4 pt (150 ml) single cream

1   Put the toasted almonds in a plastic bag and
break them up into small pieces with a rolling
pin.
2   Liberally grease a 2 pt (1.2 litre) basin with
butter and put a circle of greaseproof paper in the
base. Scatter half of the broken flakes all over the
inside of the basin.
3   In a bowl, cream the butter and sugar. Then
beat in the eggs a little at a time. Add the
almond essence, ground almonds and the rest of
the nuts. Fold in the flour a bit at a time along
with 2–3 tablespoons of milk to get a softish
consistency.
4   Spoon this mixture into the basin. Cover first
with greaseproof paper and then foil.
5   Steam for 1½ hours (see notes on steaming,
page 10).
6   While the pudding is cooking, make the
sauce: put a small heavy-based pan on the scales
and slowly pour in the warmed syrup. Watch the
scales, so that when it is getting towards the 5 oz
(150 g) mark you can slow down.

7   Add the butter, soft brown sugar and white
sugar. Heat gently until the sugars are melted.
Bang the wooden spoon up and down, you will
hear if the sugar is really dissolved. Give the
mixture just another 5 minutes, then take it off
the heat.
8   Very slowly pour the single cream into the
hot mixture, stirring all the time. Thin down
even further if you wish with more cream or just
milk.
9   Serve the pudding with the butterscotch
sauce.

FIGGY PUDDING WITH CRÈME ANGLAISE

Serves 5–6

6 oz (175 g) dried figs
7 fl oz (200 ml) milk
5 oz (150 g) self-raising flour
1 teaspoon baking powder
5 oz (150 g) caster sugar
4 oz (125 g) shredded suet or packet suet
2 oz (50 g) fresh white breadcrumbs
grated rind and juice from 1 small orange
1 size-1 or size-2 egg, beaten
butter, for greasing

Crème Anglaise
1 vanilla pod
20 fl oz (600 ml) mixed milk and single
  cream
1½ oz (40 g) caster sugar
1 teaspoon cornflour
4 size-1 or size-2 eggs, beaten

1   Snip the stalks off the figs with scissors and
chop the fruit into small pieces about the size of
raisins. Put in a pan with the milk and cook
gently until soft.
2   Sift the flour and baking powder into a large
mixing bowl, stir in the sugar, suet, breadcrumbs
and orange rind and mix well. Add the figs with
the milk, orange juice and beaten egg. Mix well.
3   Grease well a 2½ pt (1.5 litre) basin and put

a circle of greaseproof paper in the base. Spoon the mixture into the basin. Cover first with greaseproof paper and then foil.

4   Steam for about 2 hours (see notes on steaming, page 10).

5   While the pudding is cooking, make the Crème Anglaise: put the vanilla pod in a pan with the milk, bring this to a boil and set it aside.

6   In a large heatproof bowl, mix the sugar and the cornflour. Then use a balloon whisk to beat the eggs gradually into the sugar and cornflour. Whisk until this mixture is smooth.

7   Now take the vanilla pod out of the milk (wash and dry it for future use). Reheat the milk and pour it over the egg mixture, stirring all the time. Suspend this bowl over a pan of simmering water and stir continuously, until the custard has thickened and coats the back of the wooden spoon. Stand the bowl of hot custard in a bowl of icy water to stop it cooking. Allow to cool, then reheat gently in the bowl suspended over a pan of simmering water when required.

HELSTON PUDDING

Serves 4–5

Helston is in Cornwall and my jokey friend Jean suggested that this is perhaps what the dancers ate after the Floral Dance! Anyway it is a bit like a light Christmas Pudding.

2 oz (50 g) plain flour
2 oz (50 g) ground rice
2 oz (50 g) breadcrumbs
4 oz (125 g) mixed fruit
2 oz (50 g) suet
1 oz (25 g) chopped candied peel
1/2 teaspoon mixed spice
1/2 teaspoon bicarbonate of soda
little milk

1   Put all the dry ingredients, except the bicarbonate of soda, into a large bowl and mix well.

2   Dissolve the bicarbonate of soda in a little milk, add this to the bowl together with enough milk to give a softish but not sloppy mix.

3   Grease well a 1 1/2 pt (850 ml) pudding basin and put a circle of greaseproof paper in the bottom. Spoon the mixture into the greased basin. Cover with greaseproof paper and foil.

4   Steam in a saucepan of boiling water for 2 hours (see notes on steaming, page 10).

ORANGE & LEMON PEEL PUDDING

Serves 4

For maximum flavour buy whole crystallized orange and lemon peel quarters, then chop them up yourself.

3 size-1 or size-2 eggs, beaten
2 oz (50 g) plain white flour, sieved
10 fl oz (300 ml) milk
pinch of salt
2 oz (50 g) crystallized lemon peel, finely chopped
2 oz (50 g) crystallized orange peel, finely chopped
1 teaspoon baking powder
butter, for greasing

1   Put the eggs in a roomy bowl and beat in the flour gradually.

2   Stir the milk into the mixture then whisk it well with a hand-held electric mixer or a stick blender. Now add the salt, chopped peel and baking powder. Mix well.

3   Grease well a 1 pt (575 ml) basin and put a circle of greaseproof paper in the bottom. Pour the mixture in to the basin. Cover with greaseproof paper and foil.

4   Steam for 1 1/2 hours until firm. Put a skewer into the pudding to check as you would a cake. (See notes on steaming, page 10.)

AROMATIC APPLE PUDDING AND CUSTARD

Serves 6

6 oz (175 g) self-raising flour, sifted
3 oz (75 g) packet suet
1½ lb (675 g) cooking apples
3 oz (40 g) caster sugar
knob of butter, plus more for greasing
5 cloves, or to taste

Packet Custard (makes 10 fl oz / 300 ml)
1 rounded dessertspoon custard powder
1 dessertspoon sugar
10 fl oz (300 ml) milk

1   In a bowl, mix the flour and the suet.
Measure out ¼ pt (150 ml) water and use just enough of it to make a soft but not sticky dough.
2   Turn the mixed dough out on a floured board and roll it out to a biggish circle, bearing in mind the size of the basin. Cut out a wedge of pastry equivalent to one-quarter of the whole circle. Set this aside for the lid.
3   Grease a 1½ pt (850 ml) pudding basin well and put a circle of greaseproof paper in the bottom. Ease the rest of the pastry into the basin, taking care to moisten the cut edges to help them join together. Use your fingers to move the pastry into position.
4   Peel, core and chop the apples. Mix them in a bowl with the sugar and cloves. Now tip this mixture into the pastry-lined basin along with the butter, taking care to scrape the sugar on top.
5   Now roll out the reserved pastry to make a lid. You may find you have a pan lid the right size to act as a giant cutter. Moisten the pastry lining and the lid edge. Cover the pudding with the pastry lid and nip the two pastry edges together to make a good seal.
6   Cover first with greaseproof paper and then foil and steam for 2 hours. (See notes on steaming, page 10.)
7   Towards the end of cooking time, make the custard. To cook in a microwave: whisk the custard powder and sugar into the cold milk. Cook on high for just over 4 minutes, whisking

hard every minute. I use a loose-headed loop whisk. Make sure you cover the base of the jug with the whisk to prevent the custard powder setting. To cook conventionally: in a pan, whisk the custard powder and sugar into the cold milk. When the powder has dispersed, take up a wooden spoon and stir continuously over a gentle heat until the mixture has thickened.

APPLEY PUDDING WITH PEEL AND CURRANTS

Serves 4

This is a different kind of steamed apple pudding. There is no pastry to make as breadcrumbs are used for a lighter result. They may be made either by processing crustless slices of white bread or grating an uncut crustless loaf on a metal grater.

4 oz (125 g) fresh white breadcrumbs
2 oz (50 g) packet suet
1½ oz (40 g) sugar
1 large Bramley cooking apple, peeled, cored and finely chopped
1 oz (25 g) finely chopped peel
2 oz (50 g) currants
2 size-1 or size-2 eggs, beaten
2–3 tablespoons milk

1   In a large bowl mix all the dry ingredients with the eggs and just enough milk to give a soft consistency.
2   Grease well a 1½ pt (1 litre) pudding basin and put a circle of greaseproof paper in the bottom. Spoon the mixture into the basin. Cover first with greaseproof paper then with foil.
3   Steam for 2 hours. (See notes on steaming, page 10.)

SIMPLE MINI SPONGES WITH FRESH FRUIT SAUCES

Makes 6

Individual steamed sponge puddings are brought into the luxury class with some accompanying fresh fruit sauces. Use dariole moulds or disposable individual foil cases.

4 oz (125 g) caster sugar
4 oz (125 g) butter or margarine, softened
6 oz (175 g) self-raising flour
pinch of salt
2–3 drops of vanilla essence
2 size-1 or size-2 eggs, beaten
2 tablespoons milk

1 Grease well 6 individual dariole moulds or foil basins and drop a tiny circle of greaseproof paper into the bottom of each one.
2 Cream the butter or margarine with the sugar and the vanilla essence.
3 Mix the flour and salt and beat this into the butter mixture, a little at a time, alternating with small amounts of the beaten eggs. Fold in just enough milk to give a softish consistency.
4 Spoon into the little moulds and cover each with foil.
5 Steam for 45–50 minutes. Because they are so small it is easier to steam them in a proper steamer. If you have to use a pan, do not let the water boil too fiercely in case the puddings fall over. Test with a skewer to see if they are cooked through.

Fruit Sauces
You can use just about any fruit as a sauce. In the past such sauces were nearly always cooked and thickened with cornflour and sieved. I really do not think this is necessary. I certainly like to see pieces of fruit. Since these fruits are not cooked, or just lightly cooked, they must be eaten within 2 days, unless you decide to freeze what is left.

Fresh Apricot Sauce: Stew ripe apricots in a little lightly sweetened water. Liquidize with a stick blender or food processor.

Fresh Raspberry Sauce: Very ripe raspberries do not need to be cooked. Just liquidize with a little water and sugar

Fresh Strawberry Sauce: The same goes for ripe strawberries – no cooking needed.

Fresh Blackcurrant Sauce: Stew ripe blackcurrants in water with sugar. Their powerful flavour means you need much less fruit. Liquidize with a stick blender or food processor.

Fresh Gooseberry Sauce: The earlier the gooseberries the greener will be the sauce. Top and tail each berry and stew gently in water barely to cover. Sweeten to taste. Liquidize with a stick blender or food processor.

TRADITIONAL GOLDEN SYRUP PUDDING

Serves 4

The original – and some will say the best – way to steam this sponge pudding is with the golden syrup inside the basin. I prefer to steam the pudding first, then pour the warm syrup over.

2 large tablespoons of golden syrup, plus more for serving
4 oz (125 g) butter or margarine, softened, plus more for greasing
4 oz (125 g) caster sugar
5 oz (150 g) self-raising flour, sieved
2 size-1 eggs, beaten

1 You will need a 1½ pt (1 litre) pudding basin well greased and with either 2 large tablespoons of golden syrup in the base or if you are doing it my way, with just a small greaseproof paper circle in the bottom of the basin.
2 In a large mixing bowl, put the butter, sugar, flour and eggs. Beat well with a wooden spoon or with a hand-held electric beater until the mixture is smooth and creamy.
3 Spoon this into the basin. Cover with greaseproof paper and foil.
4 Steam for about 1¾ hours. (See notes on steaming, page 10.)
5 To serve: run a knife round the edge, turn the pudding out on a serving dish and pour a little hot golden syrup over the top. Hand round with extra hot syrup or custard.

APPLE & MANGO ROLY-POLY

Serves 6–8

This is a strange marriage, but it works. Peel the mango over a bowl to catch the juice. Stand the fruit on its narrow end and take a wide slice off each side. Cut the fruit across in cubes inside the ovals this reveals then turn each oval inside out and slice off the cubes. Recover as much fruit as you can from round the stone. You can get quite nice cans of mango slices if you are in a hurry or can't find fresh.

Suet Pastry
6 oz (175 g) self-raising flour, sieved, plus more for dusting
3 oz (75 g) packet suet
1 size-6 or size-7 egg
hot custard, to serve (optional)

Filling
1 lb (450 g) cooking apples, chopped (peeled weight)
1 ripe mango, peeled and cubed (as described above)
2 oz (50 g) caster sugar

1 Put a large pan of water on to boil and get a pudding cloth ready (one side of a clean pillow case would do) and some string.
2 Make the pastry: mix the flour and suet in a bowl. Beat the egg in a little water and use this to mix into the flour and suet to make a firm dough.
3 Roll the dough out to a thickness of about ½ in (1 cm). Spread the chopped apples over it, then sprinkle over the mango pieces and the sugar.
4 Roll the apple roly-poly up and nip the ends together very carefully. Put the roly-poly in the cloth, sprinkle dry flour under the pudding and over it. Roll this up and tie firmly at each end.
5 Sink the pudding roll in the pan of boiling water, being careful not to let the water go off the boil. Top up with boiling water and boil for 1½ hours.
6 Serve in slices, with some mango juice poured over each slice and perhaps some hot custard.

St Stephen's Pudding

Serves 6

This is a rather ritzy steamed pudding, served with brandy butter no less.

3 oz (75 g) packet suet
2 oz (50 g) self-raising flour, sieved
4 oz (125 g) fresh breadcrumbs
4 oz (125 g) black raisins, plus a few extra
2 oz (50 g) soft brown sugar
2 Bramley apples
grated rind of 1 lemon
1 size-1 or size-2 egg
about 3 tablespoons milk
butter, for greasing

Brandy Butter

3 oz (75 g) soft butter (unsalted if you can get it)
3 oz (75 g) caster or soft brown sugar
2 tablespoons brandy
dash of lemon juice

1 Well ahead and ideally the day before, make the brandy butter: use a deepish bowl and beat the butter until it is really soft and pale. Add the sugar a little at a time and continue beating. Gradually beat in the brandy just a teaspoon at a time and lastly the lemon juice. This is an arm-aching job if using a wooden spoon, so use a stick blender or an electric blender if you can. When everything is well mixed, transfer the butter to a dish. Cover it and chill in the fridge for a few hours as the brandy flavour takes time to percolate. It will taste even better on the second day.

2 Grease well a 2 pt (1.1 litre) basin and drop a circle of greaseproof paper in the bottom.

3 In a large bowl, mix the suet, flour, breadcrumbs, raisins and sugar really well.

4 Peel and grate the apples straight into the mixture. Add the lemon rind and mix again.

5 Whisk the egg into the milk and pour this into the bowl. Mix well. Add a little more milk if the pudding is stiff.

6 Put into the basin a spoonful of raisins, then spoon the pudding mixture on top. Cover with greaseproof paper and foil.

7 Steam for 2 hours. (See notes on steaming, page 10.) Serve with the brandy butter.

'When Eve upon the first of Men
The apple press'd with specious cant,
Oh! what a thousand pities then
That Adam was not Adamant!'

A Reflection, Thomas Hood.

APPLE CHARLOTTE

Serves 6

I always think of this pudding of apples and bread as a hot version of summer pudding. It was said to have been created for Queen Charlotte, the wife of King George III, by her French Cook. A charlotte mould is made of tin and shaped like a soufflé dish, but with slightly sloping sides and two little 'lugs' or handles. I think the other kind of charlotte was probably the one dreamed up for a Queen. The mould is lined with sponge fingers or pieces of plain cake and filled with a bavarois (flavoured whipped cream set with gelatine).

1½ lb (675 g) Bramley cooking apples
2 oz (50 g) caster sugar
4 oz (125 g) butter, plus more for greasing
about 8 slices of bread from a large thickly
      sliced loaf, crusts removed

1   First cook the apples: peel, core and slice thinly. Add 1 oz (25 g) of the measured sugar and 1 oz (25 g) of the measured butter to the pan and just a tablespoon of water. Aim to have a very thick firm purée. Cook gently and beat to a purée. Set this aside to cool.
2   Butter a charlotte mould or a soufflé dish about 6 in (16 cm) across fairly generously and sprinkle sugar all round the sides and the base.
3   Next melt the rest of the butter. Brush one side only of the bread pieces going down on the bottom of the mould. Next cut the bread in even rectangles, brush these with butter too and set these round the inside of the container (the buttered side of the bread pieces go next to the mould), overlapping slightly and at the bottom. Overlap the ends on the bottom pieces as shown in the diagram on the right. Press hard on the joins. There should be no gaps.
4   Preheat the oven to gas6/400°F/200°C.
5   Once the bread lining is complete, spoon in the apple mixture. A gentle tap will help the apple to settle and you can then cover the surface with a 'crazy-paving' of leftover bread pieces. If the side pieces stand up above the apple you can turn them in under the lid. Find a small plate or saucer which will sit on top of the charlotte.
6   Set on a baking sheet and bake for 30 minutes. Remove the saucer and bake for a further 10 minutes to allow the top to toast.
7   To serve: run a knife round the outside of the mould. Set a large serving plate upside down on top of the tin mould and, holding the plate in place, swiftly invert the dish so that the pudding is right way up on the serving dish. Serve hot.

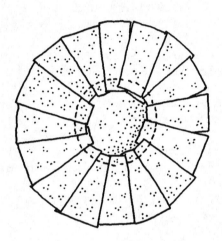

STEAMED WALNUT PUDDING

Serves 4

I saw this recipe in Margaret Costa's Book *Four Seasons Cookery*. It is such a good idea that I tried it and like it very much. Look for good walnuts which are pale and moist. I get mine from my greengrocer who sells them loose.

3 oz (75 g) crushed walnuts (a food
      processor make an easy job of this), plus
      2 tablespoons of coarsely chopped
      walnuts
3 size-1 or size-2 eggs
2 oz (50 g) caster sugar
4 oz (125 g) plain sponge cake, cut into
      small squares
butter, for greasing

1 Grease a 1½ pt (1 litre) pudding basin generously with butter, then scatter the chopped walnuts round the sides and bottom.
2 Separate the eggs and beat the egg yolks with the sugar until thick and pale. Stir in the crushed walnuts and cut sponge cake. Whisk the egg whites until they are very stiff and fold into the walnut mixture.
3 Spoon into the pudding basin. Cover first with greaseproof paper and then foil.
4 Steam for 30–35 minutes. (See notes on steaming, page 10.)

MICROWAVE APRICOT & ALMOND PUDDING

Serves 2

This pudding cooks in 7 minutes on high in the microwave. It is best eaten on the day it is made.

2 tablespoons apricot jam
2 oz (50 g) butter or margarine, softened
2 oz (50 g) caster sugar
1 size-1 egg, beaten
2–3 drops of almond essence
4 oz (125 g) self-raising flour, sifted
4 tablespoons milk
2 no-soak dried apricots, cut very small
custard, to serve

1 Spoon the jam into the bottom of a 1 pt (600 ml) basin.
2 Put the butter or margarine, sugar, egg, almond essence, flour, milk and finely chopped apricot in a large bowl and beat until smooth. Spoon into the basin and cover with greaseproof paper or a saucer.
3 Cook in the microwave on high for 7 minutes, turning the bowl round halfway. Allow another 5–6 minutes standing time to finish cooking.
4 Serve hot with custard.

LEMON POND PUDDING

Serves 6

Said to have come from Sussex, this delectable suet pudding is always described with the lemon left whole inside. I have tried it with the lemon cut up in chunks and it works well and everybody can get a piece. The pond occurs when you first cut into the pudding and the buttery lemon sauce flows out.

8 oz (225 g) self-raising flour
pinch of salt
4 oz (125 g) packet suet
6 oz (175 g) soft brown sugar
4 oz (125 g) hard butter, cut into small cubes
2 small thin-skinned lemons, topped and tailed and cut into small chunks

1 Sift the flour and salt together and stir in the suet. Mix to a soft but not sticky dough with about 8 tablespoons of water.
2 On a floured board, roll the dough out to a thickness of about ¼ in (5 mm) in a rough circle. Cut out one-quarter of the circle and set this aside for the lid.
3 Grease well a 1½ pt (1 litre) pudding basin and ease the dough into it to line it, taking care to moisten the cut edges so that they will stick together. Use your fingers to work the dough fairly smoothly up the sides and with a slight overhang.
4 Put half the sugar and half the butter into the basin. Toss the chopped lemon in the rest of the sugar, then turn all that into the basin with the butter on top.
5 Roll out the pastry for the lid. Moisten the top of the lining pastry and set the lid on. Make a good seal. I use scissors to trim off the excess pastry. Cover the basin first with greaseproof paper and then with foil on top, tucking it well under the rim.
6 Steam for 4 hours, topping up with boiling water as needed. (See notes on steaming, page 10.)

GUARDS PUDDING

Serves 4–6

Like spotted dick, this is always said to be one
of the puddings that men remember with
longing. If you use good home-made raspberry
jam it will be even better than you remember.

4 oz (125 g) soft brown sugar
4 oz (125 g) soft butter or margarine, plus
    more for greasing
3 tablespoons raspberry jam
1/2 teaspoon bicarbonate of soda
4 oz (125 g) brown breadcrumbs
2 size-1 or size-2 eggs, beaten
pinch of salt

1   In a roomy mixing bowl, cream the sugar and
butter or margarine until pale and light. Beat in
the jam.
2   Dissolve the bicarbonate of soda in a tiny
amount of hot water. Stir this in with the
breadcrumbs, eggs and salt. Mix well.
3   Butter generously a 1 1/2 pt (850 ml) pudding
basin. Turn the mixture into the basin.
4   Steam for about 2 1/2 hours. (See notes on
steaming, page 10.)
5   The pudding is very moist and light so leave
it in the pudding basin for 10 minutes after
cooking. You could put it in a low oven to keep
it hot. Turn out gently on to a serving plate.

CHOCOLATE SPONGE PUDDING WITH BUTTERSCOTCH SAUCE

1/2 oz (15 g) cocoa (not drinking chocolate)
7 1/2 oz (215 g) self-raising flour
pinch of salt
3 oz (75 g) butter or margarine, cut into
    pieces, plus more for greasing
4 tablespoons milk
1 size-1 egg

2–3 drops of vanilla essence
Butterscotch Sauce (see Toasted Almond
    Sponge and Butterscotch Sauce, page
    174), to serve

1   Sift the flour, cocoa and salt into a roomy
bowl.
2   Stir in the butter and rub it in as if you are
making pastry. When you get to the stage when
the mixture looks liked damp breadcrumbs stir
in the sugar.
3   In a small jug, whisk together the milk, egg
and vanilla essence. Pour this into the flour
mixture and beat together to a soft consistency.
Add a drop more milk to the mixture if you
think it is necessary.
4   Butter a 1 1/2 pt (1 litre) basin and put a circle
of greaseproof paper in the base. Turn the
mixture into the buttered basin. Cover with
greaseproof paper and then foil.
5   Steam for 2 hours. (See notes on steaming,
page 10.) Serve with butterscotch sauce.

INDIVIDUAL STICKY TOWERS AND STICKY SAUCE

Makes 4–5

Towers
2 oz (50 g) soft brown sugar
2 oz (50 g) soft butter, plus more for
    greasing
1 size-1 egg, beaten
4 oz (125 g) plain flour, sifted
1/4 oz (10 g) baking powder
about 1 fl oz (25 ml) milk
1 oz (25 g) chopped walnuts
1 oz (25 g) finely chopped dates

Sticky Sauce
14 oz (400 g) can of condensed milk
2 tablespoons golden syrup
2 oz (50 g) caster sugar
4 oz (125 g) butter

1   You will need 4 or 5 dariole moulds (small metal moulds shaped like a tower). Grease them well and put a tiny circle of greaseproof in each one.
2   In a roomy bowl, cream the sugar and butter until pale and fluffy. Beat in the egg a little at a time.
3   Fold in the flour and the baking powder. Add the milk to achieve a dropping consistency, adding a little extra, if needed. Stir in the chopped walnuts and dates.
4   Divide the mixture between the 4 or 5 moulds, filling each no more than half-full. Cover each mould with foil.
5   Steam for about 45 minutes. (See notes on steaming, page 10.)
6   While the towers are cooking, make the sauce: in a small heavy-based saucepan, combine all the ingredients. Cook very gently until you achieve a nice toffee colour.

Georgie Porgie Pudding and Pie
Kissed the girls and made them cry.

Nursery Rhyme and skipping song

SPOTTED DICK

Serves 4

Another all-time favourite – a steamed roll of suet pudding.

3 oz (75 g) fresh white breadcrumbs
3 oz (75 g) self-raising flour, plus more for dusting
3 oz (75 g) packet suet
2 oz (50 g) caster sugar
6 oz (175 g) currants
grated rind of 1 lemon
1 size-1 egg, beaten
4 tablespoons milk, plus more if needed
custard, to serve

1   You will need a pan of boiling water big enough to take a 'Swiss roll' of spotted dick wrapped in paper and then in foil.
2   In a roomy bowl, thoroughly mix the breadcrumbs, flour, suet, sugar and currants, together with the grated rind of 1 lemon.
3   Make a well in the centre, add the beaten egg and enough milk to form a soft but not sticky dough.
4   Turn the dough out on a floured board and pat out to a neat rectangle. Then shape the mixture into a fat roll. Wrap this loosely first in floured greaseproof paper, screwing up the ends like a giant sweet, then over-wrap the paper with foil. Fasten tightly at each end.
5   Slide this parcel into a steamer and steam for 2 hours or, if you have no steamer, find something like a sugar basin turned upside down and put a plate on it and the pudding on top of that. (Anything to raise the 'roll' out of the water, but big enough to allow the spotted dick to lie down!) See notes on steaming, page 10.
6   Serve hot with custard.

CLOUTIE DUMPLING FROM SCOTLAND

Serves 10–12

This is a boiled fruit pudding very like a Christmas Pudding mix, but with a very different texture. The 'skin' of the pudding is the very desirable part of this traditional fare. Silver charms and the old silver threepenny bits were wrapped tightly in greaseproof paper and buried in the pudding. A 'cloutie' or 'clout' is a cloth.

Once the pudding has been boiled, have ready a large empty mixing bowl and a sinkful of cold water. Lift the pudding out with strong tongs, dunk it once very briefly in the cold water and then put into the mixing bowl. This cold water treatment helps to prevent the pudding from sticking to the 'clout'. Untie the string and let the cloth hang over the sides. Now cover the pudding and bowl with the serving dish. We would call this an 'ashet' in Scotland. Hold tightly to the plate on the top and place your hand underneath the bowl. Turn the whole lot over and you should have your dumpling on its serving dish. Peel off the cloth and leave it to soak before washing it. The surface of the pudding will be quite sticky.

Long ago, the much-prized shiny thick skin would be formed by leaving the pudding in front of the fire and turning it frequently. You can get the same effect by 10–15 minutes in a very low oven.

1 level teaspoon bicarbonate of soda
1 lb (450 g) self-raising flour
fat pinch of salt
8 oz (225 g) raisins
8 oz (225 g) mixed dried fruit
1 large carrot, peeled and grated
1 medium cooking apple, peeled and grated
2½ oz (65 g) packet grated suet
1 large teaspoon mixed spice
1 level teaspoon ground ginger
1 size-3 egg
1 tablespoon black treacle
flour, for dusting

1   You will need string, a 24 in (60 cm) square of cotton from an old clean sheet or pillowcase and a large pan. A jam pan will do, but improvise a lid with a double thickness of wide foil so that you can tuck it over the edge to keep all the steam in.
2   In a large mixing bowl or clean washing-up bowl, mix the dry ingredients very thoroughly. Stir in any wrapped-up charms if you wish, followed by all the other ingredients. Stir in a little water to achieve a stiffish mixture.
3   Now rinse your cloth out in hot water, wring it well and lay it out. Sprinkle some flour in the centre where the dumpling is going to sit. Turn the mixture out on to this and sprinkle more flour all over. Gather up the edges of the cloth and tie it 'Dick-Whittington'-style, leaving a little room for the pudding to expand. It is a good plan to put an old plate in the bottom of the pan of boiling water and sit the dumpling on it. The water should come two-thirds of the way up the pudding.
4   Bring to the boil, turn down the heat to a gentle level and boil for 3 hours. If the plate stops rattling, you'll know that the water needs to be topped up.

GRACE'S CHRISTMAS PUDDING

Serves 10

I cannot understand why so many people buy their Christmas Puddings. It is extremely easy to make your own. No skill is needed. Unlike making a Christmas cake, the cooking could not be easier. If you like a really dark sticky pudding, the earlier in the year you make it the better. Some go as far as making puddings one Christmas to eat the following year! Another way to achieve a dark pudding is to boil it for twice as long as the recipe states.

This quantity will make one big pudding in a 3 pt (1.75 litre) basin, or one 2 pt (1.1 litre) plus one ½ pt (300 ml), or one 1½ pt (1 litre) pudding plus one 1 pt (600 ml).

2 oz (50 g) almonds, blanched, skinned and
  chopped
2 oz (50 g) cut mixed peel
1 medium-size cooking apple or carrot,
  peled and grated
8 oz (225 g) fresh white breadcrumbs
2 oz (50 g) plain white flour
7 oz (200 g) shredded packet suet
9 oz (250 g) soft brown sugar
8 oz (225 g) raisins
8 oz (225 g) currants (Greek Vostizza
  currants are tiny and have no seeds)
8 oz (225 g) sultanas
1 rounded teaspoon mixed spice
grated rind and juice of 1 lemon
4 size-3 eggs, beaten
3 tablespoons brandy
butter, for greasing

1   Put all the ingredients in a large mixing bowl
and mix very thoroughly. Leave the mixture to
stand for a couple of hours.
2   Prepare a steamer or a large pan of hot water
with a lid.
3   Grease the pudding basin(s) and put a circle
of greaseproof paper in the bottom(s). Spoon the
mixture in but do not fill the basin(s) to the top.
Cover with greaseproof paper and foil.
4   Steam for 6 hours for the big pudding and 4
hours for smaller ones. See page 10 for notes on
steaming.
5   To reheat on Christmas day: 2–3 hours in the
steamer will be sufficient.

INDIVIDUAL CHRISTMAS
PUDDINGS

There are several handle-less cups I keep and
use for small Christmas puddings. Actually the
quantity is enough for two small portions. The
only drawback is that you cannot have too
much water in the steaming pan since it should
not come up more than half-way, therefore you
have to keep an eye on the water level. These
little puddings also heat up well in the
microwave cooker.

VEGETARIAN CHRISTMAS
PUDDINGS

Suet which has not been derived from an
animal, and is therefore acceptable to
vegetarians, is now available.

NO-SUGAR, NO-FLOUR
CHRISTMAS PUDDING

Serves 8

The idea for this pudding came from Margaret
Costa again. I have made one or two changes.
She suggests serving the pudding with whipped
cream flavoured with grated orange peel.

4 oz (125 g) mixed candied peel, cut finely
2 oz (50 g) glacé cherries, cut small
12 oz (325 g) raisins
4 oz (125 g) currants (Greek Vostizza
  currants have no seeds)
2 oz (50 g) chopped almonds
6 oz (175 g) white breadcrumbs
6 oz (175 g) shredded packet suet
$1/2$ teaspoon ground cinnamon
$1/2$ teaspoon freshly grated nutmeg
4 size-3 eggs
3 tablespoons brandy
$1^1/2$ fl oz (75 ml) brown ale
butter, for greasing

1   Grease well a 2 pt (1.2 litre) basin and put a
circle of greaseproof paper in the base.
2   In a large bowl, mix the fruit, nuts,
breadcrumbs, suet and spices. Whisk the eggs in a
separate bowl, then add to the big bowl along with
the brandy and enough of the ale to give a soft but
not runny consistency. Mix very thoroughly.
3   Spoon into the basin. Cover first with
greaseproof paper then with foil.
4   Steam for 5 hours (see page 10).
5   On the day, give it another 3 hours. This
pudding should be eaten within 6 weeks.

BAKED PUDDINGS

CHOCOLATE SUPREME

Serves 6–8

4 oz (125 g) soft butter
4 oz (125 g) caster sugar
2 size-1 or size-2 eggs, beaten
1 oz (25 g) cocoa
2–3 drops of vanilla essence
4 oz (75 g) self-raising flour
1 level teaspoon baking powder
1½ oz (40 g) chocolate chips
little milk, if needed
chilled single cream, to serve

1   Preheat the oven to gas4/350°F/180°C and slide a baking sheet in the oven to heat up. You will need a 1½ pt (1 litre) ovenproof dish.
2   Cream the butter and sugar together until pale and fluffy.
3   Add the eggs just a little at a time, beating hard between each addition.
4   Mix the cocoa with a little hot water and beat this paste into the egg mixture along with the vanilla essence.
5   Sift the flour and baking powder together and fold into the butter mixture along with the chocolate chips. Add a little milk to achieve a soft but not sloppy consistency.
6   Spoon into the ovenproof dish. Place on the hot baking sheet and bake for about 30–40 minutes or until there is no wobble. Place your hand lightly on the middle of the sponge and you will know if the pudding is still liquid underneath.
7   Serve with chilled single cream.

CHOCOLATE SURPRISE PUDDING

Serves 4–5

There is a lemon version of this pudding, the sponge rises up and underneath it there is the surprise – a sauce to eat with the pudding – magic!

Sponge
1 rounded tablespoon cocoa (not drinking chocolate)
3 oz (75 g) self-raising flour
3 oz (75 g) caster sugar
4 oz (125 g) butter or margarine, softened, plus more for greasing
2 size-1 or size-2 eggs, beaten

Sauce
1 rounded tablespoon cocoa
1½ oz (40 g) chopped walnuts
4 oz (125 g) demerara sugar
10 fl oz (300 ml) strong coffee (3 heaped teaspoons coffee granules in 10 fl oz (300 ml) boiling water)

1   Preheat oven to gas4/350°F/180°C. Grease a 2 pt (1.2 litre) ovenproof dish.
2   Sieve the cocoa and flour into a mixing bowl. Add the sugar, butter or margarine and the eggs. Beat well until the mixture is smooth. Spoon into the ovenproof dish.
3   To make the sauce: first mix the cocoa, nuts and half the sugar and sprinkle this over the top of the uncooked pudding.
4   Put the remaining sugar in the hot coffee. Stir to dissolve it then pour over the uncooked sponge.
5   Bake for about 50 minutes: test with a skewer to see if the sponge is cooked.

LEMON SURPRISE PUDDING

Serves 2

This is a lighter and more delicate pudding than the Chocolate Surprise. Bake it in an ovenproof dish with a capacity of 1½ pt (1 litre).

2 oz (50 g) soft butter
3½ oz (90 g) caster sugar
grated rind and juice of 1 lemon
2 size-3 eggs, separated
1 level tablespoon plain flour, sifted
10 fl oz (300 ml) milk

1   Preheat the oven to gas4/350°F/180°C.
2   Beat the butter, sugar and lemon rind until pale and fluffy. Beat in the two egg yolks, one at a time.
3   Fold in the sifted flour in alternating spoonfuls with the milk. Lastly add the lemon juice.
4   Whisk the egg whites until stiff and fold these into the sponge mixture.
5   Spoon into the dish and bake for about 45 minutes. Serve fairly quickly.

MINCEMEAT SPONGE

Serves 4

This is a baked sponge with mincemeat underneath, using the easiest of all sponge recipes – all-in-one.

4 oz (125 g) self-raising flour
1 teaspoon baking powder
4 oz (125 g) caster sugar
4 oz (125 g) soft margarine
2–3 drops of vanilla essence
2 size-1 or size-2 eggs, beaten
10 oz (275 g) mincemeat
1 chopped apple (optional)

1   Preheat the oven to gas4/350°F/180°C. You will need a greased 2 pt (1.2 litres) ovenproof dish or pie dish. Have ready a small roasting tin with hot water, in which to bake the pudding. This helps to avoid scorching the mincemeat while the sponge is cooking.
2   Into a large mixing bowl, sift the flour and the baking powder. Add all the other ingredients except the mincemeat and apple, if using.
3   Beat this mixture thoroughly. If you have a hand-held electric mixer the job will be faster. The mixture should be softish. If not add a drop of water to loosen the texture.
4   Now spread the mincemeat in the bottom of the dish. Add the chopped apple to bulk it up if you wish and spread the sponge mixture on top.
5   Bake for about 40 minutes. Do the wobble test to check that the sponge is done: place your hand lightly on top of the sponge. You will easily detect if the mixture is still liquid underneath.

Variations
Stewed Fruit: Apple, rhubarb, apricot etc. Strain off some juice.

Jams: Raspberry, strawberry, apricot jam, etc. These can be pleasant, but counteract their sweetness with some added lemon juice.

Golden Syrup: Again I think this is improved with a strong dash of lemon juice.

Note
In all of the above puddings, be sure to bake the sponge in a 'bain-marie', that is a bath of water. I use a small roasting tin with the water half-way up the dish.

LEMON MERINGUE PUDDING

Serves 8

Another all-time favourite for which you need an 8 in (30 cm) pre-baked pastry shell. I use a flan tin with a loose bottom or a flan ring on a greased baking tin.

6 oz (175 g) Shortcrust Pastry (see page 16)
juice and grated rind of 2 large lemons
7 oz (175 g) caster sugar
1½ oz (40 g) cornflour (about 3 level tablespoons)
½ oz (15 g) butter, plus more for greasing
2 size-1 eggs, separated

1   Preheat the oven to gas 5/375°F/190°C and put a baking sheet in to heat up. Grease a flan tin well (see above).
2   On a floured board, roll out the pastry and use to line the greased flan tin. Line the inside of the pastry with foil and fill with dried beans. Set the flan on the hot baking sheet and bake for 20 minutes. Remove the foil and beans and return the flan to the oven for a further 5 minutes if it is pale. Allow to go cold in the tin.

To make the filling in the microwave
1   Into a microwave measuring jug, put the lemon rind and lemon juice and make up to 10 fl oz (300 ml) with cold water. Add 3 oz (75 g) of the sugar and the cornflour. Whisk hard and put the jug in the microwave on high for a total of about 4 minutes, but whisk every minute.
2   When the mixture is thick, take out of the microwave and beat in the butter and egg yolks. Pour into the flan case and allow to go cold.

To make the filling in a pan
1   First put the lemon juice in a measuring jug and top up with water to 10 fl oz (300 ml). Pour into the pan with the lemon rind, cornflour and 3 oz (75 g) of the sugar. Whisk hard to disperse the cornflour. Then take a wooden spoon and stir all the time over a moderate heat until thick.
2   Remove from the heat and beat in the butter and 2 egg yolks. Pour this into the pastry case.

Meringue Topping
1   Turn the oven down to gas 2/300°F/150°C. In a clean bowl, whisk the reserved egg whites until stiff using an electric mixer or hand-held electric whisk.
2   Whisk in the remaining sugar at about a tablespoon at a time, whisking all the time. Spread the meringue, which should be stiff, all over the lemon filling. Use the flat blade of a knife to seal the meringue topping and use the point of a skewer to make decorative whirls.
3   Place the pie on a baking sheet and bake for about 40 minutes, or until the meringue is tipped with colour and crisp outside and soft within.

EVE'S PUDDING

Serves 4–5

This is very like Apple Sponge, but this time the apples go in uncooked.

1 lb (450 g) cooking apples, peeled, cored
**   and thinly sliced**
2 oz (50 g) demerara sugar
grated rind and juice from 1 lemon
3 oz (75 g) butter or margarine, softened
4 oz (125 g) self-raising flour, sifted
1 size-1 or size-2 egg, beaten
little milk

1   Preheat the oven to gas 4/350°F/180°C.
2   Arrange the apples in the bottom of a 1½ pt (1 litre) pie dish and sprinkle over them the lemon rind and juice, the sugar and a dash of water (about 2 tablespoons).
3   In a bowl, cream the butter and sugar until light and fluffy. Now beat the egg in a little at a time, beating well after each addition.
4   Fold in flour, adding just enough milk to give a soft consistency. Spread over apples, ensuring it goes right to the edge all round.
5   Bake for 40 minutes. Check that the sponge is cooked through: if not, give it more baking time.

Variations
You could flavour the apples with ground cinnamon (1 level teaspoon) or cloves (2–3 whole cloves).

BATTER PUDDINGS

FRENCH CLAFOUTIS

Serves 6–8

This delightful pudding is nearly always made with cherries. In the old recipe books the dish is cooked with whole cherries, stones and all. Unless you have a cherry-stoning gadget I should just use canned cherries.

1½ lb (675 g) black cherries
3 size-1 or size-2 eggs
3 oz (75 g) plain white flour
3 oz (75 g) sugar (you may not need as much
    as this with canned fruit)
15 fl oz (450 ml) warm milk
knob of butter, plus more for greasing
rum and/or crème fraîche, to serve
    (optional)

1   You will need a buttered ovenproof dish big enough for the cherries to lie in a single layer. Preheat the oven to gas 7/425°F/220°C.
2   Rinse, dry and remove the stalks and stones from the cherries, if fresh; drain the cherries if canned.
3   Beat the eggs with a fork in a big jug. Whisk in first the flour and then the sugar. Pour this mixture gradually over the warm milk, whisking as you do.
4   Lay the cherries in the buttered dish and, after a final whisk, pour the batter over the cherries. Scatter flakes of butter all over the top.
5   Set the dish on a baking sheet and bake for 25–30 minutes. It is often served warm, with a drop of rum poured over each serving. It is also nice with crème fraîche.

Variations
I have had this same dish served within a pastry case. The flan was made with shortcrust and would have been put in the oven raw with the filling already in. Fresh apricots or thinly sliced fresh pears, flavoured with almonds, would be lovely in place of the apples.

YORKSHIRE BATTER PUDDING

Makes 12 small puddings

It was not until I came to live in Yorkshire that I heard of sweet Yorkshire puddings. The puddings themselves were made in the usual way, but served with a sweet sauce.

4 oz (125 g) strong plain flour
pinch of salt
1 size-1 egg
10 fl oz (300 ml) milk
white vegetable fat

1   Preheat the oven to gas 7/425°F/220°C.
2   In a large jug, whisk together all the ingredients. A hand-held electric whisk is a great energy-saver. Keep whisking until bubbles appear on the surface and the batter is smooth. (Many people like to leave the batter standing at this point, but I cannot say that I have noticed much difference.)
3   Put a small piece of fat in the base of 12 deep pattie tins. Put them in the oven until they get very hot indeed.
4   Give the batter one last whisk and half-fill each tin.
5   Bake for about 30 minutes, until the puddings are risen and crisp.
6   Serve with a sweet sauce.

Suggestions for sweet sauces:
Melted jam sharpened with lemon juice was popular long ago.
A fresh fruit sauce would be good, e.g. lightly cooked and sweetened fresh apricots liquidized or liquidized and sweetened fresh raspberries.
Golden syrup melted with lemon juice and a tiny amount of water.

NORMANDY APPLE BATTER

Serves 6–8

1½ lb (675 g) crisp eating apples
1½ oz (40 g) butter
1 tablespoon vegetable oil
1 tablespoon sugar
small glass of apple spirit, such as Calvados,
    or brandy
icing sugar, to dust
chilled single cream, to serve

Batter
3 oz (75 g) plain flour
3 size-3 eggs
10 fl oz (300 ml) rich milk

1   Preheat the oven to gas4/350°F/180°C. You will need a fairly shallow ovenproof gratin dish.
2   Peel, core and slice the apples, but not too thinly.
3   Mix the butter and oil in a frying pan. Heat it up and fry the apple slices briefly. Do not let them disintegrate.
4   Arrange the lightly cooked apples in the gratin dish. They do look better if you set them overlapping in a neat pattern. Sprinkle over the sugar.
5   Deglaze the buttery frying pan with the glass of Calvados or brandy and pour these juices all over the apples. Allow to cool.
6   Make the batter: using an electric whisk if you can, beat together the flour, eggs and milk until the mixture is very smooth. Pour this over the apples.
7   Set the dish on a baking sheet and bake for about 1 hour, or until the batter is set. Sprinkle with a spoonful of icing sugar knocked through the sieve and serve with chilled single cream.

FRUIT FRITTERS

For about 8 pieces

Dipped in a light batter and deep-fried in fresh oil, fruit fritters are delicious – especially with a scoop of good ice-cream.

This simple batter works well. I have tried different, more elaborate, batters without much success – with and without oil, with and without egg white.

Batter
4 oz (125 g) white self-raising flour
2 teaspoons caster sugar, plus more for dusting

1   Whisk the flour and sugar together with 6 fl oz (200 ml) water until the batter is smooth and creamy.

Suggestions for Fruit to Fry
Banana, peeled and cut into chunks.
Apple, peeled, cored and cut into thick slices.
Dates are particularly nice with a crunchy outside.
Pineapple, fresh is best of all, cut in slices, but canned pineapple is good too, though it must be drained and dried properly.

Check that the fruit to be fried is dried on kitchen paper. Use fresh oil which has not been used for anything else.

1   Heat some sunflower oil for deep-frying.
2   Lower the chunks of fruit in the batter on the end of a skewer, draw out, allow to drip for a second, then carefully drop into the hot oil. Fry in batches of just 4 pieces at a time.
3   Drain on kitchen paper and dust with caster sugar. Eat as soon as possible. They go soft very quickly.

CRÊPES SUZETTES

In the *Farmhouse Kitchen* books for our TV programme all recipes got their English name and no French names were allowed, so Crêpes Suzettes became Orange Pancakes!

They are, however, very special pancakes. They are not very fast if you have to do a stack, so I have two 6 in (15 cm) iron frying pans on the go at once. They are only used for pancakes and mine now have a good non-stick finish.

To serve the pancakes, I use another frying pan – this time cast-iron with a non-stick finish. This is brought to the table with the brandy still burning with a blue flame and the pancakes sitting in a delicious sauce.

Pancake Batter
4 oz (125 g) plain flour, sifted
pinch of salt
2 size-1 or size-2 eggs
10 fl oz (300 ml) milk and water mixed
1 oz (25 g) caster sugar
grated zest from 1 small orange
little white vegetable fat
knob of butter

Sauce
¼ pt (150 ml) orange juice
1 oz (25 g) caster sugar
grated rind from 1 small orange
grated rind and juice from 1 small lemon
3 tablespoons orange liqueur (Cointreau or
    Grand Marnier)
2 oz (50 g) butter
2 tablespoons brandy, for flaming

1   An electric whisk takes the hard work out of pancakes, so sieve flour into a large jug (I use a 3 pt (1.75 litre) microwave plastic jug).
2   Add all the other pancake ingredients and whisk until you have a smooth thinnish batter. The first pancake will tell you if the batter is too thick or too thin. (I usually keep a fork in the jug with the batter so that I can give the batter a quick whisk before every pancake.)
3   Melt about 3 oz (75 g) white vegetable fat in a small pouring jug and add a knob of butter to melt in it as well.

4   Now heat your pan and pour in a little melted fat. Swirl this around to coat the pan and pour the excess back into the jug. Turn the heat down to moderate, then pour a little batter into the pan. Swirl this mixture round by lifting the pan by the handle. There should be just enough batter to cover the pan with a thin film. The fat should sizzle as the batter hits the hot pan. Cook the pancake briefly until the surface bubbles. Flip the pancake over with a small egg slice and cook for a minute on the other side. Actually you do not really need to cook the pancake on both sides. If it is thin enough, cooking one side only will be fine.
5   Stack the pancakes on top of each other on a plate sitting over a pan of simmering water. Cover them with foil as well.

Making the sauce
1   Put all the ingredients except the brandy in a large frying pan and allow to heat through gently.
2   Now fold each pancake in two, then over again to make a triangle. Set these triangles in a overlapping circle round the pan with the sauce. Tip the pan so that the sauce gets into and over the pancakes. Heat up again very gently.
3   To flame the hot pancakes (and they must be hot) put the brandy in a metal ladle and hold this over a candle to heat up. Tip the brandy gently to the edge of the ladle bowl and it should light up. If it doesn't it means that the brandy is not hot enough. Once it is flaming, pour the brandy over the pancakes in the frying pan and serve as soon as the flames have died down. You can do the flaming bit at the table but, as a precaution, have a large mat down to protect the cloth and the table in case of accidents.

CHURROS

Serves about 6

I had my first *churros* in a seaside fairground near San Sebastian in Spain. Sprinkled with sugar, they were crunchy and addictive. The stallholder operated a dangerous-looking system. The sweet batter was piped in a huge fat spiral on an iron plate. This plate was fixed to a chain contraption which lowered the plate into a vat of boiling oil. It was most impressive – out came the plate with a huge spiral of churros which were swiftly cut into sticks and dredged with sugar for the queue.

8 oz (225 g) plain white flour
1 tablespoon vegetable oil
pinch of salt
1 teaspoon sugar
¼ teaspoon lemon essence
sunflower oil, for frying
caster sugar, for dusting

1   Sieve the flour on to a piece of greaseproof paper.
2   Put the oil and 1 pt (600 ml) water, the salt, sugar and essence in a pan and bring it slowly to a boil. Tip all the flour into the water at once. Turn the heat down low. Beat the mixture until it turns into a smooth, shiny and very thick paste. Leave this to cool down for about 10 minutes.
3   Fit a ½ in (1 cm) star or plain icing tube into a strong icing bag. Beat the thick batter again and if it is too stiff add a little more water.
4   Heat the oil to a depth of about 3 in (7.5 cm) in a not-too-deep pan. Pipe the batter in lengths straight into the hot oil (this is not easy if your pan is too deep or narrow) and fry briefly until brown and crisp. Lift out with a perforated spoon and drain on kitchen paper.
5   Dredge with caster sugar and serve. It is easier if two people do the frying bit. A pair of scissors to chop off the batter is another help.

MAPLE SYRUP PANCAKES

Serves 6

Sometimes called French pancakes, these are baked on saucer tins or saucers if you do not possess the small shallow baking tins used usually for curd or ground rice tarts.

1 small lemon
15 fl oz (450 ml) milk
2 oz (50 g) butter, softened, plus more for greasing and to serve
2 oz (50 g) caster sugar
2 size-1 or size-2 eggs, beaten
4 oz (125 g) plain flour
6 tablespoons maple syrup, to serve
2 tablespoons lemon juice

1   Preheat the oven to gas5/375°F/190°C. Liberally butter 6 small baking tins or old saucers.
2   Using a swivel-bladed potato peeler, take the peel from the lemon, avoiding the white pith, or use a sharp knife and peel it like an apple.
3   Put the peel in a pan with the milk and heat gently for about 10 minutes. Then set aside to cool.
4   In a large bowl, cream the butter and sugar until pale. Beat in the eggs a little at a time, adding a spoonful of flour if the mixture looks as if it is separating.
5   Gradually stir in the flour and the flavoured milk. Continue beating until you have a smooth consistency.
6   Divide the mixture between the saucers and bake for about 15–20 minutes.
7   Serve with maple syrup, with the lemon juice added to cut the sweetness. You could also dilute the syrup very slightly with water if you find it too strong.

RHUBARB STIRABOUT

Serves 2–3

This is a very nice name and the method of making the batter is very different. You can use other fruit such as plums, but cut them quite small.

2 oz (50 g) soft butter or margarine, plus
    more for greasing
4 oz (125 g) plain flour
2 oz (50 g) caster sugar
1 size-1 or size-2 eggs, beaten
¼ pt (150 ml) milk
10 oz (275 g) early forced rhubarb
icing sugar, to dredge

1   Preheat the oven to gas7/425°F/220°C. Grease a 1½ pt (1 litre) pie dish.
2   Rub the butter or margarine into the flour, as if you were making pastry. Stir in the sugar.
3   Whisk the egg into the milk and gradually stir this into the butter and sugar mixture to make a fairly stiff batter.
4   Top and tail the rhubarb. Wipe the stalks, then chop into small pieces. Stir these into the batter. Add just a little more milk if needed to make the batter pour.
5   Pour the batter into the pie dish, set on a baking sheet and bake for about 30 minutes.
6   Dredge the top with icing sugar to serve.

"'No business before breakfast, Glum!" says the King. "Breakfast first, business next."'

The Rose and the Ring, William Makepeace Thackeray

MILK PUDDINGS

All milk puddings can be reduced in fat content by using skimmed or
semi-skimmed milk. Sugar too can be replaced, especially in the boiled puddings,
by adding artificial sugar substitute at the end of cooking time when the
pudding has cooled down a bit.

RICE BOILED & EATEN WITH STEWED FRUIT

Serves 4–6

Creamy boiled rice pudding is not often made
now, but it has one big advantage in that it
takes much less time to cook than the famous
baked rice pudding. It does have a drawback in
that you must stay in the kitchen with it and
stir often. Use pudding rice with a round grain.

1½ oz (40 g) rice
1 pt (600 ml) milk, plus extra if necessary
1 oz (25 g) sugar, or more to taste

1   Put the ingredients in a pan and stew gently
for about 25–30 minutes. Test the grain, adding
more milk if necessary.
2   Taste for sugar; you may like a sweeter finish.

Stewed Fruit
Most kinds of stewed fruit go with rice. Prunes
used to be a great favourite in school and they
can be excellent. I prefer the big fat ones from
California, stewed until really soft.

Jam
A good spoonful of high-quality sharp jam, like
blackcurrant or damson, is delicious.

Variation
Fat black raisins tossed into the rice for about 10
minutes before the end of cooking.
A lovely vanilla flavour goes well with creamy
rice. Put a whole vanilla pod in while cooking
the rice. Afterward, remove, wash and dry the
pod for future use.

RICE BOILED & GRILLED TO SIMULATE BAKED RICE

Once the rice is soft and creamy, turn it into a
heatproof dish and slide it under a hot grill.
Watch carefully until it is golden – it is not
quite as good as on a baked pudding, but it
isn't bad at all.

TRADITIONAL BAKED RICE PUDDING

Serves 6

I remember reading somewhere that Simpson's
in the Strand baked their famous rice pudding
over two days!

1½ oz (40 g) round-grain pudding rice
1–1½ oz (35–40 g) caster sugar
1 pt (575 ml) milk, plus extra if necessary
knob of butter

1   Preheat the oven to gas3/325°F/160°C.
2   Put all the ingredients uncovered in a
heatproof oven dish and place in the slow oven to
bubble gently for 2 hours.
3   During the first hour, stir twice to prevent a
skin forming.
4   During the last hour, slide a fork under the
skin to move the pudding round a bit. Add a
little more milk if necessary. The finished rice

should not be stiff, but moist and creamy.

Variations

Unrefined soft brown sugar gives a caramel
flavour to the rice.
Vanilla extract – just 2 or 3 drops – is very good.
Grated nutmeg added at the beginning of
cooking is liked by some.

MILLIONAIRE'S RICE PUDDING

Serves 6

A simple luxurious variation on the basic recipe.

2 oz (50 g) round-grain pudding rice
thinly cut rind of 1 small lemon
7 fl oz (200 ml) double cream
1½ oz (40 g) caster sugar
grated chocolate, to decorate

1   Boil the rice with the lemon rind in plenty of
water.
2   When the grains are soft, strain off the rice
and rinse it with cold water. Set the rice to go
cold in the fridge.
3   Whip the cream with the sugar until it is at
the floppy stage. Fold into the rice and pour into
small individual dishes.
4   Decorate with chocolate.

Note

Do not fold the cream into the rice until a couple
of hours before serving. The rice will otherwise
start to expand again and soak up the cream. It
will taste fine, but does not look as good as with
the separate grains.

MILLIONAIRE'S RICE PUDDING WITH FRUIT

Serves 6

2½ oz (65 g) round-grain pudding rice
1 pt (575 ml) milk, plus more if necessary
1 vanilla pod
1½ oz (40 g) caster sugar
1 rounded teaspoon powdered gelatine
2 tablespoons orange juice
1 small firm-textured dessert apple
3 oz (75 g) firm red strawberries
3 tablespoons double cream

Sauce
13 oz (275 g) strawberries
½ oz (15 g) caster sugar

1   Simmer the rice and milk in a roomy pan
until the rice is soft and creamy. Add more milk
if needed.
2   Stir in the sugar and allow to go cold.
3   Sprinkle the gelatine over the orange juice in a
little cup or jug. Allow the gelatine about 3
minutes to swell, then stand the cup in a pan of hot
water and heat and stir until the gelatine melts. Stir
this gelatine mixture into the cooled rice.
4   Peel and core the apple and cut into small
dice. Chop the strawberries up into small pieces.
Add the fruit to the rice mixture and stir gently.
5   Whip the cream to the floppy stage and fold
that into the rice and fruit. Pour into a glass dish
or individual glass dishes and put in a cool place
to set.
6   Make the sauce: hull the strawberries and
liquidize with a stick blender or a food processor.
Stir in sugar to taste and chill.
7   Serve both the rice and sauce very cold.

Variation

Instead of the apple and strawberries, add about
1½ oz (40 g) raisins plumped up with rum or
fruit liqueur (a tablespoon of rum or liqueur is
about enough). A few seconds in a microwave in
a spoonful of water will help to soften the
raisins quickly, then drain off the water and add
the alcohol.

GROUND RICE PUDDING

Serves 4–6

In old recipe books this is often given as a baked pudding. The ground rice is simmered in the usual way then, when it is thick, a beaten egg is stirred in and the whole lot poured into a baking dish and set in the oven to brown. I find this ends up very heavy and stodgy. I much prefer the simple boiled and sweetened ground rice poured over stewed fruit. Stewed plums are particularly nice.

Like most milk puddings it takes time to thicken and it should be stirred frequently. If the ground rice has to stand for some time it will form a thick skin on top. It is easier to lift this off than to try to beat it in again.

1 pt (575 ml) milk
2 oz (40 g) ground rice
1 oz (25 g) caster sugar

1   Bring the milk and ground rice to a boil. Turn down the heat, stir often and simmer until the mixture is thick. Add more milk if the mixture gets too stiff.
2   Stir in the sugar and serve.

MICROWAVE PACKET CUSTARD

Serves 4–6

This simply made custard is easily cooked in a jug in the microwave for 6 minutes. I use a very large 3 pt (1.75 litre) plastic jug with a rounded inside base. I whisk the custard with a 75p loop-headed whisk and the rounded base of the jug means that the custard powder does not escape the whisk.

1 pt (575 ml) milk
2 heaped dessertspoons custard powder
1 tablespoon sugar

1   Put the cold milk in the jug first, followed by the custard powder and sugar. Whisk thoroughly and set in the microwave on full power for 2 minutes.
2   Whisk and cook for 2 minutes again. Then repeat, making 3 whiskings and 6 minutes altogether.

Note
If this custard stands for any time it will form a skin. It is better to lift this off and discard it since it will not beat down smoothly again.

REAL POURING CUSTARD

Serves 4–6

Proper custard is made with egg yolks, vanilla and cream. Cook it in a double-boiler – that is one pan sitting on top of, or inside, a bottom pan in which the water is simmering. If you have not got such a thing you can suspend a heatproof bowl over a pan of simmering water. The bowl bottom should not touch the water.

The addition of a tiny bit of cornflour is not traditional, but it does help to stabilize the egg yolks and prevent the mixture separating. (If it starts to look granular it can be rescued if you take it off the heat and beat hard.) Some people never use a double boiler or the bowl. They simply cook the custard over just a thread of heat, stirring constantly. When you taste the custard you will know why it is worth all the bother.

10 fl oz (300 ml) whipping cream, plus
   more if necessary
3 size-1 or size-2 egg yolks
1 level tablespoon caster sugar
1 small teaspoon cornflour
2–3 drops of vanilla essence (the pure kind
   has a superior flavour)

1   Put the cream in a small pan and heat it almost to boiling.

2   In a roomy bowl, whisk together the egg
yolks, sugar, cornflour and vanilla until smooth.
3   Pour half of the very hot cream into the bowl.
Whisk it hard, then pour the whole lot back into
the pan. Start stirring at once.
4   Once the cream has thickened you will see
whether or not you need to add extra cream (or
milk) to get the right consistency.
5   This custard can be eaten hot or cold.

CRÈME ANGLAISE

Serves 6–8

This is 'THE' custard cream to go on top of a
trifle or in the bottom of tartlets topped with
fresh fruit.

6 size-1 or size-2 egg yolks
4 oz (125 g) caster sugar
1½ oz (40 g) plain white flour
1 teaspoon cornflour
1 pt (575 ml) milk
1 small teaspoon pure vanilla essence
icing sugar, to dust

1   Put the egg yolks in a roomy bowl with
1 tablespoon of the measured sugar. Whisk until
pale and thick.
2   Sift the flour and cornflour through a sieve
into the egg yolk mixture. Whisk this in
carefully but smoothly.
3   Put the remaining sugar, the milk and the
vanilla into a pan and bring to a boil. Pour about
one-third of the hot milk mixture over the egg
yolk and flour, whisking as you do this. Pour the
rest of the milk in as well.
4   Now pour this egg mixture into a clean pan.
Simmer and stir without stopping for about 2
minutes, or until the mixture thickens.
5   Pour into a bowl and sift some icing sugar
over the surface. This helps to prevent a skin
forming and can be stirred in later.

CRÈME CARAMEL

Makes 6

The normal way to cook these custards is in a
bain-marie in the oven (a roasting tin with
water halfway up the miniature soufflé dishes).
My oven was full one day, so I steamed them on
top of the stove with the lid on the steamer. It
was fine, but I could only cook 4 at a time.

4 oz (125 g) granulated sugar
1 pt (575 ml) milk
3 size-1 or size-2 eggs
2–3 drops of pure vanilla essence

1   Preheat the oven to gas4/350°F/180°C. You
will need 6 heatproof ramekin dishes sitting in a
roasting tin with hot water in it.
2   Make the caramel: put the sugar in a heavy-
based pan over a medium heat. Allow the sugar
to start to melt underneath, then start shaking
the sugar from side to side, lifting the pan off the
heat to do so. Eventually all the sugar will melt.
Pour a little into the bottom of each dish. Do not
use anything to stir the caramel, just shake.
3   Put the pan with the remains of the caramel
still in it back on the heat. Pour in the milk,
eggs and vanilla essence. Whisk until smooth.
Pour this slightly warm liquid into the 6
ramekins.
4   Set the roasting tin in the oven and bake
until the custards are set, about 40 minutes.
Leave to go cold. For maximum caramel liquid
leave in the fridge for 1 or 2 days. By this time
all the caramel will have melted.
5   To serve: run a thin-bladed knife round each
custard and shake it down into a pudding bowl
or plate. I prefer a bowl, but a plate does look
better.

CARDAMOM CUSTARD

Cardamom is a delicious unexpected flavour in this custard.

10 cardamom pods, left whole but split
1 pt (575 ml) milk, plus a little extra
3 size-1 or size-2 eggs
1½ -2 oz (40–50 g) caster sugar
pumpkin seeds, for sprinkling
crisp biscuits, to serve

1 Preheat the oven to gas4/350°F/180°C. You will need 6 heatproof ramekin dishes sitting in a roasting tin with hot water in it.
2 Crush the cardamom pods slightly and put them in a pan with the milk. Bring this slowly to the boil, then simmer for 2–3 minutes. Set aside to go cold and to allow the cardamom flavour to infuse the milk.
3 Strain off the milk and top up to the 1 pt (575 ml) mark again. Warm the milk briefly and whisk in the eggs (I use a rotary whisk) and the sugar.
4 Now pour the custard into the 6 dishes. Set them in a roasting tin with hot water halfway up the sides. Bake for about 40 minutes or until the custard is set.
5 Allow to go cold and serve sprinkled with pumpkin seeds and accompanied by a crisp biscuit.

SEMOLINA PUDDING

Serves 4–6

1½ oz (40 g) semolina
pinch of salt
1 pt (575 ml) milk
1 dessertspoon caster sugar
stewed fruit or jam, to serve

1 In a medium-size bowl, mix the semolina and salt with some of the cold milk.
2 Boil the rest of the milk and pour about ¼ pt (150 ml) of the hot milk on to the semolina. Whisk, then tip that mixture back into the pan. Stir in the sugar.
3 Stirring all the time, cook the semolina until it is thick and soft. Spoon it out into small bowls and serve at once with stewed fruit or jam.

ORANGE SEMOLINA

Serves 4–6

1½ oz (40 g) semolina
pinch of salt
1 pt (575 ml) milk
1 dessertspoon caster sugar
2 tablespoons concentrated orange juice
    (the kind you dilute with water)
2 oz (50 g) dark chocolate, grated
grated rind from ½ small orange

1 Follow the instructions as in the recipe above, up to the end of step 2.
2 Stirring all the time, cook the semolina until it is thick and soft. Stir in the concentrated orange juice.
3 Pour into individual glass dishes and allow to go cold. Sprinkle with the mixed grated chocolate and orange zest.

CHOCOLATE RICE

Serves 6

1½ oz (40 g) round-grain pudding rice
1 pt (575 ml) milk, plus more if necessary
1 oz (25 g) sugar, or more to taste
5 oz (150 g) good–quality plain chocolate
1 tablespoon Crème de Cacao
½ pt (300 ml) double cream (at room
  temperature)
1 dessertspoon drinking chocolate powder

1   Simmer the rice in the milk until very tender
and creamy, adding extra milk if necessary. It is
important to keep stirring the rice while it is
cooking. Stir in sugar and set aside to cool.
2   Spoon the rice into 6 small glass pudding
dishes.
3   Break the chocolate into small pieces and
melt it in a large bowl. Stir in the Crème de
Cacao and the double cream. Whip the mixture
to the floppy stage, then divide between the
glasses. Smooth over and sprinkle with the
drinking chocolate.
4   Serve chilled.

INDIAN CARROT DESSERT

Serves 6

This unusual dessert is so rich that you could
not eat much more than would fit into a tiny
custard or coffee cup.

1 lb (450 g) fresh juicy carrots, scraped and
  finely grated
2 oz (50 g) cashew nuts, coarsely chopped
4 oz (125 g) caster sugar
1¼ pt (750 ml) milk
7 cardamom pods
3 oz (75 g) ghee or butter

1   In a large pan, put the carrots, cashew nuts,
sugar and milk. Heat until the sugar dissolves,
then lower the heat and go on cooking and
stirring every now and then until almost all the
liquid has been absorbed or evaporated.
2   While this is cooking, take the seeds out of
the cardamom pods and crush these in a mortar
with a pestle.
3   When the milk has all but been absorbed, melt
the ghee or butter in a clean pan. Stir in the carrot
mixture and cook, stirring, for just 2–3 minutes.
Stir in the cardamom grounds and serve warm.

BLANCMANGE

Serves 6

The word blancmange means just one thing to me – a white rabbit. I expect this was one way to get a reluctant child to eat a milk pudding. I dare say the one I remember came out of a packet. This recipe is a world away from a packet blancmange. You will need a 1 pt (575 ml) jelly mould or a rabbit mould or 6 small glass pudding dishes.

½ pt (300 ml) milk
4 oz (125 g) ripe red strawberries, plus 6 extra
1–2 drops of vanilla essence
1–2 drops of pink or red food colouring (optional)
1 sachet of powdered gelatine
4 oz (125 g) caster sugar
¼ pt (150 ml) single cream

1 Put the milk into a big jug or bowl.
2 Hull the strawberries, chop them up a bit and drop into the milk.
3 Liquidize the strawberries, milk and vanilla essence with a stick blender. Drop in 1–2 drops of food colouring if you wish and blend again. Set this jug or bowl aside.
4 Put ¼ pt (150 ml) water into a small bowl. Sprinkle the gelatine over and allow to stand for a couple of minutes. Now set the bowl in a pan of gently simmering water and stir until the gelatine melts. Stir in the sugar until it has dissolved as well.
5 Now pour this gelatine and sugar mixture into the flavoured milk along with the cream. Blend this briefly and pour into a wetted mould or into 6 individual glass dishes and set aside to go cold.
6 Serve with a perfect strawberry sliced on top of each portion.

STRAWBERRIES & SEMOLINA

Serves 6

I was in a very grand restaurant and this is what was on the dessert menu. It sounded odd but I had to find out what it was. I have had to guess at the semolina bit, but it was wonderful.

½ pt (300 ml) milk
8 cardamom pods
1¼ oz (35 g) semolina
1 oz (50 g) sugar, plus more for sprinkling
¼ pt (150 ml) single cream
1 sachet of gelatine powder
1 lb (450 g) ripe strawberries

1 You will need 6 dariole moulds (little metal shapes like plant-pots) or 6 small ramekins and 6 greaseproof paper circles, one for each mould.
2 First flavour the milk: put it into a pan with the shelled and lightly crushed cardamom seeds. Bring this to a boil. Turn off the heat and put on a lid. Leave to infuse for 30 minutes.
3 Strain off the milk. Add the semolina and sugar and cook gently until the semolina starts to get thick. Stir in the cream and set this mixture aside.
4 Put ¼ pt (150 ml) of water in a small bowl and sprinkle the gelatine over. Leave it to soak for a couple of minutes, then set the bowl in a pan of simmering water. Stir until the gelatine melts. Pour this mixture into the semolina and stir well. Pour into the moulds and leave to set in the fridge.
5 Hull the strawberries and put one half of them in a bowl and liquidize these with just a sprinkling of sugar, using a stick blender or a food processor. Pour the strawberry sauce into a glass jug. Cut the rest of the strawberries in quarters and divide between 6 flat plates.
6 When the semolina towers are set and chilled run a thin knife blade round each mould to release – one on each plate. Peel off the greaseproof paper and serve with the strawberry sauce trickling down one side of the semolina tower and over the strawberries.

FRUIT PUDDINGS & DESSERTS

PIES AND TARTS GALORE

The traditional deep British fruit pie has a top and bottom crust. These can be made several ways:

In a straight-sided flan tin – usually about 8–9 in (20/23 cm) across and 1½ –2 in (2.5–5 cm) deep.

In a pie tin with sloping sides and about the same size.

On a flat baking sheet – providing the filling is not too juicy you can make a pie on the flat by piling up the filling and sealing the pastry tightly round it.

The amount of pastry needed for a pie of the dimensions above is 8 oz (225 g). The quantity of filling needed is about 1½ lb (675 g) to fill the pie.

Note

All pies with a bottom crust should sit in the oven on a preheated metal baking sheet. The heat from this helps to cook this bottom layer of pastry quickly. The sheet goes in when the oven is switched on for preheating. It is also much easier to lift a pie in and out of an oven if it is on a baking tray.

TRADITIONAL DOUBLE-CRUST APPLE PIE

Serves 6–8

8 oz (225 g) Shortcrust Pastry (see page 16)
milk or milk and beaten egg, to glaze
caster sugar, to glaze

Filling
1½ lb (675 g) Bramley apples
1 oz (25 g) caster sugar
lemon juice, to taste (about 1 tablespoon)

1 Preheat the oven to gas6/400°F/200°C and put a metal baking sheet in to heat up.
2 Make the pastry and let it rest for 30 minutes in a plastic bag. This helps to make the pastry more elastic and less liable to shrink.
3 Prepare the fruit while the pastry is resting: peel and core the apples and chop into cherry-sized pieces. Stew in a pan with the sugar and 2 tablespoons water. Do not fully cook the apples, just enough to get some juices out. Set aside to go cold.
4 Now grease the tin thoroughly. Divide the pastry in two and roll one half out on a lightly floured board roughly to fit the tin. Lift the rolled pastry on your rolling pin and set down in the middle. Ease into position, pushing the sides well down so that you have very little to trim away.
5 Now transfer the fruit to the pie tin. Use a perforated spoon to do this or set the apple in a nylon sieve and allow the juice to drain off.
6 Roll out the rest of the pastry into a circle to fit the pie. You might have a pan lid to act as a giant cutter or a round plate to use as a pattern. Wet the upper edge of the bottom crust and the under edge of the pastry lid. Cover the pie and seal the edges securely by fluting the pastry all round or pressing a fork down all round the edge.
7 Brush the top with milk or milk and egg and dust with sugar. Make a steam vent in the centre.
8 Set the pie on the hot baking sheet and bake for about 30 minutes.

Variations

The pastry can be any variation on shortcrust, such as rich shortcrust or wholemeal shortcrust. Apples mix happily with cloves – 4 or 5 whole cloves would be plenty stirred in with the fruit. Cinnamon is also lovely with apples – about 1 level teaspoon would be enough mixed in with the apples.

Raisins are often added to apples – 3 oz (75 g) would be enough.

Apple & Blackberry Tart is a classic combination – 1 lb (450 g) apples with ½ lb (225 g) blackberries. Cranberry & Apple Tart is another good pairing – 1 lb (450 g) apples with ½ lb (225 g) cranberries. Cranberries are very tart so check the flavour.

Mincemeat & Apple mincemeat is sweet, so I suggest 1¼ lb (550 g) apples plus ¼ lb (125 g) mincemeat. (Do not cook the mincemeat, but just stir it into the drained apple.)

Rhubarb: because rhubarb 'falls' so much during cooking (especially the early forced rhubarb) you will need 2½ lb (1.1 kg) to start with. Stew briefly, drain and sweeten to taste.

Rhubarb and Ginger Tart is particularly nice. Use about 1 heaped teaspoon of ground ginger. Put this in to stew with the fruit, then strain as before, then sweeten.

Plums: stew plums in order to get the stones out. Drain the fruit thoroughly then sweeten to taste.

Blueberries: these are much more readily available than they used to be. Stew briefly and drain well, then sweeten the fruit to taste.

Apricots: use fresh or dried fruit. Stones have to be removed from the fresh fruit and the dried fruit needs soaking and stewing.

FLANS

One crust only and that is, of course, the bottom one. These, are nearly always pre-baked – 'baked blind' is the correct term. The crust can be either pastry or crushed biscuit. They are often baked in the same tins as described earlier for double crust pies, 8–9 in (20–23 cm) across and 1½ –2 in (2.5–5 cm) deep. A loose-bottomed tin is a big advantage. Other flans are now often baked like the French open tarts in big, very shallow fluted tins about 10 in (25 cm) across.

On the whole pastry is usually richer for an open flan. It is baked in the usual way, with a lining of foil topped with dried or ceramic beans. Baked until golden, then the foil and beans are removed and the flan given 5 more minutes in the oven.

The crème pâtissière which goes in the bottom of these flans is very rich. However, once this is made it is easy to assemble the flan.

CRÈME PÂTISSIÈRE

Enough for 3 small flans

4 size-1 or size-2 eggs, plus 2 extra yolks
8 oz (225 g) caster sugar
2 oz (50 g) plain white Flour
18 fl oz (650 ml) milk
2–3 drops of pure vanilla essence

1   Put the eggs plus the egg yolks in a large bowl with about 2 oz (50 g) of the measured sugar. Whisk hard until the mixture is pale and fluffy.
2   Sift the flour through a sieve and into the bowl. Whisk this in thoroughly.
3   Bring the milk and the remaining sugar to a boil and pour this on the egg mixture with one hand and whisking hard as you go.
4   Pour this hot mixture into a clean pan, bring to the boil over a gentle heat and cook for a couple of minutes, or until thickened.
5   Then stir in the vanilla and pour into another bowl. Leave to go cold.

Fruit

This is when your imagination and artistic flair can go mad. Spoon the rich cream into the base of the flan (having first put it on a flat serving dish). The raw ripe fruit goes on top of the cream and a glaze goes on top of the fruit. Any mixture of fruit is good and colours are important too.

Raspberries: see that you use the ripest fruit you can find and set the berries close together.

Strawberries: they sit better if they have been halved and are very ripe and juicy.

Pears: fresh and very juicy slices are lovely, but they do need to be brushed in lemon juice to prevent them discolouring. Toasted flaked almonds scattered over pears look and taste good.

Apricots: stew them carefully and drain well or use canned fruit. Fresh apricots tend to collapse but their flavour is very much better than any others.

Peaches: a bit like apricots for going very soft. The newer canned ones in their own juice are excellent.

Glaze

Strained apricot jam or melted redcurrant jelly
are both used to brush over the fruit on an open
flan. This gives a shine and also adds sweetness.
Apricot jam: warm the jam by standing the open
jar in a pan of water. Now sieve out the pieces of
fruit and you will be left with the glaze.
Redcurrant jelly: again stand the open jar in a
pan of water to melt the jelly or scoop out 2 or
3 tablespoons and heat carefully in a small pan.

Use a soft brush to glaze the tarts then leave
to set.

HONEYED PIE

Serves 6–8

You make this pie flat on a greased baking sheet.

8 oz (225 g) Shortcrust Pastry (see page 16)

Filling
4 oz (125 g) honey
1 oz (25 g) butter, plus more for greasing
6 oz (175 g) currants (look for Vostizza currants
   – they are tiny and virtually seedless)
1 oz (25 g) mixed peel, chopped
1 oz (25 g) ground almonds
1 oz (50 g) whole almonds, chopped

grated rind of 1 lemon plus 2 tablespoons
   lemon juice
1 teaspoon mixed spice
1 tablespoon milk
caster sugar, for sprinkling
flour, for dusting

1   Preheat the oven to gas6/400°F/200°C and
grease a baking sheet.
2   Divide the pastry into two and roll one half out
on a floured board to a circle about 7 in (17.5 cm)
across. You may be able to use a plate or a cake tin
as a template. Lay this on the pastry and cut round.
3   Lay the pastry circle on the greased baking
sheet. From the trimmings, cut a ½ in (1 cm)
strip (you may have some joins) to go all round the
outside edge of the pastry circle. Wet the edges
first so that the narrow strip will stick. This strip
is just an added seal to keep the juices in the pie.
4   For the filling: soften the honey and butter in
a good sized pan and stir in the rest of the
ingredients, except the milk and caster sugar. Set
the filling aside until it is cold.
5   Pile the fruity filling on the pastry base
neatly, then roll out another circle of pastry. Wet
the upper side of the sealing strip and set the lid
over the pie. Press the edges together and trim
off any excess pastry. Flute the pastry edge by
nipping the pastry upwards at regular intervals
to make a decorative edge.
6   Brush over the pie with milk. Make a steam
vent on the top and scatter some caster sugar over.
7   Bake for 25–30 minutes until brown.

LINZERTORTE

Serves 6

This very famous Austrian recipe sounds more like a glamourous gâteau than a pastry flan filled with cranberry jam. The reason for its popularity is that the pastry is made with nuts and this rich taste is a perfect foil for the sharp jam. You can use ground almonds, walnuts or hazelnuts for the pastry. Named after the town of Linz, elaborately made lattice-work 'lids' were used for the torte, looking like a many-petalled flower. Other filling suggestions are raspberry or redcurrant jam. I am using a much more simple lattice top.

Rich Ground Almond Pastry
7 oz (200 g) plain white flour
2 oz (50 g) icing sugar, plus more for
    dusting
1 level teaspoon cocoa
¼ teaspoon ground cinnamon
5 oz (150 g) butter, cut into small pieces
3 oz (75 g) ground almonds
1 size-1 or size-2 egg, beaten
1–2 drops of real almond essence
1 tablespoon Kirsch
1 egg yolk, beaten, to glaze
little milk, to glaze
icing sugar, to dust

Filling
7 oz (200 g) fresh cranberries
2 wide strips of zest from a lemon
4 oz (125 g) granulated sugar

1   First make the pastry: sift the flour, icing sugar, cocoa and cinnamon into a large bowl.
2   Stir in the butter and rub into the mixture until it all looks like damp breadcrumbs. Stir in the almonds.
3   Whisk the egg lightly. Stir in the almond essence and the Kirsch. Now using a long-bladed knife, stir and mix the egg into the pastry and bring together. If the mixture is dry, add a tiny amount of water. Sprinkle the dough with flour, wrap it in a plastic bag and set aside for 45 minutes to rest.

4   While the pastry is resting, make the jam filling: put the fruit, lemon zest and 4½ fl oz (135 ml) water in a pan. Bring to the boil, cover and turn down to a simmer for 10 minutes. Stir often and watch that it does not burn. Check that the fruit is soft, if not give it a few more minutes. Stir in the sugar. When it has dissolved, take the pan off the heat and set it aside to go cold. Remove the lemon zest.
5   To assemble the flan: you will need a loose-bottomed flan tin about 9 in (23 cm) across and with shallow sides. Butter this very thoroughly, especially if the tin is fluted. Preheat the oven to gas5/375°F/190°C. Set a baking sheet in the oven.
6   First cut off and set aside a piece of dough weighing about 4 oz (125 g) for the lattice top.
7   Roll the rest of the dough out to a big circle, about 10 in (25 cm) across. Lift on your rolling pin and drop in the centre of the tin. Spread out and work pastry up the sides of the tin with your fingers. It may break, but just patch it up by pushing the pastry together again. Try to get the pastry up and over the rim of the tin slightly.
8   Now spread the jam filling over the base of the flan. You may not want all of it but whatever you do, set aside 1 tablespoon to be used later.
9   Now roll out the rest of the pastry and cut out narrow strips of about ½ in (1 cm) wide. If you have a pastry roller which gives a fancy edge, so much the better. Aim to have at least 6 strips which will stretch across the widest part of the flan. Now lay the strips in a lattice pattern across the jam as neatly as you can. If you have the patience to basket-weave the pastry this looks good. Mix the egg yolk with a drop of milk and brush the underside edge of each strip of pastry to stick it to the sides of the flan.
10 Neaten the top edge of the flan either with an even narrower strip of pastry to go right round and on top of the lattice ends or just take a fork and press it all the way round. Take a narrow brush and go over all the lattice work with the egg yolk and milk mixture.
11 Set the flan on the baking sheet in the oven for about 30 minutes. Keep a close eye on it, because nut pastry soon burns.
12 Once the flan is out of the oven take the reserved jam filling and dot a little into each space between the lattice work. Serve warm and with a decorative dusting of icing sugar.

WET NELLIE

Serves 6–8

The other name for this Liverpudlian speciality is Lord Nelson Cake. It is very sweet unless you are generous with the lemon juice.

8 oz (225 g) Shortcrust Pastry (see page 16)
8 oz (225 g) cake crumbs (from a Madeira
   cake or a sponge cake)
grated rind and juice from 1 lemon
3 oz (75 g) currants
4 oz (125 g) golden syrup, warmed
4 tablespoons milk
butter, for greasing
little milk, for glazing
caster sugar, for sprinkling

1 Preheat the oven to gas5/375°F/190°C. Set a baking sheet in the oven to heat up. Grease well an 8 in (18 cm) shallow sandwich tin.
2 Cut the pastry in two, roll one piece out and use to line the tin. Trim off any excess pastry.
3 Put the cake crumbs in a bowl with the lemon rind and currants and mix.
4 Put a small pan on your scales and pour the golden syrup into it, watching carefully for the 4 oz (125 g) mark to come up. Stir the lemon juice and milk into the syrup.
5 Add the crumb mixture to the syrup mixture. Stir well then pour into the pastry.
6 Roll out the rest of the pastry to form a lid, sealing the edges well by brushing with milk. Trim off any excess pastry, brush the top with milk and scatter some caster sugar over.
7 Set the pie on the hot baking sheet and bake for about 30-35 minutes or until brown.
8 Allow to cool down a bit before eating as the syrup stays very hot. In fact, I prefer this tart when it is served cold.

RICH LEMON TART

Serves 6

Look for lemons which have thin skins and feel heavy. The rock-hard giants rarely have as much juice.

Pastry
5 oz (150 g) plain white flour, plus more for dusting
3 oz (75 g) butter, plus more for greasing
1 oz (25 g) caster sugar

Filling
4 lemons
2 size-1 or size-2 eggs, plus 2 extra yolks (reserving the whites)
4 oz (125 g) caster sugar
¼ pt (150 ml) single cream

Decoration
julienne strips of lemon rind

crème fraîche, to serve (optional)

1   Preheat the oven to gas6/400°F/200°C and put a baking sheet in to heat up. Grease well an 8 in (20 cm) flan tin with a loose base.
2   Make the pastry by whizzing the flour, butter and caster sugar in a food processor. When the mixture looks like crumbs, turn down the speed a bit and dribble about a tablespoon of cold water into the machine while it is running. As soon as it has gathered into a lump, stop the machine. Scrape it out and, with a little flour, work it into a ball. Wrap in a plastic bag and set it aside to rest for 30 minutes.
3   While the pastry is resting, make the julienne of lemon rind for the decoration. Using one of the lemons, cut 2 large slices from it by standing the lemon on the stalk end and slicing one oval from each side. Squeeze and reserve the juice from the two ovals and the middle bit of the lemon. Cut the ovals into 2 rectangles, turn them over and, using the flat of a knife, slice off the white pith. Take care to keep the lemon peel whole. It does not matter if all the pith does not come away, as long as you have the lemon skin.

Now, with your sharpest knife, cut these rectangles into very fine strips. Put the lemon strips in a pan with ¼ pt (150 ml) water to cover. Add the 2 oz (50 g) caster sugar. Stir to dissolve it and simmer until the peel goes translucent. Set aside to go cold, then drain and pat dry the lemon rinds with kitchen paper.
4   Roll out the pastry on a lightly floured board and use to line the flan tin, taking care to ease the pastry into position without stretching it. Now line the flan case with a square of foil or greaseproof paper and fill it with baking beans.
5   Set the flan on the hot baking sheet and bake for about 20 minutes. Take the flan out of the oven, remove the foil and beans and brush the inside of the flan with the reserved egg white. Return the flan to the oven for just 5 minutes. Take it out and allow it to cool down. Turn the heat down to gas3/325°F/160°C.
6   Make the filling by grating the rind from 3 lemons, squeezing the juice from 2 of the lemons and adding to the juice from the first lemon.
7   Whisk the 2 eggs and 2 extra yolks with the sugar for 2 minutes, until pale and frothy. Whisk in the grated lemon rind, lemon juice and cream. Pour this filling into the pastry case (still in its tin).
8   Set the flan on the hot baking sheet and bake for about 30 minutes or until the lemon filling is just set. Allow to cool.
9   Serve the lemon tart with the lemon julienne scattered over the top and perhaps a spoonful of crème fraîche with each serving.

YORKSHIRE CURD TART

Serves 6–8

I live in Yorkshire, so when I have a visitor from far away I always make one of these tarts to show how very nice they can be. Curds used to be sold by the milkman and were easily bought in all the supermarkets. Nowadays I know that only at my local open market can I buy curds. However, it is an easy job to make your own curds using the method handed down for generations.

6 oz (175 g) Shortcrust Pastry (see page 16)

Homemade Curd
2 pt (1.2 litre) Channel-Island milk or gold-
    top
1 heaped teaspoon Epsom Salts

Filling
½ oz (15 g) butter, melted
1 oz (25 g) currants, plus extra for
    sprinkling
1 size-1 or size-2 egg, beaten
1 tablespoon golden syrup
1 tablespoon rum (optional)

1   Well ahead, make the curds: bring the milk
to a boil and stir in the salts.
2   Stir well and remove the pan from the heat.
The curds should start to form almost at once.
Leave to go cold. (Note: if this does not start to
separate, return the pan to the heat and add
another half teaspoon of Epsom salts.)
3   Drain the curds and rinse briefly under cold
water. You should have about 13 oz (375 g)
curds.
4   Preheat the oven to gas6/400°F/200°C and
place a baking sheet in the oven to heat up.
Grease a 7–8 in (18–20 cm) flan tin or flan ring
set on a greased baking sheet. (If you are using
the ring on a baking sheet you will not need the
hot sheet in the oven.)
5   Roll out the pastry on a lightly floured board
and line the flan tin with it. Trim off excess
pastry.
6   Make up the filling by first breaking up 8 oz
(225 g) of the curds (use the rest for breakfast
with honey) and then adding all the other filling
ingredients except the rum. Stir thoroughly and
pour the filling into the raw pastry flan. Scatter a
few extra currants over the surface.
7   Set the flan on the hot baking sheet and bake
for about 30 minutes, when the pastry should be
brown and the filling just set. Do not over-bake.
Eat on the same day, either hot or cold. Dribble
the tablespoon of rum over the freshly baked hot
filling, if you wish.

PEAR & GINGER PUFFS

Serves 4

You could make this tart with canned pears, but
they are not quite as nice as fresh ones.

4 large fat firm pears
4 oz (125 g) caster sugar
2 tablespoons vanilla essence
about 8 oz (225 g) frozen puff pastry, defrosted
2 fat knobs of crystallized ginger, plus 2
    tablespoons of the syrup
vanilla ice-cream, to serve
butter, for greasing

1   Preheat the oven to gas6/400°F/200°C and set
a baking sheet in it to heat up. Grease a 10 in
(25 cm) flan tin.
2   First, partially cook the pears: peel and cut
each pear in two. Remove the core. In a large pan
or deep frying pan big enough for the pear halves
to lie in one layer if possible, lay each cored pear
half flat and barely cover with water. Add the
sugar and the vanilla essence. Bring to a gentle
boil and simmer until the pears have softened
slightly, about 30 minutes unless your pears are
rock-hard and you will then have to continue
cooking. Drain the pears and set them aside.
3   Pour away about half of the sweetened water.
Boil the rest down to about 2 tablespoons. Stir in
the ginger syrup and set this aside for later.
4   Now roll out the pastry to a circle a little
bigger than the flan tin base. Lift the pastry on
to the flan tin. Turn the edges over towards the
centre to make a narrow border. Prick the pastry
all over the centre.
5   Set the drained and dried pears on the circle,
with the narrow bits towards the centre. Now
carefully slice the pears lengthwise into 4 slices,
taking care to avoid cutting the pastry.
6   Brush the reserved syrup over the pears. Set
the flan base on the hot baking sheet and bake
for about 20 minutes until the pastry is cooked
and well-risen.
7   Chop the crystallized ginger finely. Brush
over the tart again with the syrup, scatter the
ginger over the top and serve with a scoop of
vanilla ice-cream.

DRIED APRICOT PIE

Serves 4–6

Dried apricots often give an intensity of flavour which is sometimes missing in fresh ones. Soak them first overnight to cut down on the stewing time.

8 oz (225 g) Sweet Shortcrust (see page 17)
butter, for greasing

Filling
2 oz (50 g) caster sugar
8 oz (225 g) dried apricots, soaked
    overnight in cold water
2 cloves
1 in (2.5 cm) stick of cinnamon

Custard
2 size-1 or size-2 eggs
2 oz (50 g) caster sugar
10 fl oz (300 ml) milk, warmed
4 fl oz (100 ml) Cointreau

1   Preheat the oven to gas5/375°F/190°C and put a baking sheet in the oven to heat up. Grease an 8 in (20 cm) flan tin with a loose base (grease the tin thoroughly, especially if it is fluted).
2   Roll out the pastry on a lightly floured board and use to line the flan tin. Ease the pastry into position, pushing it well down the sides so that it doesn't shrink. Chill for 30 minutes.
3   Line the pastry with foil and fill with baking beans. Set the flan tin on the hot oven tray and bake for just 10 minutes. Remove the tin from the oven.
4   Make the filling: dissolve the sugar in 10 fl oz (300 ml) water and cook the apricots in this until they are very soft. Lift the apricots out and dry them on kitchen paper, then chop up coarsely. Reduce the syrup in the pan by boiling it gently. Add the cloves and the cinnamon to give it flavour. Continue cooking until you have a thick syrup. Strain the syrup and set aside for later.
5   Make the custard: in a heatproof bowl, whisk the eggs and sugar until they are pale and fluffy. Stir in the warm milk and the Cointreau. Set the bowl over a small pan of simmering water and cook gently until the custard thickens, stirring often. Set this aside to go cold.
6   To assemble the pie: put the oven heat up to gas7/425°F/220°C and put the apricots into the flan. Pour the custard over the apricots barely to cover and bake for just 7–8 minutes. Remove the pie from the oven if the custard has set.
7   Allow to cool down slightly, then brush over with the flavoured syrup two or three times, allowing the syrup to dry between each brushing.

'The rule is, jam tomorrow and jam yesterday - but never jam today.'

Alice Through the Looking Glass, Lewis Carroll

PUFF PASTRY FRUIT GALETTE

Serves 6–8

Swiftly made, this pudding looks very impressive.

8 oz (225 g) frozen puff pastry, defrosted
1 size-6 or 7 egg, beaten
1 oz (25 g) caster sugar
small tub of Mascarpone cheese
4 oz (125 g) green seedless grapes
4 oz (125 g) black seedless grapes
1 firm kiwi fruit
4 oz (125 g) perfect raspberries
2 tablespoons redcurrant jelly
butter, for greasing
flour, for dusting
chilled cream, to serve

1   Preheat the oven to gas5/375°F/190°C. Lightly grease a baking sheet.
2   Roll out the pastry on a lightly floured board and cut an oblong about 10 in (25 cm) by 8 in (20 cm).
3   Roll the pastry trimmings together again and cut four strips 1 in (2.5 cm) wide to fit round the top edge of the pastry. Brush this edge first with the beaten egg so that the strips will stick. Cut the corners to fit. Nick the top edge of the border all the way round, then brush again with the egg. Prick the centre of the pastry all over to stop it rising too much.
4   Set the pastry on the baking sheet and bake for 15–20 minutes or until the pastry is cooked. Set aside to cool.
5   Put the cool cooked pastry on a flat serving dish. Stir the caster sugar into the Mascarpone cheese and spread this inside the pastry border in a thin layer. Now add the fruit. Peel and chop the kiwi fruit into small chunks. It is usual to set the fruit in rows, but pack it tightly together.
6   Glaze the fruit lightly by melting down the redcurrant jelly and brushing over the fruit. Serve with chilled cream.

STEWED FRUIT WITH CUSTARD OR ICE-CREAM

Strictly speaking, fruit should be poached – not stewed – in a small quantity of syrup. The quantity and richness of the syrup varies according to the juiciness of the fruit. Fruit with a lot of juice like plums, cherries, raspberries and rhubarb are best cooked in a small quantity of syrup, while less juicy fruits like apples, pears and gooseberries call for a lighter syrup but more of it. The syrup should be made before the fruit is added. I do not think we enjoy anything like as much sugar as we used to do with fruit, particularly apples; by the way, these should not be sliced straight into a bowl of water to preserve their colour but straight into the sweetened poaching water. Apples can soak up too much water.

Certain pies call for flavourings like grated lemon, orange rind, cloves, cinnamon, vanilla, a leaf or two of lemon balm, and so on. All are good variations with apples. Elderflower syrup with gooseberries is an old favourite. Ginger with rhubarb, and orange too. All these help to make the fruit more interesting, especially at the end of a season when, say, cooking apples are getting quite mild in flavour.

Very sour fruit like blackcurrants and damsons have a powerful flavour and need a lot of sugar, while many cultivated blackberries are very tasty when compared with the wild ones and therefore need less sugar to sweeten them.

To use sugar substitute, of course, the fruit must be cooked and cooled before the sweetener can be added. Its ability to taste sweet evaporates when mixed with anything hot. It does work well and is a great boon for anyone trying to cut down on sugar and for diabetics.

Stewed – or should I say poached – fruit and custard remains a firm favourite in family eating and is often a necessity if you grow fruit in any quantity. Packet Custard and Real Custard recipes are on pages 196–7. Fruit and ice-cream are a good combination too – think of the glorious combination of poached blackberries dribbling over vanilla ice-cream.

APRICOT OMELETTE

Serves 2

This is a rare pudding these days and yet it is very versatile, since you can fill the omelette with many fruit stuffings – from cherries and apple to passion fruit pulp and mango slices. Perhaps the only drawback is that an omelette is best eaten straight from the pan and since one omelette is enough for two, any more would have to wait.

I bought myself an omelette pan long ago. It is copper and is not used for anything else. An unblemished non-stick pan does a good job, but notice I said unblemished. If you haven't got an omelette pan, increase the number of eggs according to your pan.

2 size-1 or size-2 eggs
1 dessertspoon caster sugar
¾ oz (20 g) butter
2 apricots, chopped, lightly stewed and
  sweetened, well drained

1   Take a fork and stir the eggs together with the sugar. There is no need to whisk or beat.
2   Put an empty 6 in (15 cm) omelette pan on a moderate heat and wait until it is hot. Add the butter and turn up the heat. Swirl the butter round to coat all the pan and the rounded sides as well.
3   When the butter is frothy pour in the eggs. It will set immediately on the base so, lifting the pan up, draw the fork from the outside towards the middle and, tipping the pan, allow the uncooked egg to run off the top of the omelette. Do this about 3 times, when the top of the omelette will look wrinkled like a prune. Take off the heat while the top is still wet.
4   Have ready your fruit. It should also be warmed and 2 tablespoons would be enough. Set the fruit on one side of the omelette. Flip over the other side to cover it. Slide it out of the pan straight on a warm plate.

SOUFFLÉ OMELETTE

Serves 2

This is a slightly different texture of omelette and it can be flavoured with grated lemon rind and juice or left plain, just sweetened, and served with a spoonful of crème fraîche or fruit.

2 size-1 or size-2 eggs, separated
1 dessertspoon caster sugar
¾ oz (20 g) butter
1 spoonful of hot fruit
cream, to serve (optional)

1   Preheat the grill and heat up your omelette pan (see previous recipe) over a moderate heat.
2   In a small bowl, whisk the egg yolks and sugar until pale and creamy.
3   In another bowl, whisk the egg whites until they are stiff and quickly fold these into the yolk mixture.
4   When the pan is hot, turn up the heat. Add the butter and swirl it round to coat the pan all over and up the sides. Pour in the omelette mixture. Draw a fork over the omelette from side to middle to allow the wet egg to roll down on to the base of the pan just as you would an ordinary omelette. This should take no more than 10–15 seconds.
5   Flash the omelette under the hot grill to finish cooking and serve at once, with a spoonful of hot fruit in the middle or just plain with whipped cream.

Variations
Lemon rind and juice whisked in with the eggs. filled with lightly cooked apples or morello cherries in the omelette, or raw chopped pears and hazelnuts, or raw chopped strawberries etc.

CHOCOLATE & ORANGE SOUFFLÉ

Serves 4

Properly speaking, a soufflé is baked and hot. This is a set mousse presented in such a way that it looks like its hot counterpart.

You will need a small straight-sided soufflé dish measuring about 5 in (15 cm) across, with a capacity of 1 pt (600 ml). Prepare the dish by putting a double-thickness collar of greaseproof paper round the dish, rising about 2 in (5 cm) above the rim. I fix mine with an elastic band.

2 teaspoons gelatine
6 oz (175 g) dark good-quality chocolate
grated rind of 1 orange (1 tablespoon)
2 teaspoons instant coffee powder
4 size-1 or size-2 eggs, separated
2 oz (50 g) caster sugar
¼ pt (150 ml) whipping cream

Orange Sauce
1 orange
2 teaspoons arrowroot
14 fl oz (200 ml) orange juice
1 teaspoon orange flower water

1   Sprinkle the gelatine over 3 tablespoons of water in a cup or small bowl. Set this aside for 3 minutes, then stand the cup in a small pan of simmering water. Stir until the gelatine dissolves.

2   Break up the chocolate and put it in a heatproof bowl with the orange rind and coffee powder. Set the bowl over a small pan of simmering water and allow it to melt. Stir gently, then stir in the gelatine mixture and remove from the heat.

3   In yet another bowl, whisk the egg yolks and the sugar until thick and creamy. Stir the chocolate and gelatine mixture into the egg mixture then set this aside to cool and start to go thick. Wait for this to happen.

4   Stir in the cream. Lastly, in another bowl, whisk the egg whites. Gently but thoroughly fold these into the chocolate mixture. Set the soufflé dish on a plate, then pour the mixture into the dish. It will rise above the dish level. Chill.

5   While the mousse is setting, make the sauce: peel the orange and the other orange left over from the mousse as if you were peeling apples. Section the orange segments out by holding the orange in your hand and using a sharp knife to cut down between the lines of white pith (this is easier than it sounds). Reserve the juice. Cut the orange segments into small pieces.

6   Mix the arrowroot with a little of the orange juice. Place the rest of the juice, sugar and orange flower water in a pan. Heat and stir until the sugar dissolves. Stir some of the hot juice into the arrowroot mix and then tip that back into the pan of hot juice. Stir continuously until the juice thickens. Strain through a fine sieve, if you wish, then stir in the fresh orange pieces.

BLACKBERRY SOUFFLÉ

Serves 6

This is another so-called 'soufflé' which I just set with gelatine and egg white. I always dislike the puce colour of blackberries and cream together, so I serve the cream separately with this pudding.

You will need one big soufflé dish about 7–8 in (18–20 cm) across, with a capacity of 2 pt (1.2 litre). Tie a double collar of greaseproof paper round the dish, or fasten as I do with a strong elastic band.

2 lb (900 g) ripe blackberries
2 oz (50 g) sugar or more to taste
2 packets of gelatine
whites of 4 eggs
crisp biscuits, to serve

1   Stew the blackberries in water until they are soft. Then strain and push the berries through a nylon sieve to get rid of the seeds. This is time-consuming I have to admit, but there is no other way. Some people say that to blend the berries with a stick blender makes it easier to sieve. See that you regularly scrape away the purée from under the sieve. I use a big tablespoon to push the fruit back and forward and I end up with just a fistful of seeds to throw away.
2   Measure the purée and make it up to just under the 2 pt (1.2 litre) mark with water. Taste and sweeten the purée. I would use 2 oz (50 g) caster sugar. Stir this in.
3   In a small bowl, put about 4 tablespoons of cold water. Sprinkle the 2 packets of gelatine over the surface and set it aside for about 3 minutes to allow the gelatine to swell. Now set the bowl in a small pan of simmering water and wait until the liquid is clear. Use a teaspoon to stir it round a bit. Stir the gelatine into the blackberry purée and leave it in a cool place until it is beginning to set – this is important.
4   At this point stir it up again. In a clean bowl, whisk the egg whites until they are firm but not too stiff. Stir one big tablespoon of whipped egg white into the purée to loosen it up and then fold the rest of the whipped egg white fairly gently

but carefully. When the egg white has all been folded in, pour this bowlful into the prepared soufflé dish allowing the level to rise inside the paper collar and above the soufflé dish rim. Chill in the fridge to serve and serve with crisp biscuits.

LEMON SOUFFLÉ

Serves 2

You will need a small soufflé dish with straight sides and a capacity of about 3/4 pt (450 ml). Fix a double collar of greaseproof paper round the outside so it stands about 2 in (5 cm) above the rim. Tie it or fasten with an elastic band.

2 size-1 or size-2 eggs, separated
4 oz (125 g) caster sugar
juice and rind of 1 lemon
1 heaped teaspoon powdered gelatine
¼ pt (150 ml) double cream

1   Whisk the egg yolks and sugar until pale and thick. Stir in the lemon rind.
2   Put the lemon juice in a heatproof bowl and sprinkle over the gelatine. Leave to soften for 4–5 minutes, then place the bowl over a small pan of simmering water until the liquid is clear and smooth. Stir with a teaspoon.
3   In yet another bowl, whip the cream until it gets to the floppy stage. In another bowl, whisk the egg whites to soft peaks.
4   Stir the gelatine mixture into the egg and sugar mixture. Using a rubber spatula, fold in the whipped cream. At this point if the mixture is not showing signs of setting wait until it does (you could put it in the fridge and then beat it down again). Give the egg whites a final whisk, then fold into the pudding mixture and pour into the soufflé dish. Level the surface and chill.

Note

To remove the paper without damaging the soufflé you can pull the paper with one hand and with the other hold a knife upright against the outside of the soufflé and on the paper. Pull against the knife.

POACHED PEACHES IN WINE

Serves 4

Peaches can often be disappointing in flavour and texture. One good way of rescuing them is by adding wine and sugar.

4 hard peaches
1½ oz (40 g) caster sugar
¾ pt (450 ml) sweet wine
½ teaspoon of vanilla extract

1   Preheat the oven to gas4/350°F/180°C.
2   First skin the peaches: set them in a small bowl one at a time and cover with boiling water. Leave for 2–3 minutes, then dunk into cold water and remove the skin. Cut the peach in half and remove the stone.
3   Stir the sugar into the wine along with the vanilla. Set the peaches cut side down in a shallow baking dish which will take all 8 side by side. Pour over the wine mixture. Cover with foil and bake gently for about 45 minutes or until the peaches go soft. Sometimes it takes considerably longer than 45 minutes, so turn the fruit over and continue cooking.
4   Lift the peaches into a serving dish or dishes and chill. Boil down the liquid in which the peaches were cooked to a thickish syrup. Pour into a jug.

STUFFED PEACHES

Serves 4

Poached Peaches in Wine, cooked as above
    to step 3
8 ratafia or amaretti biscuits, crushed
2 oz (50 g) finely chopped almonds
¼ pt (150 ml) double cream

1   Lay the peaches cut side up in a large flat dish.

2   Mix the crushed biscuits and nuts in a bowl and stir in a teaspoon or two of the sweet wine syrup – just enough to hold the crumbs together. Now divide the stuffing between the peaches.
3   Whip the cream and spoon a dollop on top of each peach or use a piping bag to force a large star on each peach. Pour the reduced syrup round the fruit.

Note
If the peaches are very round and won't lie down, cut a thin sliver off the rounded bottom of each one so that it sits more easily.

PEACHES POACHED IN REDCURRANT JUICE

Serves 4

4 hard peaches, prepared as in Poached
    Peaches in Wine above to end of step 2
8 oz (225 g) redcurrants
2–3 oz (50–70 g) sugar
whipped cream, to serve

1   Strip the redcurrants off the stems and stew gently in water to cover. When the berries have popped, sieve the fruit by pushing it back and forward across a nylon sieve to extract as much purée as possible. Add more water if you need to make up to 10 fl oz (300 ml). Now sweeten this extract to taste. Try 2 oz (50 g) sugar first and dissolve it in the juice.
2   Pour the liquid over the peaches. Cover with foil and bake at gas6/400°F/200°C for about 45 minutes, turning the fruit over halfway through. Serve with whipped cream.

WARM STRAWBERRIES

Serves 2

Strawberries should never be cooked, but in this recipe they are just warmed through by the sauce which goes over them. This is not so easy to do for more than 2 people. The fried bread should be served straight out of the pan.

2 slices of good-quality white bread
about 2 oz (50 g) butter
granulated sugar, for sprinkling
8 oz (225 g) ripe strawberries, hulled and
    cut in half

Orange Syrup
1 small orange
little orange juice
2 level tablespoons sugar
knob of butter

1   First make the syrup: grate the peel from the orange and set it aside. Squeeze the juice then put it in a measuring jug. Top up to the 5 fl oz (150 ml) mark with carton orange juice. Stir in 2 level tablespoons of sugar and half of the rind. Simmer this juice in order to reduce it a little and add more sugar if you wish, plus a knob of butter.
2   Butter the bread on both sides and sprinkle on a light dusting of granulated sugar. Melt 1 oz (25 g) of butter in a small frying pan and fry the bread on both sides until very crisp.
3   While the bread is still hot, cut each slice into two triangles and set on two warm plates. Scatter the strawberries on top and pour over a little of the orange syrup.

HOT RASPBERRIES IN A SOUR CREAM BATTER

Serves 6

The sour cream gives a delicious and unusual bite to this batter pudding.

1 lb (450 g) raspberries
2 oz (50 g) caster sugar
Cassis (blackcurrant liqueur)
2 size-3 eggs
10 fl oz (300 ml) sour cream
1 oz (25 g) plain white flour
1 oz (25 g) caster sugar

1   Preheat the oven to gas2/300°F/150°C.
2   Tip the raspberries into a flat ovenproof dish (sometimes called a gratin dish) and scatter the sugar over evenly. Dribble a very small amount of Cassis over the berries and slip the dish into the warm oven to get the juices running.
3   To make the batter: whisk the eggs, sour cream, flour and sugar together until smooth. When the berries are hot, pour over the batter.
4   Set the dish on a baking sheet and bake for about 45 minutes, or until the batter is golden. Serve hot or cold.

BAKED YELLOW PLUMS WITH AN APRICOT PURÉE SAUCE

Serves 4

We used to call yellow plums 'egg plums'. I do not know why, except that they are rather large and egg-shaped.

8 large yellow plums
8 oz (225 g) vanilla sugar

Apricot Purée Sauce
8 oz (225 g) fresh ripe apricots
½ teaspoon grated lemon rind
1 oz (25 g) sugar

1 Preheat the oven to gas4/350°F/180°C.
2 Make up a syrup by melting the vanilla sugar in 10 fl oz (300 ml) water. Simmer for a minute or two.
3 Stone the plums by cutting into the stone all round the fruit. A quick twist and the two halves should come apart. Discard the stones.
4 Set the plums in a flat ovenproof dish, cut sides down, and pour over the syrup. Cover and bake gently until the fruit is soft. Set aside.
5 Make the sauce: cut the apricots and stone them. Liquidize the fruit with a stick blender and stir in the lemon rind and the sugar. Keep stirring until the sugar melts.

HOT APRICOT SOUFFLÉ

Serves 2 or 3

4 oz (125 g) dried apricots, soaked overnight in cold water to cover
1 vanilla pod
1½ oz (40 g) sugar
2 tablespoons Grand Marnier
whites of 3 size-1 or size-2 eggs
butter, for greasing

1 Preheat the oven to gas6/400°F/200°C. Butter a soufflé dish with a capacity of 1½ pt (1 litre).
2 First poach the apricots and vanilla pod in the water in which the apricots have been soaking. Stir in the sugar. When very soft, drain off the water, squeezing out much as possible. Liquidize the fruit with the Grand Marnier.
3 Whisk the egg whites until very stiff and fold into the apricot purée as carefully as possible. Spoon into the soufflé dish.
4 Set it on a baking sheet and bake for about 20–25 minutes. Serve at once.

HOT CHOCOLATE & CHERRY SOUFFLÉ

Serves 6

6 oz (175 g) bitter chocolate
4 oz (125 g) very ripe sweet cherries, stoned and chopped
2 tablespoons brandy
2 oz (50 g) caster sugar, plus more for sprinkling
4 size-1 or size-2 eggs, separated, plus whites of 2 extra eggs
butter, for greasing
caster sugar,

1 Preheat the oven to gas6/400°F/200°C and put in a baking sheet.
2 Break up the chocolate and put it into a heatproof bowl with the brandy. Set the bowl over a small pan of simmering water.
3 Grease a 2 pt (1.2 litre) soufflé dish with butter and sprinkle some caster sugar inside too. Scatter the chopped cherries in the bottom.
4 Whisk the egg yolks with the sugar until creamy.
5 In a large bowl, having washed the beaters and dried them thoroughly, whisk the egg whites until they are stiff.
6 When the chocolate is smooth and liquid, stir it into the yolk and sugar mixture.
7 Use a metal spoon to take 2 tablespoons of the whisked egg whites and stir this into the chocolate mixture. This will soften the mixture and make it easier for the next step.
8 Fold the rest of the egg whites into the chocolate mixture and, as quickly as possible, scrape it out again with a rubber spatula and into the soufflé dish over the cherries.
8 Set the dish on the baking sheet and bake for about 30 minutes. Serve at once.

APPLE SQUARES

Makes 9 small squares

The base of this hot pudding is like shortbread but more crunchy – a perfect foil for the cinnamon apples.

3 oz (75 g) butter, cut into small pieces, plus
    more for greasing
6 oz (175 g) plain white flour, sieved
3 oz (75 g) unrefined soft brown sugar

Topping
1½ oz (40 g) chopped almonds
1 extra-large Bramley apple, or 2 small ones
1 tablespoon soft brown sugar
1 level teaspoon ground cinnamon
1 oz (25 g) butter
ice-cream or chilled single cream, to serve

1   Preheat the oven to gas6/400°F/200°C.
2   Rub the butter into the flour until the mixture looks like breadcrumbs, then stir in the soft brown sugar.
3   Grease a shallow 7 in (18 cm) square tin and then spread the mixture loosely in it. Scatter the chopped almonds on top of the base.
4   Peel, core and slice the apples fairly thinly. Press the slices into the base mixture in overlapping rows.
5   Mix the tablespoon of soft brown sugar with the cinnamon and sprinkle this all over the apples. Dot with tiny pieces of butter.
6   Bake for 35–40 minutes.
7   Serve cut in squares, with ice-cream or chilled single cream.

BAKED BANANAS

Serves 4

The easiest of all baked banana recipes is to bake the unpeeled fruit for about 20 minutes in a moderate oven (gas 5/375°F/190°C) until the skins are black and the insides soft and runny.

Split the skins and eat the banana with a teaspoon. Fine for Bonfire Night, but here is something a little more elegant although just as easy.

I've only just discovered that I can flake hazelnuts in my food processor. They are so good that they have been going into everything!

4 large bananas
2 tablespoons fresh lemon juice
2 fl oz (50 ml) fresh orange juice
2 oz (50 g) soft butter
pinch of nutmeg
pinch of cinnamon
icing sugar, to dust
1½ oz (20 g) flaked hazelnuts

1   Preheat the oven to gas6/400°F/200°C.
2   Put the lemon and orange juices in a roomy bowl. Chop the bananas into thick chunks and toss in the juice.
3   Scoop the bananas and the juice into a large shallow ovenproof dish (sometimes called a gratin dish). Put the butter in a small bowl and work the nutmeg and cinnamon into it. Then dot the bananas with tiny bits of the spiced butter.
4   Cover with foil and bake for about 10 minutes, or until the bananas have softened.
5   Sprinkle icing sugar over the top and scatter over the hazelnuts. Slip back into the oven for 2 more minutes uncovered, then serve.

CARAMELIZED APPLES

Serves 2

I have to admit I never used to think of frying apples but, in fact, for a really quick pudding this is a doddle. The addition of the Calvados (apple brandy) is probably rather extravagant, but it is divine. Try ordinary brandy if you have no Calvados.

2 small dessert apples
2 oz (50 g) butter

1 tablespoon caster sugar
1 tablespoon soft brown sugar
1 tablespoon Calvados or brandy
about 1 tablespoon double cream

1 Melt the butter in a frying pan and turn down the heat. Cut the apples in 4 and then cut each one again so that you have 8 slices from each apple. Take out the cores. If the apples are really small, cut each half into 3.
2 Now fry the apples in the butter with care until soft, turning them often. Transfer to 2 warm plates and keep hot.
3 Sprinkle the two sugars over the buttery juices in the pan and cook until the sugar melts. Add the Calvados or brandy, followed by just a dash of cream.
4 Pour this hot caramel sauce over the apples and serve at once.

PLUM DUMPLINGS

Serves 4

We ate apple dumplings when young and we each had a whole apple wrapped in pastry and drowned in custard. A plum dumpling is more my size nowadays.

4 ripe Victoria plums
1 oz (25 g) hard butter, plus more for
   greasing
8 oz (225 g) Shortcrust Pastry (see page 16)
1 size-6 or 7 egg, beaten
caster sugar, for sprinkling
thin cream or custard, to serve

1 Preheat the oven to gas7/425°F/220°C and put a baking sheet in the oven to heat up.
2 Wipe and stone the plums, but try to open the plums on one side only.
3 Cut the butter into 4 and put a piece inside each plum.
4 Roll out the pastry thinly and cut it into four large squares. Set one plum on each square of pastry and roll it up like a parcel. Set the parcels, seam side down, in a well buttered heatproof dish. Brush the pastry all over with the beaten egg and sprinkle sugar over.
5 Bake for about 25–30 minutes.
6 Serve with thin cream or custard.

BANANA & COCONUT ROLLS

Serves 4

4 large bananas
lemon or lime juice
3 oz (75 g) desiccated coconut (fresh
   coconut is even better)
2 oz (50 g) demerara sugar
1 tablespoon rum
1 oz (25 g) butter, plus more for greasing
crème fraîche, to serve

1 Preheat the oven to gas4/350°F/180°C. Generously butter a large shallow heatproof dish.
2 Cut the bananas in two and brush all over with lemon or lime juice.
3 In a shallow dish, mix the coconut and the demerara sugar. Roll each banana in this and coat well. Set the rolls side by side in the ovenproof dish, sprinkle with rum and then flake the butter all over the fruit.
4 Bake for about 15–20 minutes.
5 Serve with a dollop of crème fraîche.

RUM-TUM-TUM

Serves 3

A rich omelette flavoured with banana, rum and demerara sugar.

3 size-1 or size-2 eggs, separated
2 oz (50 g) demerara sugar
grated rind & juice of 1 lemon
pinch of salt
1 large banana
3 tablespoons rum
1½ (40 g) butter

1   Put the egg yolks and one-quarter of the measured sugar with just 1 teaspoon of the lemon rind in a bowl. Whisk lightly.
2   In another bowl, whisk the egg whites with the salt.
3   For the filling: liquidize the banana. Stir in the remaining lemon rind and 1 tablespoon of rum. Heat gently.
4   For the topping: melt 1 oz (50 g) of the butter and the rest of the sugar in a small pan and let it cook for just a few seconds, then remove from the heat. Stir in 1 teaspoon lemon juice and the last 2 tablespoons of rum.
5   To make the omelette: melt the remaining butter in a 7 in (18 cm) omelette pan. Preheat the grill.
6   Fold the egg mixtures together and pour into the hot butter. Cook gently until set underneath. Slip the pan under the grill to firm up the top.
7   Scoop the banana mixture on to one half of the omelette and flip over the other half. Slip on to a serving dish.
8   Cut into 3 pieces and serve with the reheated topping.

RHUBARB & APRICOT WOBBLE

Serves 4

This recipe is based on one given to my TV programme *Farmhouse Kitchen* by Anne Wallace, a fellow Scot. You will need 4 decorative glass dishes, like old-fashioned champagne glasses.

1½ (40 g) dried apricots
1½ lb (675 g) pink early rhubarb
4 oz (125 g) caster sugar
1 packet of gelatine
grated rind and juice of 1 orange
3 tablespoons double cream

Decoration
4 tablespoons whipped cream
thread-fine strips of dried apricot

1   Soak the apricots overnight in 5 fl oz (150 ml) cold water and next day stew them in the same water until they are very soft.
2   Preheat the oven to gas3/325°F/160°C. Wash and trim the rhubarb, slice it and put it in a casserole (which has a lid). Stir in the sugar and cook in the oven (no water is needed) until soft.
3   Strain the juice from the rhubarb into a measuring jug. There should be about ¾ pt (450 ml). Set this aside to cool (reserve the rhubarb and use it for another dish).
4   Drain the apricots in a nylon sieve and mix the orange juice with the strained apricot juice. Pour this into a small bowl and sprinkle over the powdered gelatine. Allow this to stand for 3–4 minutes. Then stand the bowl in a small pan of gently simmering water and stir until the gelatine melts.
5   Stir the gelatine liquid into the rhubarb juice. Pour about half a cup of this into a bowl and set this aside. Pour the rest equally into the four glass dishes. Put these to set in the fridge.
6   Liquidize the apricots with a stick blender. Stir in the finely grated orange rind, the cream and the ½ cup of jelly, stirring this mixture all the time to keep it liquid until the jelly has set in the glasses. When it does set, pour the creamy

mixture equally into the 4 glasses and allow this
to set too.

7   To serve: spoon a whirl of whipped double
cream on each jelly and decorate with a few strips
of dried apricots.

Not Quite Christmas

Serves 6

This jelly imitates the shape of a Christmas
pudding and the port gives it a lovely flavour.

To blanch almonds, pour boiling water over
them and leave until cool enough to handle.
The skins should then slip off.

1 lb (450 g) dark grapes (look for seedless
  ones)
1¹/₂ packets of a dark jelly (blackcurrant or
  blackberry)
¹/₄ pt (150 ml) port
2 oz (50 g) raisins
2 oz (50 g) chopped blanched almonds
pouring cream, to serve

1   Rinse the grapes and dry them. Then cut
them in two and deseed if necessary.
2   Make up the jelly according to the packet
instructions, but use the ¹/₄ pt (150 ml) port as
part of the water measurement. I found it easier
to make up the jellies one at a time and then
measure out a bare 1¹/₂ pt (1 litre) needed for the
recipe.
3   Wet a 3 pt (1.75 litre) pudding basin and
pour in the liquid jelly.
4   Add the grapes, raisins and nuts. Stir
occasionally until it sets.
5   Turn out on a flat plate and stick a sprig of
holly on top. Serve with pouring cream.

Apricots with a Fudge Sauce

Serves 4

The apricots for this dish must be soft and
juicy: if not stew or bake them briefly in a little
water, then strain.

You can buy apricot kernels in Chinese
grocers – at least that is where I got mine. If
you are strong enough to crack the apricot
stones you find a lovely moist kernel inside,
which you also have to skin.

8 very ripe apricots
apricot kernels, to decorate

Fudge Sauce
8 oz (225 g) unrefined soft brown sugar
¹/₂ oz (15 g) butter
2 tablespoons thin cream or milk

1   First make the fudge sauce: in a heavy-based
pan, cook gently the sugar, butter and cream or
milk. Stir over a low heat until the sugar
dissolves, then bring up to a gentle boil for just
2–3 minutes. Remove from the heat and set
aside.
2   If the apricots are whole, cut them in two and
remove the stones. Set the fruit in the bottom of
a flat dish in a single layer.
3   Warm up the fudge sauce again to boiling
point, then pour it over the fruit. Leave it aside
to go cold. Decorate with apricot kernels.

STREUSEL-TOPPED GLORIOUS GOOSEBERRIES

Serves 6–8

1½ lb (675 g) gooseberries
2 oz (50 g) butter
6 oz (175 g) soft brown sugar
2 teaspoons fresh ginger, peeled and grated

Topping
8 oz (225 g) plain white flour, sifted
5 oz (150 g) butter
4 oz (125 g) demerara sugar
1 teaspoon ground ginger

1   Preheat the oven to gas4/350°F/180°C.
2   Top and tail the gooseberries. Melt the butter in a large pan, stir in the soft brown sugar, add the gooseberries and ginger. Cover the pan and stew gently for about 5 minutes, or until the gooseberries start to look yellow. Remove from the heat and allow to go cold. Strain off most of the juice and tip the fruit into a deep ovenproof dish like a large soufflé dish.
3   To prepare the topping: rub the butter into the flour and stir in the demerara sugar and ground ginger. Sprinkle about 2 tablespoons of water over the crumbs as this encourages a really crunchy finish.
4   Spoon the topping over the fruit, set the dish on a baking sheet and bake for 25–30 minutes.

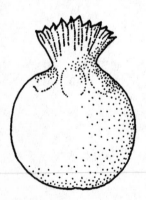

APPLE DUMPLINGS WITH FILO

Serves 4

These dumplings are not quite the right shape, but they are quick and easy.

1 packet of frozen filo pastry, defrosted
melted butter

Filling
4 eating apples
1½ oz (40 g) butter
1 level tablespoon soft brown sugar
½ teaspoon ground cinnamon
2 oz (50 g) raisins

1   For the filling: peel, core and chop the apples then cut into pieces (sugar-cube size).
2   Melt the butter and sugar and add the cinnamon, apples and raisins. Cook gently. Aim to have the apples just slightly undercooked. Remove from the heat and leave to cool down.
3   Preheat the oven to gas6/400°F/200°C. Cut the filo into even squares and set aside the strips. Use three squares for each serving and set them on top of each other at different angles. Brush melted butter between each layer of pastry.
4   Spoon the apple mixture into the middle of each pastry portion. A tablespoon will be plenty I think. Gather up the pastry to form a 'Dick Whittington' bundle. Some writers have described them as 'money bags'. Squeeze the 'neck' of the bag and the pastry will stick together.
5   Repeat this until the apples have been used up. Brush a little more melted butter all over the little 'bags' and especially over the frilly bits at the top.
6   Bake for about 10–12 minutes until golden. Avoid over-baking which makes the pastry too crisp.

SWEET PEAR PIZZA

Serves 6–8

I remember doing pizzas on TV and we thought
we were very daring to suggest a sweet pizza.
Then we were using proper bread dough
bottoms. Here I suggest you buy some frozen
puff pastry or, if you are pushed for time, a thin
crispy pizza base from the supermarket.

8 oz (225 g) frozen puff pastry, defrosted, or
    a pizza base
1 oz (25 g) butter, plus more for greasing
5 oz (150 g) caster sugar
3 ripe pears, peeled, cored and sliced (but
    not thinly sliced)
2 tablespoons Mascarpone cheese

1 Preheat the oven to gas5/375°F/190°C.
Grease a big baking sheet.
2 On a lightly floured board and, using a long
rolling pin, roll out the pastry to a large circle
about 10 in (25 cm) across.
3 Set the pastry ring on the greased baking
sheet and leave it while you prepare the pears.
4 Melt the butter over a high heat and stir in
the sugar. Shake this about a bit and, when the
sugar has melted and become a golden liquid,
turn down the heat a bit and add the pears. Keep
tossing and shaking them about and, if they start
to stick, pour in a little water. Do not let them
go soft and mushy.
5 Arrange the pears on the pastry. Drop blobs
of the Mascarpone here and there.
6 Bake for about 15–20 minutes, when the
pastry should be well risen. Serve warm.

DATE & WALNUT PORTIONS WITH FUDGE SAUCE

Serves 12–16

8 oz (225 g) block dates, cut small
8 fl oz (225 ml) boiling water
3 oz (75 g) butter, softened, plus more for
    greasing
7 oz (200 g) caster sugar
1 size-1 or size-2 egg, beaten
1 teaspoon vanilla essence
10 oz (275 g) self-raising flour, sieved
1 level teaspoon baking powder
3 oz (75 g) walnuts, chopped

Fudge Sauce
8 oz (225 g) soft brown sugar
6 oz (175 g) butter
1/4 pt (150 ml) double cream
small can of evaporated milk or carton of
    single cream

1 Preheat the oven to gas2/300°F/150°C. Grease
a roasting tin measuring about 8x12 in (20x
30 cm) and line the base with greaseproof paper.
2 Pour the boiling water over the chopped
dates. Bring to the boil and set aside to go cold
before you start the pudding.
3 In a large bowl, cream the butter and sugar.
Add the egg a little at a time and beat well. Stir
in the cold dates with the water, the vanilla, flour,
baking powder and two-thirds of the walnuts.
4 Mix well, spoon into the tin and level the
surface. Scatter the remaining chopped walnuts.
5 Bake for about 25–30 minutes, or until the
pudding is firm.
6 To make the sauce: put the sugar, butter and
double cream in a heavy-based pan over a low
heat. Once the sugar has dissolved, bring up the
heat a little to a gentle boil. Boil for just 2–3
minutes and set aside.
7 Slide a knife round the pudding to loosen the
sides and cut into squares. Serve with the fudge
sauce reheated and thinned down with the
evaporated milk or cream.

OATY APPLE SPONGE

Serves 6–8

1 lb (450 g) Bramley cooking apples, peeled, cored and thinly sliced
6 oz (175 g) light muscovado sugar
6 oz (175 g) butter, softened, plus more for greasing
2 size-1 or size-2 eggs, beaten
4 oz (125 g) self-raising wholemeal flour
1 teaspoon baking powder
2 oz (50 g) rolled oats
1 teaspoon ground cinnamon
2–3 tablespoons milk
icing sugar, to dust
custard, to serve

1   Preheat the oven to gas5/375°F/190°C. Grease a 2 pt (1.2 litre) shallow ovenproof dish.
2   Arrange the apples in the bottom of the dish and sprinkle with 2 oz (50 g) of the measured sugar. Dot with 2 oz (50 g) of the measured butter.
3   Place the rest of the sugar and butter in a roomy bowl with the eggs, wholemeal flour, baking powder, oats, ground cinnamon and milk. Beat thoroughly for 2–3 minutes, adding more milk if needed to obtain a soft consistency. Spread this mixture evenly over the apples.
4   Set on a baking sheet and bake for 25–30 minutes, until well risen and firm. Test the sponge with the flat of your hand and you will know if it is still liquid underneath and needs longer in the oven.
5   Dust with icing sugar and serve hot with custard.

BLACKCURRANT, APPLE & MINT CRUMBLE

Serves 6

Crumble
5 oz (150 g) butter, plus more for greasing
5 oz (150 g) plain white flour
3 oz (75 g) caster sugar

Fruit
2 Granny Smith apples
1 oz (25 g) butter
2 oz (50 g) caster sugar
10 big mint leaves
4 oz (125 g) blackcurrants (well drained, if frozen)

1   Preheat the oven to gas5/375°F/190°C. Grease a deep pie dish with a 1½ pt (1 litre) capacity.
2   Prepare the crumble: chop the butter into pieces and rub into the flour. Stir in the sugar, dribble 1 tablespoon of water over the top and stir it in. Set aside.
3   Prepare the fruit: peel, core and slice the apples, but not too thinly. Melt the butter in a heavy pan and add the sugar. Toss in the apples and cook them carefully, shaking the pan all the time to prevent sticking. Aim at having some bite left. Turn the apples into the pie dish, snip the mint leaves over the apples and then spread the blackcurrants over the top.
4   Tip the crumble over the fruit and press down gently. Set the dish on a baking sheet and bake for about 35 minutes, or until the crumble is golden. Serve warm.

BLACKBERRY & APPLE CRUMBLE

Serves 6

Using the same crumble topping as in the previous recipe.

Fruit
1 lb (450 g) cooking apples
2 oz sugar
8 oz (225 g) blackberries

1   Follow previous recipe to end of step 1.
2   Peel, core and slice the apples and barely

cover with water. Stew gently until just
beginning to fall. Drain off the water and
sprinkle over the sugar and stir it in.
3   Drain the apples again and pour into the pie
dish, spread the blackberries on top and stir
them in.
4   Cover the fruit with the crumble topping. Set
the dish on a baking sheet and bake for 35
minutes, or until the topping is crisp and golden.

Posh Peach Crumble

Serves 6

4 ripe juicy peaches (or bottled or canned)
3 oz (75 g) butter
4 oz (125 g) plain flour
2 oz (50 g) caster sugar, plus more for fruit
    if necessary
1 oz (25 g) chopped almonds
2 oz (50 g) amaretti biscuits
whipped cream, to serve
2–3 drops of real almond essence

1   Slice the peaches in two and remove the
stones, then pour boiling water over them and
leave until the skins will slip off easily. Set the
fruit side by side in a shallow oven dish which
will take 8 peach halves lying closely side by
side. It will be a tight fit. Sprinkle over some
sugar if you think they need it.
2   Make the crumble by rubbing the butter into
the flour until the mixture looks like breadcrumbs.
Stir in the sugar, almonds and the coarsely crushed
biscuits. Dribble a tablespoon of water through the
crumble and spread it over the fruit.
3   Set the dish on a baking sheet and bake for
about 30 minutes. Serve with whipped cream
flavoured with 2–3 drops of real almond essence.

*'Every Millionaire.' according to Ronald Firbank, loves a 'baked apple'. Perhaps it would be a good
idea to try something richer, sweeter and more likely to be appreciated by those not yet accustomed to
the austerity of extreme wealth.*

STRAWBERRY MILLE FEUILLE

Serves 6

This famous French recipe name translates as 'a thousand leaves'. While a good home-made flaky pastry is very much superior to the commercial variety, I have to admit that it is very much quicker to buy it frozen. However do try the fast New Flaky Pastry recipe on page 19 some time so that you can compare the texture and flavour. The words flaky and puff have, I think, come to mean the same thing. The word 'puff' used to refer to the pastry we called 'rough puff' and which is not so much used nowadays. Commercial flaky pastry is sold in 8–9 oz (225–250 g) packs.

4 oz (125 g) New Flaky Pastry (see page 19)

Filling
8 oz (225 g) perfectly ripe strawberries, plus extra for garnish

Vanilla Cream
9 fl oz (250 ml) milk
vanilla pod or ½ small teaspoon vanilla essence
3 yolks from size-1 or size-2 eggs
2 oz (50 g) caster sugar
1 oz (25 g) plain flour
little single cream

1   Preheat the oven to gas 7/425°F/220°C.
2   Roll the pastry out on a lightly floured board and cut to a 12 in (30 cm) square. Use a ruler to mark this square of pastry into 3 equal strips and cut. Set these strips on a damp baking sheet (run it under the tap and pour all the water away but do not dry).
3   Prick them all over with a fork, then bake for about 12 minutes or until the pastry is brown – watch carefully as it soon burns. Remove the baking sheet and leave the pastry to cool down.
4   Make the rich vanilla cream: bring the milk with the vanilla pod or essence to the boil and set it aside for the vanilla flavour to strengthen. In a

bowl, whisk the egg yolks and sugar until the mixture is pale and creamy. Now add the flour to this bowl, but do it through a sieve and then stir it in. Reheat the milk and pour about one-quarter of it on the egg, sugar and flour mixture, whisking hard all the time. Return this bowlful to the rest of the milk, still in the pan. Over a low heat, whisk as the liquid thickens, then change to a small wooden spoon. When the mixture comes together and tastes fully cooked (you can easily tell if the flour tastes raw), scoop into a bowl.
5   If the mixture is very thick, add just a spoonful of single cream to thin it down. It should be thick enough to sit in the pastry layers and not run out, but not so thick that it is too stiff to spread.
6   To assemble the mille feuille: divide the vanilla cream in two. Set one slice of pastry on a flat plate or tray. Spread with one half of the cream. Press half of the cut strawberries into the cream. Cover with the next layer of pastry and repeat the layers of cream and strawberries. Top with the last layer of pastry. Dredge this thickly with icing sugar.
7   Decorate if you wish by heating long metal skewers on your hob and, with a thick oven glove to protect your hand, lay the hot skewers one at a time on the icing sugar to mark lines in the icing sugar in a criss-cross pattern.
8   Serve within 2–3 hours, surrounded by whole strawberries.

FRUIT COBBLER

Serves 6

I was given a bottle of elderflower cordial and it had been sitting unopened for ages. I have always used real elderflowers to make a lovely gooseberry jelly early in the year, but their season is short. It eventually dawned on me that I could use the cordial. This is another way of using it. The cobbler topping is very often made up into little scones, but I think this pudding is much nicer with the scone topping in large dollops straight into the fruit.

2 lb (900 g) gooseberries, topped and tailed
3–4 oz (75–125 g) sugar
2 fl oz (50 ml) elderflower cordial
1 heaped tablespoon preserving sugar
    (coarse crystals)

Scone Topping
4 oz (125 g) block margarine or butter
8 oz (225 g) self-raising flour
1 heaped teaspoon baking powder
1 oz (25 g) caster sugar
6 fl oz (160 ml) milk

1   Preheat the oven to gas7/425°F/220°C and
put a baking sheet in the oven to heat. You will
need an ovenproof baking dish at least $2^1/_2$ in
(6 cm) deep and with a capacity of 3 pt
(1.75 litres) and measuring 9 in (23 cm) across.
2   If the gooseberries are very hard, cut each one
in two and pour them into the baking dish. Stir
in the sugar and the cordial – only 3 oz (75 g)
sugar if you like the fruit fairly sharp.
3   Make up the scone topping: cut the
margarine or butter into chunks. Sift the flour
and baking powder. Add the sugar, then rub in
the fat until the mixture looks like damp
breadcrumbs. Now mix swiftly with the milk to
a soft dough. This could all be done in a food
processor using the pulsing action so that the
mixing is light.
4   Use a tablespoon to set the sticky dough in
dollops on top of the fruit. Scatter the preserving
sugar on top.
5   Set the dish on the hot baking sheet and bake
for 25-30 minutes. Check with a skewer that the
topping is fully cooked.

RHUBARB & ORANGE COBBLER

I tried the previous recipe out with
2 tablespoons of concentrated orange cordial in
with the rhubarb and the grated rind of a small
orange mixed with the scone dough. It was
excellent.
    If the rhubarb is late in the season and hard
it would be better to stew it slightly in advance.
Drain it well and then add the orange.

PEACH AND ALMOND COBBLER

For the fruit filling I would be inclined to use
canned peaches, well drained and flavoured
with 2–3 drops of almond essence. Some whole
skinned almonds would be nice too.
    For the topping: carry through the almond
flavouring with $1^1/_2$ oz (40 g) flaked almonds
chopped into the scone dough.

*'We may say of angling as Dr Boteler said of strawberries: "Doubtless God could have made a better
berry, but doubtless God never did"; and so (if I might be judge) God never did make a more calm,
quiet, innocent recreation than angling.'*

Izaak Walton

BREAD PUDDINGS

POOR KNIGHTS OF WINDSOR

Serves 4

I have always known this name for a pudding and yet I have never heard of it being used. It sounds like something a nanny would make for her charges.

2 rounds of thick-cut white bread
1/4 pt (150 ml) milk
1 1/2 oz (40 g) sugar
1 size-1 or size-2 egg, beaten
knob of butter

1   Cut the crusts from the bread and cut each slice into 3 strips.
2   Arrange 3 flat dishes (old fashioned soup-plates) side by side. Put the milk in one, sugar in the next, and egg in the third.
3   Put a knob of butter in a frying pan. Dip the bread briefly into the milk back and front, then in the sugar back and front, then in the beaten egg. Shake off the surplus egg and fry in the butter. You have to be quite quick as this is nothing like as simple as it sounds.

POSH KNIGHTS OF WINDSOR

I have read that the Spaniards say this is a much better recipe. I agree. Beat 2 egg yolks into a glass of sweet sherry. The bread is dipped into this mixture and then fried in oil back and front. When crisp it is sprinkled with icing sugar and cinnamon.

PAIN PERDU

Serves 4

This is a French version of the Poor Knights recipe, which is often served to accompany a compote of fruit.

2 teaspoons vanilla sugar
1/4 pt (150 ml) milk
4 large slices of brioche
1 size-1 or size-2 egg, beaten
knob of butter
granulated sugar, for sprinkling

1   Stir the vanilla sugar into the milk and lay two flat dishes side by side. Pour the sweetened milk in one dish and the beaten egg in the other.
2   Put a frying pan on the hob to heat up.
3   Dip the brioche slices first in the sweet milk, then quickly back and front into the beaten egg. Shake off any surplus egg.
4   Put a knob of butter into the frying pan. When it is frothing, put in the brioche and fry quickly on both sides.
5   When crisp, sprinkle over a little granulated sugar.

BROWN BETTY

Serves 5–6

This homely old-fashioned pudding is based on breadcrumbs and fruit. Use either 1 lb (450 g) apples, 1 lb (450 g) plums, or 1 1/2 lb (675 g) rhubarb.

1 lb (450 g) plums, halved and stoned
5 oz (150 g) caster sugar
6 oz (175 g) fresh white breadcrumbs
1 oz (25 g) butter, melted
hot custard or cream, to serve

1   Preheat the oven to gas6/400°F/200°C. You will need a heatproof oven dish with a capacity of about 3 pt (1.75 litres) and about 9 in (23 cm) across and 2¹⁄₂ in (6 cm) deep.
2   Out of the measured sugar, set aside 2 oz (50 g) and out of the fresh breadcrumbs set aside 2 oz (50 g).
3   In the dish, layer the fruit, sugar and crumbs, ending with fruit.
4   Stir the reserved sugar into the melted butter and stir in the reserved breadcrumbs. Spread this over the fruit.
5   Bake for 30 minutes or until brown.
6   Serve with hot custard or cream.

TOFFEE APPLE CHARLOTTE

Serves 4

1¹⁄₂ lb (675 g) apples (Bramley and Cox's mixed)
4 oz (125 g) soft brown sugar
pinch of ground cinnamon
pinch of ground cloves
1 oz (25 g) butter, plus more for greasing
about 4 large white bread slices
grated rind of 1 lemon
ice-cream, to serve

Caramel
6 oz (175 g) caster sugar
dash of lemon juice

1   Lavishly butter a shallow ovenproof dish with a capacity of about 1¹⁄₂ pt (1 litre).
2   First peel, core and cut the apples into quite small chunks. Cook them in a pan with the soft brown sugar, spices and butter. Keep stirring to prevent them sticking until you have a purée which is firm and fairly dry.
3   Make a caramel by cooking the sugar in 2 teaspoons water with a little lemon juice. Shake the pan so it goes back and forth until it melts into a light brown caramel. I find it easier to keep taking the pan off and on the heat. Pour the liquid into another flat dish. (If you have gone too far and made toffee, then add 2 spoonfuls of water

over a low heat and you will probably manage to get it dissolved – it is a slow process.)
4   Cut the crusts off the bread and cut the slices into squares (4 per slice). Dip one side only of the bread into the caramel and quickly line the dish with these pieces, with the caramel facing out. Cover the base as well, leaving as few gaps as possible. Press the bread together and pour in the cooked apple. Press down, scatter with lemon rind and seal in with more bread pieces. If there is any caramel left, pour over the top.
5   Bake on the baking sheet for 20 minutes.
6   Leave it in the dish until it sinks a bit, then run a knife round the edge and turn it out on a flat plate and serve with ice-cream.

CRUNCHY APPLE CRUMBS

Serves 4

This looks nice in tall wine glasses so that you can see the layers.

5 oz (150 g) fresh white breadcrumbs
5 oz (150 g) butter
5 oz (150 g) caster sugar
2 lb (900 g) Bramley apples
grated rind from 1 lemon
4 tablespoons whipped double cream
dark chocolate, grated into curls with a
    swivel-bladed vegetable peeler

1   Fry the breadcrumbs in a large frying pan with the butter over a low heat (it will take 15 minutes to achieve the crunchiness).
2   Once cooked, stir in 3 oz (75 g) of the caster sugar, then turn them into a flat dish to cool.
3   Peel, core and slice the apples. Cook with the remaining sugar, lemon rind and 2–3 tablespoons of water, until a thick soft purée (you could help with a potato masher). Allow to cool.
4   Layer the fried crumbs and apple purée in the glasses. Finish with the crumbs. Top with a whirl of whipped cream and the chocolate curls. Serve the same day or the crumbs will go soft.

CHOCOLATE CRUNCH

Serves 6

You will need a deep dish with a capacity of
2 pt (1.2 litres) for this recipe – a glass one
would look nice.

4 oz (125 g) butter
6 oz (175 g) fresh white breadcrumbs
2 oz (50 g) demerara sugar
2 oz (50 g) cocoa, sieved (not drinking
   chocolate)
1½ lb (675 g) cooking apples (Bramleys if
   possible)
3 oz (75 g) caster sugar
grated rind and juice of 1 lemon
¼ pt (150 ml) double cream, whipped

1   First, over a low heat, melt one-quarter of the
butter and fry the crumbs. They take a long time
and must be kept moving a lot – about 15
minutes is about right.
2   Once cooked, mix the demerara sugar and
cocoa and stir into the crumbs. Spoon the crumbs
into a dish and leave to cool down.
3   Peel, core and chop the apples. Cook slowly
with the caster sugar, the rind and juice of the
lemon and the remaining butter. Stir often until
you have a thick soft purée (use a potato masher
to help speed things up). Set aside to cool.
4   Layer the purée and the chocolate crumbs and
finish with a layer of whipped double cream.
Chill, but eat on the day it is made.

SPICED APPLE & DRIED FRUIT STRUDEL

I once saw an Austrian lady make strudel paste
and she was working on a small table which she
eventually covered with a 'cloth' of strudel
which hung down almost to the floor. Try your
hand at this if you are interested, you will find
that the texture is very good. If not you can
always fall back on frozen filo pastry.

Strudel Paste
1 size-7 egg, beaten
¼ pt (150 ml) warm water, plus more if
   necessary
2 teaspoons vegetable oil, plus more for
   brushing
8 oz (225 g) plain white flour, plus more for
   dusting
2 oz (50 g) melted butter, plus more for
   greasing
icing sugar, for dusting

Filling
2 lb (900 g) dessert apples
2 oz (50 g) melted butter
2 oz (50 g) soft brown sugar
½ teaspoon mixed spice
½ teaspoon ground cinnamon
2 oz (50 g) currants
2 oz (50 g) sultanas
1 dessertspoon lemon juice
3 oz (75 g) fried breadcrumbs

1   Preheat the oven to gas4/350°F/180°C.
Grease a large baking sheet well.
2   Prepare the filling: peel, core and chop the
apples to the size of big raisins. Put into a big
bowl and stir in all the remaining filling
ingredients except the breadcrumbs very
thoroughly. Set aside.
3   Make the strudel paste: whisk the egg into
the warm water. Stir in the oil.
4   Sieve the flour into another bowl – a good big
one this time. Stir in the egg and water mix and
work up to a soft dough, adding more warm
water if necessary. At this point put the dough to
rest for 15 minutes.
5   Knead the rested dough hard on a wooden
board or put it in a machine if you have one,
with a dough hook. When the dough is very
elastic, roll it out as far as you can on your board
with a rolling pin, then transfer it to a cloth
spread out on a table. (It is easier if you can move
round the table).
6   Brush all over the paste with oil and leave it
again for 15 minutes. By then you should be able
to pull the paste out very gently until you have
stretched it as thin as paper. Do this very slowly,
then brush the paste all over with melted butter.
7   Scatter over the crumbs and the fruit filling,

covering as much strudel as possible. Roll up, enclosing all the fruit. Slide on to the baking sheet, you will probably have to curl it round.
8   Brush over with butter and bake for about 30 minutes, or until the pastry is crisp.
9   Dust all over with icing sugar and serve warm, cut into thick slices.

BREAD & BUTTER PUDDING

Serves 2–3

This is a simple version of this pudding. Be sure to give enough time for the soaking process as the texture of the pudding relies on this.
Look for a good quality loaf either white or brown. I like to leave the crust on, especially because they become pleasantly crisp during the baking. Cinnamon is my chosen spice. Some people also like peel in the pudding.

5 oz (150 g) sliced bread (about 5 slices), buttered
2 oz (50 g) currants or raisins
2 oz (50 g) caster sugar
freshly grated nutmeg or ground cinnamon
1 size-1 or size-2 egg
10 fl oz (300 ml) milk
butter, for greasing

1   Preheat the oven to gas4/350°F/180°C. Grease a 1-2 pt (600 ml-1.2 litre) pie dish well.
2   Cut the buttered bread into triangles and arrange about one-third of them in the pie dish. Sprinkle over half of the dried fruit, just under half of the sugar and a dusting of nutmeg or cinnamon.
3   Cover with another layer of bread. Sprinkle over the rest of the dried fruit, a dusting of nutmeg or cinnamon and all but one dessertspoon of sugar.
4   Finish with a layer of bread pieces, overlapping them slightly. Sprinkle over the last of the sugar, plus a final dusting of nutmeg or cinnamon.

5   Beat the egg and milk together and pour this custard over the pudding. Allow it to soak in for 20 minutes. Check that all the bread is well soaked and press the top of the pudding down.
6   Set the dish on a baking sheet and bake for about 40 minutes, or until the custard is set and the top brown and crusty.

RICH BREAD & BUTTER PUDDING

Serves 4–6

For this one I like to use a fruited yeast loaf – not the sticky kind, but a proper bread. Soak the raisins all night if you can manage that, so that they really do soak up the rum.

6–8 slices of fruit bread
soft butter
2½ oz (65 g) raisins, soaked overnight in 1 of the tablespoons of rum
2 oz (50 g) caster sugar
2 tablespoons rum
3 size-1 or size-2 eggs
8 fl oz (175 ml) milk
¼ pt (150 ml) double cream

1   Preheat the oven to gas4/350°F/180°C. Butter a baking dish with a 2 pt (1 litre) capacity well.
2   Butter the bread slices and cut each in two.
3   Put one layer of bread on the bottom of the dish and sprinkle over half the raisins and some sugar. Dribble some rum over the bread as well.
4   Lay another layer of bread and scatter the rest of the raisins and sugar (all but a spoonful). Dribble more rum over the bread and raisins. Finish with a layer of bread, overlapping slightly. Sprinkle the last of the sugar and rum.
5   Whisk the eggs into the milk and cream and pour this slowly into the pudding. Leave it to soak for 20 minutes. Press the pudding down to encourage the bread to take up the custard.
6   After 20 minutes, put the baking dish on an oven tray and bake for about 30–40 minutes. Serve warm.

PEACH PUDDING WITH BRIOCHE

Serves 6–8

This variation and excellent idea came from a recipe by Alastair Little, one of today's famous chefs. It is a good example of an old recipe getting the kiss of life. Brioche is a sweet, rich – but light – bread originally of French origin. Nowadays all our supermarkets sell it. Look for an oblong brioche loaf. It will be easier to cut into cubes.

8 oz (225 g) brioche, cut into 1 in (2 cm)
    cubes – cut 1 in (2 cm) slices from the
    loaf and then cut into cubes
1½ oz (40 g) butter, melted, plus more for
    greasing
3 size-1 or size-2 eggs
2½ oz (65 g) caster sugar
10 fl oz (300 ml) milk
½ teaspoon vanilla extract
2 large ripe peaches, skinned, or 4 canned
    peach halves, drained and cut into cubes
½ teaspoon ground cinnamon
¼ pt (150 m) double cream
1 oz (50 g) icing sugar
2 teaspoons Armagnac

1   Preheat the oven to gas4/350°F/180°C. Butter a 2 pt (1 litre) ovenproof dish and a baking tray.
2   Toss the cubes of brioche in a roomy bowl with the 1½ oz (40 g) melted butter. Check that the bread has absorbed all the butter. Now set the cubes on a greased baking tray and bake for 10 minutes or until lightly browned. Set that aside to cool.
3   Whisk the eggs in a roomy bowl with 2 oz (50 g) caster sugar, reserving ½ oz (15 g). Bring the milk to the boil with the vanilla in a pan, then pour this in a steady stream into the egg mixture, whisking all the time. Stir in the peaches and the brioche cubes and leave aside for not less than 15 minutes – up to an hour would be even better.
4   Lower the oven to gas3/320°F/160°C. Now pour the pudding into the ovenproof dish. Mix the cinnamon with the remaining caster sugar and sprinkle this over the pudding. Set the dish on a baking tray and cook for 30–40 minutes, or until just set and the top tinged with gold.
5   Whip the double cream with the sifted icing sugar and Armagnac to the floppy stage and serve with the pudding.

COCONUT PLUM CRUNCH

Serves 4

You will need a shallow ovenproof dish large enough to take 8 plum halves in a single layer.

4 large ripe plums
1 oz (50 g) butter, softened
2 level tablespoons granulated sugar
thin custard, to serve

Topping
3 slices of white bread from a small loaf
2 oz (50 g) butter
4 level tablespoons demerara sugar
4 level tablespoons desiccated coconut
    (fresh is even better)

1   Preheat the grill.
2   Cut the plums in two and remove the stones. Set the halves in the ovenproof dish in a single layer. Dot the butter all over the fruit. Set the dish under the grill, until the fruit is evenly soft and the butter melted.
3   Take the dish out and sprinkle the sugar over the fruit. Keep the dish warm.
4   Prepare the topping: cut the bread into small cubes about ¼ in (6 mm). Melt the 2 oz (50 g) butter in a saucepan. Add the bread cubes, demerara sugar and coconut. Stir well.
5   Pile these on top of the fruit in the dish. Set the dish under the grill as far from the heat as possible. Grill gently until the bread and coconut are toasted.
6   Serve at once with thin custard.

FRIAR'S OMELETTE

Serves 6

One of the things I remember being told about cooking apples is that the finest flavour comes from a baked apple. In the old books the start of this recipe is to bake the apples for 45 minutes to 1 hour. Now, that time can be reduced very easily with a microwave cooker.

6 medium-size cooking apples
3 oz (75 g) butter, plus more for greasing
    and dotting
2 oz (50 g) caster sugar
rind from 1 lemon
pinch of ground cloves or nutmeg
4 oz (125 g) fresh breadcrumbs
4 size-1 or size-2 egg yolks
custard, to serve

1   Preheat the oven to gas5/375°F/190°C. Grease a 2½ pt (1.4 litre) ovenproof baking dish.
2   Score each apple round its middle – just with the tip of the knife. Then core each apple as well. Set the apples in a microwave dish with 4 tablespoons of water. Cook on high for 20 minutes, checking at the ten-minute stage. When they are all soft, take the dish out to cool. Scrape all the apple out of the skins.
3   Cream the butter and sugar, add the lemon rind, apple pulp and ground clove or nutmeg.
4   Sprinkle the bottom and sides of the baking dish with the breadcrumbs.
5   Whisk the egg yolks and then stir them into the apple mixture. Pour into the dish. Cover with the rest of the crumbs and dot with the butter.
6   Bake for 30 minutes, or until the pudding has set and is firm.
7   Serve with custard.

CHICHESTER LEMON PUDDING

Serves 4

I remember doing this recipe on a pudding programme. It was always difficult to time something like this which should be served immediately it comes out of the oven – before it falls. The recipe was sent by a viewer, Sheila Powell of Sussex.

4 slices of good-quality white bread
½ oz (15 g) butter
2 size-1 or size-2 eggs, separated
2 oz (50 g) caster sugar
9 fl oz (250 ml) milk
grated rind and juice from 1 large lemon

1   Preheat the oven to gas4/350°F/180°C and put a baking sheet in to heat up. Butter a 1 pt (600 ml) soufflé dish.
2   Cut the crusts off the bread and whizz them in a food processor to crumbs – rough ones, not too fine.
3   Whisk the egg yolks with the sugar and milk. Add the crumbs, lemon juice and rind.
4   In another bowl (having washed and dried the whisk beaters), whisk the egg whites until very stiff. Use a rubber spatula to fold the egg whites into the lemon mixture.
5   Scrape the mixture into the soufflé dish and put straight into the oven on the heated tray.
6   Bake for 35–40 minutes until the pudding is set and golden.
7   Serve at once before it sinks. The white inside is marbled with lemon.

RHUBARB & GINGER INSTANT CRISP CRUMBLE

Serves 6

The crumble topping can be pre-cooked in bulk and stored in a tin.

2 lb (900 g) rhubarb (early rhubarb is best)
1 level teaspoon ground ginger
3 oz (75 g) caster sugar

Crumble Topping
4 oz (125 g) butter, melted
6 oz (175 g) rolled oats
4 tablespoon fresh breadcrumbs
4 tablespoons demerara sugar

1   Preheat the oven to gas3/325°F/160°C.
2   Make the topping ahead: put the melted butter in a large bowl and stir in the oats, breadcrumbs and demerara sugar.
3   Sprinkle this mixture in the bottom of a large tin like a roasting tin and bake for about 10 minutes. Stir it once or twice during the baking. Take out of the oven and leave to cool. Crush further with a rolling pin. Store in an airtight tin.
4   Now for the pudding: first bake the rhubarb in a covered dish in the oven with the ginger. It should not need water. Strain off almost all the water and stir in the sugar.
5   Preheat the oven to gas4/350°F/180°C. Put the rhubarb and ginger in an ovenproof baking dish with a 2 pt (1.2 litre) capacity. Spread a ½ in (1 cm) layer of the breadcrumb crisp on top.
6   Bake on a tray for 15 minutes, or until the pudding is heated through. Serve warm.

QUEEN OF PUDDINGS

Serves 4

Traditionally this very light pudding with a fluffy meringue topping had strawberry jam in it. I've always thought a sharper jam like blackcurrant or even gooseberry would be better. You must choose.

grated rind of 1 lemon
3 oz (75 g) fresh breadcrumbs
15 fl oz (450 ml) milk
½ oz (15 g) butter, plus more for greasing
5 oz (150 g) caster sugar
3 size-3 eggs, separated
2 tablespoons good sharp jam like blackcurrant
caster sugar

1   Preheat the oven to gas4/350°F/180°C. Generously butter a 1½ pt (845 ml) baking dish.
2   Stir the lemon rind into the breadcrumbs and put them into the baking dish.
3   In a small pan, warm the milk, butter and 1 oz (25 g) of the measured sugar (there are 4 oz (125 g) left).
4   In another bowl, beat 3 egg yolks and the white of 1 of the eggs together, then stir in the milk, butter and sugar mixture. Pour this over the breadcrumbs and leave it to stand for 20 minutes.
5   Now set the dish on a baking sheet and bake for 25 minutes, when the pudding should have set.
6   Slightly warm the jam in the microwave (3 seconds on high). Spread it carefully over the set pudding. Reduce the oven to gas3/325°F/160°C.
7   Use an electric whisk on the 2 remaining egg whites until they are stiff. Add half of the remaining sugar, whisk again and fold in the remaining sugar. Pile the meringue on the pudding and spread it all over, sealing it to the edge. Bake for 10-15 minutes.

Variations for Queen of Puddings
Instead of jam, try crushed fresh strawberries or raspberries.

BAKED CUSTARDS

SIMPLE BAKED CUSTARD

Serves 4–6

This custard is flavoured with vanilla. Try to get the very best vanilla extract – although it costs a great deal more it does go a long way, hardly ever needing more than 2 or 3 drops per recipe.

3 size-1 or size-2 eggs
1 pt (575 ml) milk
1 oz (25 g) sugar
2–3 drops of vanilla extract

1   Preheat the oven to gas3/325°F/160°C.
2   Put the milk and vanilla and sugar in a big jug and warm it very slightly in the microwave. Stir until the sugar dissolves.
3   Drop the eggs into the warmed milk and whisk together; I use a rotary whisk or a hand-held electric mixer. Pour the custard into a flat ovenproof dish with a capacity of about 1½ pt (1 litre).
4   Set in a roasting tin and pour hot water halfway up dish to bake the custard slowly for about 1 hour. The custard should be firm. Slide a knife blade in and if it comes out clean it is done.

Variations

Grate nutmeg over the surface either before of after cooking.
Sweeten the custard with a dessertspoon of honey instead of sugar.
    This same amount of custard will make 6 individual ones in small straight-sided ramekins.

CRÈME BRÛLÉE

Serves 4

The original Crème Brûlée or 'burnt cream' is associated with Trinity College, Cambridge, where the college crest was impressed on the top of the cream with a branding iron. It is simply a rich custard cooked in a pan, set in a baking dish, with a sugared top caramelized under a grill. My son was a student at that college and swears he was never given this as a pudding!

1 oz (25 g) caster sugar, plus more for
    sprinkling
4 yolks from size-1 or size 2 eggs
1 vanilla pod
1 pt (575 ml) double cream

1   Whisk the sugar with the egg yolks until they are pale and fluffy.
2   If you have a double saucepan use it. If not use a heatproof bowl over a saucepan of simmering water. Put the double cream and the vanilla pod into the top of your double saucepan or in the bowl. Bring almost to boiling point, but do not boil. Remove the vanilla pod. Pour the hot cream over the whisked egg yolks, whisking all the time. Return all the mixture to the double pan or bowl. Stirring often, cook gently until the custard thickens.
3   Pour the custard into an ovenproof dish with a capacity 1½ pt (1 litre) and set it aside to go cold and firm up.
4   Preheat your grill so that it is as hot as it can go. Cover the cream with a thick layer of caster sugar. (A fellow food writer always describes the quantity as being as thick as a pound coin.) Put the sugared cream under the grill to caramelize the sugar. Watch it carefully and remove it before it burns. Serve chilled.

Variations

Put the custard in individual heatproof ramekins. Other people swear that demerara is the best sugar to use. I think that the unrefined golden caster sugar has the best flavour.
    If you are nervous of burning sugar, a good substitute is to buy peanut brittle and crush it with a rolling pin inside a strong plastic bag. Scatter this over the cream.
    Almond Praline is another nice nutty toffee which crushes deliciously.

FRUIT BRÛLÉE

This is probably the version most often associated with the burned sugar process. These are nearly always done in individual heatproof ramekins.

Fruits to use:
Small sweet grapes
Bananas, chopped perhaps with crystallized ginger
Blackberries, lightly cooked
Nectarines, chopped
Apricots, chopped

A spot of liqueur would be pleasant with some fruit – I do mean a spot, e.g. a fruit liqueur like Framboise, Cassis, Kirsch, Prune, Cointreau or Grand Marnier.

Cream

There are some alternatives now for whipped double cream:
crème fraîche which has a rich slightly sharp flavour and there is no need to whip;
thick Greek yoghurt, again no need to whip;
or a mixture of any of the two.

1 Fill the ramekins two-thirds full of fruit. Remember to leave room for cream and sugar. I have found that it is easier if the sugar does not sit level with the rim of the ramekins (there are less dribbles).
2 Next put in the 'cream' of your choice. If you are whipping cream, do not make it too thick. Level the cream off carefully, then set the ramekins in the fridge so that the cream is really cold and stiff.
3 Put the sugar on evenly. Heat up the grill in advance and, when you slip these dishes under, have them sitting in the grill pan or on a heatproof plate so that you have something to hold. Watch them carefully – do not leave them alone!

CARAMEL MADE IN A PAN

This is one other way to get a crisp toffee finish on your Fruit Brûlée. I think it is the easiest. You must have a heavy-based pan which is also deep. The one I use is 5 in (6 cm) deep and 7 in (18 cm) across. Non-stick pans aren't easy as the dark finish obscures the colour of the caramel. For 6 ramekins I suggest you use 6 oz (175 g) caster sugar. Some people put a dash of water in with sugar, I don't.

1 Put the pan with the sugar over a moderate heat. Watch it and when you see that the sugar is beginning to melt underneath very slightly, shake the pan so that the sugar is tossed from side to side. This way the pan is off and on the heat. Just keep it on the move but do not use a spoon – the sugar will just stick to it in a lump. Keep up this movement and all the sugar will melt.
2 When you have a rich golden colour, grip the pan handle firmly and pour the caramel over the cream. I use an upturned teaspoon in the same way as for pouring cream into a liqueur coffee to get it to stay on top. I pour the caramel over the back of the spoon and over the cream. I think it is easier to pour this caramel over a big dish of fruit and cream. However the individual ones do look good. GOOD LUCK!

Notes

Anything with crisp caramel should not go in the fridge as it will start to dissolve. Just keep it in a cool place.

If you get cold feet about the caramel, here is a very nice topping which also looks good. Several hours before the meal, sprinkle some dark molasses sugar over the cream. Do this roughly and not too much. Put the ramekins in the fridge and the sugar will trickle over the cream very nicely.

AROMATIC CUSTARD

Serves 4

8 oz (225 g) natural yoghurt
4 cardamom pods, broken up
2 yolks from size-1 or size-2 eggs
1½ oz (40 g) caster sugar
crisp biscuits or toasted brioche, to serve

1   Well in advance, put the yoghurt into a pan with the cardamom pods and all. Leave them there as long as you can.
2   Whisk the egg yolks and the sugar until they are thick and fluffy.
3   Heat up the yoghurt and, when it is warm, pour some over the egg yolk, whisking all the time. Pour this mixture back into the pan. Go on heating until the custard thickens. Fish out the bits of cardamom.
4   Pour into 4 small ramekins and put aside to set.
5   Serve with a crisp biscuit or toasted brioche.

DEEP CUSTARD PIE

Serves 4

You could not call yourself a good baker in Yorkshire unless you could make a decent custard pie. By this I do not mean a thin one in a flan tin but a deep one from a tin measuring 5 in (14 cm) at the bottom and 6 in (16 cm) at the top and 1½ in (4 cm) deep. Getting it out of the tin in one piece is another challenge.

6 oz (175 g) Shortcrust Pastry (see page 16)
8 fl oz (225 ml) milk
1 oz (25 g) caster sugar
2 size-1 or size-2 eggs
freshly grated nutmeg
butter, for greasing

1   You will need a traditional tin as above. Grease this well. Preheat the oven to gas7/425°F/220°C and put a baking sheet in the oven to heat up.
2   Roll out the pastry on a lightly floured board to about 10 in (25 cm) in diameter (if you have not made this pie before I would be inclined to make the pastry very slightly thicker than usual). Lift the pastry on your rolling pin and fit it into the pie tin as neatly as possible. Trim off the excess party and put the pastry into the fridge to rest while you make up the custard.
3   Warm the milk, add the sugar and stir to dissolve the sugar. Whisk the eggs lightly then whisk them into the milk.
4   Put the custard pie tin on the hot baking sheet in the oven (pull the shelf out slightly), pour the custard in and grate some nutmeg over the top. Close the oven door and bake at the high temperature to set the pastry for about 15 minutes. Now reduce the heat to gas6/400°F/200°C and cook for another 25 minutes, or until the custard is set.
5   Leave the pie in the oven for 5 or 6 minutes. Then drop it gently out on a clean tea towel on your outstretched hand. Immediately place a cooling wire against the base and turn the pie the right way up. Hooray!

CHOCOLATE & ORANGE CUSTARDS

Serves 5

Chocolate and orange is a wonderful combination. Make this in very small portions. Use either Terry's Orange Chocolate or a very plain good quality chocolate.

6 oz (175 g) Terry's Orange Chocolate or
    very good plain chocolate
1 oz (25 g) butter, cut into small pieces
4 yolks from size-1 or size-2 eggs
15 fl oz (450 ml) milk
1½ oz (40 g) caster sugar
2 teaspoons grated orange peel
small dash of Cointreau

1   Preheat the oven to gas3/325°F/160°C. You will need a small heavy-based pan, 5 small ramekins and a roasting tin.
2   Break the chocolate up into small pieces and melt it over a low heat. When it is liquid, draw the pan off the heat and stir in the butter pieces until melted.
3   In another bowl, whisk the egg yolks with the milk. Then strain the egg and milk mixture into the chocolate mixture. Add the sugar, orange rind and Cointreau. Pour into the ramekin dishes and stir each one lightly.
4   Pour hot water about 1 in (2.5 cm) deep into the roasting tin. Set the ramekins in the water. Bake for about 20–25 minutes or until firm.
5   Chill and serve with something crisp.

CARAMEL CUSTARD

Serves 6

Caramel
4 oz (125 g) caster sugar
4 tablespoons (2 fl oz) hot water

Custard
juice of 1 lemon
3 tablespoons of hot water
1 packet of gelatine
4 size-1 or size-2 eggs
1½ oz (40 g) caster sugar
6 tablespoons lightly whipped double
    cream

1   First make the caramel: put the sugar and 10 fl oz (300 m) water in a heavy-based pan and cook gently until the sugar has melted. Turn up the heat and watch it boil until it becomes quite golden. Take the pan off the heat and sit the pan in the sink with about 2 in (5 cm) cold water to cool it down. Now stir in the hot water and set aside.
2   Make the custard: put the lemon juice and 3 tablespoons of hot water in a small bowl. Sprinkle over the powdered gelatine. Set aside for 3–4 minutes to swell up. Now stand the bowl in a small pan of simmering water and stir until the gelatine has melted.
3   Next, separate 2 of the eggs. Put the 2 whole eggs and 1 egg yolk in a heatproof basin with the 1½ oz (40 g) caster sugar and suspend the basin over a pan of simmering water. Whisk often until the mixture thickens. Take the bowl off the heat and whisk again to cool it down a bit, before adding the caramel liquid and the melted gelatine. Stir well then leave this aside until it has almost set and looks just a bit wobbly. Stir it again and stir in the cream.
4   Stiffly beat the egg whites and fold them in. Pour into 6 individual ramekins to set.

TRIFLES

TODAY'S TRADITIONAL FAMILY TRIFLE

Serves 6–8

It's no good believing that everybody thinks it's worth making proper custard and home-made sponge for a trifle. This recipe represents what lots of people enjoy – a very simple family trifle.

1 packet of trifle sponges
large glass of sweet sherry
large tin of fruit cocktail or peaches
1 packet of custard or can or carton of
    ready-made custard
¼ pt (150 ml) double cream, or more

Decorations
red cherries
grated chocolate or chocolate drops

1   Slice 2 or 3 sponges in two and lay them to cover the bottom of a deep glass bowl.
2   Sprinkle over a large glass of sherry.
3   Drain the fruit and spoon some of the juice over the sponges so that they are all nice and moist. Spoon in the fruit on top of the sponge.
4   Make up the custard (see page 196). Aim for a thinnish custard so that it does not set too firmly. Pour the custard over the fruit and leave that to cool down.
5   Lastly, whip the cream so that it is soft rather than stiff and spoon over the trifle.
6   Decorate with red cherry pieces or grated chocolate.

JELLIED TRIFLE

This will appeal to children I think, when they see the bright colour at the bottom of the trifle bowl. Omit the sherry and the fruit juice, just put the fruit on top of the sponge, then pour a made-up jelly over the fruit and sponge and leave that to set before the layer of custard.

If you are using a good crystal bowl, take care to cool the custard and jelly before you pour them in.

ITALIAN TRIFLE

Serves 8

4 oz (125 g) boudoir biscuits
¼ pt (150 ml) strong coffee
5 tablespoons Tia Maria
1 pt (575 ml) Fresh Custard (see page 196,
   not too thin)
8 oz (225 g) Mascarpone cheese
10 fl oz (300 ml) whipping cream
1 oz (25 g) toasted flaked almonds
1 oz (25 g) cocoa powder

1   Set the biscuits in the bottom of a deep glass bowl or a large flat gratin dish. Mix the coffee and the Tia Maria and pour this over the biscuits. Leave for at least 10 minutes so that they have time to soak up the liquid.
2   In another bowl, mix the custard and the Mascarpone. Spread this mixture over the biscuits and set aside for 2 hours.
3   Lightly whip the cream. Spread this over the pudding and scatter the toasted almonds. Lastly shake the cocoa through a sieve to give the pudding a light dusting only. Chill for 1 hour before serving.

TIRAMISU – THE ORIGINAL FLAVOUR

Serves 8

The biscuit sponges we use are not quite like the Savoiardi from Italy, although you can get them in some specialist Italian and French shops. Theirs are much softer and more absorbent and nothing like as sweet as the boudoir sponge biscuits.

2 size-1 or size-2 eggs, separated
3 oz (75 g) caster sugar
12 oz (325 g) Mascarpone cheese
3 fl oz (75 ml) brandy
6 fl oz (175 ml) strong cold coffee
about 20 Savoiardi boudoir biscuits
1 oz (25 g) cocoa powder

1   Whisk the two egg yolks with the sugar until very pale and thick (do this in a large bowl). Stir in the Mascarpone cheese gradually, then beat it together until smooth.
2   Whisk the two egg whites until they stand up in stiff peaks. Fold the egg whites into the Mascarpone mixture. Scoop about one-third of the mixture into the bottom of a large flattish dish about 3 in (7.5 cm) deep and level it off.
3   Now mix the brandy into the coffee and pour this into another flat dish. Take 10 of the biscuits and dip each one briefly into the liquid and lay it down on top of the cream. If there are any spaces, use more biscuits.
4   Scoop the next third of the cream on top of the biscuits and repeat the dipping with the rest of the biscuits. Cover with the second layer of fingers, then with the last of the Mascarpone cream. Smooth the surface.
5   Cover and chill the pudding.
6   Just before serving, knock the cocoa through a sieve for a light dusting all over the top.

INDIVIDUAL COFFEE & CRUNCH TRIFLES

Serves 6

To crush the peanut brittle, put the pieces in a thick plastic freezer bag and hammer with a rolling pin.

6 boudoir biscuits
2 tablespoons rum
6 fl oz (175 ml) freshly made but cold coffee
8 oz (225 g) crushed peanut brittle
7 oz (200 g) crème fraîche

1   Break up the boudoir biscuits in pieces and put a layer in the bottom of each of 6 ramekins.
2   Mix the rum with the coffee and pour some into each pot. Aim to make the biscuits very moist.
3   Put a layer of crushed peanut brittle in next, then spoon the crème fraîche over the toffee. Smooth over the topping, then finish with another layer of crushed peanut brittle.

GRACE'S SUNDAY BEST TRIFLE

Serves 6

We grow a lot of raspberries and I always use them in this trifle. I make my own fatless sponge and real custard. You will need a flat gratin dish about 10x8 in (25x20 cm). I find it much easier to serve a shallow trifle rather than a deep one.

1½ lb (675 g) fresh or frozen raspberries
2 oz (50 g) caster sugar
½ a fatless sponge (see page 144)
1½ oz (40 g) flaked almonds
½ pt (300 ml) Real Custard (see page 196
   (450 ml) double cream

1   First cook the raspberries in about ½ in (1 cm) water with the 2 oz (50 g) sugar. Cook very, very briefly to get the juices running and set aside to go cold.
2   Cut the half sponge in two horizontally and lay the sponge in the bottom of the dish. Use the raspberry juice to moisten the sponge really well. Now use a perforated spoon to scoop up the raspberries and put them into the dish on top of the sponge.
3   Scatter the flaked almonds all over the raspberries and pour over the warm custard. Set aside to go cold.
4   Whip the cream to the floppy stage and spread in a thick layer on top of the custard. Use the point of a skewer to make whirls across the surface of the cream.
5   Chill and serve.

'Little Miss Muffet
San on a tuffet,
Eating her curds and whey;
There came a big spider,
Who sat down beside her
And frightened Miss Muffet away.'

'I have never a piece of toast
Particularly long and wide,
But fell upon the sanded floor,
And always on the buttered side.'

Chamber's Journal, James Payn

2

Five-Minute Favourites

GREEN PEPPERCORNS & STRAWBERRIES

Serves 4

This is an extension of the pepper with strawberries theme. It is not a new idea. I remember we used to say that a sprinkling of white pepper brought out the flavour of our strawberries. Nowadays I would say grind a tiny amount of black pepper over a bowl of cut strawberries, but I think the strawberries must be very ripe and sweet to benefit from this treatment.

Green peppercorns are the unripe berries of the more familiar black peppercorn in your grinder. You can get them freeze-dried and hard or preserved in brine or vinegar, when they are soft and very mild. They must be thoroughly rinsed, as in this recipe.

1 oz (25 g) icing sugar
2 tablespoons Pernod
8 oz (225 g) sweet strawberries
1 small teaspoon green peppercorns in brine, thoroughly rinsed
whipped cream or crème fraîche, to serve

1 Sieve the icing sugar into the Pernod and stir until it dissolves.
2 Cut the strawberries in two and pour over the sweetened Pernod. Add the peppercorns and give the mixture a stir.
3 Serve with a blob of whipped cream or crème fraîche.

MELON & GINGER WINE

These days, you do not often see ground ginger and sugar handed round to sprinkle on melon. It always produced a bout of sneezing in our house. However, ginger is lovely with melon and if you can mix two types of melon, such as Honeydew and Ogen, so much the better.

Cut the chilled melons in big chunks and give everyone a liqueur glass of ginger wine to pour or drink.

RED HOT PEARS & ICE-CREAM

You can do this with both fresh and canned pears. I prefer the fresh ones. One large juicy pear, like a Comice, will give 2 good portions.

Peel the pear, cut it in two and scoop out the core neatly with a teaspoon. Put each half on a flat plate and slice it down from the stem end into 5 or 6 slices. Push the slices flat to one side and fan them out slightly. Cover each pear with a cup or a bowl and heat the pear in the microwave until really hot. Start with 10 seconds and check the heat, it may need more.

Pour over a dash of a fruit liqueur, like Grand Marnier or cherry brandy, as it comes out of the microwave and heat the other half the same way. Serve with a scoop of good ice-cream.

ETON MESS

This strawberry pudding is said to have originated at the famous public school. It could not be more simple. Whip double cream to the floppy stage, fold in broken meringues and crushed or chopped strawberries. I think it looks even better if you liquidize about half of the strawberries and mix them in so that the cream is streaked with pale pink.

BUTTERSCOTCHED BANANAS

Peel and slice the bananas lengthwise and lay them tightly together in a dish which will go in the microwave. Dot all over with little bits of butter and sprinkle soft brown sugar over – not too much. Squeeze the juice from half a lemon and dribble that over too. Cover the dish with another plate or clingfilm (don't forget to puncture the film in a few places) and cook on high for 1 minute, then have a look. The bananas will soften slightly. You may need more time in the microwave, but it is always easy to have a look then decide if it needs more cooking. Eat at once.

HOT RIPE PEACHES & MASCARPONE

Fresh peaches have to have boiling water poured over them in order to skin them. (Once skinned you could heat them up in the microwave if you want them really hot). To skin the peaches: slit the skin slightly round the middle. Set each whole peach in a pudding basin so that the boiling water will cover the fruit.

While the fruit is steeping, stir some crunchy demerara sugar into 2 large tablespoons of Mascarpone cheese. Scoop out each peach from the water and slip off the skin. Set a whole peach per person in a pudding bowl (not on a plate, where it would skid about). Scatter some demerara sugar over the peach and serve with a scoop of the sweetened Mascarpone.

Note that the peaches must be very ripe for this treatment.

PEACHES IN A MELBA SAUCE

Here is a famous recipe in its simplest form. Skin some ripe peaches by pouring over boiling water. Slip off the skins, then cut the peaches in two. Remove the stones and slice the fruit. Serve with a purée of fresh or frozen raspberries, liquidized with or without a little sugar. Serve with a meringue and whipped cream or ice-cream.

POMEGRANATE PEARLS WITH ORANGE JUICE & CREAM

I have always loved pomegranates – seeds and all. You had better ask your guests in advance if they do, as lots of people hate crunching. You could say the fibre content is good for them! I have to say that getting the garnet-coloured fruit out of its skin is not a fast job. However, they do freeze well, so for the sake of the 5-minute deadline I shall assume you have them in your freezer!

One big pomegranate will give you enough fruit for 2 small portions. Squeeze the juice of 1 small orange over the fruit and divide between small dishes. I use old-fashioned stemmed sherry glasses. Reserve a few fruits. Top with a blob of whipped cream or thick yoghurt and dot over the pretty scarlet 'pearls'.

Look for ripe fruit which is heavy and the skin not too rigid. There are two methods of releasing the fruit from the pomegranate:
1 Cut the fruit in half and turn each half outside in to pull away the fruit. Do this over a bowl to catch the juice. This works better with smallish fruit.
2 The other way is to slice off the stem end so that the fruit will stand up. Take a sharp knife and cut through the skin downwards into 4 or 5 sections. Avoid piercing the fruit as much as you can. Pull out the sections and separate the glistening 'pearls' from every trace of pith.

CHILLED PAPAYA WITH RATAFIA CRUMBS

Also known as paw-paw, the exotic fruit papaya is usually pear-shaped and quite big, starting at about 12 oz (325 g). If it is ripe, it is sweet enough to be eaten straight from the skin with a teaspoon. Cut the fruit in 2 from the stem end. Scoop out the black seeds. Ratafia biscuits are small almond macaroon biscuits. Crush just 2 for each serving and sprinkle over the fruit.

FRUIT BRÛLÉE

A fast fruit brûlée probably needs rather more than 5 minutes. It is usual to chill this pudding down after it is made, but it is rather nice with the hot topping and cool fruit underneath.

Switch on the grill well ahead. Half-fill heatproof ramekins with raw slightly sharp fruit – like small seedless grapes, raspberries, peaches or pineapple. Cover with stiffly whipped cream, smooth and top with a layer of caster sugar.

Slide the pots under the grill and watch carefully so that the cream does not boil over. Eat warm (remembering that hot sugar is very hot).

HOT PEPPERED PINEAPPLE WITH A LIME & RUM SAUCE

This is another microwave recipe. Put 1 or 2 rounds of fresh or canned pineapple on a flat plate which can go in the microwave. Add just a tablespoon of the pineapple juice and heat covered for 1 minute, then check. Once hot, grind some black pepper over very lightly.

The sauce is easy: melt 2 big tablespoons of lime jelly in a small pan with a tiny dash of rum. This would do for 2 servings. Eat while warm.

PEARS WITH COTTAGE CHEESE & HOT WALNUTS

This easy starter or pudding takes less than 5 minutes. Peel and slice in 2 a large pear. Scoop out the core with a teaspoon. Spoon over about half a small carton of cottage cheese. Heat good-quality walnuts on a plate in the microwave and scatter over the cheese. Eat at once.

Heating the walnuts for just 10 seconds brings out the walnut flavour. Peeling the pear is not actually essential, you could just wipe the skin with a piece of damp kitchen paper and chop up if you wish.

FRESH LYCHEES ROLLED IN TOASTED COCONUT

Lychees have a rough pinky brown skin which slips easily off the smooth white juicy ball of fruit within, not much bigger than a grape. I love the taste and texture of this fruit. The stone is surprisingly large, but will come out easily if you just slit the flesh and squeeze it out. I also find canned and stoned lychees very good too.

To toast coconut you just just use a hot grill. Spread the coconut thinly on a baking tray and slip it under the grill. Watch carefully as it soon burns. Allow to cool down, roll the wet fruit in the coconut and serve with coconut ice-cream – bliss!

Note: fresh grated coconut is best of all, or look for coarsely grated unsweetened coconut in whole-food shops.

GRILLED APPLES & CHEESE

The combination of apples and cheese is an old favourite. Wipe and cut in 2 each dessert apple. Core and then cut into fairly thin slices. Nick out the core and then lay the slices overlapping in a flat heatproof dish. Squeeze over the juice from half a lemon. Follow that with just a sprinkling of caster sugar. Dot with butter and grill until the apples are just beginning to fall, then scatter a grated mild cheese like Wensleydale over and return to the grill until the cheese melts. Eat at once.

GRATED APPLE WITH HAZELNUTS & CRÈME FRAÎCHE

You need sweet dessert apples for this one. Peel the apples if you wish, but then grate quickly on the big holes of a steel grater. Mix in finely sliced hazelnuts (done on your food processor). Serve with a dollop of crème fraîche.

GRILLED CANNED RICE OVER GRAPES

Heat up your grill before you do anything. I forgot where I saw this, but it is a quickie as only the top is warm. Half-fill heatproof ramekins with halved seedless grapes. Top with canned rice, smooth the rice over and scatter some caster sugar over the rice. Slide the pots under the grill and watch until they turn brown, then pull out quickly and eat.

NOT QUITE CRÈME ANGLAISE

This was a tip I got from a caterer. Simply mix canned custard with double or single cream and the result isn't bad at all! Use over fruit or fruit puddings.

'But I when I undress me,
Each night upon my knees,
Will ask the Lord to bless me,
With apple pie and cheese.'

Eugene Field

YOGHURT PUDDINGS

TART APPLES, YOGHURT & GINGER CRUNCH

Serves 4

6 ginger snap biscuits
4 Granny Smith apples
2 tablespoons lemon juice
about 1 level tablespoons light muscovado
    sugar
1 carton of natural yoghurt

1   First crush the ginger biscuits. You can break these up coarsely, then give them a quick whirl in the food processor to the rough crumb stage.
2   Do not grate the apples until you are almost ready to eat them. Use the big holes on the grater. Once grated and in a bowl, pour over some lemon juice and stir this round to try and prevent browning. Now stir in a little light muscovado sugar.
3   To serve: in some tall wine glasses, layer the crushed biscuits, natural yoghurt and grated apple in narrow bands if you have a steady hand. Serve at once.

SET GREEK YOGHURT WITH A BLACKCURRANT SAUCE

Serves 4

This set yoghurt can take the powerful flavour of blackcurrants.

1 carton set Greek yoghurt
crisp biscuits, to serve

Blackcurrant Sauce
8 oz (225 g) blackcurrants
about 3 oz (75 g) sugar

1   To make the sauce: liquidize the blackcurrants, reserving a few whole ones for decoration. Then stir in sugar to taste.
2   If you want a smooth sauce, pass this mixture through a nylon sieve.
3   Serve in pretty glasses with a scoop of yoghurt and the sauce over the top. Decorate each with 2 or 3 whole blackcurrants and serve with a crisp biscuit.

YOGHURT BANANAS & PEANUT BRITTLE

Get peanut brittle in a sweet shop. Put the pieces in a strong plastic bag and hammer with your rolling pin. Chop the bananas into a small bowl of natural yoghurt. Stir in some peanut brittle but leave enough for a topping. Divide and serve with some crushed peanut brittle on top.

BRAMBLE & YOGHURT BRÛLÉE

Another simple way to imitate a real brûlée. Switch on your grill as early as you can. Crush and sweeten some very ripe brambles (blackberries), but avoid using too much sugar. Spoon about 1 big tablespoon of fruit into small heatproof ramekins. Top with chilled thick yoghurt and smooth this over. Cover with a thickish layer of demerara sugar. Slide the pots under the hot grill and watch carefully as this melts. Pull out quickly if the sugar starts to get too brown.

POSH JELLY & CREAM

Serves 4

As early as you can, put a jug in the fridge with 5 fl oz (150 ml) very cold water. Add a handful of ice cubes and put the glasses in the fridge too.

½ packet of raspberry jelly
1 tablespoon port
8 oz (225 g) fresh or frozen raspberries
3 oz (75 g) Mascarpone cheese
2 tablespoons thick Greek yoghurt

1   Make up the jelly: cut the jelly in pieces and put in a heatproof measuring jug with the port and enough water just to cover the jelly.
2   Melt this in the microwave – about 1 minute on full power. Look at it after 40 seconds and give it a stir. Give it another 40 seconds.
3   When melted, take the ice-cold water out of the fridge and pour this into the jug to come just under the ½ pt (300 ml) mark. Take the cold glasses out of the fridge and divide the jelly between them. Divide the raspberries between the glasses, dropping them into each jelly, but reserving a few for decoration. Put the glasses back in the fridge to set.
4   Stir the Mascarpone and yoghurt together and, when the jelly has set, spoon this mixture on top of the jelly. Top each glass with a couple of the reserved raspberries.

GREEK YOGHURT WITH A BAKED CRUNCHY TOP

See page 220 for a streusel mixture to have ready-baked in a tin for this instant pudding. Use to top a dollop of thick cold yoghurt, then perhaps add a few grapes.

Another easy topping is made by toasting or baking dry 2 slices of plain sponge cake until crunchy, then crumbling the result and mixing it with chopped almonds.

TOASTED ALMONDS AND RUNNY HONEY OVER GREEK YOGHURT

Toast either chopped or flaked almonds under a hot grill. Watch carefully and do not answer the phone! Set honey can be turned quickly into runny honey in the microwave. Spoon as much as you need into a bowl and microwave, covered, for 10 seconds to begin with, then more if necessary.

Spoon the thick chilled yoghurt into nice glass dishes. Dribble over the runny honey while it is nice and warm and top with the toasted almonds. Eat at once.

A 17th-century French visitor wrote a glowing appreciation of English puddings:

'They make them fifty several ways. Blessed be he that invented pudding.'

HOMEMADE YOGHURT

Homemade natural yoghurt is cheap to make. A wide-necked flask which is gleamingly clean inside is a good container, but it can also be made in a clean jug or bowl. All you need is milk and a starter. The easiest form of starter is a large tablespoon of natural yoghurt (either commercial or homemade).

Both UHT and sterilized milk make rather thin yoghurt. Try to use whole milk, silver- or gold-top.

1 pt (600 ml) milk
1 level tablespoon plain yoghurt
2 oz (50 g) dried skimmed whole milk
   powder

1 Heat the milk to just above blood heat (110°F/43°C).
2 Whisk in the plain yoghurt and skimmed milk powder.
3 Transfer this mixture to a wide-necked flask or jar or jug which had been rinsed with boiling water and dried. Cover with a lid or a plate and set in a warm place like an airing cupboard. The flask should be fine anywhere, but the aim is to keep the mixture at an even temperature for 4–6 hours. Do not open the airing cupboard door to have a look until the 4 hours are up. Have a quick look and shake. If the yoghurt wobbles you will know it has worked.
4 Once set, this yoghurt should be put in the fridge for a further 4 hours to thicken. Take the cover off the flask and just cover with a plate.

Variation:
Replace the milk powder with a large dollop of cream (about 1 heaped tablespoon).
Thicker yoghurt is easily managed. Set the cooked and cooled yoghurt in an immaculate clean square of cotton (a large old hankie will do). Tie up with string and hang up over a bowl to catch the drips.

Chilled thick yoghurt goes extremely well with:
Brandied apricots
Rum-soaked raisins
Cherries in cherry brandy
Clementines in brandy

BOUGHT ICE-CREAM TARTED UP

CHRISTMAS PUDDING ICE-CREAM

This simple idea could be the alternative to a hot Christmas pudding. All that is needed is some softened vanilla ice-cream and a piece of Christmas pudding or Christmas cake (preferably homemade). Cut the Christmas pudding or cake into 1/2 in (1 cm) slices and then into cubes. Discard any crumbs and stir the cubes into the ice-cream very gently and re-freeze.

You could if you wished make the ice-cream into a pudding shape and serve it with a sprig of holly on top. All you do is line a suitable bowl with cling-film and spoon the ice-cream into that, pushing it well down to get a neat shape, then freeze. To serve, take it out of the freezer and put into the fridge to thaw slightly. Lift out the cling-film and set the iced pudding on a plate. Do not allow it to thaw too much. You must keep an eye on it.

MINT ICE-CREAM & SHAVED CHOCOLATE CURLS

Commercial mint ice-cream always tastes rather artificial to me. This home-produced version is very nice but should be eaten within 2 weeks of being made. You need peppermint oil, which you can get from a chemist. Although initially quite expensive for a tiny bottle, you only ever need 2 or 3 drops at any one time. It is also the mint you need to make real peppermint cream sweets. Add also some finely chopped bright green mint leaves which add both colour and flavour.

Use vanilla ice-cream and allow it to soften enough to stir and mix in 2 or 3 drops of real oil of peppermint and have ready finely chopped fresh unblemished mint leaves and stir these in as well. Once stirred together put the ice-cream back in the freezer until needed. It should be in a plastic box with a tight lid to prevent the peppermint from tainting other foods.

To make coarsely chopped chocolate for the topping: take a bar of good plain chocolate and freeze it hard. Using a swivel-bladed vegetable peeler, cut chunky curls off the side of the block of chocolate.

LEMON CURD & ICE-CREAM

You need a tasty homemade lemon curd for this and perhaps some grated lemon peel. Soften the ice-cream and stir in the lemon curd and lemon peel, then re-freeze.

ICY LIME WITH A GREEN SAUCE

Soften some ice-cream and stir in the juice and finely grated green peel from a lime. Re-freeze at once. To make the green sauce, melt 2 large tablespoons of lime jelly marmalade, add 1 tablespoon of lime juice and a few peeled and chopped pistachio nuts which are also pale green.

COCONUT SURPRISE ICES

Serves 8–10

This is a more elaborate pudding but the basis is plain vanilla ice-cream. You will need about 10 washed-out squat yoghurt cartons.

8 oz (225 g) desiccated coconut
1½ pt (1 litre) firm vanilla ice-cream (not the softer whipped kind)
about 20 small seedless grapes
10 small meringues, broken up

1   To toast the coconut, spread it in a grill pan and toast under a moderate heat in the grill. Take great care as it burns easily.
2   Allow the ice-cream to soften slightly. Fill each of the cartons about three-quarters full. Return them to the freezer.
3   When the ice-cream has firmed up, one at a time, take the cartons out, scoop out a cavity in the middle, put in a couple of grapes and some crumbled meringue. Seal up again with the ice-cream, smooth over and return to the freezer.
4   When frozen, again remove the cartons one at a time and unmould the ice-cream. Put the toasted coconut in a deep tin (a small roaster) and roll the ice-cream in it, using your hands to shape them into rough balls. Wrap the ball loosely in foil and return to the freezer until needed. Repeat the procedure with all the other cartons.
5   To serve: remove the balls from the foil and set each one in a pudding bowl.

CREAMY TOFFEE SAUCE OVER RICH VANILLA

Serves 4

This simple sauce is a real quickie.

½ pt (300 ml) good-quality vanilla ice-cream

Creamy Toffee Sauce
2 oz (50 g) white marshmallows
2 oz (50 g) butter
2 oz (50 g) creamy toffees

1   In a small heavy-based pan, put all three sauce ingredients together and melt very slowly. Keep stirring. Pour over balls of the good vanilla ice-cream and serve at once.

MELTED MARS BAR OVER COFFEE ICE-CREAM

Cut a Mars Bar into thin slices. Put into a small heavy-based pan with 2 tablespoons of liquid whipping cream. Melt over a low heat. Remove from the heat and stir in 2 teaspoons of strong coffee and more cream until you get to the texture for pouring. Serve over coffee ice-cream.

FLAKY BAR & STRAWBERRY ICE

Chop fresh strawberries and stir into softened vanilla or strawberry ice-cream. Return to freezer. Serve with crushed milk chocolate flake bar scattered over and a few fresh strawberries.

FRESH FRUIT SAUCES OVER ICED YOGHURT

You can buy yoghurt ice-cream or frozen yoghurt dessert. Failing these, a very good-quality ice-cream with a fresh fruit sauce is delightful.

FRESH APRICOT

Lightly stew the apricots in a little water. Drain and remove stones. Liquidize with a stick blender and sweeten very lightly.

FRESH RASPBERRY

Use a blender to liquidize the raspberries. Sweeten very lightly. Serve with a few whole berries on the side. (Note: if you want to remove seeds – I do not bother – it can be done through an extremely fine-mesh cone strainer.)

FRESH STRAWBERRY

Use a stick blender to reduce the strawberries to liquid. Add a little sugar. Serve with a few whole berries on the side.

FRESH BLACKCURRANT

This strongly flavoured berry needs to be diluted slightly with water. Stew 4 oz (125 g) blackcurrants in a little water until soft. Liquidize, then sweeten to taste. For a smooth sauce strain through a nylon sieve.

FUDGE TOPPING FOR VANILLA ICE AND ORANGES

Serves 6–8

1½ pt (850 ml) vanilla ice-cream
4–6 oz (125–175 g) mandarin oranges, drained and dried

Fudge Topping
5 oz (150 g) golden syrup, warmed
2 oz (50 g) butter
2 oz (50 g) caster sugar
3 oz (75 g) soft brown sugar
4 fl oz (100 ml) double cream

1   Soften the ice-cream and stir in drained and dried mandarin oranges. Re-freeze.
2   Make the sauce: using a heavy-based pan, first put the pan on your scales and weigh out the syrup (having warmed the tin it should be easy to pour). Watch the dial carefully as it goes in (5 oz / 125 g is about one-third of a 1 lb / 450 g tin).
3   Now add the butter and sugars and melt slowly. Keep stirring. When melted, remove from the heat. Cool slightly, then stir in the double cream. If it is still too thick, dilute with a little water or more cream.

GINGERED ICE

The ginger preserved in syrup is the best type to use for this ice-cream. Soften the ice-cream slightly and quickly stir in finely chopped ginger and a spoonful of the ginger syrup. Re-freeze.

Serve with a crisp biscuit and chopped ginger sprinkled over each serving.

RICH CHOCOLATE SAUCE OVER DOUBLE CREAM ICE-CREAM

Buy really top-quality cream ice-cream and make this rich Chocolate Sauce to go over it.

6 oz (175 g) soft brown sugar
½ pt (300 ml) milk
½ oz (15 g) butter
2–3 drops of vanilla essence

Put all the ingredients into a heavy-based pan and bring very slowly to a boil. Simmer for 5 minutes, stirring all the time.

MAPLE SYRUP SAUCE WITH CHOPPED PECANS AND VANILLA ICE-CREAM

Maple syrup has a distinctive flavour. Take some single pouring cream and stir into it a spoonful of maple syrup at a time, until you get the strength you like. Chop some pecan nuts and sprinkle them over plain ice-cream and follow that up with the sauce.

EASY CHOCOLATE SAUCE

The rich chocolate spreads which are on sale in jars will make a fast sauce. Use a whisk to mix the thick paste with cream or just milk. Pour the liquid on a little at a time and whisk hard.

EASY HAZELNUT SAUCE

As with the Easy Chocolate Sauce above, whisk some hazelnut spread into cream or milk in the same way. You could add some chopped hazelnuts to the mixture as well.

3

Chocolate Delights

CHOCOLATE FONDUE TO ACCOMPANY FRESH STRAWBERRIES

Makes 2 pt (1.1 litres)

To finish a summer party this fondue would be perfect with a basket of fresh ripe strawberries. Other fruit could be used, like chunks of pineapple or cherries on sticks, but the strawberry – with its green stalk at one end – is perfect for dipping.

6 size-1 or size-2 egg yolks
6 oz (175 g) caster sugar
1 miniature bottle of Orange Curaçao or
    3 tablespoons of any other fruit liqueur
8 oz (225 g) best-quality dark chocolate,
    broken into pieces
3 tablespoons strong dark coffee
1 pt (575 ml) double cream
8 oz (225 g) soft unsalted butter

1   In a heatproof bowl, whisk the egg yolks and the sugar until pale and thick. Whisk in the liqueur.
2   Set the bowl over a pan of simmering water to cook the custard gently, whisking often. Then, when the mixture is hot, take the bowl off the pan and sit it in a bowl of ice-cold water and whisk until cool.
3   Into another heatproof bowl, put the dark chocolate pieces and set this over the pan of simmering water to melt it. Stir the cold coffee and the cream into the melted chocolate.
4   Take the chocolate, cream and coffee off the heat and beat the butter in a little at a time.
5   Blend the chocolate and coffee mixture in with the egg yolk and sugar. Keep warm. If too thick stir in extra coffee or liqueur.

BITTER CHOCOLATE FONDUE WITH GRISSINI

This fondue is exactly the same recipe as the previous one, except that the chocolate should be top-quality bitter chocolate, with a high percentage of cocoa solids (60-70%). The sugar quantity is also lower, 3 oz (75 g) caster sugar instead of 6 oz (175 g).

Plain grissini – thin crisp bread sticks from Italy – are a lovely plain crunchy accompaniment for the bitter chocolate.

RICH CHOCOLATE BLANCMANGE AND FRESH ORANGES

Makes 4 or 6 tiny portions

Blancmange was usually a milk pudding set with cornflour. This is also a milk pudding, but set with gelatine and good chocolate.

1 packet of gelatine
4 oz (125 g) Terry's Chocolate Orange,
    broken into pieces
5 fl oz (150 ml) milk
5 fl oz (150 ml) double cream
4 large juicy oranges

1   Put 5 fl oz (150 ml) water in a bowl and sprinkle the gelatine over. Set it aside for 3 minutes. Then set the bowl over a pan of simmering water. Stir the gelatine to encourage it to melt.
2   Now melt the chocolate orange pieces in the milk. Do this slowly, stirring every now and then. When liquid, stir the chocolate mixture into the gelatine mixture, followed by the double cream.
3   Pour into 4 wetted glass dishes or 6 small wetted moulds.
4   To peel the oranges: take a sharp paring knife

and, over a bowl to catch the juice, peel the oranges as if you were peeling an apple. Cut down deep enough to take the pith off as well. Now holding an orange in one hand, slice down between each section and cut out the orange segments free from white pith. This is much easier than it sounds. Remove all the orange segments and then squeeze what's left to give you lots of juice. Repeat with the remaining oranges and chill the bowl of orange segments.
5   To serve: unmould each chocolate pudding and set on a flat plate with a circle of fresh orange slices and a little juice.

CHOCOLATE & ORANGE MOUSSE WITH ALMOND TUILES

Serves 6–8

6 oz (175 g) top-quality plain dark chocolate
1 oz (25 g) caster sugar
½ oz (15 g) butter, softened
2 dessertspoons Cointreau
3 size-1 or size-2 eggs, separated
about 24 Almond Tuiles (see page 262)

1   Break the chocolate into pieces and melt it in a pan with 3 fl oz (75 ml) water. Do this over a low heat and, once it has melted, stir in the sugar. Remove from the heat once the sugar has also dissolved. Allow this chocolate mixture to cool down a little (this is important).
2   Stir in the butter, followed by the Cointreau and lastly by the egg yolks. Stir gently but thoroughly.
3   In a clean bowl, whip the egg whites until they are stiff and fold them into the chocolate mixture.
4   Spoon into custard glasses or small coffee cups. Chill and serve with the almond tuile biscuits.

ORANGE & CHOCOLATE CUSTARDS

Makes 6

6 oz (175 g) plain dark chocolate, broken into pieces
1 oz (25 g) butter
4 size-1 or size-2 egg yolks
15 fl oz (450 ml) milk
1 oz (25 g) caster sugar
2 teaspoons finely grated orange rind
2-3 tablespoons Grand Marnier or other orange liqueur

1   Preheat the oven to gas3/325°F/160°C.
2   Put 1 tablespoon of water and the chocolate in a small heavy-based pan and melt it over a low heat. When it has melted, take the pan off the heat and allow it to cool down a bit.
3   Add the butter a little at a time, stirring gently.
4   Whisk the egg yolks with the milk. Stir this into the chocolate mixture, followed by the sugar, orange rind and Grand Marnier.
5   When all is amalgamated, pour the custard into 6 ovenproof ramekins.
6   Stand the pots in a roasting tin with hot water in it which comes halfway up the pots. Bake for about 25 minutes, until the custard is firm.
7   Serve hot or cold.

HOT CHOCOLATE SOUFFLÉ

Serves 6–8

4 oz (125 g) plain dark chocolate
2 tablespoons strong black coffee
2 oz (50 g) vanilla sugar
6 size-1 or size-2 eggs, separated
butter, for greasing
icing sugar, to decorate
chilled single cream, to serve

1   Preheat the oven to gas6/400°F/200°C. Butter a 2 pt (1.2 litre) soufflé dish.
2   Break the chocolate into small pieces and put it in a heavy-based pan with the coffee and the sugar. When melted, stir until smooth. Allow to cool down before the next step.
3   In another bowl, whisk 4 of the egg yolks until they are fluffy. Stir these into the chocolate mixture. (Keep the remaining egg yolks for enriching a sauce.)
4   In yet another bowl, whisk the 6 egg whites until stiff, then fold them into the chocolate and egg yolk mixture. Spoon immediately into the soufflé dish.
5   Set the dish on the baking sheet and bake for about 30 minutes, until the soufflé is risen. Dust with icing sugar and serve at once with chilled single cream.

COLD CHOCOLATE SOUFFLÉ

Serves 4–6

You will need a 6–7 in (16–18 cm) soufflé dish. Tie a collar of doubled greaseproof paper round the outside of the dish which is deep enough for the paper to stand about 2 in (5 cm) above the rim. Use a piece of string or an elastic band to hold it in place. See that the join overlaps by a least 2 in (5 cm).

2 packets of gelatine
3 oz (75 g) plain dark chocolate
1 pt (575 ml) milk
4 size-1 or size-2 eggs, separated
3 oz (75 g) caster sugar
½ pt (300 ml) double cream, whipped
extra whipped cream or grated chocolate, to decorate

1   In a medium-sized bowl, sprinkle the gelatine over 4 tablespoons of water and leave to soak for 3-4 minutes. Now set the bowl over a pan of simmering water to allow it to melt. Stir with a spoon until the gelatine is clear.
2   Put the chocolate in a pan with the milk and place over a low heat to allow it to melt. Stir until smooth and then bring the heat up almost to boiling point.
3   In another bowl, whisk the egg yolks and sugar until pale and thick. Pour the hot milk and chocolate over the yolk mixture, whisking all the time. Set this bowl over a pan of simmering water, stirring constantly, until the custard coats the back of the spoon.
4   Stir in the melted gelatine and set the chocolate mixture aside to cool down and start to set. It is important that you wait until the mixture is on the point of setting.
5   In yet another bowl, beat the egg whites until they are stiff. First fold the whipped cream into the chocolate mixture followed by the egg whites. Pour into the prepared soufflé dish and set it aside in the fridge to firm up.
6   Decorate the top of the soufflé with whipped cream rosettes or grated chocolate. Serve chilled.

LUXURY HOT CHOCOLATE DRINK

For 2

In Spain they serve this for breakfast, with Churros (see page 192) to dip in it.

3 oz (75 g) plain dark chocolate
1 level tablespoon caster sugar

8 fl oz (225 ml) milk
1 fl oz (30 ml) brandy or vodka
whipped cream, to decorate
grated chocolate, to decorate

1   Break the chocolate into pieces and dissolve
with the sugar in 2 fl oz (60 ml) of milk over a
low heat. Stir gently.
2   When the chocolate has melted, stir in the
remaining milk.
3   Pour into 2 hot beakers and stir in the brandy
or vodka.
4   Top with whipped cream and sprinkle with
grated chocolate. Serve at once with the churros.

LIGHT & DARK CHOCOLATE CUPS

Makes 24 tiny ones

5 oz (150 g) plain dark chocolate
4 tablespoons single cream
6 oz (175 g) milk chocolate
2 oz (50 g) butter
2 size-1 or size-2 egg yolks
4 chocolate buns
about 2 tablespoons rum, brandy or sherry
24 whole almonds

1   Melt the plain dark chocolate in a bowl. Set
over a pan of simmering water. Using a brush,
paint the inside of 24 foil sweet cases fairly
thickly with the melted chocolate. Now turn the
cases upside down to dry and harden on a baking
tray lined with non-stick paper. Put to set in the
fridge.
2   To make the pale chocolate filling: put the
cream in a small heavy-based pan and break the
milk chocolate into it. Melt over a low heat and,
once melted, take the bowl away from the heat.
3   Allow the chocolate mixture to cool and then
stir in the butter a little at a time. Next beat in
the egg yolks and set aside to cool until firm.
4   Meanwhile, take the chocolate cups out of
their foil cases and set them on a big flat plate.
Break up the chocolate buns and put in a bowl.

Dribble rum or other alcohol over the crumbs so
that they are really moist. Put a small teaspoon of
this in each cup.
5   Beat the filling again, fit a piping bag with a
1/2 in (1 cm) star nozzle. Pipe a whirl of pale
chocolate in each dark chocolate cup. Set a brown
almond on top of each cup.

PALE CHOCOLATE BAVAROIS

Serves 4

2 size-1 or size-2 eggs, separated
2 oz (50 g) caster sugar
6 fl oz (175 ml) milk
8 oz (225 g) milk chocolate
2 teaspoons powdered gelatine
3 fl oz (75 ml) double cream, whipped
toasted flaked almonds, to decorate

1   In a large mixing bowl, mix the egg yolks
and half the measured sugar.
2   Put the milk in small pan and bring it slowly
to the boil. Pour this hot milk over the egg yolk
mixture, whisking all the time. Return this
mixture to the pan and stir with a wooden spoon
until the custard thickens.
3   Break up the chocolate into pieces and add to
the hot custard. Stir until it dissolves. Remove
from the heat and decant it into a large bowl.
4   Sprinkle the gelatine over 2 tablespoons of
water in a small bowl and leave it to swell (about
3 minutes). Now set the bowl in a pan of
simmering water and allow it to melt. Stir
carefully. Then stir the liquid gelatine into the
chocolate mixture.
5   In another bowl, whisk the egg whites until
they are quite stiff. Add the remaining caster
sugar and whisk again.
6   With a large metal spoon or a big spatula,
fold first the whipped cream and then the egg
whites into the chocolate mixture.
7   Pour into a big glass dish and chill.
8   Decorate with toasted flaked almonds and
serve with a crisp biscuit.

AMARETTO & CHOCOLATE TERRINE WITH APRICOT SAUCE

Serves 4

You will need a small plastic storage box about 4 in (10 cm) square.

4 oz (125 g) plain chocolate, broken into
    pieces
2 oz (50 g) caster sugar
2 size-1 or size-2 eggs, separated
3 tablespoons Amaretto liqueur
2 heaped teaspoons gelatine
5 fl oz (150 ml) double cream, whipped

Apricot Sauce
6 oz (175 g) fresh apricots
1 oz (25 g) caster sugar

1   Put the broken chocolate into a heatproof medium-sized bowl over a pan of simmering water. Stir gently until it dissolves. Allow to cool a little.
2   Now stir in the sugar, egg yolks and liqueur. Stir until the sugar dissolves.
3   Put 2 tablespoons of water in a small bowl. Sprinkle the gelatine over the surface. Leave it aside to swell a bit. Set the bowl in a small pan of simmering water to melt. Now stir the melted gelatine into the chocolate mixture.
4   Stir in the whipped double cream.
5   In another bowl, beat the egg whites until stiff. Fold these into the chocolate mixture and pour into the plastic box. Aim to have a depth of about 1 in (2.5 cm). Set aside to firm up.
6   To make the sauce: if the apricots are very ripe, cut in two and remove the stones. Using a stick blender or a food processor, reduce the fruit to a purée. Stir in sugar to taste. If the apricots are hard, stew them in a little water until soft. Drain them and remove the stones. Reduce to a purée as described.
7   To serve, run a knife round the outside edge of the terrine and turn it out. Slice into 4 or 6, depending on your appetite. Place 1 slice on each plate and pour the apricot sauce over one side of it.

BRANDY & CHOCOLATE TRUFFLE MARQUISE

Serves 10

The use of gelatine in a recipe is often a real 'turn off' for some cooks, so when I saw this idea of 'setting' a chocolate filling using marshmallow I adapted the suggestion for this highly calorific cake.

5 oz (150 g) digestive biscuits, crushed
2 oz (50 g) almond macaroons, crushed
3 oz (75 g) butter, plus more for greasing
16 oz (450 g) good-quality plain chocolate,
    broken into pieces
4 oz (125 g) marshmallows
7 tablespoons brandy
1 pt (575 ml) double cream
1/2 pt (300 ml) single cream

1   Grease lightly a 9 in (23 cm) deep cake tin with a loose base or a spring-form tin with movable sides and put a circle of greaseproof paper in the base, or use a 2 lb (900 g) loaf tin lined with cling-film.
2   First mix the digestive and the macaroon crumbs. Melt the butter and stir into the mixture so that the crumbs are all well coated. Press into the base of the cake tin. Level it off, but do not hammer it down too much.
3   Set 2 pans of simmering water on the hob. In a heatproof bowl set over one, put the chocolate. In another, put the marshmallows and all but 2 tablespoons of the brandy. Stir each frequently. Once melted, take the bowls from the heat and set them aside to cool for at least 5 minutes.
4   In yet another bowl, whip the cream to the floppy stage. Scoop half of the cream into the chocolate bowl and the other half into the marshmallow bowl. Use a gentle folding movement to blend the cream in. Now blend the two bowlfuls together. Spoon the mixture into the cake or loaf tin, level the surface and set in the fridge to firm up.
5   To serve: stir the reserved brandy into the chilled single cream as a sauce and unmould and cut the marquise in wedges.

CHOCOLATE-BASED SAUCES FOR PUDDINGS & ICES

CHOCOLATE SAUCE USING COCOA

Serves 6

6 oz (175 g) unrefined light muscovado
    sugar or soft brown sugar
3 oz (75 g) cocoa, sieved
10 fl oz (300 ml) milk
½ oz (15 g) butter
2–3 drops of vanilla extract

1   In a heavy-based pan over a gentle heat, slowly melt all the ingredients above. I use a small loop-headed whisk to disperse the dry cocoa. Stir often.
2   To keep the sauce warm once you have made it, stand the jug in a pan of gently simmering water.

MARS BAR SAUCE

Serves 4

1 normal-size Mars bar
5 fl oz (150 ml) whipping cream
2 teaspoons strong coffee
little milk, if necessary

1   Chop the Mars bar into thin slices, then put these into a heavy-based pan together with the cream and coffee. Melt slowly over a gentle heat.
2   To thin the sauce, if necessary, add a few spoonfuls of milk.

Variation
A melted Mars Bar mixed with coffee icing make an excellent topping for éclairs.

QUICK CHOCOLATE SAUCE

Serves 4

4 oz (125 g) plain chocolate, broken into pieces
5 fl oz (150 ml) evaporated milk

1   Put the chocolate and the milk in a small heavy-based pan and melt the chocolate slowly.

FUDGE SAUCE

Serves 6

5 oz (150 g) golden syrup (one-third of a 1 lb /
    450 g tin)
2 oz (50 g) butter
2 oz (50 g) caster sugar
3 oz (75 g) unrefined light muscovado sugar
    or soft brown sugar
4 fl oz (100 ml) double cream

1   A good way to measure golden syrup or any other sticky thing is to warm the syrup by standing the opened tin in a pan of simmering water. Next put the pan you intend to use to melt everything on the scales and pour the syrup in slowly, watching carefully when the 5 oz (150 g) mark comes up. Stir in all the other ingredients except the double cream.
2   Melt them slowly, paying particular attention to the sugar. It sometimes has small very hard balls of compressed sugar hidden in it.
3   Once these first 4 ingredients are liquid, set the pan aside and allow the mixture to go almost cold before you stir in the double cream.

CHOCOLATE & RUM SAUCE

Serves 4–6

4 oz (125 g) best-quality dark chocolate,
   broken into pieces
7 fl oz (195 ml) double cream
1 oz (25 g) butter (unsalted if possible)
2 tablespoons rum
6 oz (175 g) icing sugar, sieved

1   Put the chocolate pieces, cream and butter in
a heatproof bowl and set it over a pan of
simmering water. Stir gently.
2   Once the chocolate has melted, pour in the rum.
3   Take the bowl away from the heat and beat in
the icing sugar gradually.
4   The sauce should be quite thick. If you wish
to thin it down add more rum or cream.

CHOCOLATE FUDGE SAUCE

Serves 4–6

4 fl oz (100 ml) canned evaporated milk
3 oz (75 g) caster sugar
4 oz (125 g) plain dark chocolate, broken
   into pieces
2 oz (50 g) butter, cut into pieces
1–2 drops of vanilla extract or essence

1   In a small pan with a heavy base, heat the
evaporated milk and sugar very gently until the
sugar melts. Once this happens, bring the
mixture up to a gentle boil for about 5 minutes.
Do not stir. This will caramelize the mixture to
give the typical fudge flavour.
2   Take the pan off the heat and stir in the chocolate.
3   When the chocolate has melted, stir in the
butter and vanilla. Set aside to cool.
4   If the sauce is too thick add a little more
evaporated milk.

CHOCOLATE & CREAM SAUCE

Serves 6–8

10 fl oz (300 ml) double cream
8 oz (225 g) plain dark chocolate
2–3 drops of vanilla extract or essence

1   In a pan with a heavy base, heat about half of
double cream very, very gently.
2   Grate the chocolate into the cream or chop it
rather finely and add.
3   When the chocolate has finally melted, add
the vanilla and remaining cream.

HOT CHOCOLATE & BRANDY SAUCE

Serves 4

$3^{1}/_{2}$ oz (90 g) bitter chocolate, broken into
   pieces
$^{1}/_{2}$ teaspoon vanilla extract or essence
1 oz (15 g) caster sugar
$^{1}/_{2}$ oz (15 g) butter
2 size-1 or size-2 egg yolks
2 tablespoons brandy

1   Put into a heatproof bowl all the ingredients
except the egg yolks and brandy together with
3 fl oz (75 ml) of water.
2   Set the bowl over a pan of simmering water
and stir lightly. When eventually the chocolate
has melted, take this bowl away from the heat
and set it aside to cool down a bit.
3   Then beat in the egg yolks, followed by the
brandy. If the mixture is too thick add another
spoonful of water.

4

Biscuits to Accompany Creamy Puddings or Ice-cream

A really crisp biscuit is a joy, especially with soft creamy puddings. The contrast in texture is always good, but do remember that home-made biscuits are not treated as commercial biscuits so as to stay crisp for months. They need to be taken out of their storage tin just before they are needed.

To crisp up biscuits which have gone soft, heat the oven to gas4/350°F/180°C, set the biscuits out on a baking tray and bake for 10 minutes. All biscuits are soft when hot, but they crisp up as they cool.

ALMOND TUILES

Makes about 24

Tuile is the French word for 'tile'. The biscuits are baked and when still soft, draped over a handle to make them curved like a tile.

2 oz (50 g) butter (unsalted if possible), plus more for greasing
whites from 2 size-1 or size-2 eggs
4 oz (125 g) vanilla sugar
2 oz (50 g) plain flour, sifted
1 oz (25 g) flaked almonds, crushed into tiny pieces

1   Preheat the oven to gas4/350°F/180°C. Have ready a large baking sheet covered with non-stick paper and a broomstick handle, cleaned and lightly greased. (Sometimes a rolling pin is used instead, but I think it is too thick to give the right shape).
2   Melt the butter until it is runny and, while it cools down, whisk the egg whites to a froth – quite lightly in fact. Add the sugar and whisk again.
3   Using a light hand, mix the flour, almonds and melted butter into the egg white and sugar mixture.
4   Dot teaspoons of the mixture over the baking tray, leaving plenty of space, as they spread to about 2 in (5 cm) across. Press each teaspoonful down lightly before baking.
5   Bake for about 7 minutes, or until the biscuits are golden.
6   Use a wide spatula or a small egg slice to lift the biscuits off the tray while they are still warm and drape them over the broomstick to stiffen up in a curve. If they break, just lay them back on the baking sheet to warm up and soften again. Push the broken edges together; they usually seal up.
7   When cold, store in an airtight tin.

HAZELNUT TUILES

Makes about 24

whites from 2 size-1 or size-2 eggs
4 oz (125 g) vanilla sugar
2 oz (50 g) butter (unsalted if possible)
2 oz (50 g) plain flour, sifted
1 oz (25 g) ground hazelnuts
1 teaspoon hazelnut oil (if you have it)

The method is exactly the same as for the Almond Tuile recipe above.

CHOCOLATE ALMOND TUILES

Makes about 24

whites from 2 size-1 or size-2 eggs
4 oz (125 g) vanilla sugar
2 oz (50 g) butter (unsalted if possible)
bare 2 oz (50 g) plain flour, sifted
1 oz (25 g) flaked almonds, crushed into tiny pieces
1 level teaspoon cocoa

The method is more or less the same as for the Almond Tuile recipe above, the only difference is that the cocoa should be sifted with the flour.

LANGUES DE CHAT

Makes 24–30

These wafer-thin biscuits are easy to make and look good, with their darker edge and pale centre. I have never managed to get them shaped evenly like the commercial ones. My cat's tongues are definitely crooked.

2 oz (50 g) caster sugar
2 oz (50 g) unsalted butter, softened
whites from 2 size-1 or size-2 eggs
2 oz (50 g) plain white flour
2 drops of vanilla essence

1   Preheat the oven to gas5/375°F/190°C. You will need a large baking sheet lined with non-stick baking paper, and a piping bag fitted with a ¼ in (5 mm) plain nozzle.
2   In a large bowl, beat the sugar into the butter until the mixture is pale.
3   Stir the egg whites together slightly, then beat them a little at a time into the creamed butter and sugar.
4   Sift the flour on top of your biscuit mixture and fold this in together with the vanilla essence fairly gently.
5   At this point you can just dot teaspoons of the mixture all over the baking sheet, keeping them well apart. If you want the traditional cat's-tongue shape, however, spoon the mixture into your piping bag and pipe 2 in (5 cm) lengths on the trays.
6   Bake for just 6–8 minutes, or until pale gold and edged with brown. Leave to cool down and crisp up on the tray, then store in an airtight tin.

RATAFIA BISCUITS

Makes about 30

These tiny almond macaroons are sold at great expense in boxes. They are often used crushed in trifles or served with coffee or for decoration on a pudding. They used to be flavoured with 'ratafia essence' which was similar to almond essence. I used to use it for marzipan, but have not seen it for a long time.

whites from 2 size-1 or size-2 eggs
4 oz (125 g) ground almonds
1 oz (25 g) ground rice
2 drops of almond essence
8 oz (225 g) caster sugar (vanilla-flavoured if possible)

1   Preheat the oven to gas¼ /230°F/110°C. You will need 2 baking sheets lined with non-stick baking paper and a piping bag with a ¼ in (5 mm) plain nozzle.
2   Whisk the egg whites until they are stiff.
3   Put the ground almonds, ground rice, almond essence and sugar in a bowl and rub your fingers through as if you were rubbing in (ground almonds often lump together). Now fold the almond mixture into the egg whites.
4   Spoon the meringue into the piping bag and pipe little dots of meringue about the size of a small teaspoon all over the trays.
5   Bake for about 15 minutes or until they are dry. Lift one up and let it cool down; if the bottom is still sticky, give them a little longer.
6   Allow to cool on the trays and, when cold, store in an airtight tin.

ALMOND BISCUITS

Makes about 30

These delicate biscuits need patience to roll out all the tiny balls of mixture but are worth the effort.

7 oz (200 g) butter, softened
6 oz (175 g) caster sugar
½ teaspoon vanilla extract or 1 small
  teaspoon of vanilla essence
8 oz (225 g) self-raising flour
1 teaspoon bicarbonate of soda

1   Preheat the oven to gas4/350°F/180°C. You will need 2 large baking sheets covered with non-stick baking paper.
2   Cream the butter and sugar together until pale and fluffy. Add the vanilla extract or essence and beat that in.
3   Sieve the flour and the bicarbonate of soda and stir into the rest of the ingredients. If the mixture is very stiff, add 1 or 2 teaspoons of water. Knead lightly.
4   Roll into balls about the size of big marbles and set them well apart on the baking sheets. Press each one down with the flat of a knife or the back of a fork.
5   Bake for about 15 minutes, or until they are golden brown.
6   When cold, store in an airtight tin.

CRISP SPONGE BISCUITS

Makes about 24

These biscuits are based on a fatless sponge mixture and would make an excellent base for a trifle. They are also very good sandwiched together in pairs with whipped cream.

3 size-1 or size-2 eggs
3 oz (75 g) caster sugar
3 oz (75 g) plain white flour

1   Preheat the oven to gas3/325°F/160°C. You will need two large baking sheets covered with non-stick baking paper.
2   Use an electric mixer or hand-held whisk to beat the eggs with the sugar, until you have a billowing bowlful of pale cream mixture. It takes me 6-7 minutes to get to this stage.
3   Using a nylon sieve, shake the flour through and on to the egg mixture in three lots – that is, about 1 tablespoon at a time. Fold the flour in with a flexible spatula or a large metal spoon. Do not try to fold in every bit of flour, but get the next tablespoon in and then the next. I use a spatula and find that the 'figure-of-eight' movement works for me.
4   When all the flour has been incorporated, use 2 spoons to drop blobs all over the baking sheets. Scoop up with one spoon and push it off with the other. The biscuits do spread, but not all that much.
5   Bake for about 20 minutes, or until the tops are quite brown. When cold, they should lift cleanly from the non-stick paper.
6   Store in an air-tight tin.

CRISP CHOCOLATE SPONGE BISCUITS

Makes about 24

This is exactly the same as the previous recipe, except that to make the biscuits chocolate-flavoured you must take 2 teaspoons of flour out of the measured 3 oz (75 g) and replace it with 2 teaspoons of cocoa (not drinking chocolate).

Instead of round biscuits as in the previous recipe, you can make finger shapes using éclair tins. These oblong tins should be well greased and I put a narrow strip of non-stick baking paper in the base of each mould. Spoon about a small dessertspoon of mixture into each oblong, pulling it gently to fit. Do not overfill and do not bake for as long as the sponge biscuits, only about 15 minutes. They are not as crisp as the biscuits in the first recipe.

DOIGTS DE DAMES

Makes about 30

Translated this means 'ladies' fingers'. Based on meringue, you can make these easily if you can use a piping bag.

whites from 2 size-1 or size-2 eggs
pinch of salt
pinch of cream of tartar
4 oz (125 g) caster sugar

1 Preheat the oven to gas¼ /230°F/110°C. You will need a baking sheet lined with non-stick baking paper, and a piping bag with a narrow nozzle about ½ in (1 cm) either star-shaped or plain.
2 Using an electric mixer or a hand-held mixer, whisk the egg whites, salt and cream of tartar until very firm indeed. You should be able to turn the bowl upside down without the filling running out!
3 Still running the mixer, add the sugar about 1 tablespoon at a time and mixing well between each addition. Do not rush this bit, as adding the sugar too quickly will spoil the meringue. When the mixture is glossy and very stiff it is ready.
4 Scoop the meringue into the icing bag with the nozzle fitted and pipe neat straight fingers, about 4 in (10 cm) long (do not overfill the bag – just under half-full is about right). You can also pipe dozens and dozens of meringue stars if you get fed up with the fingers.
5 Bake for as long as possible – a minimum of 1½ hours, when the meringue will look quite cream in colour. Bake longer to get a very dry result. (Although some people like meringues with a chewy centre.)
6 Allow to get quite cold and store in an airtight tin.

CHOCOLATE FRIDGE BISCUITS

Makes about 40

This method of baking biscuits is easy. You make up a dough, roll it into a cylinder, then set it in the fridge. When it has firmed up, you slice off wafer-thin biscuits and bake them. However, you must judge the texture of your biscuit dough. Too hard and you will not be able to cut anything; too soft and the mixture collapses. A really thin knife blade which is very sharp helps to shave off really paper-thin slices. The cut shape is never a perfect round, but they are crisp and thin.

1 size-1 or size-2 egg
7 oz (200 g) caster sugar
7 oz (200 g) plain flour
1 teaspoon baking powder
2 oz (50 g) grated chocolate
½ teaspoon vanilla extract or 1 small
teaspoon vanilla essence
4 oz (125 g) butter or soft margarine

1 Stir the egg and sugar together.
2 Sift the flour and baking powder into a large bowl and stir in the chocolate and vanilla.
3 Melt the butter or margarine and put the egg and sugar mixture in with the flour. Stir in the butter or margarine to make a soft dough.
4 Knead the dough lightly and form it into a sausage. Roll on the work top to smooth the sides, wrap in foil and leave in the fridge to firm up or put in the freezer to store for longer.
5 Preheat the oven to gas4/350°F/180°C. You will need 2 baking sheets covered with non-stick paper.
6 Take the sausage of dough out of the fridge or freezer and allow it to soften slightly. Shave off thin biscuits and set the biscuits on the non-stick paper. If the slices start to come off curled, do not try to straighten them – the heat of the oven will do that perfectly.
7 Bake for 15–20 minutes. Leave to cool down and harden on the baking tray.
8 When cold store in an airtight tin.

FLORENTINES

Makes about 16

A delicious concoction of nuts, peel and chocolate. You can make Florentines any size you wish – 1 heaped teaspoon of the mixture will spread to about 3 in (7.3 cm) across.

5 fl oz (150 ml) double cream
3 oz (75 g) caster sugar
4 oz (125 g) flaked almonds
3 oz (75 g) mixed chopped glacé cherries, chopped raisins and chopped candied peel
½ oz (15 g) butter
1 level tablespoon self-raising flour
6 oz (175 g) plain dark chocolate, broken into pieces

1   Preheat the oven to gas5/375°F/190°C. You will need a large baking sheet covered with a sheet of non-stick baking paper.
2   In a thick-bottomed pan, heat the cream and sugar slowly, stirring to encourage the sugar to dissolve. Once the sugar dissolves, bring the mixture to the boil.
3   Tip in the nuts, fruit, butter and flour. Remove the pan from the heat and mix well.
4   Place small teaspoonfuls of the mixture about 6 in (15 cm) apart and bake for about 10 minutes, or until they are quite brown. Remove the tin from the oven and allow them to go cold.
5   To melt the chocolate: put the pieces in a heatproof bowl set over a pan of simmering water. Stir gently and remove from the pan once the chocolate is liquid. Spread the chocolate on the flat side of each Florentine and use a fork to mark the chocolate with wavy lines. (I wonder if this is to imitate Florentine embroidery!). Leave to dry.
6   Store in an airtight tin.

MADELEINES

Makes 12–18

Said to be the French version of fairy cakes, these plain buns are often to be seen in the pâtisseries of France. I have bought them in the past and sometimes thought they were old and stale! Freshly made, however, they are lovely. Traditionally they are baked in little shell-shaped tins, which are a nuisance to clean afterwards.

4 oz (125 g) self-raising flour
4 oz (125 g) caster sugar
very finely grated rind of 1 lemon
2 size-1 or size-2 eggs, beaten
4 oz (125 g) butter, melted, plus more for greasing
icing sugar, for dusting

1   Preheat the oven to gas5/375°F/190°C. Grease well some madeleine moulds or flattish pattie tins, or use paper bun cases set in bun tins.
2   Sift the flour into a big bowl and stir in the sugar and the finely grated lemon rind. Gradually add the beaten eggs and mix well.
3   Fold in the melted butter a little at a time and spoon the mixture into the moulds – not more than half-full.
4   Bake for just 12–15 minutes, until well risen and golden.
5   Cool on a wire rack and store in an airtight tin.
6   To serve: shake some icing sugar through a tea strainer and knock the strainer gently to achieve a light 'veil'.

GINGER THINS

Makes about 40

This is another variation on the Fridge Biscuit (see page 264). This time the raw paste is pressed into the bottom of a loaf tin so that the finished biscuit is a small rectangle.

8 oz (225 g) plain white flour
1 teaspoon ground ginger
1 teaspoon bicarbonate of soda
1 oz (25 g) light soft brown sugar
4 oz (125 g) golden syrup
2 oz (50 g) butter or margarine, plus more
    for greasing

1   Grease and line the base and the long sides of a 1 lb (450 g) loaf tin. This helps you to lift the paste out of the tin. One strip of greaseproof is enough.
2   Sift the flour, ginger and bicarbonate of soda into a large mixing bowl. Stir in the sugar.
3   To weigh out the golden syrup: first warm the tin by taking off the lid then stand it in a pan of simmering water. Put a small pan on the scales and weigh into it the 4 oz (125 g) of syrup. Transfer the pan to a low heat on the hob and add the butter or margarine. Wait until the butter has melted, then stir this mixture into the dry ingredients. Mix well.
4   Press this soft dough into the base of the loaf tin and level it off. Set in the fridge for about 1½ hours. It should be hard but sliceable.
5   Preheat the oven to gas3/325°F/160°C. Line a large baking tray with non-stick paper. Slide a knife down the ends of the block in the tin and use the greaseproof paper to pull it out.
6   Using a sharp knife with a thin blade, pare off very, very thin slices and put them on the non-stick paper. They do not spread much. If the slices have a curl, leave them alone as the heat in the oven will make them lie down.
7   Bake for about 12 minutes, when they will be a 'ginger snap' colour. Take out of the oven and set aside to go cold. Store in an airtight tin.

Variation
Chop about 1 oz (25 g) of preserved ginger and sprinkle a few bits on top of each biscuit before baking.

'There were cakes and apples in all the chapels.'

R. H. Barham

5

Meringues, Mousses, Jellies, Creams and Ices

MERINGUES

BROWN SUGAR CHOCOLATE MERINGUES

Makes about 18

Meringue
whites from 2 size-1 or size-2 eggs
pinch of salt
big pinch of cream of tartar
4 oz (125 g) soft brown sugar

Dipping Chocolate
6 oz plain dark chocolate

Filling
2 teaspoons cocoa
5 fl oz (150 ml) double cream

1   Preheat the oven to gas ¼ /225°F/110°C. You will need a large baking sheet lined with non-stick baking paper (rub a spot of margarine under each corner of the sheet to help the paper to stick in position). You will also need a large piping bag and nozzle.
2   To make the meringues: using an electric or a hand-held mixer, whisk the egg whites, salt and cream of tartar in until you have a billowing stiff foam. Do not hurry this stage. The mixture will be snowy white. While the machine is still running, sprinkle the sugar in, 1 tablespoon at a time and whisking hard between each addition. You should have a glossy stiff meringue.
3   You can perfectly well just spoon the meringues on the paper using 2 spoons, one to lift and the other to push off. The rough heaps do look attractive but since we intend to dip the meringues in chocolate, fit a ½ in (5 mm) star nozzle into a large piping bag, scoop about half of the meringue into it and pipe nice big whirls of meringue. Refill the piping bag and finish the meringue. Depending on the size, you should make about 18.
4   Bake the meringues for at least 1½ hours and up to 3 hours to get a really dry centre.

5   Break up the chocolate and put the pieces in a small heatproof bowl over a pan of simmering water. Stir gently and, when liquid, dip the base of each meringue in the chocolate. Shake off the excess and set the meringues chocolate bottoms down on the non-stick paper. Repeat this with all the meringues.
6   Just before serving, sandwich the meringues: first mix the cocoa with 1 tablespoon of boiling water to a smooth paste. Then, when cool, beat in a spoonful of double cream. Finally, pour over all the cream and use a hand whisk to whip the cream until it is stiff and a pale chocolate colour.
7   Serve with a little fresh fruit, like a small pile of strawberries or sharp grapes.

WALNUT & CHOC MERINGUE GINGERS

Makes 12

You will need very finely chopped walnuts for this recipe.

whites from 3 size-1 or size-2 eggs
6 oz (175 g) caster sugar
2½ oz (65 g) walnuts, very finely chopped
6 oz (175 g) plain chocolate, broken into
   pieces
5 fl oz (150 ml) double cream

1   Preheat the oven to gas ¼ /225°F/110°C. You will need a large baking sheet lined with non-stick baking paper. Also a large piping bag with a ½ in (5 mm) plain nozzle. (Do not use a star, as the nuts might get stuck).
2   Whisk the egg whites until they are very stiff indeed and snowy white. Spoon in the sugar, about 2 oz (50 g) at a time, whisking hard between each addition. When all the sugar is incorporated you should have a stiff and glossy meringue. At this point fold in the walnuts.

3 Scoop about half of the meringue into the piping bag and pipe 3 in (7.5 cm) long fingers about 1 in (2.5 cm) thick. You should get about 24 fingers.

4 Bake the meringue fingers long and slow, from about 1½ hour to 3 hours. (1½ hours if you like a chewy centre or 3 hours for a very dry centre). When cold, take the meringues off the trays and store in an airtight tin.

5 Melt the chocolate in a heatproof bowl over a pan of simmering water. Stir lightly, then dip each meringue finger into chocolate and shake off the surplus. (I found it was easier to dry off one end before dipping the opposite end!). Set the fingers on the non-stick paper to dry.

6 Sandwich the fingers not more than 2 hours before they are needed. Whip the cream stiffly to sandwich the pairs – use a piping bag if you wish.

Note

The meringue fingers will store quite happily in a tin, but dip them into chocolate and fill the meringues on the day you intend to eat them.

Spotted Meringue Baskets with Cream & Fruit

Makes about 10

These meringues do not take as long to dry out in the oven – about 30–35 minutes. The high chocolate content is probably the reason.

I put the chocolate in my food processor; it makes a lot of noise but the chocolate comes out in tiny nibs which is ideal for this recipe. Chocolate can also be grated.

whites from 2 size-1 or size-2 eggs
pinch of salt
pinch of cream of tartar
6 oz (175 g) caster sugar
4 oz (125 g) grated dark chocolate

Filling
10 fl oz (300 ml) double cream, whipped
Fresh strawberries, raspberries or grapes, or
   a mixture

Coulis
10 oz (275 g) fresh raspberries or
   strawberries
1 oz (25 g) caster sugar

1 Preheat the oven to gas2/300°F/150°C. You will need a large baking sheet lined with a sheet of non-stick paper. Also a large piping bag fitted with a ½ in (5 mm) plain nozzle.

2 Use an electric mixer to beat the egg whites, salt and cream of tartar to a very firm snow. Now whisk in the sugar, about 2 oz (50 g) at a time, whisking hard between additions. You should have a glossy and very stiff meringue. Fold in the grated chocolate and spoon half of the meringue into the piping bag with the plain piping nozzle.

3 You could draw 2½ in (6 mm) circles all over the non-stick paper, but you will soon do it easily without. Pipe a flat ring of meringue and then pipe a 'wall' on top of the outer edge. You will be able to do it in one spiralling movement eventually.

4 Set these in the oven to bake for about 30–35 minutes. Take them out of the oven to cool down. Store in an airtight tin.

5 For the filling: whip the double cream and put a spoonful in each nest. Be fairly generous and then top with whichever fruit you have chosen.

6 To serve the baskets: first make a coulis by reducing the raspberries or strawberries to a purée. Add the sugar and stir it until it melts. Spoon some coulis on each plate and set a meringue basket on top.

MERINGUE SHAPES

Just as in icing cakes, meringue can be shaped in different ways using a filled piping bag and either a plain or star nozzle. The star nozzle is probably the most popular and useful and you can use either a ½ in (1 cm) nozzle or a much bigger 1 in (2.5 cm) one. The smaller ½ in (1 cm) is more versatile.

With it you can make lots of tiny stars or much bigger ones to sandwich together with whipped cream. With care, you can make circles which then look good with a grouping of a glacé cherry and some angelica leaves stuck on with icing. A Christmas one looks pretty with miniature holly leaves and berries in coloured marzipan. The ½ in (1 cm) star can fashion crosses for kisses, with a red marzipan heart in the centre, or just fingers of meringue or shell-shaped miniatures.

The shell shape uses the same technique as in royal icing. The nozzle is held close to the paper and you squeeze down, up and over, pulling the meringue back towards you so that it comes to a point. It is nothing like as difficult as it sounds on paper. Meringue nests or baskets are always useful and, with practice, you can shape one all in one movement.

The plain nozzle is useful when finely cut fruit or nuts have been mixed with the meringue. There is much less chance of it sticking with the plain nozzle. Dozens of tiny plain dots about the size of a small marble make a simple decoration round the edge of a mousse or cold creamy dessert. Make them a little bigger for nibbling with coffee. The plain nozzle is just as easy to use for circles, crosses and baskets.

Large discs of meringue make ideal layers with fruit and cream for a party dessert. A layer of meringue is also nice sandwiched with two layers of a delicate sponge and cream and fruit. Three layers of meringue look good with, say, a chocolate filling and the top layer of meringue spread with the chocolate filling then encrusted with sliced almonds.

MERINGUE MUSHROOMS

Serves about 6

This is an old favourite which is more suited to a youngish party. The mushrooms are set in a field of jelly. There will probably be more meringues than you need, so sandwich those with whipped cream for the adults.

Field
1 packet of lime jelly
1 oz (25 g) desiccated coconut
green food colouring

Meringue
whites from 2 size-1 or size-2 eggs
4 oz (125 g) caster sugar

Chocolate Buttercream
1 teaspoon cocoa
1 tablespoon boiling water
2 oz (50 g) soft butter
1 heaped tablespoon sieved icing sugar

1   Preheat the oven to gas ¼ /225°F/110°C. You will need a baking sheet covered with a sheet of non-stick baking paper, and a piping bag with a ½ in (1 cm) plain nozzle.
2   Make the meringue: whisk the egg whites until they are very stiff indeed. Spoon in the sugar, 1 tablespoon at a time, whisking hard between each addition. When all the sugar is in you should have a glossy and very, very firm meringue. Spoon this into the piping bag.
3   You need to pipe about 10 fingers of meringue about 3 in (7.5 cm) long and about ½ in (1 cm) wide to make the mushroom stems. Then you need the mushroom caps, so pipe 10 smooth round caps. To do this hold the nozzle in one place near the paper and squeeze and pull. They should be about 2 in (5 cm) across.
4   Bake the mushroom stems and caps until they are fairly dry – 3 hours to be on the safe side. When cold, store in an airtight tin.
5   Make the chocolate buttercream: mix the cocoa with the hot water, then beat this into the butter and icing sugar for a softish mixture.
6   On the day of serving, make up the jelly, but

cutting down on the quantity of water so that the jelly will be stiff. Use ³/₄ pt (450 ml) of total liquid instead of 1 pt (575 ml). Pour the jelly into a flattish gratin dish so that there is a depth of about 1¹/₂ in (3.5 cm). Leave to firm up in the fridge.

7   Meanwhile, put the desiccated coconut in a cup or bowl with 3 drops of green colouring and rub it in with your fingers. Set this aside and, when the jelly is firm, sprinkle the coconut over the surface.

8   To make up the mushroom field: use a thin sharp knife to slice off the end of each meringue finger. Spread a layer of chocolate buttercream on the flat underside of the meringue caps. Take a knife and make a slit in the jelly and hold the slit open with the knife. Drop a stem of mushroom in. Repeat this all over the jelly. Set a mushroom cap on each stalk. Serve within 2 hours.

PETITS VACHERINS

Makes 6

These are individual vacherins made with hazelnuts and a very nice apple filling.

Meringue
whites from 4 size-1 or size-2 eggs
8 oz (225 g) caster sugar
4 oz (125 g) ground hazelnuts

Filling
1³/₄ lb (800 g) Bramley apples, peeled, cored and thinly sliced
3 oz (75 g) caster sugar
1 oz (25 g) butter
1 tablespoon lemon juice
10 fl oz (300 ml) double cream

Decoration
whole hazelnuts
icing sugar

1   Preheat the oven to gas3/325°F/160°C. You will need 2 baking sheets lined with non-stick baking paper. Draw 3 in (7.5 cm) circles all over the papers.

2   Whisk the egg whites until they are very firm indeed. Spoon in the sugar, about 2 oz (50 g) at a time. Whisk hard between every addition until you have a very stiff glossy meringue. Fold in the ground hazelnuts.

3   Put a good dessertspoon of meringue on each circle and spread it out to the pencil marking on the baking sheet (for 6 vacherins you will need 18 circles of meringue – 3 rings per serving).

4   Bake for about 30 minutes. Take the meringues out of the oven and allow them to cool. Store in an airtight tin.

5   To make the filling: cook the apples with the sugar, butter and lemon juice. Simmer with the lid on, but keep an eye on it so that the apple does not stick. Take the lid off and beat the apple to a purée, then continue to cook gently so that you end up with a thick purée. Set this aside to cool.

6   About 2 hours before your guests are due, whip the cream until it forms soft peaks. Scoop into another bowl about one-third of the cream and set this aside for decoration.

7   The apple purée should be thick with no loose juice. At this point you could put it to drain in a nylon sieve. When really thick, fold it into the whipped cream.

8   Place 1 meringue round on a flat serving plate and spread a layer of apple and cream. Put another meringue round on top and spread more apple and cream. Finally top with a third meringue round. Repeat with the rest of the meringue rounds on other plates.

9   To serve: whip up the reserved cream and put a blob on top of each vacherin (you could pipe a whirl if you wish). Top with a whole hazelnut and then shake icing sugar through a tea strainer to make a dusting of icing sugar all over each vacherin.

MERINGUES CHANTILLY

Makes 12–14

Crème chantilly is sweetened whipped cream, flavoured with real vanilla. This used to be done by splitting the vanilla pod in two and then adding it to the cream. The tiny black seeds from the pod gave the cream a very speckled appearance. Now we can use vanilla extract – a powerfully flavoured essence with no black dots.

The shape of these meringues has always been described as 'wiggles' in our house – perhaps 'scribbles' would be a better description. I cannot think how to say it in words only in a drawing.

I am colouring one half of the meringue pink so that the wiggly sandwich can be pink on one side and white on the other.

Meringue
whites of 3 size-1 or size-2 eggs
6 oz (175 g) caster sugar
1–2 drops of red food colouring

Filling
½ pt (300 ml) double cream
2–3 drops of vanilla extract

1   Preheat the oven to gas ¼ /225°F/110°C. You will need a large baking sheet covered with non-stick baking paper, and a large piping bag with a ½ in (1 cm) star nozzle.
2   Make the meringue: whisk the egg whites at high speed until they are firm and white. Start to add the sugar, 2 oz (50 g) at a time, whisking hard between additions. When all the sugar has gone in you should have a firm glossy meringue. Spoon half of the meringue into the piping bag. Add the food colouring to the rest of the meringue in the bowl and give it another whisk to distribute the colour. Add more colour if it is too pale.

3   Pipe the wiggles on the non-stick paper. Hold the nozzle almost on the paper and squeeze and pull away following the shape I have described. When the white meringue is finished, spoon the pink meringue into a clean bag fitted with the ½ in (1 cm) star nozzle and pipe them out too.
4   Bake for not less than 1½ hours and longer if you want a crisp meringue.
5   Make the filling: whip the cream with the vanilla extract until it is stiff and pipe or spoon the cream on a white wiggle and top it with a pink one. Repeat until the cream and meringues are used up.

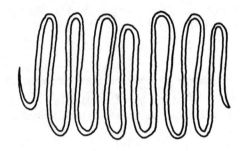

USES FOR MERINGUES

- Crushed, they are famous for the crunchy sweetness in the famous fresh strawberry pudding Eton Mess, see page 242.
- Light fatless Swiss roll with a filling of raspberries, crushed meringue and cream.
- Instead of a piped whirl of cream on top of a light syllabub you could plant a whirl of meringue. It would look good, especially if the meringue was of the brown sugar variety.
- I have used broken meringues to stir into softened ice-cream which then goes back into the freezer to firm up again.
- Ice-cream Surprises (see page 250): the broken meringue is buried in an ice-cream ball.
- Rolled in toasted coconut.
- As part of a Peach Melba (see page 243).

MOUSSES

MANGO MOUSSE

Serves 6

Getting the ripe delicious fruit from a mango can be a messy business if it is truly ripe. The way I do it is to stand the mango on end and slice down each side of the fruit to obtain two large ovals. Cut the fruit inside each oval in a criss-cross pattern and then turn the oval inside-out and slice off the fruit. Cut the fruit as best you can from the large oval stone.

15 fl oz (450 ml) milk
3 size-3 egg yolks
2½ oz (65 g) caster sugar
1 packet of gelatine
1 ripe mango, stoned (see above)
8 oz (225 g) quark or soft cheese
grated chocolate or whipped cream, to
    decorate

1   Bring the milk to a boil and remove from the heat.
2   In a bowl, whisk the egg yolks and sugar together. Slowly pour some of the hot milk over the egg mixture, whisking all the time. Tip this back into the pan with the rest of the milk and cook gently, stirring all the time until the custard thickens slightly. Remove from the heat and stand the saucepan in a bowl of cold water.
3   Put 3 tablespoons of water in a small bowl, sprinkle over the gelatine powder and set it aside to expand. After 3 minutes, set the small bowl in a pan of simmering water. Stir the gelatine to encourage it to dissolve.
4   When the gelatine is clear, pour it into the cooled custard mixture.
5   Liquidize the mango thoroughly with a blender or food processor. Then stir it into the quark or soft cheese.

6   Wait until the gelatine mixture is on the point of setting, then stir in the mango mixture and pour into a 2 pt (1.2 litre) ring mould or about 6 small ramekins. Set aside to firm up.
7   To unmould the ring: press all round the edges to loosen the top part and sit the ring on a hot wrung-out tea towel. Turn out on a flat serving plate. Decorate with grated chocolate or whipped cream.

KIWI FRUIT UNDER A VANILLA CREAM

Serves 6

4 firm kiwi fruits, peeled and cut into small
    chunks
8 oz (225 g) soft cream cheese
3 size-3 eggs
finely grated rind of ½ lemon (1 teaspoon)
2–3 drops of vanilla essence
2 oz (50 g) caster sugar
chopped nuts, to decorate

1   Divide the kiwi fruit between 6 small ramekins, reserving 6 pieces for decoration.
2   Whisk the soft cheese, eggs, lemon rind, vanilla and caster sugar in a heatproof bowl. Set this over a pan of simmering water and stir until it thickens slightly.
3   Remove the pan from the heat and pour the hot cream over the kiwi fruit. Set aside to firm up, preferably in the fridge.
4   When set, decorate with some chopped nuts and a piece of the reserved fruit.

TANGERINE MOUSSE

Serves 6

You will need a 5 in (12.5 cm) diameter soufflé dish. Wrap a double collar of greaseproof paper round the dish so that it stands about 2 in (5 cm) above the rim. Fasten the paper on with an elastic band exactly on the rim of the dish or tie string round tightly.

2 tablespoons lemon juice
1 packet of gelatine
3 size-1 or size-2 eggs, separated
2 oz (50 g) caster sugar
4 large tangerines
¼ pt (150 ml) warm milk
5 tablespoons crème fraîche
4 tangerines, for decoration

1 Put the lemon juice in a small bowl and sprinkle the gelatine over the surface. Leave it aside for 3 minutes.
2 In a medium-size bowl, whisk the egg yolks and the caster sugar until pale and thick. Now grate the peel off the 4 tangerines (I use the biggest hole on my grater). Stir this peel into the egg yolk mixture.
3 Reheat the milk and pour this gradually over the egg yolk mixture, whisking all the time. Set this bowl over a pan of simmering water and cook gently until the mixture thickens. Do not let it boil. Once the custard coats the back of a wooden spoon it is ready.
4 Peel the 4 grated tangerines and chop the fruit finely, removing as much pith as possible from each segment and saving any juices.
5 Set the bowl with the gelatine in the simmering water and stir until the gelatine is clear. Stir the gelatine into the egg mixture, along with the chopped tangerines and juices. Leave aside and give a stir every now and then.

6 Once the mixture has cooled down and is on the point of setting, fold in the crème fraîche.
7 Lastly use an electric whisk to beat the egg whites until they stand up in stiff peaks. Fold this into the fruit cream. Spoon into the soufflé dish and chill until set.
8 Decorate with the segments of fruit from the tangerines.

FLUFFY BLACKCURRANT MOUSSE

Serves 5–6

1 packet of gelatine
12 oz (450 ml) fresh ripe blackcurrants
2½ oz (65 g) caster sugar
6 oz (175 g) double cream, whipped
whites of 3 size-1 or size-2 eggs

1 Put ¼ pt (150 ml) of water in a small heatproof bowl and sprinkle over the gelatine. Set this aside to expand.
2 Top and tail the blackcurrants as best you can and discard any berries which are not really black and juicy. Now liquidize the berries until smooth (or almost smooth). Stir in the sugar.
3 Set the gelatine bowl over a pan of simmering water and stir to dissolve. When this is clear, stir into the sweetened fruit purée. Follow this with the whipped cream and set the bowl aside to firm up a bit and go cold.
4 Stiffly beat the egg whites and fold these into the fruit mixture.
5 Pour into 6 small glass dishes and chill overnight.

RASPBERRY MOUSSE

Serves 6–8

You will need a glass bowl or a 5 in (12.5 cm) diameter soufflé dish with a double greaseproof paper collar tied round to stand 2 in (5 cm) above the rim.

12 oz (325 g) perfect raspberries, hulled
2 oz (50 g) caster sugar
1 packet of gelatine
4 size-1 or size-2 eggs, separated
grated zest from 1 lemon
6 oz (175 g) crème fraîche or double cream

1 Put the raspberries in a bowl and sprinkle with about half of the sugar. Leave for a few minutes and stir to break up the fruit and melt the sugar. Reserving a few of the best-looking raspberries for decoration, liquidize the berries with a stick blender or a food processor. At this point if you want rid of the seeds you must pass the berries through a very fine mesh sieve (I do not bother to do this).
2 Put 4 tablespoons of water in a small bowl and sprinkle the gelatine over. Leave aside to swell up.
3 Whisk the egg yolks and the rest of the sugar in a small bowl. Fold in the lemon zest and set aside.
4 Set the bowl with the gelatine in a pan of simmering water and stir until it dissolves and is fairly clear. Stir in the lemon juice. Set aside to cool.
5 Now stir the cooled gelatine and lemon into the egg yolk and sugar mixture.
6 Next fold in the crème fraîche or cream, followed by the raspberry purée.
7 In a largish bowl, whisk the egg whites until they stand in stiff peaks. Fold this into the raspberry purée.
8 Pour into the bowl or prepared dish. Set aside to firm up.
9 Serve decorated with the reserved fresh raspberries.

STRAWBERRY MOUSSE

Serves 4

12 oz (325 g) ripe juicy strawberries
1½ oz (40 g) caster sugar
8 oz (225 g) fromage frais, or lightly whipped double cream
white of 1 size-1 or size-2 egg

1 Reserving 4 good-looking specimens for decoration, blend the strawberries with a stick blender or in a food processor. Add the sugar and blend again.
2 Fold the fromage frais or whipped double cream into the strawberry purée.
3 In another bowl, whip the egg white until it is standing in stiff peaks. Fold this into the strawberry mixture.
4 Pour into 4 glass dishes and put in the fridge to chill and set.
5 To serve: decorate with one of the reserved whole perfect strawberries on each. Leave the green stalk on the berry, slice the fruit 3 or 4 times downwards without cutting fully through and fan out slightly.

FLUFFY ORANGE MOUSSE WITH GRAND MARNIER

Serves 4–5

Grand Marnier is an orange liqueur. You could also use Cointreau.

2 large thin-skinned and juicy oranges
2 tablespoons lemon juice
1 packet of gelatine
2 tablespoons Grand Marnier or other orange liqueur
3 oz (75 g) sugar
3 size-1 or size-2 eggs, separated
½ oz (15 g) toasted flaked almonds

1 Finely grate the rind from 1 orange only. Squeeze the juice from both oranges and mix it with the lemon juice.

2 Put 4 tablespoons of water in a small bowl, sprinkle the powdered gelatine over and leave it to soak. After 2–3 minutes, stand the bowl in a small pan of simmering water. Stir the gelatine to encourage it to dissolve and, once clear, set it aside.

3 Stand another cup or bowl in hot water and pour in the liqueur. When the liqueur is very hot, take the pan off the heat.

4 In a large bowl, stir 2 oz (50 g) of the measured sugar into the egg yolks. Whisk this mixture hard with an electric whisk if you have one. Pour in the hot orange liqueur and whisk again (about 5 minutes whisking in all). The mixture should now be quite thick.

5 Pour the orange juice into the egg yolk mixture (strain it if you don't like the bits). Add the orange rind and whisk again.

6 Stir the gelatine mixture, pour this into the orange one and stir well to amalgamate. Set this bowl aside, but keep giving it a stir so that it doesn't set too much.

7 In a very clean bowl, whisk the egg whites until they are stiff and dry. Whisk in the remaining sugar and whisk again.

8 By this time the orange mixture should be on the point of setting. Fold in the egg whites until evenly mixed.

9 Pour into 4 or 5 nice individual glass dishes or into 1 big glass serving dish. Put in the fridge to chill and set.

10 When set and chilled, serve with the toasted flaked almonds scattered on top.

SNOWY MOUSSE

Serves 8

Based on Greek yoghurt and double cream, this white mousse is a perfect foil for coloured fresh fruits of all kinds.

You will need a plain 2½ pt (1.4 litre) ring mould or 8 glass dishes for individual portions.

1½ packets of gelatine
2 size-1 or size-2 eggs, separated
1 oz (25 g) caster sugar, plus more to serve
1 tablespoon runny floral honey
½ pt (300 ml) Greek ewes'-milk yoghurt
  (not the set kind)
½ pt (300 ml) double cream
colourful fruit, to serve

1 Put 4 tablespoons of cold water in a small bowl, sprinkle over the gelatine and set it aside to expand.

2 Whisk the egg yolks with the sugar and runny honey until thick. An electric hand-held whisk is best. (If the honey is stiff, a few seconds in the microwave will help.) Now whisk in the yoghurt.

3 Set the bowl with the gelatine in a pan of simmering water. Stir to help it dissolve and, when clear, take the pan off the heat and allow to cool.

4 In another bowl, whip the cream to the soft and floppy stage.

5 If you are using a ring mould, rinse it out with water but do not dry it.

6 In yet another bowl, whisk the egg whites until they are stiff.

7 Beat or whisk the cooled gelatine mixture into the egg and yoghurt mixture. Then fold in the floppy cream. Lastly fold the whipped egg whites in as well.

8 Spoon the mixture into the ring mould or glasses. Bang the ring mould to knock out any air bubbles. Smooth the top(s) and leave to set.

9 Serve with colourful fruit, like raspberries, strawberries and redcurrants. Put the cut strawberries in a bowl with the fresh raspberries and redcurrants, layering with caster sugar. Turn the fruit over in the sugar and chill.

Apricot Mousse with Ginger Thins

Serves 4

2 size-1 or size-2 eggs, separated
2 oz (50 g) caster sugar
8 oz (225 g) can of apricot halves, drained and liquidized
1 packet of gelatine
2 tablespoons lemon juice
¼ pt (150 ml) double cream
Ginger Thins (page 267), to serve

1 Put the egg yolks, sugar and apricot purée into a clean bowl and set it over a pan of simmering water. Stir the egg yolks to break them up and cook gently until the mixture forms a smooth thinnish custard.
2 Sprinkle the gelatine over the surface of the hot apricot mixture and use a whisk to help dissolve it completely. Remove the bowl from the heat and stir in the lemon juice. Cool until almost set (you can hurry this along by standing the bowl in another bowl full of cold water with some ice cubes), keeping the mixture fairly liquid by stirring frequently.
3 Whip the cream to the floppy stage and then fold into the apricot mixture.
4 In another bowl, whisk the egg whites to the soft peak stage and fold these into the fruit mixture.
5 Spoon into a large serving dish or into 4 individual ones.
6 When set, serve with Ginger Thins.

Coffee & Chocolate Mousse

Serves 6

4 oz (125 g) best-quality plain chocolate
4 size-1 or size-2 eggs, separated
3½ oz (90 g) butter, cut into small pieces and at room temperature

1 tablespoon brandy
1 tablespoon very strong coffee
2 level dessertspoons icing sugar, sieved
3 tablespoons double cream
toasted almonds or a whirl of double cream, for decoration

1 Break the chocolate into small pieces and put it in a medium-sized bowl set over a pan of simmering water.
2 Once the chocolate has melted, take the bowl away from the heat. Stir in the egg yolks gently. Add the pieces of butter and stir again gently to help them to dissolve. Add the brandy, strong coffee and icing sugar. Stir again and then stir in the cream.
3 In another bowl, whip the egg whites until thick and firmish. Fold into the chocolate mixture. Spoon into 6 small glass dishes and allow to set.
4 Decorate with toasted almonds or a whirl of cream. This pudding improves after a day in the fridge.

Black Coffee & White Chocolate Mousse

Serves 6

The clever idea of mixing strong coffee and white chocolate like this came originally from the imaginative food writer Rosamond Richardson.

1 packet of gelatine
3 tablespoons cold very strong black coffee (preferably brewed from beans)
6 oz (175 g) good-quality white chocolate
1½ oz (40 g) soft butter
1 oz (25 g) caster sugar
4 size-1 or size-2 eggs, separated
4 oz (125 g) Greek yoghurt, beaten until smooth
crisp biscuits, to serve

1 First sprinkle the gelatine over the cold coffee in a small bowl. Leave it aside to expand.
2 Break up the white chocolate and put it in a small heatproof bowl set over a pan of simmering water. (White chocolate is not as liquid as dark chocolate.)
3 In a medium-sized bowl, cream the butter and sugar until fluffy, then beat in the softened chocolate a bit at a time.
4 In yet another bowl, whisk the egg yolks and stir them into the butter and chocolate mixture.
5 Set the coffee and gelatine bowl in a pan of simmering water and, when the gelatine has dissolved and become clear, stir this into the mixture, followed by the Greek yoghurt.
6 Whisk the egg whites until stiff and fold gently into the chocolate mixture.
7 Pour into 6 small glass dishes or ramekins and leave aside to set.
8 Serve with a crisp biscuit.

CHOCOLATE AND ORANGE MOUSSE

Serves 6

6 oz (175 g) plain cooking chocolate
1 small juicy orange
½ oz (15 g) butter, cut into tiny pieces
3 size-1 or size-2 eggs, separated
¼ pt (150 ml) double cream, whipped
1 teaspoon caster sugar

1 Break up the chocolate and put it into a medium-size bowl. Set this bowl over a pan of simmering water.
2 Grate the rind from the orange and squeeze the juice.
3 Take the bowl with the melted chocolate off the heat and stir in the butter, orange rind and juice. Mix well.
4 In another bowl, whisk the egg yolks lightly, then beat them a little at a time into the

chocolate mixture.
5 Stir in the whipped cream.
6 In yet another bowl, beat the egg whites until they are stiff, then whisk in the caster sugar.
7 Fold the egg white mixture into the chocolate mixture. Spoon into 6 small glass dishes and leave to set.

COFFEE MOUSSE

Serves 6

1 large can of evaporated milk (14 fl oz / 400 ml)
1 packet of gelatine
5 oz (150 g) caster sugar
4 large teaspoons instant coffee granules
3 oz (75 g) crisp peanut brittle, to decorate

1 Pour the evaporated milk into a large jug or bowl and set in the fridge to chill for at least 1 hour, covered with a plate.
2 Put 2 tablespoons of water in a small bowl and sprinkle the gelatine over the top. Set this aside to swell up.
3 Using an electric whisk if you have one, whisk the evaporated milk until it is thick and then whisk in the sugar a bit at a time.
4 Set the gelatine bowl over a pan of simmering water and stir until it becomes clear and free from lumps. Stir in the coffee granules and stir until they dissolve. (Add a tiny drop of water to help this process if you need to).
5 Now slowly pour the gelatine and coffee mixture into the evaporated milk, whisking all the time.
6 Pour into 6 small dishes or ramekins.
7 Break up the peanut brittle into tiny pieces and crumbs by putting it into a thick plastic bag and hammering it with something heavy.
8 When the mousses are set, serve with the toffee sprinkled over the top.

JELLIES

GOOSEBERRY & ELDERFLOWER JELLY

Serves 2–3

Elderflowers smell of cats to me but by some magic they impart a lovely muscat taste and smell to this cloudy jelly. You could perk up the green colour with 2 or 3 drops of green food colouring stirred in before it sets.

12 oz (325 g) fresh young gooseberries (hard and green)
2 tablespoons elderflower cordial
1 tablespoon lemon juice
1 packet of gelatine
2½ oz (65 g) caster sugar, or more
2 elderflower heads (optional if available)

1   Stew the gooseberries in a pan with water to cover until they are very soft.
2   Using a slotted spoon, lift the fruit out of the water (but reserve water) and sieve it through a nylon sieve into a measuring jug, pushing the fruit back and forth and scraping the purée regularly from under the sieve. Set this aside.
3   In a small bowl, put the elderflower cordial and the lemon juice. Sprinkle the gelatine over and set this aside to swell up for 3 minutes. Now stand this bowl in a pan of simmering water and stir until the gelatine melts and the liquid is almost clear.
4   Pour the gelatine liquid into the measuring jug with the gooseberry purée and the sugar. Use some of the water from stewing the gooseberries to top the mixture up to just under the 1 pint (600 ml) mark.
5   Just before the jelly is poured out, if using shake the elderflower heads over a piece of paper and gather up the white flower heads which are perfect. Pour the jelly into 2–3 individual glasses or a flat glass dish and sprinkle the flowers over the top after it sets. Serve cool.

SWEET CIDER JELLY WITH A BRAMLEY SAUCE

Serves 6

Jelly
1 pt (600 ml) sweet cider
1 packet of gelatine

Sauce
1 large Bramley apple
2 cloves
1 level tablespoon caster sugar
1 tablespoon chopped walnuts

1   Put about ¼ pt (150 ml) of the cider in a small bowl. Sprinkle over the gelatine and set aside to expand for 3 minutes.
2   Now set the bowl in a pan of simmering water and stir the gelatine until it is dissolved and clear. Mix the melted gelatine and cider in with the rest of the cider.
3   Pour into 6 small glass dishes or wine glasses which you have just rinsed in cold water but not dried, leaving room at the top of the cider jellies for the sauce. Set aside to firm up.
4   To make the sauce: core the apple and score it lightly through the skin horizontally. Sit the apple in a bowl with 2 tablespoons of water and drop the cloves into the middle. Cook in the microwave on high for 2–3 minutes, then have a look; if not cooked through, give it another 1 minute.
5   Now scrape out the apple pulp and discard the cloves. Sweeten the pulp very lightly and allow to cool down.
6   Just before serving, spoon a little apple sauce on top of the jelly and sprinkle on some chopped walnuts.

REDCURRANT & RASPBERRY CREAM

Serves 6

8 oz (225 g) perfect ripe redcurrants
8 oz (225 g) perfect ripe raspberries
1 pt (600 ml) hot water
5 oz (150 g) caster sugar
3 level tablespoons cornflour
thick yoghurt or cream, to serve

1   Blend the redcurrants and raspberries in a food processor and put in a large pan with the hot water and sugar. Bring to a boil and stir until the sugar has dissolved. Reduce to a simmer and cook until the purée is fairly thick. Rub this purée through a very fine sieve to remove seeds
2   Put 3 tablespoons of the purée in a small bowl and stir into this the cornflour until smooth. Add some more purée, then tip the lot back into the greater amount of purée. Pour this into a small pan and simmer, stirring all the time, until the juices thicken slightly.
3   Off the heat, adjust the sugar and spoon into 6 little bowls or glasses and leave to set.
4   Serve with thick yoghurt or cream.

FRESH ORANGE JELLY

Serves 8

1 pt (600 ml) fresh orange juice, strained
pared rind from 1 orange
pared rind from 1/2 lemon
2 1/2 oz (65 g) caster sugar
2 tablespoons fresh lemon juice
2 1/2 packets of gelatine
chilled cream, to serve

1   Put the orange juice in a pan with the orange and lemon rind, 1/4 pt (150 ml) of water and the caster sugar. Set this pan over a low heat to infuse.
2   Put another 1/4 pt (150 ml) water into a small bowl and sprinkle over the gelatine. Set it aside for 5 minutes to swell up.
3   Stir the soaked gelatine and water into the pan with the orange and lemon rind. Over a low heat, keep the gelatine moving and, when all the gelatine has dissolved, pass the whole lot through a nylon strainer into a big jug. Stir in the lemon juice. Taste and adjust the sweetness if you like.
4   Turn into a nice big glass bowl to set. Serve with chilled single cream.

PASSION FRUIT JELLY & MERINGUE KISSES

Serves 4

6 ripe passion fruits
about 1/4 pt (150 ml) unsweetened orange juice
2 tablespoons lemon juice
3 oz (75 g) caster sugar
1 packet of gelatine
8 oz (225 g) thick yoghurt or fromage frais
Meringue Kisses (page 271), to serve

1   Cut 5 of the passion fruit in two and scrape out the jelly-like flesh which clings to the jet black shiny seeds. Set this in a nylon sieve and rub the seeds back and forth to extract as much juice as possible. It is a slow job. Reserve some of the black seeds.
2   Put the passion fruit juice in a measuring jug and bring up to the 4 fl oz (100 ml) mark with the orange juice. Pour this mixture plus the lemon juice and caster sugar into a small pan. Heat and stir until the sugar dissolves. Allow to cool.
3   When the contents of the pan are cold, sprinkle the gelatine over the liquid in the pan and set aside for 3 minutes until the gelatine expands. Set the pan on a low heat and whisk and stir until the gelatine dissolves. Stir the juices into the yoghurt or fromage frais, just a little at a time. If you wish, stir a teaspoon of the black seeds into the mixture.
4   Pour into the 4 glass dishes (wine glasses look nice) and leave aside in a cool place to set.
5   Serve decorated with the seeds from the remaining passion fruit and with Meringue Kisses.

FRUIT WINE JELLIES

Makes 4

1 fresh lemon
2 oz (50 g) caster sugar
1 packet of gelatine
2 fresh ripe peaches
1/2 pt (300 ml) peach wine
whipped cream or Mascarpone cheese, to
    serve

1   Grate the rind from the lemon and squeeze
the juice.
2   Put 8 fl oz (225 ml) water in a pan with the
grated rind and the sugar. Heat gently and then,
when it does come to a boil, remove the pan from
the heat.
3   Put the lemon juice in a small bowl. Sprinkle
over the gelatine and leave it to soak for a few
minutes, then stand the bowl in a small pan of
simmering water to allow the gelatine to
dissolve. Stir often and, when the liquid is clear,
pour it into the lemon-flavoured water.
4   Pour this mixture through a sieve and set it
aside to go cool (the peach wine does not go in
until later).
5   Meanwhile, pour boiling water over the
peaches to cover and then leave to stand for a few
minutes. Then skin and cut each peach in half
and remove the stones. Cut the fruit in slices or
chunks and divide between the 4 glass dishes.
6   If the lemon water is cool and thickening, stir
in the peach wine. Mix well and pour into the
glasses on top of the fruit. Put in a cool place to set.
7   Serve with a spoonful of whipped cream or
Mascarpone on top.

JELLIED FRUIT PUREÉS

Serves 4–6

1 lb (450 g) fresh or frozen blackberries
juice of 1 lemon
1 packet of gelatine
1 1/2 oz (40 g) caster sugar

1   Reserving 12 perfect blackberries for
decoration, barely cover the rest of the berries
with water and stew gently until the berries are
soft. Remove from the heat and mash the fruit
down to a pulp with a potato masher.
2   Put the lemon juice in a small bowl, sprinkle
the gelatine over and leave to expand for about 3
minutes. Now set the bowl in a small pan of
simmering water and stir until the gelatine
dissolves. Stir in the sugar.
3   Using a nylon sieve over a measuring jug,
push the fruit and water through. Scrape back
and forward with a big metal spoon to work the
pulp through the sieve, leaving the pips behind.
Scrape all the pulp from the underside of the
sieve too. Pour the gelatine mixture into the
measuring jug as well and make up to 1 pint
(600 ml) with water. At this point check if you
think you want more sugar in the jelly.
4   Pour into 4–6 small glass dishes or ramekins
and leave to set.
5   Serve with 2 or 3 perfect berries on top of
each portion.

ROSE JELLY WITH CRYSTALLIZED ROSE PETALS

Serves 4

1/2 pt (300 ml) rose wine
2 tablespoons triple-distilled rose water
    (sold by delis or specialist food shops)
juice of 1 lemon
1 packet of gelatine
1 oz (25 g) caster sugar, plus more for
    sprinkling
about 12 sweet-scented rose petals
white of 1 size-6 or size-7 egg

1   To make the jelly, pour the wine and rose
water into a big measuring jug. Put the juice
from the lemon in a small bowl and sprinkle the
gelatine over it. Set aside for 3 minutes to allow
the gelatine to expand. Now set the bowl in a

small pan of simmering water and stir until the gelatine dissolves. Stir in the sugar and stir until that dissolves too. Pour this mixture into the wine. Top up the liquid to the 1 pint (600 ml) mark with water or wine, pour into 4 glasses and set aside in the fridge to set.

2   To crystallize the rose petals: nip out the part of the petal which was attached to the rose – it is quite hard and is often white or green. Now very lightly whisk the egg white. Take a pastry brush and paint the petals one at a time with egg white (back and front). While the egg white is still wet, use a spoon over a dish to pour caster sugar all over the petal (back and front). Set the petal to dry on a piece of non-stick baking paper. It will crisp up as it dries and is very nice to eat.

3   Set the rose petals on the jellies just before your serve them.

VICTORIAS IN PORT WINE JELLY

Serves 4–6

1 medium-size orange
¼ pt (150 ml) port
4 oz (125 g) caster sugar
12 oz (325 g) fresh ripe Victoria plums,
    halved and stoned
1 packet of gelatine
chilled single cream, to serve

1   With a sharp knife, pare 3 wide strips of peel from the orange and squeeze the juice.

2   Pour the port and orange juice into a measuring jug. Top up with water almost to the ¾ pint (450 ml) mark.

3   Put this liquid into a saucepan with the sugar and orange rind. Heat gently until the sugar dissolves, then bring to a boil. Reduce to a simmer, remove the orange rind and put in the plums. Simmer for just about 3–4 minutes, or until the plums are tender. Set the pan aside and fish out as many skins as you can.

4   Put 5 tablespoons of water in a small bowl, sprinkle over the gelatine and leave aside for 3

minutes. Now set the bowl in a pan of simmering water and stir until the gelatine dissolves. Pour this dissolved gelatine into the plums.

5   Rinse a 1½ pt (1 litre) glass or china serving dish with cold water. Pour the water away, but do not dry the dish. Pour the jelly and plums in and set aside to go cold and firm up. Alternatively, you could spoon the jelly and fruit into wetted individual serving dishes.

6   Serve with chilled single cream.

APPLE JELLIES & BANANA CRISPS

Serves 4

12 oz (325 g) cooking apples
1 packet of gelatine
¼ pt (150 ml) apple juice
1–2 oz (25–50 g) caster sugar
banana crisps (from whole-food shops and
    some greengrocers)

1   Peel, core and chop the apples coarsely. Put in a saucepan with ¼ pt (150 ml) water. Bring to the boil, reduce to a simmer and cook until the apples are soft.

2   Sprinkle the gelatine over the fruit. Liquidize the apples with the cooking water, using a stick blender or a liquidizer. Pour into a measuring jug. Stir in the apple juice and enough water to reach the 1 pt (600 ml) mark. Sweeten to taste (the amount will depend on how sweet the apple juice was).

3   Pour into 4 glasses or serving dishes and, when set, cover the top with coarsely crushed banana crisps.

BRAMLEY JELLY & WENSLEYDALE CHEESE

Use the same recipe as above, but look for Bramley cooking apples. Set the jellies in straight-sided ramekins. To serve, turn each jelly out on a flat plate and set a wedge of creamy Wensleydale cheese beside it.

RASPBERRY JELLY

Serves 6

1½ lb (675 g) fresh or frozen raspberries
4 oz (125 g) caster sugar
7 fl oz (200 ml) red wine
3 packets of gelatine
whipped cream, to serve

1   Put the fresh or drained frozen fruit, sugar, wine and 7 fl oz (200 ml) water in a pan, bring to the boil and then simmer for only 3 minutes. Remove from the heat and allow to cool.
2   One sachet at a time, sprinkle the gelatine over the hot fruit and whisk to dissolve each one. Taste and add more sugar if you wish.
3   Pour into a wetted 2¼ pt (1.25 litre) ring mould or flat dish and leave aside to set.
4   Serve with whipped cream.

PEACHES & BRISTOL CREAM

Serves 6

15½ oz (435 g) can of sliced peaches in syrup
about 4 tablespoons Bristol cream sherry
2 tablespoons lemon juice
1 packet of gelatine
about 1 oz (25 g) caster sugar
icing sugar, for dusting

1   Drain the syrup from the peaches and pour it into a measuring jug. Take half of the peaches and add them to the syrup. Use a stick blender or food processor to blend the peaches and syrup to a purée. Stir in the sherry and set aside.
2   Put the lemon juice in a small bowl and sprinkle over the gelatine. Leave it for 3 minutes to swell up. Now set the bowl in a small pan of simmering water and stir until the gelatine dissolves completely. Pour into the peaches and stir hard. Bring the liquid peaches up to the 1 pt (600 ml) mark with water in the measuring jug.
3   Taste and add more sugar or sherry to taste, then pour into 6 ramekins or small dishes and set in the fridge to firm up.
4   To serve: turn each mould out on a flat plate and set 2 or 3 peach slices on the side. Dust icing sugar over through a sieve at the last minute.

GLOWING FRUIT SALAD JELLY

Serves 6–8

2 packets of gelatine
1 pt (600 ml) white grape juice
2 oz (50 g) caster sugar
2 large oranges
4 oz (125 g) green seedless grapes, halved
4 oz (125 g) black seedless grapes, halved
1 nectarine, stoned and thinly sliced
4 oz (125 g) fresh raspberries, or frozen and
   drained
2 oz (50 g) melon balls from a honeydew
   melon
2 oz (50 g) watermelon chunks, deseeded

1   Put ¼ pt (150 ml) of water into a small bowl and sprinkle over the 2 packets of gelatine. Allow to soak for 3 minutes, then set the bowl in a small pan of simmering water. Stir until the gelatine is clear. Set aside to cool for 10 minutes.
2   Put ¼ pt (150 ml) grape juice in a small pan with the sugar. With a sharp knife, pare the zest from the oranges and add to the grape juice. Simmer for about 10 minutes.

3   Now stir in the remaining grape juice. Finally, stir the gelatine mixture in as well and set aside. Fish out and discard the pieces of orange zest.

4   Put all the prepared fruit in a large bowl or dish. Take a sharp knife and peel all the pith from around the two oranges, then take out the segments of fruit and allow the juice to drop down on the fruit as you do it. I find it easier to segment the oranges by holding one in my left hand and slicing down between the fruit and the pith to loosen the segment. Add the orange segments to the bowl of fruit.

5   Pour the jelly over the fruit and then set it aside to firm up in the fridge, about 2 hours. Cover with a plate or cling-film if it is to be left longer.

JUNKET

Makes 4 or 6 small ones

My brother hated this 'jellied milk', but I always loved the silky texture.

However, getting rennet in the shops is not always as easy as it might be. The liquid has a limited shelf-life, so it is difficult for most stores to stock something for which they are rarely asked. The food writer Philippa Davenport wrote recently that her local Waitrose stocks Burgess rennet essence. If you do find it, take careful note of the expiry date as the rennet will probably not work as well after that date.

½ pt (300 ml) gold-top milk (called 'breakfast milk' in some stores)
10 fl oz (300 ml) single cream
1 level dessertspoon vanilla sugar
1 teaspoon of liquid rennet

1   Pour the milk, cream and sugar into a pan and warm gently to blood heat (98°F/37°C, or when you can put your finger in the liquid and hold it there for 30 seconds comfortably – use a sugar thermometer if you have one).

2   Take the pan off the heat and put 4 small glasses or bowls on a tray. Now stir the rennet into the warm milk and stir it round. Divide between the dishes, set the tray in a corner where it will be undisturbed at room temperature and leave for 3 hours. It can go in the fridge once it has set, but not before.

Variation

Coffee junket: add 4 teaspoons of strongly flavoured coffee to the milk.

PORT & PRUNE JELLY

Makes 6 small portions

12 oz (325 g) dried prunes, soaked overnight in water to cover
1 packet of gelatine
grated rind and juice of 1 lemon
¼ pt (150 ml) port

1   Stew the soaked prunes in the soaking water (with perhaps a little extra) until they are squashy. Reserve water. Remove stones and use a stick blender to reduce the fruit to a purée.

2   Sprinkle the gelatine over the purée, reheat and stir until the gelatine dissolves. Pour the purée into a measuring jug, add the lemon juice and rind together with the port and enough of reserved water to bring the level up to the 1 pt (600 ml) mark. Taste and add sugar if you wish.

3   Pour into 6 small dishes or ramekins and set in the fridge to firm up.

CREAMS

LEMON COTTAGE CHEESE & GOLDEN SULTANAS

Serves 6

In old recipes, cottage cheese was sieved to break it down. In fact, it never does reduce to a smooth cream and there is always a soft grainy texture – even with a food processor.

Soak the golden sultanas in 2 or 3 teaspoons of water – 30 seconds in the microwave cooker would plump them up quickly.

3 oz (75 g) unsalted butter
10 fl oz (300 ml) milk
1 packet of gelatine
8 oz (225 g) plain cottage cheese
1 heaped teaspoon grated lemon rind and
    2 tablespoons lemon juice
3 oz (75 g) caster sugar
2 oz (50 g) golden sultanas
single cream, to serve

1   In a heatproof bowl, put the butter and milk. Sprinkle the gelatine over the surface. Set the bowl over a pan of simmering water to cook gently. Whisk the gelatine into the milk, then stir until all is smooth.
2   Take the bowl off the heat and set it aside to thicken. Give it one last whisk to make sure that it is smooth and the gelatine has melted. Set aside to go cold.
3   Using a stick blender or food processor, blend the cottage cheese, lemon rind, lemon juice and sugar into the cooled cream.
4   Pour into 6 small ramekins.
5   To serve: turn the creams out on flat plates, scatter with the golden sultanas and serve with a little single cream.

TIA MARIA CREAMS

Serves 6–8

3 size-1 or size-2 egg yolks
2 oz (50 g) caster sugar
2 tablespoons Tia Maria liqueur
1 packet of gelatine
15 fl oz (450 ml) milk
½ pt (300 ml) double cream
chopped nuts, to decorate

1   In a large heatproof bowl, put the egg yolks, sugar and one of the tablespoons of Tia Maria. Suspend this bowl over a pan of simmering water and whisk the contents until they are pale and thick.
2   Sprinkle the gelatine over the surface of the egg yolk mixture and whisk it in. Add the milk to this mixture, whisking well to get the gelatine to dissolve. Go on cooking this mixture gently until it is smooth.
3   Take the bowl from the heat and leave it until the mixture is cool. Now stir in the second tablespoon of Tia Maria. Set the bowl aside and, when it starts to set, stir in half of the double cream.
4   Spoon the cream into 6–8 small ramekins or glass dishes and leave aside to set.
5   To serve: run a thin knife round each cream and shake it hard to unmould the cream (put the ramekin upside down on its serving plate and, using two hands to hold on tight to both plate and dish, shake the cream out). Whip the remaining double cream and put a blob on each Tia Maria cream. Sprinkle on some chopped nuts as well. Serve chilled.

APPLE SNOW & TOASTED ALMONDS

Serves 4–5

For toasted almonds, turn on your grill and scatter a thin layer of flaked almonds in your grill pan or on a metal baking sheet. Watch carefully; you want pale gold not bitter black.

1 lb (450 g) Bramley apples, peeled, cored and cut in slices
1½ oz (40 g) caster sugar
whites of 2 size-1 or size-2 eggs
1½ oz (40 g) toasted flaked almonds

1 Stew the apples with the sugar in 2 tablespoons water. Do this slowly so that they do not burn. When the apples are soft, pour off any liquid and mash the apples to a purée. Set aside to go cold.
2 In another bowl, whisk the egg whites until they are stiff. Fold these into the apple and spoon this airy mixture into 4–5 glass dishes. Sprinkle each with toasted almonds.

WINE & STRAWBERRY CREAM

Serves 6

1 lb (450 g) strawberries
3 oz (75 g) caster sugar
9 fl oz (235 ml) red wine
2 packets of gelatine
9 fl oz (235 ml) double cream

1 Set aside 3 perfect strawberries for decoration. Hull and slice the remaining strawberries and set these in a bowl with the sugar. Leave overnight, if possible, to extract as much juice as possible. Stir every now and then to dissolve the sugar.
2 Put the red wine in a small saucepan and sprinkle the gelatine over. On a low heat, allow the gelatine to dissolve. Set aside to cool.

3 Use a stick blender or a food processor to reduce the strawberries to a rough purée. Stir in the liquid gelatine and wine. Chill until the strawberry mixture is beginning to set. Stir in the cream.
4 Pour into 6 small glass dishes or ramekins.
5 When set, decorate each dish with half a strawberry.

MASCARPONE & CRÈME DE CACAO

Serves 6

This coffee-flavoured pudding is enhanced with the coffee liqueur Crème de Cacao. Mascarpone is an Italian soft cheese.

3 size-1 or size-2 egg yolks
3 oz (75 g) caster sugar
3 level teaspoons coffee granules, dissolved in 1 tablespoon hot water
1 packet of gelatine
15 fl oz (450 ml) milk
1 tablespoon Crème de Cacao
½ pt (300 ml) Mascarpone cheese (or half double cream and Mascarpone)
grated chocolate, to decorate

1 Put the egg yolks, sugar and coffee in a heatproof bowl suspended over a pan of simmering water.
2 Whisk until the mixture thickens slightly and the sugar dissolves. Sprinkle the gelatine over and whisk that in too. Stir in the milk and whisk all of this together. When the gelatine has dissolved, take the bowl off the heat and allow the mixture to cool.
3 Stir in the Crème de Cacao. Now wait until the mixture is on the point of setting, then stir in just half of the Mascarpone or cream and Mascarpone mixture.
4 Pour the mixture into 6 small glass dishes or ramekins and leave aside to set.
5 To serve: spoon some of the reserved Mascarpone or cream mixture on each cream and decorate with grated chocolate.

ELDERFLOWER CREAM POTS

Makes 6

Pick the elderflowers on the day you need them and look for absolutely perfect flowers – no brown ones at all.

2 large heads of elderflower
15 fl oz (450 ml) milk
4 size-1 or size-2 eggs, separated
3 oz (75 g) caster sugar
1 packet of gelatine
1/4 pt (150 ml) double cream

1   Put the elderflowers upside down in a pan with the milk. Bring it slowly to the boil. Switch off the heat, put a lid on and leave it to infuse. About 10 minutes will be enough.
2   Using a large bowl, whisk the egg yolks with 2 oz (50 g) of the measured sugar until pale, thick and creamy.
3   Boil up the milk again and strain it through a fine sieve into a jug. Pour this hot milk in a steady stream on the egg yolk mixture, whisking all the time. Place the bowl over a pan of simmering water and stir until the custard thickens. Set aside.
4   Put about 3 tablespoons of cold water into a small bowl, sprinkle the gelatine over and leave it to swell up. Then stand the bowl in a small pan of simmering water. Stir until it dissolves. Pour into the hot custard and stir it round. Set aside to thicken and go tepid. When almost cold, stir in the double cream.
5   In another bowl, whisk the egg whites until they are at the soft peak stage. Sprinkle over the last 1 oz (25 g) sugar and whisk again until stiff. Fold the egg whites into the custard.
6   Spoon into 6 small glasses or pots or a nice mould with a capacity of 1 1/2 pt (1 litre). (If you are using a mould, do not forget to rinse the mould with cold water and pour the water away but, do not dry it).

RICOTTA & CHOCOLATE POTS WITH BRANDY

Serves 4

Ricotta cheese is a low-fat Italian fresh cheese. It should be used within 2 days of buying it.

2 oz (50 g) golden sultanas
1 tablespoon Cognac
4 oz (125 g) Ricotta cheese
4 tablespoons fromage frais
2 tablespoons cocoa powder
2 tablespoons caster sugar

1   Put the sultanas and the Cognac in a small bowl and set aside for 20–30 minutes so that the raisins can absorb the spirit.
2   Work the Ricotta through a sieve into a biggish bowl. (You could use a stick blender on it instead). Stir in the fromage frais.
3   Sieve the cocoa into the bowl with the sugar and the raisins and any remaining Cognac. Blend again and spoon into 4 small glass dishes.
4   Chill and serve with crisp biscuits.

RUM & CHESTNUT CHOCOLATE CREAMS WITH MARRONS GLACÉS

Serves 8–10

This pudding is very rich.

6 oz (175 g) dark good-quality chocolate, broken into pieces
3 oz (75 g) butter, softened
2 oz (50 g) sugar
15 1/2 oz (435 g) tin of unsweetened chestnut purée
3 tablespoons rum
1/2 pt (300 ml) double cream
3 marrons glacés, crumbled

1   Put the chocolate pieces in a heatproof bowl over a pan of simmering water to melt.
2   In another big bowl, cream the butter and sugar and add the chestnut purée a bit at a time. Mix thoroughly.
3   Stir in first the melted chocolate, then the rum and lastly pour in the double cream.
4   Pour the dessert into 8 small glasses and chill.
5   Serve with a little marron glacé crumbled on top.

CRANBERRY CREAMS

Serves 6

8 oz (225 g) fresh or frozen cranberries
4 oz (125 g) caster sugar
2 teaspoons cornflour
8 oz (225 g) plain fromage frais
5 oz (150 ml) thick Greek yoghurt
1 packet of gelatine
¼ pt (150 ml) whipping cream, lightly
    whipped

1   Cook the cranberries in a pan with 3 tablespoons water and 2 oz (50 g) of the sugar until soft. Use a stick blender in the pan to reduce the cranberries to a purée.
2   In a small container, mix the cornflour with a little water, then stir this into the purée. Continue to cook the purée until the mixture thickens. Set aside to cool, but give it a stir every now and then.
3   In a large bowl, beat the fromage frais into the yoghurt with the remaining caster sugar.
4   Put 3 tablespoons of cold water in a small bowl, sprinkle the gelatine over and set aside to swell up for 3 minutes. Now set the bowl in a small pan of simmering water to melt the gelatine. Allow to cool slightly.
5   Fold the cooled gelatine into the fromage frais mixture, followed by the whipped cream and the cranberry mixture.
6   Spoon the cranberry cream into 6 small glass dishes or into one big one. Set in the fridge to firm up.
7   Serve cool, but not icy.

WHITE CHOCOLATE & LIME CREAMS

Serves 4

4 oz (125 g) granulated sugar
2 oz (50 g) chopped and toasted nuts
4 oz (125 g) white chocolate
juice and grated zest from 2 limes
2 level teaspoons gelatine
1 size-1 or size-2 egg, separated
2 oz (50 g) fromage frais
vegetable oil, for greasing

1   Over a low heat, dissolve the granulated sugar in a heavy-based pan and boil it steadily until it looks a rich gold. To test if it is ready, dribble a small teaspoon into a jug of cold water. If the caramel is ready it will set to a crisp in the cold water. If it stays soft, then boil the caramel a little longer.
2   Tip the toasted nuts into the caramel and pour this out on a well-oiled baking tray and leave it to set hard. Once it is set hard and cold, break up the pieces, put them into a food processor and reduce them to a sandy grit.
3   Put the pieces of chocolate in a heatproof bowl and set the bowl over a pan of simmering water. When melting, give the chocolate a gentle stir (remember that white chocolate never does go very liquid).
4   Put the lime juice and rind in a small bowl and sprinkle over the gelatine. Set the bowl in a pan of simmering water and stir every now and then to melt.
5   In another bowl, whisk the egg whites to soft peaks.
6   In yet another bigger bowl, mix the fromage frais, egg yolk and praline (toffee mixture). Stir in the lime and gelatine mixture, followed by the chocolate. Stir hard to get the chocolate to mix. Lastly, fold in the beaten egg white.
7   Spoon into 4 individual glass dishes and set aside to chill.

CHOCOLATE POTS

Makes 6

You will need 6 little containers like custard cups, or tiny coffee cups also look pretty.

6 oz (175 g) top-quality dark chocolate
12 fl oz (350 ml) single cream
1 tablespoon Earl Grey tea leaves
1 teaspoon orange flower water

1   Break up the chocolate into small pieces and put them in a heatproof bowl. Set it over a pan of simmering water.
2   In another pan, simmer the cream with the Earl Grey tea leaves for about 1 minute. Stir vigorously, then strain the cream into a large jug and stir in the orange flower water.
3   Once the chocolate has melted, pour the hot cream over it, slowly at first and stirring all the time.
4   Set the cream aside to cool down, before pouring it into the glass dishes or small cups. Chill.

GUAVA & CARDAMOM VELVET

Serves 4

I cut this recipe out of a copy of *Woman's Weekly* magazine years ago, so I have Liz Burn to thank for it.

4 oz (125 g) caster sugar
juice of 1 lemon
seeds from 2 cardamom pods
3 ripe guavas, peeled, sliced and seeds removed
4 fl oz (125 ml) very hot milk
2 level teaspoons gelatine
1 teaspoon orange flower water
8 oz (225 g) soft cream cheese
pink food colouring (optional)

1   Put the sugar, lemon juice, cardamom seeds and ¼ pt (150 ml) water in a small pan. Bring to the boil and reduce to a simmer to dissolve the sugar. Now add the guava slices and simmer for a minute, then set the pan aside to cool down. Fish out the cardamom.
2   Put the milk in a heatproof bowl and heat it up in the microwave. Sprinkle the gelatine over the surface and whisk it in. When the gelatine has dissolved, set the bowl aside to cool.
3   When cool, stir in the orange flower water and then beat in the cream cheese. Spoon about two-thirds of this mixture into 4 glass dishes and leave to set.
4   Take two guava slices out of the syrup and reserve for decoration. Purée the rest with the syrup, then mix this with the rest of the cheese mixture. If you wish, add 2–3 drops of pink colouring to this mixture so that the colour will show against the first part of the cream recipe. Pour into the glasses and set them aside to chill.
5   Serve with the reserved guava slices, to decorate the top of each cream.

ROSE CREAM

Serves 4–5

¼ pt (150 ml) milk
2 size-1 or size-2 eggs, separated
2 tablespoons vanilla sugar
1 tablespoon Kirsch
½ pt (300 ml) double cream
2–3 drops of essence of rose
4 or 5 perfect rose leaves
4 oz (125 g) plain chocolate

1   Put the milk in a small pan, whisk in the egg yolks along with half the measured sugar. Heat and stir until the mixture thickens. Stir in the Kirsch and set aside to cool.
2   Whip the cream with the rose essence to the soft peak stage.
3   In another bowl, whip the egg whites with the remaining sugar, until they are stiff. Fold these into the whipped cream.
4   Lastly fold in the custard, a little at a time,

and spoon into 4 or 5 glass dishes or one big one.
Chill.

5   To make chocolate rose leaves: first wipe the
leaves gently with damp kitchen paper. Break up
the chocolate and set it in a heatproof bowl over a
pan of simmering water. When the chocolate has
melted, use a small brush to paint the liquid
chocolate on the back of each leaf. Allow to set,
then paint on another coat. Leave to dry, then
peel away the real leaf to reveal the chocolate
ones marked with veins.

6   Decorate the top of each pudding with a
chocolate leaf (or two if you feel like doing
more).

COEURS À LA CRÈME

Makes 4

It is traditional in France to serve these little
desserts shaped like a heart. You will need four
3 in (7.5 cm) heart-shaped china or pottery
moulds and some clean muslin. Some moulds
have holes so that the muslin is not needed.

10 oz (275 g) fromage frais
3 oz (75 g) caster sugar
4 oz (125 g) soft cheese
¹/₂ teaspoon vanilla extract
8 oz (225 g) fresh raspberries
2 oz (50 g) caster sugar

1   Beat together the fromage frais, sugar, soft
cheese and vanilla extract.

2   Line the moulds carefully with muslin and
then spoon the creamy mixture into each one.
Smooth the surface. Set in the fridge and leave
overnight. (Tilt each one up slightly to allow the
moulds to drain.)

3   Next day, reserving 12 perfect raspberries to
serve, liquidize the berries with the sugar and
spoon some on each of 4 flat plates.

4   Drain off any residual moisture from the
hearts, turn one out on each plate and top with 2
or 3 reserved fresh raspberries. Chill and serve.

DOUBLE-CREAMS WITH LEMON

Serves 6

3 large lemons
6 oz (175 g) caster sugar
1 packet of gelatine
3 size-1 or size-2 eggs, separated
6 fl oz (160 ml) double cream

1   Finely grate the rind of 2 lemons and squeeze
the juice from all 3. Set aside 1 teaspoon of
grated rind for decoration.

2   Put the rest of the grated rind and the sugar
in a large bowl.

3   Put 5 tablespoons of water in a small bowl
and sprinkle the gelatine over it. Leave for 3
minutes for the gelatine to swell, then put the
bowl in a pan of simmering water and leave the
gelatine to melt. Stir gently. When clear, take
the bowl away from the heat and cool it.

4   Add the egg yolks to the lemon rind and
sugar and set this bowl over the pan of
simmering water. Whisk until the yolks are light
and fluffy.

5   Once the gelatine is cool, stir it into the egg
yolk mixture, followed by the lemon juice. Put
this aside until it is just on the point of setting.

6   In yet another bowl, whisk the egg whites
until they are stiff. Fold these into the lemon
mixture.

7   Spoon into 6 small glass dishes or into one
big bowl and set aside to firm up.

8   Whip the double cream, spoon a large blob of
whipped cream on each lemon cream and
sprinkle with the reserved lemon rind.

FOOLS

In the past, fools of all kinds were extremely smooth, having been pushed through a sieve – sometimes more than once. Nowadays, it is more common to serve fruit fools with the texture of the puréed fruit still there. Another fact worth mentioning at this point is that since these recipes are all cold, you can easily substitute artificial sweeteners for ordinary sugar. The only difference you will notice is that when the substitute is stirred in it does fizz a bit. Most sweeteners can only be used in cool or cold food as, if subjected to heat, they lose their potency.

YOUNG RHUBARB FOOL

Serves 2–3

1 lb (450 g) early pink rhubarb
1½ oz (40 g) demerara sugar
¼ pt (150 ml) double cream

1   Top and tail the rhubarb and wipe the stalks. Cut into ½ in (1 cm) pieces. Stew very, very gently with the sugar and just 2 tablespoons of water. Cover the fruit and stop cooking as soon as it is soft. This will preserve the lovely colour.
2   Drain off almost all of the juice and mash up the fruit roughly. When cold, stir in the double cream.
3   Spoon into 2–3 glass dishes and smooth over the surface. Serve chilled.

Variations

Use half custard and half cream.
Add 1 or 2 teaspoons of Pernod.
Add the finely grated rind of 1 small orange.
Use sugar substitute – omit the demerara and add the substitute at the end.

BABY GOOSEBERRY FOOL

Serves 4

Small hard green gooseberries are best.

1 lb (450 g) small hard green gooseberries
2 oz (50 g) caster sugar
2–3 drops of green food colouring (optional)
¼ pt (150 ml) double cream

1   Rinse, top and tail the gooseberries. Cut each one in two. Simmer in a pan with the sugar and 2 tablespoons of water. Cover the fruit and cook until really soft. Because the fruit needs a long time to cook, it is not easy to preserve the green colour – hence the suggestion to use food colouring.
2   Drain the fruit and blend with a stick blender or a food processor to a rough purée. Pour away any loose juice. Stir in the double cream and spoon into 4 small glass dishes, smooth over and chill.

Variations

Omit the sugar and use sugar substitute at the end of the cooking and when the fruit is cold.
Use custard or half custard and half cream.

COCONUT & PAPAYA FOOL

Serves 4

¼ pt (150 ml) canned coconut milk
8 oz (225 g) quark
1 oz (25 g) caster sugar
finely grated rind and juice from 1 lime
1 level teaspoon stem ginger, finely chopped
1 ripe papaya, peeled, halved and deseeded
toasted coconut, to serve

1 Mix together the coconut milk, quark, sugar, lime rind, juice and ginger in a large bowl.
2 Using a food processor or stick blender, blend the papaya until the fruit is smooth.
3 Fold the fruit into the quark mixture, but you can leave it just marbled which looks nice.
4 Spoon into 4 individual glass dishes or a serving bowl and chill.
5 Serve with a covering of toasted coconut.

Note
To toast coconut: spread a layer of unsweetened desiccated coconut in a grill pan and toast under the grill. Watch carefully as it burns easily.

RHUBARB FOOL WITH CRÈME ANGLAISE

Serves 6

2 lb (900 g) early rhubarb
2 oz (50 g) caster sugar
1 teaspoon grated dried orange rind, plus
    more to decorate

Crème Anglaise
3 size-1 or size-2 egg yolks
1 level tablespoon caster sugar
1 teaspoon cornflour
1 vanilla pod
8 fl oz (225 ml) double cream

1 Top and tail the rhubarb, wipe the stalks and cut them into ½ in (1 cm) pieces.
2 Put the rhubarb in a casserole with the sugar and grated dried orange rind and just 2 tablespoons of water. Put the lid on and cook either on the hob or in the oven at a moderate heat (gas4/350°F/180°C) until soft. Do not overcook or the bright colour will vanish. When the fruit is soft, drain it in a sieve, then mash it down roughly.
3 To make the Crème Anglaise: whisk the egg yolks, caster sugar and cornflour in a medium-sized bowl. Put the vanilla pod in a pan with the double cream and bring this slowly to the boil. (Give the vanilla pod a jab or two with a fork to encourage it to release more flavour.) Fish out the vanilla pod. Now whisk the hot cream into the egg yolk mixture, a little to begin with then more and more. Whisk constantly. Return all of this mixture to the pan and whisk over a gentle heat until the custard thickens. Once this happens, sit the pan in a sink of ice-cold water to stop the custard over-cooking. Leave to go cold.
4 Mix the drained rhubarb into the custard and pour into 6 individual serving glasses or pots. Chill.
5 When ready to serve, decorate with dried and grated orange rind.

Note
To dry orange rind: peel the orange as if you were peeling an apple. Slice off as much pith as possible. Leave the rind in a warm place to dry out. I leave mine on the hob. When very dry, store in a jar.

'Better some of a pudding than none of a pie.'

Constance Spry

KIWI FOOL

Serves 6

1½ lb (675 g) ripe kiwi fruit
8 fl oz (225 ml) Crème Anglaise (see
   previous recipe)
3 oz (75 g) caster sugar
8 oz (225 g) thick Greek yoghurt

1   Peel the fruit, cut 6 thin round slices from a
whole kiwi fruit and set aside for decoration.
2   Purée the peeled fruit with a stick blender or
in a food processor. Add the cold Crème Anglaise
and blend again. Pour into a large bowl and stir
in the sugar.
3   Stir up the yoghurt until smooth, then fold
that into the kiwi fruit mixture.
4   Spoon into 6 individual serving dishes,
smooth over the surface and chill.
5   Serve with a round of kiwi on each dish.

MANGO FOOL

Serves 4

While the best flavour is always from the fresh
fruit, you can buy mango slices in a can. See
page 178 for getting the fruit from a mango.

1 large ripe mango
1½ oz (40 g) caster sugar
1 tablespoon lemon juice
8 fl oz (225 ml) double cream
crisp biscuits, to serve

1   Blend the mango in a food processor. Add the
sugar and lemon juice.
2   If the mango is very juicy, put the fruit in a
nylon sieve to allow it to drain (save the juice and
serve it poured over each fool).
3   Now whip the double cream until it is at the
floppy stage. Then fold in the mango mixture.
4   Spoon into 4 individual glass dishes, level the
surface and chill.
5   Serve with a crisp biscuit.

SPONGE CAKE & ORANGE FOOL

Serves 6

8 fl oz (225 ml) orange juice
2 tablespoons lemon juice
2 oz (40 g) caster sugar
1 packet of gelatine
2 slices of plain sponge cake
2 tablespoons medium sherry
whites from 2 size-1 or size-2 eggs

1   Stir the orange and lemon juices together in a
medium-size heatproof bowl. Stir in the sugar.
2   Sprinkle the gelatine over the orange juice
and leave it for 3 minutes. Now set the bowl over
a pan of simmering water and whisk the gelatine
until it dissolves. Check that the sugar has
dissolved too.
3   Set the bowl aside for the orange mixture to
firm up.
4   Meanwhile, break up the sponge cake and
divide between 6 glass dishes or wine glasses.
Mix the sherry with 1 tablespoon water and pour
over the sponge cakes so that they are really
moist.
5   Stir up the orange mix again and, in another
bowl, whisk the egg whites until they are stiff.
Fold these into the orange mixture and, when all
the egg white has disappeared, spoon into the
prepared dishes or glasses. Chill and serve.

SYLLABUBS

In the following syllabub recipes sugar substitute can replace caster sugar but cut the amount. I find most sugar substitutes very sweet.

MRS MOXON'S LEMON POSSET

This Robert Carrier recipe is the very first syllabub I ever enjoyed. He probably based his recipe on Elizabeth Moxon's. I base my recipe on his!

Serves about 10

1 pt (575 ml) double cream
¼ pt (150 ml) dry white wine
grated rind and juice of 2 lemons
whites of 4 size-1 or size-2 eggs
sieved icing sugar, to taste

Decoration
1 tablespoon finely grated orange rind
2 tablespoons caster sugar
3 thin orange slices

1   In a large bowl, whisk the double cream with the wine and lemon rind until it is stiff.
2   In another bowl, beat three-quarters of the egg whites until they stand in peaks. Fold these into the cream mixture and add icing sugar to taste.
3   To decorate the rim of each small wine glass, put the orange rind in a pudding bowl, the caster sugar in another bowl and the remaining lightly beaten egg white in yet another. Dip the rim of each glass first in the egg white, then in the orange rind and finally in the sugar. Set aside to allow the egg white to dry.
4   Very carefully spoon the fluffy syllabub into the glasses, sprinkle orange peel on top and set a quarter of a slice of orange on the rim.

LEMON & YOGHURT SYLLABUB

This extremely nice syllabub is from Rosamond Richardson's book *Sweet Thoughts*.

Serves 6

1 lb (450 g) low-fat natural yoghurt
6 tablespoons skimmed milk powder
4 level tablespoons sugar substitute
grated peel from 2 lemons and
    4 tablespoons fresh lemon juice
2 oz (50 g) chopped pale walnuts
white of 1 size-1 or size-2 egg

1   In a large bowl, mix the yoghurt with the dried milk. Stir in the sugar substitute, lemon juice and the lemon rind, reserving ½ teaspoon of the lemon rind for decoration. Mix well and set aside for at least 45 minutes to allow the mixture to thicken.
2   Stir in the chopped walnuts, reserving a little for decoration.
3   Whip the egg whites until stiff and fold them into the cream mixture.
4   Spoon into 6 small glass dishes or one big one and decorate with a little of the reserved lemon peel and chopped walnuts. Set aside in the fridge to firm up.

ORANGE PEEL SYLLABUB

Serves 6

grated rind and juice of 1 juicy orange
¼ pt (150 ml) white wine
2 oz (50 g) caster sugar
½ pt (300 ml) double cream
preserved orange peel (the kind you put in a
    cake)

1   In a covered bowl, soak grated orange rind in
the orange juice and white wine overnight.
2   Next day, strain off the orange rind and
discard it. Add the sugar to the wine mixture
and stir to dissolve it.
3   Whisk the double cream with the juice and
wine mixture to the floppy stage. Spoon into 6
small glasses or a bowl and set aside to firm up.
4   Serve chilled, with the finely chopped
preserved peel on top. (If you have whole peel,
soak the piece in hot water to remove the sugar,
then cut in very fine strips for the top decoration).

ORANGE LIQUEUR SYLLABUB

Serves 6

There are many orange liqueurs available, some
with famous names like Cointreau and Grand
Marnier. I also had a bottle from Cyprus which
was excellent.

grated rind and juice of 1 orange
4 tablespoons orange liqueur
½ teaspoon vanilla extract
2 oz (50 g) caster sugar
1 lb (450 g) crème fraîche

1   Put the orange rind, juice, liqueur and vanilla
in a bowl to soak overnight.
2   Next day strain into a large bowl and discard
the rind, except for a teaspoon for decoration.
Add the sugar and stir until it dissolves.

3   Stir the crème fraîche into the juice and beat
it well.
4   Spoon into 6 small glasses or a bowl and set
in the fridge to chill.
5   Serve with a sprinkle of the reserved orange
rind on top.

STRAWBERRY COTTAGE CHEESE SYLLABUB

Serves 6

8 oz (225 g) plain cottage cheese
5 tablespoons sweet white wine
grated rind of 1 lemon
2 oz (50 g) caster sugar
6 oz (175 g) thick set Greek yoghurt
8 oz (225 g) ripe strawberries

1   Blend the cottage cheese, 3 tablespoons of the
white wine, the lemon rind, sugar and yoghurt
until smooth. A liquidizer or a stick blender will
give the smoothest result, or you could pass the
syllabub through a sieve.
2   Hull and slice the strawberries, reserving 3
whole ones for decoration, and set them in 6
glass dishes. Dribble about 1 teaspoon of the
remaining wine into each glass.
3   Spoon the syllabub on top and chill.
4   Serve with half a strawberry on each pudding.

ROSE WATER & RASPBERRY SYLLABUB

Serves 6

8 oz (225 g) fresh ripe raspberries
4 small teaspoons rose water
1½ oz (40 g) caster sugar
½ pt (300 ml) double cream
7 fl oz (200 ml) sweet white wine

1 Set aside 12 perfect raspberries for decoration. Break up the rest of the fruit lightly and stir in the rose water and 1 oz (25 g) of the measured sugar.
2 In another bowl, whisk the double cream with the white wine and the remaining sugar until the cream will stand up in peaks. Fold the fruit into the cream.
3 Spoon into 4 wine glasses and set in the fridge to chill.
4 Serve with 3 perfect raspberries on each pudding.

BLACKBERRY & CRÈME FRAÎCHE SYLLABUB

Serves 6

1 lb (450 g) ripe blackberries, hulled
1 tablespoon lemon juice
1½ oz (40 g) caster sugar
8 oz (225 g) crème fraîche
crisp biscuits, to serve

1 In a covered pan, stew the blackberries with the lemon juice and 2 tablespoons of water for about 8 minutes, or until the fruit is soft.
2 Push the fruit and juices through a nylon sieve, pushing the fruit backwards and forwards with a metal spoon and scraping the pulp from under the sieve at regular intervals. Discard the pips.
3 Add the sugar to the pulp and stir until dissolved. Now beat the pulp into the crème fraîche.
4 Spoon into 6 wine glasses and chill.
5 Serve with a crisp biscuit.

EVERLASTING SYLLABUB

Serves 6

The 'everlasting' refers to the fact that the syllabub will keep well in the fridge for up to a week.

rind and juice of 1 lemon
1 wine glass of dry white wine
½ pt (300 ml) double cream
1 oz (25 g) caster sugar
sponge fingers, to serve

1 Soak the lemon rind in the glass of white wine with the juice, overnight if possible.
2 Next day, pour this into a big bowl. Stir in the cream and whip until quite thick. Add the sugar.
3 Spoon into 6 small wine glasses and chill.
4 Serve with sponge fingers.

SHERRY SYLLABUB

Serves 6

½ pt (300 ml) medium sherry
3 oz (75 g) caster sugar
rind and juice of 1 lemon
1 pt (575 ml) double cream
freshly grated nutmeg

1 In a large bowl, mix the sherry, sugar, lemon rind and juice. Stir well to dissolve the sugar.
2 In another bowl, whip the cream and fold it into the sherry mixture.
3 Spoon into 6 small glasses and chill.
4 To serve: grate some fresh nutmeg on top of each pudding.

ICE-CREAM

BASIC TRADITIONAL ICE-CREAM

Serves 8–10

This ice-cream is based on a meringue mixture and needs no beating after it goes into the freezer.

3 size-1 or size-2 eggs, separated
4 oz (125 g) unrefined light muscovado sugar
½ pt (300 ml) double cream

1 Whisk the egg whites until very stiff. Add the sugar, 2 oz (50 g) at a time, whisking in well. Continue to whisk until very stiff.
2 In another bowl, whip the cream to the floppy stage.
3 In yet another bowl, beat the egg yolks.
4 Using a large plastic spatula, fold the contents of all three bowls together.
5 Spoon into a freezer-proof serving dish, cover with foil and freeze.

BASIC LOW-FAT & LOW-CALORIE ICE-CREAM

Serves 8

1 lb (450 g) crème fraîche
5 tablespoons sugar substitute
2 teaspoons vanilla essence
whites of 3 size-1 or size-2 eggs

1 Mix together the crème fraîche, sugar substitute and vanilla essence.
2 In another bowl, whisk the egg whites until very stiff. Fold these into the crème fraîche mixture and pour into a freezer box.
3 Freeze for 5 hours.

STRAWBERRY ICE-CREAM

Serves 8

This is a rather sophisticated ice-cream, based on a rich custard made with egg yolks. If you have a fast-freeze button on your fridge, switch it on.

15 fl oz (450 ml) gold-top milk (sometimes called breakfast milk)
1 vanilla pod
4 size-1 or size-2 egg yolks
2½ oz (65 g) caster sugar
12 oz (325 g) fresh strawberries
1 tablespoon lemon juice
15 fl oz (450 ml) double cream

1 Put the milk and vanilla pod in a pan. Heat gently, but do not boil, for a few minutes. Then set the pan aside for 15 minutes to allow the vanilla flavour to infuse the milk.
2 Whisk the egg yolks and the sugar in a large heatproof bowl.
3 Take the vanilla pod out of the milk. Bring the milk to the boil and pour the hot milk over the egg yolks, whisking all the time. Set this bowl over a pan of simmering water and allow the custard to cook slowly, whisking often. Once thickened, set the bowl aside to cool down.
4 Liquidize or process the strawberries with the lemon juice. Mix with the custard and the cream. Pour the mixture into a freezer-proof plastic box to a depth of 1½ in (4 cm). Cover and set in the freezer. After 1–1½ hours the ice-cream will have set round the edges but be soft and wet in the middle. I use a stick blender to reduce the ice to slush, but you can only do this in the box if the box is deep enough. You may have to decant it into a bowl. Re-freeze the ice-cream and repeat the process twice, then re-freeze with the lid securely in place.

LEMON CURD ICE-CREAM IN A FLASH

Serves 6

12 oz (325 g) lemon curd (homemade is
   best)
1 pt (575 ml) natural yoghurt

1   Fold the lemon curd and the yoghurt
together.
2   Spoon into a rigid plastic box and freeze.

ICE-CREAM LOAF

Serves 8–10

Three layers – strawberry, chocolate and
strawberry again, all coated with my favourite
peanut brittle.

8 oz (225 g) peanut brittle

Chocolate Ice-cream
2 size-1 or size-2 egg yolks
1½ oz (40 g) caster sugar
4 fl oz (100 ml) whipping cream
3–4 drops of vanilla essence
3 oz (75 g) plain chocolate, broken into
   small pieces
4 fl oz (100 ml) thick Greek yoghurt
Strawberry Ice-cream
6 fl oz (160 ml) whipping cream
6 fl oz (160 ml) thick Greek yoghurt
6 oz (175 g) sieved icing sugar
1 lb (450 g) ripe strawberries

1   First make the chocolate ice-cream: whisk the
egg yolks with the caster sugar until pale and thick.
2   Heat the whipping cream and the vanilla
essence until almost to boiling point.
3   Pour the hot mixture on the egg yolk
mixture, whisking all the time. Return this
mixture to the pan over a low heat and add the
chocolate pieces. Stir gently until the mixture is
thick enough to coat the back of the spoon. Do
not boil. Set aside to go cold.
4   Fold in the yoghurt and spoon into a plastic
box to freeze.
5   Make the strawberry ice-cream: in one bowl,
whip the cream to the floppy stage. Fold in the
yoghurt along with the sieved icing sugar. purée
the ripe strawberries and mix with the cream and
yoghurt.
6   Pour into a freezer box and freeze.
7   To assemble the ice-cream loaf: first break up
the peanut brittle, put the pieces in the food
processor and whisk to a sandy crumb. The other
way is to hammer the brittle inside a heavy
plastic bag with your rolling pin.
8   Line the base of a large deep loaf tin with a
strip of non-stick paper. Scoop the strawberry
ice-cream out of its box and into a food processor.
Whizz it until smooth. Divide it roughly in two
and set one half back in the freezer. Pour the
other into the tin and set it in the freezer at once.
9   Turn the chocolate ice-cream out and into a
clean food processor. Whizz until smooth, then
pour all of it on top of the now-frozen strawberry
layer in the loaf tin. Now put the tin back in the
freezer.
10 When that has firmed up, retrieve the
remaining strawberry ice-cream and, if it is stiff
again, it will have to be made smooth in the food
processor. Pour into the loaf tin. Return the loaf
tin to the freezer.
11 When the loaf is firm enough, spread the
broken toffee all over a sheet of foil. Run a knife
round the ice-cream and turn it out on the toffee
mixture (if it sticks, dip the tin in hot water for
just a few seconds and then turn it out). Press the
toffee on the loaf to cover just the top and sides.
Set the loaf on a flat dish, cover with foil and
return it to the freezer.
12 To serve: transfer the loaf from the freezer to
the fridge at least 15 minutes before you want to
serve it. Slice thickly.

CHILDREN'S CHOCOLATE ICE-CREAM

Serves 6

This is easy enough for a child to make, but supervision is needed to use the food processor.

1 large can of condensed milk
¼ pt (150 ml) milk
2 tablespoons cocoa, sieved and mixed with 2 tablespoons of hot water

1   Stir everything together in a bowl, then pour it into a shallow freezing tray or plastic box.
2   When frozen quite firm, turn the ice into your food processor and blend until smooth.
3   Pour it back into the freezer tray or plastic box and freeze.

LOW-CAL RASPBERRY ICE-CREAM

Serves 6

12 oz (325 g) ripe raspberries, hulled
5 level tablespoons sugar substitute
1 lb (450 g) crème fraîche
2 small teaspoons vanilla essence
whites from 2 size-1 or size-2 eggs

1   Purée the raspberries with a stick blender or in a food processor. Stir in 2 tablespoons of the sugar substitute.
2   In another bowl, mix the crème fraîche with the remaining sugar substitute and stir in the vanilla essence.
3   Now stir the raspberry purée and the crème fraîche mixture together.
4   In yet another bowl, whisk the egg whites until they are very stiff and fold these into the fruit and crème fraîche mixture.
5   Spoon into a freezer box and freeze for about 5 hours.

CHOCOLATE ICE-CREAM

Serves 8–10

2 whole size-1 or size-2 eggs, plus 2 extra yolks
3 oz (75 g) caster sugar
½ pt (300 ml) single cream
8 oz (225 ml) top-quality dark chocolate, broken into pieces
½ pt (300 ml) double cream

1   In a big bowl, whisk the eggs, egg yolks and sugar until pale and fluffy.
2   Heat the single cream and chocolate over a low heat until the chocolate has melted. Once the chocolate has melted, turn up the heat and bring to the boil. Pour immediately over the egg yolk mixture, whisking all the time.
3   Return this mixture to the pan and heat slowly until the custard coats the back of the spoon. Strain this mixture through a nylon sieve and set it aside to cool with a cover over the bowl.
4   Whip the double cream and fold it into the cooled chocolate custard.
5   Pour into a freezer box and freeze for about 2 hours, then remove from the box and whisk the mixture until smooth. Return it to the freezer and freeze until it is firm.

LOW-CAL MANGO ICE-CREAM

Serves 6

12 oz (325 g) fresh mango flesh (2 ripe mangoes – see page 178 for getting the flesh from a mango)
3 level tablespoons sugar substitute
2 small teaspoons vanilla essence
8 oz (225 g) crème fraîche
whites from 2 size-1 or size-2 eggs

1   Use a stick blender or food processor to

reduce the mango flesh to a purée. Stir the sugar substitute and the vanilla essence into the crème fraîche.

2 Mix the mango purée and crème fraîche mixtures thoroughly.

3 In another bowl, whisk the egg whites until they are stiff. Fold these into the fruit mixture.

4 Pour into a freezer box, cover with a lid and freeze for 5 hours.

BROWN BREAD ICE-CREAM

Serves 6

2 oz (50 g) fresh brown breadcrumbs
8 oz (225 g) double cream
3 tablespoons sugar
2 tablespoons orange juice
2 teaspoons lemon juice
whites from 2 size-1 or size-2 eggs

1 First toast the breadcrumbs. Preheat the oven to gas3/325°F/160°C. Spread the crumbs on a baking sheet and bake for about 20 minutes until crisp, stirring them round a bit during baking and watching them carefully. Allow to cool.

2 In a large bowl, whisk the double cream, adding the sugar and the orange and lemon juices. Stir in the cold breadcrumbs.

3 Whisk the egg whites until stiff and fold into the cream mixture.

4 Spoon into a freezer box, cover and freeze for just 2–3 hours.

5 Brown Bread Ice-cream is best eaten on the day it is made and not frozen too hard either.

FROZEN PEACH YOGHURT

Serves 6

12 oz (325 g) very ripe peaches, stoned
1 tablespoon juice and 1 teaspoon grated
    rind from ¹/₂ lemon
2 level tablespoons sugar substitute
1 pt (575 ml) thick natural yoghurt
white of 1 size-1 or size-2 egg

1 In a food processor or in a large bowl using a stick blender, reduce the fruit to a purée. Add the lemon juice, lemon rind and sugar substitute and blend again.

2 Stir in the thick yoghurt and mix well.

3 In another bowl, whisk the egg white until it is stiff. Fold this into the peach mixture.

4 Pour into a freezer box, cover and freeze.

5 Eat within 3 days as the yoghurt will crystallize.

COCONUT ICE-CREAM

Serves 8–10

2 level tablespoons cornflour
1¹/₂ pt (1 litre) whole milk
4 oz (125 g) caster sugar
4 oz (125 g) creamed coconut, cut into
    chunks
8 oz (225 g) soft cream cheese
1 tablespoon toasted coconut

1 In a small bowl, mix the cornflour to a paste with about 4 tablespoons of the measured milk.

2 Heat the remaining milk with the sugar and creamed coconut until the coconut dissolves.

3 Stir in the cornflour mixture and bring to the boil, stirring all the time. Reduce the heat and stir until very thick. Set aside to cool.

4 Beat the cream cheese into the coconut mixture, adding the toasted coconut.

5 Pour into a freezer box, cover and freeze.

BITTER CHOCOLATE ICE-CREAM

Serves 6–8

2 whole size-1 eggs, plus 2 extra yolks
1½ oz (40 g) caster sugar
½ pt (300 ml) single cream
8 oz (225 g) bitter chocolate (with a high
   percentage of cocoa solids, 60% or 70%)
½ pt (300 ml) double cream, whipped
1 packet of dark chocolate polka dots

1   In a large bowl, whisk together the whole
eggs, egg yolks and sugar.
2   In a small pan, heat the single cream and
break the chocolate into it. When the chocolate
melts, bring up to the boil and pour over the egg
yolk mixture, whisking all the time.
3   Return this mixture to the pan and set over a
low heat. Stir until the custard coats the back of
the spoon. Strain through a nylon sieve into a
bowl. Cover and set aside to cool.
4   Whip the cream and fold into cooled custard.
5   Spoon the mixture into a rigid freezer box,
cover and freeze for 2 hours.
6   Remove the mixture, whisk it well and when
smooth stir in half of the chocolate dots. Return
the mixture to the freezer box and the freezer.
7   Scatter the rest of the dots on top to serve.

KULFI WITH PISTACHIO NUTS

Serves 6–8

This famous Indian ice-cream when
traditionally made uses long slow cooking of
milk to cause it to caramelize. This recipe uses
evaporated milk as a short-cut.

1 pt (575 ml) milk
14 oz (410 g) tin of evaporated milk
2 oz (50 g) caster sugar

12 cardamom pods
2 oz (50 g) chopped pistachio nuts
2 oz (50 g) chopped and toasted almonds

1   Put the milk and the evaporated milk in a
heavy-based pan with the sugar and the
cardamoms. Bring slowly up to the boil, then
simmer for 25 minutes. Stir often to check that
the sugar has dissolved. Pour into a bowl and
store in the fridge overnight.
2   Next day, strain off the cardamoms and pour
the liquid into a plastic box.
3   Follow the directions in the previous recipe
from step 4. Just after the last time the ice-cream
is blended, stir in the nuts. Freeze covered.
4   To serve: transfer the ice-cream from the freezer
to the fridge about 30 minutes before you need it.
Serve with the toasted almonds scattered over.

STRAWBERRY ICE-CREAM WITH BALSAMIC VINEGAR

Serves 4–6

This unusual idea comes from the Italian food
writer Anna Del Conte.

1 lb (450 g) ripe strawberries
1 tablespoon balsamic vinegar
4 oz (125 g) caster sugar
¼ pt (150 ml) whipping cream

1   Hull the strawberries and whizz them in a
food processor. Turn the speed down and dribble
the vinegar in, then add the sugar.
2   Put the resulting purée into a covered bowl
in the fridge and leave for 2 hours to allow the
flavour to develop.
3   In another bowl, whip the cream to the
floppy stage and fold this into the purée.
4   Pour into a freezer tray and freeze.
5   When half frozen, turn the mixture out and
give it another whizz in the processor. Return the
mixture to the tin and freeze again.

SORBETS

Sorbets are best eaten within 2 days of being made.

APPLE & CALVADOS SORBET

Serves 4

Calvados is an apple brandy. Substitute ordinary brandy if you wish.

To pare the lemon, use a sharp knife and peel the lemon rind off as if you were peeling an apple.

6 oz (175 g) caster sugar
pared rind and juice of 1 large juicy lemon
white from 1 size-1 or size-2 egg
2 tablespoons Calvados
fresh mint leaves, to decorate

1   Measure 16 fl oz (425 ml) of water into a pan. Add the sugar and, over a low heat, stir until the sugar dissolves. Add the pared lemon rind and bring up to the boil. Boil hard for 2–3 minutes. Cover and set aside to cool.
2   Strain off the lemon syrup, pour it into a freezer tray and set in the freezer.
3   After 1 hour, or when the mixture is just beginning to freeze at the edges, whisk the egg white until stiff. Turn the part-frozen syrup into a chilled bowl. Whisk it briefly to break up the crystals, stir in the Calvados and gently fold in the stiff egg white, using a chilled metal spoon.
4   Return the mixture to the freezer tray. Part-freeze again, then repeat the whisking process and return the sorbet to the freezer.
5   Serve in chilled glasses with a sprig of fresh mint leaves.

BLACKCURRANT SORBET

Serves 6

1 lb (450 g) ripe blackcurrants (fresh or frozen)
9 oz (250 g) caster sugar
3 teaspoons lemon juice
4 tablespoons Cassis (blackcurrant liqueur)
whites from 2 size-1 or size-2 eggs

1   First put the fresh or defrosted frozen fruit in the food processor and reduce to a purée.
2   Make a syrup by stirring the sugar into 20 fl oz (600 ml) water. Heat gently until the sugar dissolves. Now mix the blackcurrants into the syrup and stir well.
3   Strain this mixture, discard the debris and stir in the lemon juice and liqueur. Taste the syrup and add more sugar if you wish or more water if the flavour is overpowering.
4   Pour into freezing trays or plastic boxes and freeze. The mixture will be half-frozen possibly after about 2 hours, but this does vary depending on the depth of the syrup.
5   Meanwhile, in a large bowl and using a stick blender or a hand-held electric mixer, whip the egg whites until stiff. Now decant the half-frozen blackcurrant syrup and add to the egg whites slowly, a big tablespoon at a time – still whisking at the same time. You should end up with a billowy mass of foam. Refreeze this foam in a larger plastic box, when it will eventually have the consistency of snow.

LEMON SORBET

Serves 4–6

1 juicy orange
4 juicy lemons
6 oz (175 g) caster sugar

1   Rinse the orange and lemons and peel off the rind as if you were peeling an apple. Put all the rind in a pan with ½ pt (300 ml) water and the sugar. Stir over a low heat until the sugar has melted, then bring up the heat and boil the syrup hard for about 3 minutes. Set the pan aside and allow to go cold.
2   Now squeeze the juice from the orange and lemons. Add this to the syrup. Strain the syrup and discard the peel. Pour the syrup into a freezer tray and freeze for about 2 hours, when the syrup should be half-frozen.
3   Tip it into a food processor and whizz to make it fairly smooth again. Refreeze the mixture until it is needed.

ORANGE LIQUEUR WATER-ICE

Serves 6–8

12 oz (325 g) caster sugar
1 tablespoon lemon juice
1 tablespoon orange juice
¼ pt (150 ml) orange liqueur, such as Grand
    Marnier or Cointreau

1   Melt the sugar in 25 fl oz (750 ml) water over a low heat. Leave to cool.
2   When cool, stir in the juice.
3   Pour the syrup into freezer trays and freeze for about 2 hours. The outside should be frozen, but the centre still slushy.
4   Decant the frozen syrup and whizz in a food processor. Stir in the orange liqueur and freeze it all once again. Repeat this whisking and freezing process once more for a better smoother result.

PASSION FRUIT SORBET

Serves 8

This recipe takes 10 passion fruit, but the addition of apple makes the expensive fruit go further.

4 oz (125 g) caster sugar
2 juicy limes
2 large apples
10 passion fruit
whites from 2 size-1 or size-2 eggs, whisked
    until stiff

1   Put ¼ pt (150 ml) water in a pan with the sugar and stir to dissolve over a low heat. Pare the rind off the limes as if you were peeling an apple and drop this into the sugar syrup. Bring up to the boil and boil for 4-5 minutes. Set this aside to go cold.
2   Squeeze the juice from the peeled limes and cut up the peeled and cored apples. Stew the apples in the lime juice until soft. Add extra water if the mixture is too thick. Push the apple mixture through a nylon sieve and add it to the cold syrup. Stir in the passion fruit, seeds and all.
3   Pour this mixture into freezing trays and freeze for about 2 hours, or until the mixture is frozen round the edges and softish in the middle. Decant this mixture into a food processor or briefly whip it up with a stick blender. Fold in the stiffly beaten egg whites and freeze until needed.

LEMON & BASIL SORBET

Serves 6–8

about 2 oz (50 g) caster sugar
pared rind and juice of 3 lemons
white from 1 size-1 or size-2 egg
12 large fresh basil leaves, shredded

1   Make a syrup with the sugar (use more if you want it sweeter) and 20 fl oz (600 ml) water. Drop the pared lemon rinds in this. Bring to the

boil and boil for about 5 minutes. Set this aside to go cold.

2   Strain out the lemon peel, add the juice and pour this flavoured syrup into a freezer tray. Put it in the freezer.

3   When half-frozen (after about 2 hours), turn the mixture into a chilled bowl and whisk it up with a stick blender or an electric hand-held whisk. Fold in the stiffly beaten egg whites and the shredded basil.

4   Return to the freezer and, after another 2 hours, whisk it all up again and re-freeze. All this whisking and re-freezing is to make sure that the sorbet is free from large ice crystals.

ASTI SPUMANTE SORBET

Serves 6

9 oz (250 g) caster sugar
1 juicy orange
1 pt (575 ml) Asti Spumante, chilled
8 oz (225 g) kiwi fruit, peeled and chopped

1   Chill 6 wine glasses.

2   Put 5 oz (150 g) of the sugar in a pan with 9 fl oz (235 ml) water. Wash the orange and peel off the orange skin using a sharp knife. Take care to pare only the skin, leave as much pith as possible behind. Stir the sugar in the pan over a low heat and, when it has dissolved, put the orange peel in. Boil for 5 minutes in order to flavour the syrup. Set this aside to cool.

3   Squeeze the juice from the peeled orange, pour this into the orange-flavoured syrup and strain this into a bowl or freezer tray. Set it in the freezer for 2 hours or until the mixture is frozen at the edges and just slushy in the middle. Decant the mixture and whip up again either with a food processor or a stick blender. Pour in the Asti Spumante, whip up again and return the mixture to freeze. Decant it once more, beat it until smooth and re-freeze.

4   To serve: divide the kiwi fruit between the glasses and sprinkle with the reserved sugar (you will not need it all). Spoon the sorbet out just before you need it, as it melts quickly.

TANGERINE SORBET

Serves 6

6 oz (175 g) caster sugar
finely grated rind and juice of 1 orange
finely grated rind and juice of 3 tangerines
finely grated rind and juice of 1 lemon
white of 1 size-1 or size-2 egg, beaten until
   stiff

1   Dissolve the sugar in $\frac{1}{2}$ pt (300 ml) water and boil this for 5 minutes. Stir in the rind and juice from the orange, the tangerines and the lemon. Set this syrup aside to go cold.

2   Strain the syrup into a freezing tray and put in the freezer. Freeze until the outside edges are hard and the centre is still wet sludge. Take out of the freezer and whisk the mixture again, using a food processor or a stick blender. Return to the freezer.

3   After 1 hour, take it out again, whisk up and fold in the stiffly beaten egg white and whisk again. Return the mixture (you will need a bigger container this time) to the freezer, covered, and freeze until needed.

LOW-CALORIE SAUCES

These sauces are useful for using over plain sponges, vanilla ice-cream and the like. By using a sugar substitute, the calorie content will be reduced. Many are based on fresh fruit, so remember to use within 3 or 4 days, or freeze.

SWEET YOGHURT SAUCE

Serves 4

2 tablespoons thick Greek yoghurt
1 small teaspoon vanilla essence
5 oz (150 g) fromage frais
2 level tablespoons sugar substitute
little milk, if necessary

1   Put all the ingredients in a bowl and mix together thoroughly.
2   To thin the sauce, if necessary, add just 1 tablespoon of milk and beat that in.

Variations
Add 1 teaspoon grated orange peel.
Add 1 tablespoon brandy.
Add 2 teaspoons Cassis (blackcurrant liqueur).

APRICOT SAUCE

Serves 4

Unless the apricots are very ripe and juicy the fruit would need to be lightly cooked. Cut the fruit in two, remove the stone and stew with a little water until soft. Drain and use.

8 oz (225 g) ripe apricots, stoned and
    chopped
8 fl oz (225 ml) Crème Anglaise (see page
    174)
1 dessertspoon lemon juice
1 small teaspoon sugar substitute
little milk, if necessary

1   Use a stick blender or a food processor to blend the first three ingredients until smooth, except for the speckled effect of the skin.
2   Taste the sauce and add the sugar substitute if you need it. If the sauce is too thick, thin down with a spoonful of milk.

WHITE WINE SAUCE

Serves 4

This is not quite as low in calories, with the honey and sweet wine. You could omit the honey and add extra sugar substitute if you wish.

1 wine glass of sweet white wine
juice and 1 heaped teaspoon grated peel
    from 1 lemon
1 level tablespoon cornflour
3 size-1 or size-2 egg yolks
2 tablespoons runny honey
2 level tablespoons sugar substitute

1   In a medium-sized heatproof bowl, put the glass of wine and the lemon juice and rind. Whisk the cornflour into this.
2   In another bowl, whisk the egg yolks and the honey until thick. Now whisk this into the wine mixture and set the bowl over a pan of simmering water. Whisk until the sauce thickens.
3   Remove from the heat and, when the sauce is cold, stir in the sugar substitute.

LOW-CAL CRÈME ANGLAISE

See recipe on page 174. Omit the sugar and add sugar substitute at the end of cooking.

MELBA SAUCE

Serves 4

Sauce Melba is named after a world-famous singer Nellie Melba. Peach Melba was created in her honour – poached peaches, cream and ice-cream with a fresh raspberry sauce. In the past, this raspberry sauce would have been sieved to remove the seeds and this is still done by some chefs. You do need to have a very fine metal sieves. I usually just leave them in.

10 oz (275 g) ripe fresh or frozen raspberries
2 teaspoons lemon juice
1 level tablespoon sugar substitute

1   Go over the raspberries and remove any which are under-ripe. Sprinkle over the lemon juice.
2   Use a stick blender or a food processor to reduce the fruit to a purée. Taste and sweeten with the sugar substitute, according to your preference.
3   If too thick, add a tiny amount of water.

COOKED FRUIT SAUCE

Both apple and rhubarb make a well-flavoured sauce. The method is the same for both.

Stew the peeled, cored and chopped apples or rhubarb in a little water until soft. Reduce to a pulp with a liquidizer or food processor and sweeten lightly with sugar substitute.

Variation
Sharpen with lemon juice, orange rind or add ground cloves or cinnamon.

PALE CHOCOLATE SAUCE

Serves 4

3 oz (75 g) white chocolate
1½ oz (40 g) soft unsalted butter
1 teaspoon cocoa powder, sieved
2 teaspoon vanilla essence
2 level tablespoons sugar substitute

1   Break the chocolate up into small pieces and set it in a small heatproof bowl over a pan of simmering water.
2   When soft, remove from the heat and beat the butter into the chocolate.
3   Put ½ pt (300 ml) water in a pan and, stirring all the time, add first the chocolate mixture then the cocoa. Simmer gently until the sauce thickens slightly, about 5–6 minutes.
4   Remove the pan from the heat, leave it aside to go cold and then stir in the vanilla essence followed by the sugar substitute.

SIMPLE CHOCOLATE & COFFEE SAUCE

Serves 3–4

3 oz (75 g) plain dark chocolate, broken into pieces
1 heaped teaspoon instant coffee granules
1 teaspoon cocoa powder, sieved
2 teaspoons vanilla essence
2 level tablespoons sugar substitute

1   Put the broken chocolate in a pan with ½ pt (300 ml) water and melt it over a low heat, stirring all the time.
2   When it has melted, stir in the coffee followed by the cocoa powder (use a whisk if the cocoa is slow to dissolve). Stir constantly over a low heat until the sauce thickens slightly. Set it aside to cool.
3   Stir in the vanilla essence followed by the sugar substitute.

COOKED BLACKCURRANT SAUCE

Serves 6

Although I do not usually sieve a fruit sauce, I make an exception with blackcurrants.

12 oz (325 g) fresh or frozen blackcurrants
1 level tablespoon cornflour
3 tablespoons sugar substitute

1   Put the blackcurrants in a pan and barely cover with water. Cook gently until soft.
2   Push the blackcurrants and water through a sieve to remove all the pips and debris. Put the resulting liquid into a pan and heat gently.
3   Put the cornflour into a small bowl and mix to a paste with a little cold water.
4   Pour some of the blackcurrant over the cornflour and mix to a smooth consistency. Turn back into the pan with the rest of the juice, stirring all the time. Bring to the boil. Remove from the heat and, when cool, stir in sugar substitute to taste.
5   Serve hot or cold.

CHANTILLY CREAM SAUCE

Serves 3–4

½ teaspoon vanilla extract or 1 small
    teaspoon vanilla essence
8 oz (225 g) crème fraîche
2 level tablespoons sugar substitute
white of 1 size-1 or size-2 egg

1   Stir the vanilla extract or essence into the crème fraîche, followed by the sugar substitute.
2   In another bowl, whip the egg white until it is firm. Fold into the cream mixture.
3   This delicate sauce must be used on the day it is made.

SMOOTH PEACH SAUCE

Serves 4

2 large very ripe peaches
8 oz (225 g) thick Greek yoghurt
2 level tablespoons sugar substitute

1   Cut the peaches in two and discard the stones.
2   Chop the fruit into a medium-sized bowl add the yoghurt and the sugar substitute. Blend until smooth.

CRÈME FRAÎCHE LEMON SAUCE

Serves 4–6

4 oz (125 g) crème fraîche
¼ pt (150 ml) plain set yoghurt
juice of 2 lemons
2 level tablespoons sugar substitute
little skimmed milk, if necessary

1   Stir all the ingredients together.
2   If too thick, add more lemon juice or a spoonful of skimmed milk.

COOKED ORANGE SAUCE

Serves 4–5

I have always thought sweet orange sauces lacked the true flavour of oranges until I worked out this one.

1 level tablespoon plain white flour
1 tablespoon finely grated orange peel
3 oz (75 g) fromage blanc
1 size-1 or size-2 egg yolk
4 fl oz (100 ml) concentrated orange juice
   (I use a frozen one)
1 tablespoon lemon juice
3 tablespoons sugar substitute
4 oz (125 g) crème fraîche
a little skimmed milk, if necessary

1   In a heatproof bowl, mix the flour, orange peel and fromage blanc.
2   Whisk the egg yolk into the orange juice, then stir this into the fromage blanc mixture.
3   Set this bowl over a pan of simmering water and whisk until the sauce thickens. Remove from the heat and set aside to cool.
4   Stir in the lemon juice, sugar substitute and the crème fraîche. If the sauce is too thick, stir in more orange juice or a little skimmed milk.

SKIMMED-MILK CRÈME PÂTISSIÈRE

Makes about $1/_2$ pt (300 ml)

about $1/_2$ pt (300 ml) skimmed milk
2 size-1 or size-2 egg yolks
1 tablespoon warm runny honey
1 oz (25 g) plain flour
$1/_2$ teaspoon vanilla extract or 1 teaspoon
   vanilla essence
3 level tablespoons sugar substitute

1   Put the milk in a pan to heat up (but not boil).
2   In a large bowl, whisk the egg yolks with the honey until pale. Sift the flour over the top and whisk in until smooth.
3   Gradually whisk the warm milk into this mixture and return the whole lot to the pan. Simmer over a low heat, whisking all the time until the sauce is thick. Set it aside to cool down.
4   Stir in the vanilla and sugar substitute. Thin down with more skimmed milk if you wish.

'Dis-moi ce que tu manges, je te dirai ce que tu es.'
(Tell me what you eat and I will tell you what you are.)

Physiologie du Goût, Jean-Anthelme Brillat-Savarin

'Little Jack Horner
Sat in the corner
Eating a Christmas Pie;
He put in his thumb,
And pulled out a plum,
And said, What a good boy am I!'

6

Treats and Celebrations

LARGE GÂTEAUX

SPONGE & PASSION FRUIT DESSERT

Serves 12

This gâteau consists of two thin layers of feather-light sponge with a 'filling' of a passion fruit and cream cheese mould. The pale-cream gâteau looks dramatic, speckled with the edible shiny black seeds of the passion fruit.

Sponges
3 size-1 or size-2 eggs
3 oz (75 g) vanilla sugar
3 oz (75 g) plain white flour
butter, for greasing

Passion Fruit Mould
4 passion fruit (look for wrinkled skin, but not deeply wrinkled)
3–5 tablespoons smooth unsweetened orange juice
2 large tablespoons fresh lemon juice
3 oz (75 g) caster sugar
1 packet of gelatine
8 oz (225 g) fromage frais

Topping
1 tablespoon of brandy
5 fl oz (150 ml) double cream

Sauce
2 tablespoons brandy
10 fl oz (300 ml) chilled single cream

Making the sponges
1   Using an electric mixer, whisk the eggs and the sugar until they double in volume and are pale and very thick.
2   Meanwhile, grease 2 straight-sided 8 in (20 cm) sandwich tins and base-line with two 8 in (20 cm) circles of greaseproof paper. Preheat the oven to gas 2/300°F/150°C.
3   Sieve about one-third of the flour over the surface of the egg and sugar mixture. Using a flexible spatula and a figure-of-eight movement, fold this in. Do not overwork the mixture. I usually just do this 3 or 4 times, then sieve the next one-third over and mix this in lightly and repeat with the last of the flour. (Some people prefer to do this with a large metal spoon, but I like the flexible rubber – or soft plastic – spatula which gets right down to the bottom of the bowl). I take care to cut through the mixture with the sharp edge of the spatula in order to keep the mixture as fluffy as possible.
4   When all the flour has been incorporated, pour the sponge mixture into the two tins. (You can weigh the tins to divide the sponge mixture evenly). Level the sponges using a knife very lightly over the surface.
5   Bake for about 30 minutes, or until the sponges have firmed up and are golden all over. Set aside to cool for 10 minutes, then run a knife round the outside edge and turn each sponge out on a wire rack to cool. Peel off the lining paper with care. Set aside or store lightly covered until needed.

Make the passion fruit mould
you will need an 8" (20 cm) springform tin
1   Cut each passion fruit in 2. Use a sharp teaspoon to scoop out the filling, reserving 3 shells. Do this into a nylon sieve sitting over a measuring jug. Use a stainless steel spoon to scrape the passion fruit pulp and seeds backwards and forwards to extract as much pulp and juice as possible. (If the fruit is very small, you could add another passion fruit if you wish). Use a knife to scrape the pulp from under the sieve. Set aside about 2 tablespoons of seeds.
2   Pour some of the smooth orange juice into the passion fruit pulp to bring the level up to 4 fl oz (100 ml). Pour this into a pan. Add the sugar and dissolve over a low heat. Remove the pan from the heat.
3   Put the lemon juice in a small bowl and sprinkle the contents of the gelatine packet over the surface. Allow this to stand for about 3 minutes, then sit the bowl in a pan of simmering water and stir until the gelatine is clear and

dissolved. Stir this into the passion fruit and orange mixture. Allow to go cold.

4 Stir the fromage frais in a bowl and gradually add the passion fruit mixture until it is all incorporated, then add 1 tablespoon of seeds.

5 Drop one of the sponges in the base of an 8 in (20 cm) springform tin. Pour the fromage frais mixture on top and set aside to firm up.

Assemble the gâteau

1 Make the topping by stirring the brandy into the double cream and whip this until it reaches the soft-peak stage. Set aside.

2 Cover the top of the mould with the second sponge and release the sides of the tin.

3 Set the gâteau on a flat serving plate.

4 Whip the remaining cream again and spread a thick layer neatly on top of the gâteau. Position the three empty passion fruit shells back to back in the centre of the dessert to expose the pretty pink and white pearly insides. Scatter a few black seeds over the white cream. (Pour boiling water over the reserved seeds, drain and pat dry in kitchen paper to reveal their intense blackness).

5 Make the sauce by stirring the brandy into the chilled single cream and serve to accompany the gâteau cut in wedges.

CHOCOLATE MOUSSE GÂTEAU WITH MINI FLORENTINES

Serves 6–8

Base
8 oz (225 g) plain chocolate ginger biscuits or plain ginger biscuits
3 oz (75 g) butter
1 tablespoon golden syrup

Chocolate Mousse
2 teaspoons gelatine
6 oz (175 g) dark bitter chocolate
2 large teaspoons instant coffee granules
4 size-1 or size-2 eggs, separated

2 oz (50 g) caster sugar
5 fl oz (150 ml) whipping cream, whipped

Mini Florentine Topping
2 oz (50 g) butter
11/2 oz (40 g) caster sugar
1 tablespoon thick double cream
2 oz (50 g) flaked almonds
1 oz (25 g) candied peel, finely chopped
1 oz (25 g) glacé cherries, finely sliced
4 oz (125 g) dark plain chocolate

Making the base
1 Crush the biscuits in a food processor.
2 Put the butter and syrup in a pan and warm gently. When melted, stir in the biscuit crumbs. Stir well until all the crumbs are coated.
3 Press these evenly over the base of an 8 in (20 cm) loose-based cake tin, but do not compact them too much. Set aside to cool down and firm up.

Making the chocolate mousse
1 Put 3 tablespoons of cold water in a small cup or bowl, sprinkle the gelatine over the surface and leave it to stand for 3 minutes. Now set the bowl or cup in a pan of gently simmering water and stir until the gelatine dissolves.
2 Put another pan of simmering water on the hob and set a bowl in it. Break up the chocolate into small pieces and melt it in the bowl with the coffee granules and 3 more tablespoons of water. When the chocolate has melted, stir in the dissolved gelatine.
3 In another bowl, whisk the egg yolks and the caster sugar until pale and very thick. Stir the chocolate mixture into the egg yolk and sugar. Set this aside until beginning to set. Stir in the cream.
4 In yet another bowl, whisk the egg whites until thick. Fold the egg whites into the chocolate mixture. Set the bowl aside until the chocolate mousse is almost set, then turn it gently into the cake tin and put in the fridge to set.

Making the florentines

1 Preheat the oven to gas4/350°F/180°C. You will need a large baking sheet lined with non-stick baking paper and a 2 in (5 cm) metal biscuit cutter.

2 In a small heavy pan, melt the butter over a low heat and stir in the sugar. When the sugar has melted, stir in the cream and boil gently for about 1 minute. Stir in the nuts, peel and cherries. Remove from the heat.

3 Drop very small teaspoons of the mixture in little mounds all over the paper. Press the mounds down slightly, keeping them well apart.

4 Bake for about 8–10 minutes, or until the florentines have spread and are a rich golden brown. Remove the tray from the oven.

5 When the florentines start to stiffen but before they become hard, use the metal biscuit cutter to cut neat circles. Carefully lift up the trimmings and reheat to make more florentines. Leave to harden on the baking sheets.

6 Break up the chocolate into small pieces and set in a small bowl in a pan of simmering water to melt. Spread the plain side of each Florentine with chocolate and mark wavy lines with a fork in the chocolate before its sets.

Assembling the gâteau

1 Remove the chocolate mousse from the tin (you could leave it sitting on the base if you wish) and set on a big flat serving dish.

2 Set the florentines either stuck round the sides of the gâteau or just flat round the base or set them on the top, half on and half off.

RUM & PRALINE GÂTEAU

Serves 12

This gâteau is based on a fatless chocolate sponge drenched with a rum flavoured syrup and filled with whipped cream. The whole of the gâteau is covered with almond praline. The contrasting texture of the soft sponge and the crunchy praline is wonderful.

Almond Praline

4 oz (125 g) flaked almonds
2 oz (50 g) whole blanched almonds, chopped
6 oz (175 g) caster sugar
oil, for greasing

Chocolate Sponge

3 size-1 or size-2 eggs
3 oz (75 g) caster sugar
3 oz (75 g) plain white flour
2 heaped teaspoons cocoa
butter, for greasing

Rum Syrup

2 tablespoons rum
1 teaspoon icing sugar

Filling and Coating

5 fl oz (150 ml) double cream, whipped

Making the praline

1 Choose a heavy-based pan or very clean frying pan. Turn all the nuts and sugar into the pan and, over an extremely low heat, allow these to caramelize together. Keep the nuts moving by lifting the pan and shaking the contents back and forth. The toffee will eventually turn a rich golden caramel colour. To test that the mixture will set, use cold water in a heatproof glass jug. Into this dribble one small teaspoon of the mixture. If it sets to a crisp then take the toffee off the heat.

2 Have ready a sheet of foil about 10 in (25 cm) square, brushed all over with oil. Pour the praline on to the foil and spread it out as far as you can, pushing the nuts into a single layer. Leave to harden.

3 Break the praline up into pieces and reduce them to a coarse crumb in your food processor. Be careful to stop the machine before it goes too far. Another important point – be absolutely sure the processor is bone dry. Set the praline aside.

Making the chocolate sponge

1 Preheat the oven to gas3/325F/160°C. You will need an 8 in (20 cm) cake tin well greased and base-lined with a circle of greaseproof paper.

2 Use an electric mixer or hand-held mixer to whisk the eggs and the sugar until it is a very thick pale fluff; it usually takes my machine 5–7 minutes.

3 Remove 1 big teaspoon of flour from the 3 oz (75 g) and return it to the flour bag. Now stir in

the cocoa. Take the mixing bowl away from the machine and, using a nylon sieve, sprinkle about one-third of the flour all over the surface of the egg and sugar.

4   Use a soft plastic or rubber spatula to fold in the flour. I use a figure-of-eight movement. Do not over-mix, but get the next one-third of flour sieved over the sponge mixture. Fold that in roughly, then sieve in the last of the flour. When all the flour has been folded in, pour this mixture into the prepared cake tin and smooth the surface.

5   Bake for about 40 minutes, or until the sponge is beginning to shrink from the sides of the tin.

6   Remove the sponge from the oven and leave it to settle for about 10 minutes. Now run a thin knife round the outside of the sponge to check that it is loose, pressing the blade hard against the cake tin side to avoid slicing bits off the cake. Turn it out on your outstretched hand, peel off the lining paper and set the sponge to go cold on a wire tray.

Assembling the gâteau

1   First cut the sponge in two horizontally and place the bottom half on the serving plate.

2   Make the rum syrup: in a small jug, mix the rum with 2 tablespoons of water and stir in the icing sugar. Dribble about half of the mixture over the base of the gâteau. Spread about 2 tablespoons of whipped cream on the sponge and top with the other half sponge. Press this on gently. Sprinkle the rest of the rum syrup over the sponge top. (At this point you could make up more of the rum syrup if you like a strong rum flavour and sprinkle even more of it over the sponge.)

3   To finish off the gâteau: whip the cream again if it has flopped slightly and spread it in a thin layer all over the top and sides of the sponge. This does not need to be particularly neat as it is going to be covered.

4   Now comes the messy bit: sprinkle the coarse almond praline all over the cream. Getting the toffee on the sides is messy. I use my hands to 'clap' it on after I've got the top well covered. The bits which fall on to the serving plate can be lifted on a palette knife and pressed into any bald bits.

5   Serve chilled in wedges. A scoop of praline ice-cream would go well with it.

GRAND MARNIER & CARAQUE CHOCOLATE GÂTEAU

Serves 12

Chocolate and orange flavours dominate this gâteau, using the orange liqueur Grand Marnier and a topping for the swirled rich custard of poached kumquats and chocolate caraque (chocolate curls).

Sponge Base
6 oz (175 g) dark bitter chocolate, broken into pieces
3 oz (75 g) butter, plus more for greasing
3 oz (75 g) caster sugar
3 size-1 or size-2 eggs, separated
2 oz (50 g) ground almonds
3 oz (75 g) flour
2 tablespoons Grand Marnier

Rich Custard Topping
1 level dessertspoon cornflour
15 fl oz (450 ml) milk
1 size-1 or size-2 egg
2 oz (50 g) caster sugar
2 teaspoons gelatine
7 oz (200 g) cream cheese
10 fl oz (300 ml) double cream
2–3 drops of vanilla extract

Caraque
4 oz (125 g) dark bitter chocolate

Decoration
4 firm and unblemished kumquats
2 oz (50 g) caster sugar
2-3 drops of vanilla extract

Making the sponge base
1   Preheat the oven to gas4/350°F/180°C. You will need a deep 8 in (20 cm) loose-based cake tin greased and base-lined with a circle of greaseproof paper.
2   Into a large heatproof bowl, put 3 oz (75 g) of the chocolate with the butter. Set the bowl over a pan of simmering water. When this has melted and is smooth, remove it from the heat. Stir in the sugar, egg yolks, nuts and flour and beat until smooth. Allow to cool a little.
3   Whisk the egg whites in another bowl until they are stiff. Fold these into the chocolate mixture and pour into the prepared tin.
4   Bake for about 40 minutes, or until the sponge is risen and set. Take the sponge out of the tin after 5 minutes and allow it to cool on a wire tray. Meanwhile wash and dry the tin.
5   When the sponge is cool, return it to the tin. Mix the Grand Marnier with two teaspoons of water and sprinkle this all over the sponge.

Making the rich custard topping
1   In a medium pan, whisk the cornflour into the cold milk, followed by the egg and the sugar. When the cornflour has dispersed, change to a wooden spoon and heat the custard gently, stirring all the time, until it thickens. Sprinkle the gelatine over the surface of the hot custard and stir it in. Scoop this mixture into a bowl to cool and keep covered. When it is cold, whisk in the cream cheese and the cream very thoroughly. Transfer half of this mixture to another bowl.
2   Stir the vanilla extract into one bowl. Melt the other 3 oz (75 g) chocolate in a bowl over a pan of simmering water. When liquid, stir this into the second bowl of custard. You now have a bowl of pale vanilla custard and another of chocolate custard.

Making the caraque
1   In a small heatproof bowl, melt the chocolate by standing the bowl in a pan of simmering water. When liquid, pour and spread the chocolate out on a marble slab or a hard plastic surface. Allow the chocolate to cool but not set. It is not always easy to catch the chocolate at the right temperature to make the chocolate rolls.
2   Using a small clean paint stripper, hold the metal blade at an angle and push it against the firm chocolate to encourage it to roll. If it is too hard the chocolate just shatters. Use up all the chocolate.

Assembling the gâteau
1   Give each bowl of custard another stir, then drop large alternating spoonfuls of each custard

in the tin. Take a knife and swirl the custards together so that the effect will be marbled.

2   Smooth the surface and press the chocolate rolls all over. Leave aside to set.

3   Lastly prepare the kumquats: cut off and discard each end from the kumquats. Slice the rest into thin circles. Melt the sugar in the 4 fl oz (100 ml) water, add the vanilla and the slices of fruit. Turn the heat down to a simmer and cook gently until the slices become translucent (5–6 minutes). Scoop them out with a slotted spoon and allow to dry off.

4   Serve the gâteau with the kumquats decorating the gâteau all round the top edge or just scattered among the chocolate rolls. Serve in wedges. The creamy filling should be marbled with pale cream and chocolate.

5   You could gild the lily and stir more Grand Marnier into some single cream as a sauce – about 1 tablespoon liqueur to 10 fl oz (300 ml) of chilled single cream.

FRUIT & CREAM CARDAMOM SPONGE GÂTEAU

Serves 8

This delightful Swiss-roll-type dessert is delicately flavoured with the exotic spice cardamom which goes very well with sweet dishes. The number of cardamom pods used does seem very high, but for the authentic flavour do not use less. The final effect is not at all strong.

Sponge Roll
3 oz (75 g) plain white flour
20 green cardamom pods
3 size-2 or size-3 eggs, beaten
3 oz (75 g) vanilla sugar
butter, for greasing

Filling
8 oz (225 g) fruit, such as fresh ripe strawberries or fresh dry raspberries or drained canned mandarin oranges, chopped small
5 fl oz (150 ml) double cream

1   Preheat the oven to gas6/400°F/200°C. You will need a greased Swiss roll tin 8 x 12 in (20.5 x 30.5 cm) base-lined with greaseproof paper.

2   Sieve the flour into a bowl. Remove the cardamom seeds from their pods and crush the seeds thoroughly. (Use a pestle and mortar or, if you have a rolling pin with a flat end, you could use that in a cake tin.) Sieve these into the flour. Any residue can be crushed again to get it fine enough.

3   In a large bowl and using an electric mixer or hand-held electric one, whisk the eggs and vanilla sugar until they are very, very thick and creamy pale. Stir the flour and crushed cardamom seeds well, then fold lightly into the egg mixture, a big tablespoon at a time.

4   When all the flour is incorporated, spoon the mixture into the prepared tin and level the surface lightly.

5   Bake for about 12–15 minutes until pale and golden.

6   Cut a piece of greaseproof paper a bit bigger than the tin and cover it generously with caster sugar.

7   Take the sponge out of the oven and allow it to cool for a few minutes. Now run a knife round the edge to make sure it is loose then turn the sponge out and directly on to the sugar-covered paper, with the short end in front of you.

8   Take a sharp knife – a long one if you have one – and trim the two long edges (they are often quite crisp). Now, using the greaseproof paper, roll the sponge up with the paper inside and leave it to cool down.

9   Prepare the filling: lightly whip the cream and stir in the fruit.

10 When the sponge is cold, unroll it. Spread with the fruit and cream mixture and re-roll.

11 Set it on a serving dish with the join underneath and serve cut in generous slices.

SUPERB STRAWBERRY GÂTEAU

Serves 12

I saw this extravagant gâteau at the Savoy Hotel in London. There are a lot of edible trimmings for the cook and her helpers and the gâteau is finished on top with a disc of palest pink marzipan. It looks terrific.

Genoese Sponge

5 fl oz (150 ml) beaten egg (about 4 size-1 or size-2 eggs)
4½ oz (140 g) caster sugar
4½ oz (140 g) plain flour, sifted
butter, for greasing

Filling

16 fl oz (425 ml) double cream
1 oz (25 g) caster sugar
1 packet of gelatine
3 tablespoons Cointreau or other orange liqueur
24 perfect strawberries, wiped and hulled

Topping

2–3 drops of pink food colouring
2½ oz (65 g) natural marzipan (not yellow)

1   Preheat the oven to gas4/350°F/180°C. You will need an 8 in (20 cm) well-greased round cake tin with a circle of greaseproof paper sitting in the base. Also an 8 in (20 cm) greased spring-form cake tin about 2½ in (6 cm) deep, base-lined with a circle of greaseproof paper.
2   To make the Genoese sponge: whisk the eggs and sugar in a bowl set over a pan of simmering water. Use an electric hand-held whisk for speed and keep the heat low and the flex well out of the way. Whisk until the mixture is very thick and pale and almost doubled in volume. Remove the bowl from the heat. Continue to whisk until the mixture is cool, sieve the flour over the egg mixture in 2 or 3 lots and fold it in as lightly as possible.
3   When all the flour is incorporated, turn the still fluffy mixture into the cake tin and bake for about 35 minutes until risen and firm. Remove

from the oven and allow to cool down a bit. Now run a thin knife round the outside edge to make sure the sponge is loose. Turn it out on your outstretched hand, peel off the paper carefully and set the sponge on a wire rack to cool down.
4   Using a long sharp knife, slice the sponge in two pieces horizontally so that you have two discs.
5   To make the set cream filling: whip the cream with the icing sugar until thick. Remove 2 tablespoons of cream and reserve in a small covered bowl.
6   Put 5 tablespoons of water in a small bowl. Sprinkle over the gelatine and allow it to soak for 3 minutes. Now set the bowl in a pan of simmering water and stir to dissolve the gelatine. Stir in the liqueur and set aside to cool until tepid but not setting. Stir the gelatine mixture into the whipped cream.
7   Set one disc of sponge in the base of the spring-form tin. Press it down flat, spoon the cream mixture in and spread it evenly. Now arrange 16 of the whole strawberries in a circle round the edge of the gâteau with their tips pointing downwards. Quarter the remaining strawberries and arrange them in the centre, pushing a few down deep.
8   Now lay the second disc of sponge on the cream and press down gently. Spread the two reserved tablespoons of cream on top of the sponge. Chill the gâteau for 20 minutes in the freezer.
9   While the gâteau is chilling, work the pink food colouring into the marzipan until it is a delicate even pink. Roll it out with a little cornflour until big enough to cover the top of the gâteau – about ¼ in 5 mm) thick. Press it down on top of the cream.
10 Remove the sides from the spring-form tin and, with a hot sharp knife, trim the edges of the gâteau into an octagonal shape.
This will expose the strawberries and the filling and give the edible trimmings I mentioned at the start. Serve chilled and cut in wedges.

GRAND DESSERTS

SUMMER PUDDING WITH A MADEIRA CREAM

Serves 7–8

This is my favourite English pudding and needs little cooking. Use any mixture of red fruit, but do include cherries if you can. You will need a 7 in (18 cm) soufflé dish or pudding basin.

12 oz (325 g) ripe cherries, stoned and halved
4 oz (125 g) blackcurrants, topped and tailed
4 oz (125 g) redcurrants, topped and tailed
8 oz (225 g) raspberries, hulled
5 oz (150 g) caster sugar
10–12 slices of good-quality thinly sliced white or wholemeal bread

Madeira-flavoured Pouring Cream
2 tablespoons Madeira
10 fl oz (275 ml) single cream

1 Put fruit in a large pan with 5 tablespoons of water and stew gently for just 5 minutes until fruit is soft. Stir in sugar well. Allow to go cold.
2 Trim the crusts off the bread and cut some of the slices in 2 lengthwise. Line the bottom of the dish or basin with triangles of bread which overlap slightly to give a tight fit. Press the joins hard. Now line the side of the dish with the long strips of bread overlapping each other so that there are no gaps. Press all the joins hard.
3 Use a slotted spoon to transfer the fruit to the bread-lined dish or basin. Press down gently and add enough juice to soak the bread. Save the rest of the juice. Make a lid of bread for the pudding and find a saucer which will sit inside the dish or basin. Put a weight on the saucer, like another saucer. Chill in the fridge overnight.
4 To serve: invert the pudding on a serving plate and use the reserved juice to cover any white bread spots still showing. Serve cut in wedges, with the reserved juice and with the pouring cream made by mixing the Madeira into the cream.

BANOFFI PIE

Serves 12

14 oz (400 g) can of condensed milk
3 oz (75 g) butter
8 oz (225 g) digestive biscuits, crushed
3 small bananas or 2 huge ones
1 tablespoon lemon juice
5 fl oz (150 ml) double or whipping cream, softly whipped
3 oz (75 g) dark chocolate, grated

Sauce (optional)
2 bananas
1 tablespoon lemon juice

1 First boil the large tin of condensed milk: simply put it unopened in a deep pan, covered with water, and boil steadily for 2 hours. Allow to go cool. The milk sets to a soft toffee.
2 Melt the butter and stir in the crushed digestive biscuits until they are well coated. Press the biscuits into the base of an 8 in (20 cm) loose-bottomed flan tin and set aside to firm up.
3 Slice the bananas into thick rounds and toss in a bowl with the lemon juice.
4 Open up the cooled can of condensed milk, spoon it over the biscuit base and set it in the fridge to firm up.
5 Drain the bananas and set the slices on top of the toffee, reserving some for decoration.
6 Spoon the cream over the bananas roughly and return to the fridge to firm up.
7 To serve: scatter the reserved bananas on top of the cream, followed by the grated chocolate. Serve in small wedges.
8 To make the optional sauce: liquidize the bananas with the lemon juice. Do not make up until almost ready to eat.

Note
Do not freeze this particular gâteau, as the bananas will go black.

TOFFEE & VANILLA DESSERT WITH RASPBERRY SAUCE

Serves 8–10

This vanilla dessert is based on a simple recipe called 'honeycomb mould' which I used a lot to go with all the fruit from my garden. Here it is much grander, with the addition of cream and real vanilla extract. The toffee gives an added crunch and looks very pretty with its jagged shards.

4 size-1 or size-2 eggs, separated
10 fl oz (300 ml) Channel-Island milk
    (breakfast milk)
10 fl oz (300 ml) single cream
4 oz (125 g) caster sugar
1 teaspoon vanilla extract
1 packet of gelatine
4 oz (125 g) granulated sugar
oil, for greasing

Raspberry Sauce
8 oz (225 g) fresh raspberries
1 teaspoon icing sugar

1   Whisk the egg yolks with the milk, cream, caster sugar and vanilla extract. Set aside.
2   Dissolve the gelatine by first sprinkling it over 2 tablespoons of water in a small bowl. Leave this to soak for 3 minutes, then set the bowl in a pan of simmering water and stir until it is clear.
3   Now turn the milk and cream mixture into a pan and heat gently, stirring often. Do not allow to boil. Off the heat, stir in the dissolved gelatine and set this aside to cool.
4   When the mixture is just about to set, in a clean bowl, whisk the egg white until stiff. Fold into the cream mixture, pour into a shallow flat dish and leave to set in the fridge
5   Put the granulated sugar in a small heavy-based pan over a moderate heat. At the first sign that the sugar is going to melt, shake the pan so that the sugar moves around and keep it moving.

Eventually it will dissolve into a rich golden liquid. Take the pan off the heat and dribble this toffee all over an oiled sheet of foil about 10 in (25 cm) square in as thin a stream as you can and in every direction. You will be fine if there is a lip on your pan; I do not find this easy with pans with the usual rolled-over top edge as the stream is too thick. I usually use a big tablespoon, but I have to admit I always lose a lot as it sticks to the spoon. Anyway, leave the toffee to set.
6   Make the sauce: if the raspberries are ripe and soft, just purée them in a food processor or liquidizer along with the icing sugar. If the raspberries are firm, stew them very briefly in a little water (2 tablespoons) then liquidize.
7   Break the toffee into pieces (not too large) and press them into the vanilla so that they stand up in jagged shards. Serve with the Raspberry Sauce.

LAYERED CRANBERRY MOUSSE GÂTEAU

Serves 6–8

Base
6 oz (175 g) digestive biscuits, crushed
3 oz (75 g) butter, melted, plus more for
    greasing

Cranberry Mousse
6 oz (175 g) fresh cranberries
5 fl oz (150 ml) red wine
1 packet of raspberry jelly
4 oz (125 g) caster sugar
4 oz (125 g) cream cheese
finely grated rind (1 teaspoon) of 1 lemon,
    plus 1 large tablespoon of lemon juice
white of 1 size-1 or size-2 egg

1   Make the base: grease an 8 in (20 cm) spring-form tin. Stir the crushed biscuits into the melted butter and press these into the base of the tin in an even layer and up the sides of the tin slightly. Set aside to firm up.
2   Make the cranberry mousse: cook the

cranberries in the red wine until they are soft. Now strain the fruit through a nylon sieve. Use a metal spoon to push the fruit back and forward to extract as much pulp as possible, scraping it from underneath the sieve. Put the pulp juice and wine in a small pan over a gentle heat. Stir in the jelly squares and the sugar. Stir until the jelly is liquid. Now set this aside and allow to cool almost to setting point.

3   In another bowl, beat the cream cheese with the lemon rind and juice. Stir in 4 tablespoons of the wine jelly. Leave this to firm up slightly.

4   Pour about half of the remaining jelly into the biscuit crust and set this in the fridge to set. Pour the rest of the jelly into a flat dish and set aside.

5   Once the jelly in the crust has set, whip the egg white until it is very stiff and fold this into cream cheese mixture. Pour on top of the jelly and allow this to set also.

6   Release the gâteau from the tin and set it on a flat dish. Turn out the extra jelly on a piece of wet greaseproof paper and chop into cubes with a wet knife. Decorate the top of the gâteau with the chopped wine jelly and serve in wedges.

ALMOND & BRANDY RUSSE

Serves 8–10

A nutty cream dessert surrounded by a castle of sponge boudoir biscuits, traditionally this pudding is served with a ribbon tied round the upright biscuits as if to hold them together.

You will need a straight-sided deep cake tin or soufflé dish measuring 7 in (18 cm) across, base-lined with a circle of non-stick paper.

6 oz (175 g) unsalted butter, softened
6 oz (175 g) caster sugar
2–3 drops of almond essence
1 tablespoon brandy
3 size-1 or size-2 eggs, separated
4 oz (125 g) ground almonds
3 oz (75 g) whole almonds, skinned and
    toasted, plus more for decoration

12 oz (325 g) crème fraîche
about 14 boudoir biscuits
white of 1 size-6 or size-7 egg, for assembly

Sauce (optional)
2 tablespoons brandy
10 fl oz (300 ml) single cream

1   Cream 5 oz (150 g) butter and the sugar until light and frothy. Stir in the almond essence and the brandy. Beat in the egg yolks, then add the ground almonds and beat again.

2   Now stir in the whole toasted almonds, then fold in the crème fraîche.

3   In another bowl, whisk the egg whites until they are frothy. Add the remaining sugar. Whisk again to stiff peaks. Fold the egg whites into the almond mixture and set this aside.

4   To line the prepared deep cake tin or dish, take a sharp knife and slice off a little from the long side of each biscuit to help it lock together. Whisk the egg white lightly and dip the two long ends of each biscuit in the egg white. Stand the biscuits side by side with the sugary side out to line the tin or dish. When it comes to the last biscuit you may have to cut a neat wedge to lock the whole thing together.

5   Now pour the almond mixture into the biscuit case and smooth over the surface. Set the gâteau in the fridge overnight to set.

6   To serve: turn the tin upside down on a serving plate and the charlotte should slip out without any trouble. Tie a ribbon round the middle and decorate the top with more whole almonds. Serve in narrow wedges. For an optional sauce, stir 2 tablespoons of brandy into 10 fl oz (300 ml) single cream.

LARGE CHEESECAKES

COOKED BLACKCURRANT CHEESECAKE

Serves 12

Of all fruits, I think blackcurrants marry better than any other with a rich cheesecake. This baked one is based on a recipe from Rosamond Richardson. The cottage cheese gives an interesting texture.

Base
8 oz (225 g) digestive biscuit crumbs
1 tablespoon runny honey
3 oz (75 g) butter, melted

Filling
1 lb (450 g) cottage cheese
2 tablespoons runny honey
4 size-1 or size-2 eggs, separated
5 tablespoons orange juice
1 tablespoon lemon juice
2 teaspoons vanilla essence
4 oz (125 g) fromage frais
3 oz (75 g) self-raising flour, sieved

Topping
2 lb (900 g) fresh blackcurrants, topped and
    tailed
1 heaped teaspoon cornflour
5 oz (150 g) caster sugar
1 tablespoon lemon juice

1   First make the base: stir the crushed biscuit crumbs and honey into the melted butter and mix well to coat the crumbs. Press these into the base of an 8 in (20 cm) greased flan tin with a loose base. Set the crumb base in the fridge to firm up.
2   Preheat the oven to gas8/450°F/230°C.
3   Put the cottage cheese into a liquidizer and whizz to a purée. Turn the purée into a bowl and, using a hand-held electric whisk, beat in the honey

very thoroughly. Add the egg yolks one at a time. Continue beating, adding the orange and lemon juice, vanilla, fromage frais and the sieved flour.
4   In another bowl, whisk the egg whites until they are stiff and fold these into the cheese mixture. Pour into the flan tin.
5   Set the tin on a low shelf in the oven, immediately turn down the oven to gas2/300°F/150°C and bake for 40–50 minutes. Leave the cheesecake in the oven with the door half open for 3 hours. Then set it in the fridge overnight.
6   Make the topping: put half of the blackcurrants into a liquidizer with the lemon juice and cornflour and blend to a purée. Pour into a small pan and cook gently until thickened, stirring often. Strain into a jug and stir in the sugar. Set the rest of the blackcurrants in a packed layer over the cheesecake. Dribble the sauce all over the fruit and save the rest as a sauce.
7   Allow to set firm, then set the cheesecake on a flat plate and serve.

UNCOOKED ORANGE & LEMON CHEESECAKE

Serves 8

Base
8 oz (225 g) digestive biscuits, crushed
3 oz (75 g) butter, melted
1 teaspoon mixed spice

Filling
1 packet of lemon jelly, cut into pieces
1 size-1 or size-2 egg, separated
5 fl oz (150 ml) milk
juice and rind of 1 lemon
juice and rind of 1 small orange
8 oz (225 g) Edam cheese, grated
1 tablespoon caster sugar
10 fl oz (300 ml) double cream

Decoration
fine thin half-moon slices of fresh orange and fresh lemon

1   Make the base: stir the crushed biscuits into the melted butter along with the mixed spice.
2   Press the buttery crumb into the base of an 8 in (20 cm) flan tin with a loose base and level them off. Set in fridge to firm up.
3   Make the filling: dissolve the jelly in 2 tablespoons of hot water in a medium heatproof bowl set over a pan of simmering water. In another bowl, whisk the egg yolk and milk. When the jelly is liquid, pour the egg and milk mixture into it. Continue to heat this mixture without boiling it for 2–3 minutes.
4   Remove the bowl from the heat, add the lemon and orange rinds and juices and finally the Edam cheese. Process this mixture until it is fairly thick and smoothish. Set aside to cool until on the point of setting.
5   In another bowl, whisk the egg white until stiff. Stir in the caster sugar and whisk again.
6   In yet another bowl, whisk the cream to the floppy stage. Spoon half of this cream into a separate bowl and fold the egg white and the other half of the cream into the cheese mixture.
7   Pour into the flan tin, smooth the surface and put in the fridge to set.
8   To serve: set the orange and lemon slices all round. Whip up the remaining cream and use to pipe whirls of the reserved cream round the cheesecake edge.

CRANBERRY CHEESECAKE WITH TOASTED DIGESTIVES

Serves 8

8 oz (225 g) digestive biscuits, crushed
3 oz (75 g) butter, melted, plus more for greasing
2 tablespoons runny honey
8 oz (225 g) fresh or frozen cranberries
4 oz (125 g) caster sugar
2 teaspoons cornflour
8 oz (225 g) plain fromage frais
5 oz (150 g) thick Greek yoghurt
1 packet of gelatine
5 fl oz (150 ml) whipping cream, lightly whipped

1   Preheat the oven to gas4/350°F/180°C. Grease an 8 in (20 cm) spring-form tin and line with a circle of non-stick baking paper and put a strip of non-stick baking paper round the sides as well.
2   Stir the digestive biscuit crumbs into the melted butter and runny honey. Pour this mixture into the base of the spring-form tin and level it.
3   Bake for 10 minutes then set aside to cool.
4   Stew the berries in a pan with 2 tablespoons of water and 2 oz (50 g) of the sugar until soft.
5   Mix the cornflour with a little water, stir into the berries and cook, stirring, until thickened. Set aside to cool but stir every now and then.
6   In a bowl, beat together the fromage frais, yoghurt and remaining sugar.
7   Put 3 tablespoons of water in a small bowl and sprinkle the gelatine over. Set aside to swell for 3 minutes, then set the bowl in a pan of simmering water and stir to melt the gelatine.
8   Fold this mixture into the fromage frais mixture along with the whipped cream.
9   Spoon first the cranberry mixture over the biscuit base and leave that to set in the fridge. Once this has set, pour the fromage frais mixture on top of the cranberry one. Spread evenly and chill to set.
10 To serve: release the tin and set the cheesecake on its base on another plate. Serve cut in wedges.

UNCOOKED RICH CHOCOLATE SPONGE CHEESECAKE

Serves 12

This cheesecake is rather deep, so I suggest you make a cardboard ring lined with foil.

Chocolate Sponge Base
2 size-1 or size-2 eggs
2 oz (50 g) caster sugar
1½ oz (40 g) plain white flour
½ oz (15 g) cocoa, sifted

Filling
4 oz (125 g) plain dark chocolate
4 oz (125 g) white chocolate
6 teaspoons gelatine
1½ lb (675 g) soft cream cheese (skimmed milk)
10 fl oz (300 ml) single cream
4 oz (125 g) caster sugar
5 fl oz (150 ml) double cream, whipped

Make the chocolate sponge base
1 Preheat the oven to gas5/375°F/190°C. Grease an 8 in (20 cm) cake tin and line with a circle of greaseproof paper.
2 In a large bowl, whisk the eggs and 2 oz (50 g) of sugar until very, very thick.
3 Sift the flour and cocoa together and fold into the whisked egg mixture as lightly as possible. Pour into the prepared tin.
4 Bake for about 20–25 minutes, or until the sponge is springy to touch.
5 Take out of the oven and allow to rest for 5–10 minutes, then turn the sponge out on a wire rack. When cool, remove the lining paper.

Making the Cheesecake
1 First put the sponge base on a large flat serving dish.
2 Cut a strip of card long enough to go right round the sponge, with a slight overlap and about 3 in (7.5 cm) deep. Line the inside of the cardboard ring with foil, then fit it round the sponge tightly and staple it together. Cover the staples with a strip of sticky tape on the outside.
3 To make the filling: break up the chocolate, putting the white chocolate in one bowl and the plain chocolate in another. Set these 2 bowls over 2 pans of simmering water. (Note that white chocolate does not become as liquid as dark.)
4 Put 4 tablespoons of water in yet another bowl and sprinkle the gelatine over. Leave to swell up for 5 minutes, then set this bowl in a pan of simmering water and stir until dissolved and clear.
5 In a large bowl, beat together the cream cheese, single cream and sugar. Fold in the whipped double cream and the gelatine mixture.
6 Divide this mixture into two bowls and stir the melted dark chocolate into one and the melted white chocolate into the other. Allow to set slightly.
7 Take two large tablespoons and spoon the chocolate mixtures alternately over the chocolate sponge. Now take a skewer and swirl them together to get a marbled effect. Set the cheesecake in the fridge to set.
8 To serve: remove the cardboard collar and serve cut in wedges.

UNCOOKED BRAMLEY APPLE CHEESECAKE

Serves 8–10

Base
3 oz (75 g) butter, melted
6 oz (175 g) chocolate digestive biscuits, crushed

Filling
1 lb (450 g) Bramley apples, peeled, cored and chopped
2 size-1 or size-2 eggs, separated
1 packet of gelatine
8 oz (225 g) cream cheese
5 fl oz (150 ml) plain yoghurt
4 oz (125 g) caster sugar
2–3 drops of green food colouring

Decoration
4 or 5 marzipan apples and leaves

Making the base
1   Stir the crushed biscuits into the melted butter until they are well coated. Press into the base of an 8 in (20 cm) flan tin with a loose base, but do not hammer down too much. Chill.

Making the filling
1   Cook the apples in just 1 tablespoon of water until soft. Beat in the egg yolks and set aside to cool.
2   Put 5 tablespoons of water in a small bowl and sprinkle over the gelatine. Set this aside for 3 minutes until the gelatine swells, then set the bowl in a pan of simmering water and stir until dissolved.
3   Put the cream cheese, yoghurt, sugar and apple purée in a mixing bowl. Whisk together until smooth. Whisk in the gelatine and a few drops of green food colour. Pour into the tin to cover the base. Chill until set.
4   Turn out and serve with the marzipan apples and leaves grouped together neatly to one side and accompanied by chilled single cream.

COOKED LEXIA RAISIN & VANILLA CHEESECAKE

Serves 6–8

Lexia Raisins are the big fat sticky ones. Look out for seeds when you are chopping them.

Base
6 oz (175 g) plain flour
4 oz (125 g) butter, plus more for greasing
3 oz (75 g) caster sugar

Filling
2 oz (50 g) unsalted butter, softened
3 oz (75 g) caster sugar
1 lb (450 g) soft cheese
3 size-1 or size-2 eggs
1 teaspoon vanilla extract
1 oz (25 g) cornflour
5 oz (150 g) thick Greek yoghurt
3 oz (75 g) Lexia raisins, chopped
icing sugar, for sprinkling
ground cinnamon, for sprinkling

1   Preheat the oven to gas2/300°F/150°C. Grease an 8 in (20 cm) loose-bottomed cake tin.
2   Sift the flour into a bowl. Cut up the butter and rub it in carefully. Stir in the sugar. Sprinkle this mixture evenly over the base of the tin and press it down lightly with the back of a spoon.
3   Bake for 20 minutes.
4   To make the filling: beat the butter and sugar until light and fluffy. Add the soft cheese and beat well. Beat in the eggs one at a time and stir in the vanilla essence, cornflour, yoghurt and raisins.
5   Set the tin on a baking sheet and pour this mixture in.
6   Bake for 50–60 minutes, until firm around the edges. Leave to cool in the oven until it is cold, then chill.
7   When ready to serve, sift icing sugar all over, then cinnamon all round the edge. (I use a tea strainer and knock it gently to give a light dusting).

MERINGUES

RIPE PEACH & CREAM PIE WITH A FRESH PEACH SAUCE

Serves 12

This is a dessert to make in high summer, with peaches which are at their peak of flavour and dribblingly juicy.

Meringue Case
whites of 3 size-1 or size-2 eggs
pinch of salt
pinch cream of tartar
6 oz (175 g) caster sugar

Filling
3 size-1 or size-2 egg yolks
3 oz (75 g) caster sugar
grated rind and juice of 1 large lemon
10 fl oz (300 ml) double cream
4 large fresh peaches
1 teaspoon icing sugar

1   Make the meringue case: preheat the oven to gas ¼/200°F/90°C. Line a baking sheet with non-stick baking paper on the underside of which has been drawn a circle about 9 in (23 cm) across.
2   Using an electric mixer or a hand-held electric mixer, whisk the egg whites until they are frothy. Add the salt and cream of tartar and whisk hard until the mixture is like a firm snow. Add the caster sugar, about 2 oz (50 g) at a time, whisking hard after each addition. When all 6 oz (75 g) has been added, you should have a glossy stiff meringue.
3   Spoon this out over the circle on the non-stick baking sheet and, with a wide spatula, shape into a nest with a thick layer of meringue on the bottom and a wall of meringue all round. Or, if you have a really large piping bag, fit it with a ½ in (5 cm) star nozzle and pipe the nest out, finishing with a row of meringue stars on top of the wall.

4   Bake for at least 3 hours, or up to 5 for a really crisp meringue. (Some people do this overnight and if the oven is a hot one, they prop the door open).
5   Once baked, leave the nest to cool down and then lift from the non-stick paper and store in a tin until needed.
6   To make the filling: beat the egg yolks and sugar in a medium-size bowl and stir in the lemon rind and all but 1 tablespoon of the juice. Set the bowl over a pan of simmering water to cook the custard. Stir constantly until the mixture forms a thick smooth cream. Set this aside to cool.
7   In another bowl, whisk the cream to the floppy stage. Fold two-thirds of the cream into the lemon custard and set the rest of the cream to one side for decoration.
8   Pour boiling water over 2 of the peaches and skin them carefully. Remove the stones, slice the peaches and fold them into the cream.
9   Scoop the peaches and cream into the meringue nest. Skin another peach, slice that and set these slices all over the creamy filling.
10 Whip the rest of the cream again and use to pipe large stars all over the pie.
11 To make the sauce: pour boiling water over the last peach, skin and liquidize the flesh with the icing sugar and reserved lemon juice. If it is very thick, you could thin it down slightly with a little white wine.

FALLEN ANGELS WITH CRÈME ANGLAISE

Serves 8–10

These delicate poached meringues are palest cream on a light lemon-coloured sauce and streaked with caramel – they are irresistible.

Crème Anglaise
4 size-1 or size-2 egg yolks
2 oz (50 g) caster sugar
1 level teaspoon cornflour
15 fl oz (450 ml) hot milk
1 tablespoon brandy (optional)

Fallen Angels
whites from 4 size-1 or size-2 eggs
2 oz (50 g) caster sugar

Caramel
4 oz (125 g) caster sugar

1   To make the Crème Anglaise: in a medium bowl, whisk the egg yolks and the sugar. Sprinkle the cornflour over and whisk again. Pour over the hot milk and whisk again. Set this bowl over a pan of simmering water and stir constantly until the mixture thickens. Add more milk to thin it down to the consistency of pouring cream and add the brandy if you wish. Pour into a large shallow gratin dish, cover and set aside.
2   Make the Fallen Angels: whisk the egg whites until they are very stiff indeed, then add the sugar gradually, whisking hard until you have stiff shiny meringue.
3   Bring a sauté pan (a deep frying pan would do) about two-thirds full of water to the boil and turn the heat down to a simmer. Add big dessertspoonfuls of the meringue to the simmering water. Try to shape the meringues with two spoons into neat ovals. Keep the meringues well apart and poach for about 5 minutes, turning them over halfway through. Drain the poached meringues thoroughly on kitchen paper. Set them aside until almost ready to serve.

4   Make the caramel: in a small heavy pan, put the sugar over a medium heat. Toss the sugar back and forth as the bottom sugar starts to melt. Keep it all moving, but do not use a spoon as it just gets clogged up. Eventually the sugar will turn to a rich caramel. Set the pan in cold water to stop it cooking further.
5   Just before serving, pile the meringues on top of the Crème Anglaise and dribble the caramel back and forth in long straight lines.

INDIVIDUAL BAKED ALASKA

Serves 4

This dinner-party special is still fun to do. I think it is easier to make individual ones as long as there are no more than 4 at the table.

1 small oblong carton of chocolate ice-cream
whites from 3 size-1 or size-2 eggs
6 oz (175 g) caster sugar

1   Preheat the oven to gas6/400°F/200°C.
2   Cut the block of ice-cream into 4 and set each block on an ovenproof plate (a tea plate is about the right size). Put the plates in the freezer to get the ice-cream really hard.
3   Make the meringue as described in the previous recipe and put it in a piping bag with a ½ in (1 cm) star nozzle.
4   Your guests just must wait for this one. Take the plates out of the freezer one at a time and quickly pipe the meringue all over each ice-cream. I do it in long sausages. If the meringue has gaps, take a spoon and smooth over the meringue. Take care to judge the amount of meringue for each ice.
5   Slide the plates into the oven and, when the meringue is golden-tipped, take it out.
6   Set each hot plate on a cool plate at the table and warn everyone that the plates are hot.

WALNUT & LEMON MERINGUE GÂTEAU

Serves 8–10

Meringue
whites from 4 size-1 or size-2 eggs
pinch of salt
pinch of cream of tartar
9 oz (250 g) caster sugar
5 oz (15 g) best-quality walnuts, finely chopped

Filling
10 fl oz (300 ml) double cream
4 tablespoons homemade Lemon Curd

1   Make the meringue: preheat the oven to gas½/250°F/120°C. Line 2 big baking sheets with non-stick baking paper, having drawn three 8 in (20 cm) circles on the underside of the paper.
2   Using an electric mixer, whisk the egg whites until they are frothy. Add the salt and cream of tartar and whisk hard until firm and snowy. Start adding the sugar, 2 tablespoons at a time, whisking hard between additions. When all the sugar has been incorporated you should have a glossy stiff meringue. Take the bowl away from the machine and, by hand, fold the chopped walnuts into the meringue.
3   Divide the meringue evenly between the 3 circles. Take a small spatula and spread the meringue out to the pencilled line.
4   Bake for about 3 hours, or until the meringue is dry and brittle. Leave the discs to cool, then lift from the non-stick paper and store in an airtight tin.
5   To assemble the gâteau: first whip the double cream quite firmly then fold in the lemon curd. Set the first disc flat side down on a large flat plate. Scoop half of the lemon cream on the meringue and spread it out. Cover the first layer with another meringue disc and top with the rest of the cream and lemon filling, then add the last meringue layer with the rough side uppermost. Press down very gently.
6   Serve on the day it is made. The meringue circles themselves would store for several weeks in an airtight tin.

BAKED APPLE & BLACKBERRY IN A STARRY SHELL

Serves 6

The idea for this pudding came from Margaret Costa. It is very good indeed hot, and almost as nice cold. The sharpness of the fruit is a lovely foil for the meringue.

6 small Bramley apples
8 oz (225 g) blackberries
8 oz (225 g) sugar
little bramble or redcurrant jelly

Meringue
whites from 3 size-1 or size-2 eggs
6 oz (175 g) caster sugar

1   Preheat the oven to gas2/300°F/150°C. You will need a fairly shallow pan big enough to take the 6 apples in one layer, and a shallow heatproof gratin dish.
2   First peel and core the apples and stuff each one with a few blackberries. Boil 15 fl oz (450 ml) water in the pan and add the sugar. When it has dissolved, turn down the heat to a simmer and set the apples in the pan. Cover and poach gently, so that the apples do not collapse but stay in shape. Baste the tops of the apples so that they take on a little pink colour.
3   When they are tender, lift out of the water and set them well apart in the bottom of the shallow gratin dish. Spoon a little sugar on top of the blackberries, but not too much. Allow to go cold.
4   Now make the meringue: whisk the egg whites until they are frothy. Add the salt and cream of tartar. Whisk again until the whites are firm and snowy. Add the sugar, 2 tablespoons at a time, whisking hard between each addition. When the sugar is finished you should have a stiff glossy meringue.
5   Scoop this into a large dry piping bag fitted with a ½ in (1 cm) star nozzle and pipe the meringue mixture closely around each apple in circles of stars. Leave the tops of the apples open.

Pipe any spare meringue on the base of the dish.
6   Bake about 15–20 minutes, or until the meringue is brittle and just beginning to colour.
7   Fill up the centres with a spoonful of bramble jelly or something sharp like redcurrant jelly and serve at once. This pudding does not stay crisp for long.

CHOCOLATE CHIP MERINGUE GÂTEAU

Serves 8

Three layers of chocolate-chip meringue sandwiched with white chocolate ganache in one layer and dark chocolate ganache in the other. You can chop the chocolate in your food processor, as I do.

Meringue
whites from 3 size-1 or size-2 eggs
4 oz (125 g) caster sugar
pinch of salt
pinch of cream of tartar
6 oz (175 g) grated dark chocolate, plus
     more to decorate
Filling
3 oz (75 g) white chocolate, broken into pieces
2 oz (50 g) sugar
3 oz (75 g) plain chocolate, broken into pieces
1 pt (575 ml) double cream

1   Make the meringue: preheat the oven to ¹⁄₄/325°F/110°C. Line 2 big baking sheets lined with non-stick paper, having drawn two 8 in (20 cm) circles in pencil on the underside of one paper and one circle on the other.
2   Whisk the egg whites until they are frothy. Add the salt and cream of tartar. Whisk hard until the whites are firm and snowy. Start to add the sugar, 2 tablespoons at a time, whisking hard between each addition. When all the sugar has been used up you should have a glossy firm meringue. Take the bowl away from the machine and fold the chocolate chips in by hand, reserving 1 tablespoon for decoration.

3   Divide the mixture between the circles and smooth the meringue out to fit the pencil lines.
4   Bake for about 25 minutes only. Keep watching them in case they get too brown. Take them out and allow to cool and firm up.
5   To make the fillings: in 1 heatproof bowl, put the white chocolate with 1 oz (25 g) caster sugar and 3 tablespoons of water; in another heatproof bowl, put the plain chocolate with 1 oz (25 g) caster sugar and 3 tablespoons of water. Set each bowl over a pan of simmering water to melt, then set aside to go cold.
6   Whip the double cream and divide it in 2 other bowls. Stir the white chocolate mixture into one and whip until thick. Stir the dark chocolate mixture into the other. Whip each bowl of cream again.
7   To assemble the gâteau: set the first circle of chocolate meringue on a large flat plate, flat side down, spread a thick layer of white chocolate ganache on it and set the second meringue layer on top. Spread the second layer of meringue with a thick layer of dark chocolate mixture, add the top meringue layer and press down quite gently.
8   Mix the remaining creams together and whip again to stiffen it up if you have to. Spread a layer of ganache round the sides of the gâteau, using a flexible spatula. Try to make the coating as smooth as you can. Finally coat the top and smooth that out carefully. Scatter over the reserved chocolate chips and set aside to chill.
9   Serve cut in wedges – small ones!

NOT A ROUND PAVLOVA

Serves 8

The fruit in the original Pavlova, made to honour the ballerina, was kiwi fruit and passion fruit. This time the meringue is in the shape of a casket – oblong instead of round. It is much easier to serve in this shape. The soft brown sugar gives a slightly caramel flavour to the pale coffee-coloured meringue.

Meringue
whites from 3 size-1 or size-2 eggs
pinch of salt
pinch of cream of tartar
6 oz (175 g) soft brown sugar

Filling
¼ pt (150 ml) double cream
2 kiwi fruits
4 passion fruits

1   Make the meringue: preheat the oven to gas¼ /200°F/90°C. Line a baking sheet with non-stick baking paper, having drawn (in pencil) a rectangle on the underside of the paper, measuring 5 x 9 in (12.5 x 23 cm). You will need a large piping bag fitted with a ½ in (1 cm) nozzle.

2   Whisk the egg whites until they are frothy, then add the salt and cream of tartar and continue whisking until they are stiff and snowy white. Gradually add the sugar, 1 tablespoon at a time, whisking hard between each addition. You should have a firm glossy meringue.

3   Turn the meringue out on the pencilled rectangle and shape a casket with a fairly thick meringue base and a 'wall' all round. Alternatively, spoon out one-third of the meringue on the rectangle and spread it out in an even layer. Give the rest of the meringue a final whisk, then spoon it into the large piping bag fitted with a ½ in (1 cm) star nozzle and pipe a closely packed row of stars all round the outside edge of the rectangle, then pipe a second row of stars on top of the first one.

4   Bake for at least 3 hours and up to 5 hours for a very crisp result. Set aside to go cold and store in an airtight tin.

5   Make the filling: whip the double cream to the floppy stage and pile it into the meringue case. Peel and slice or chop the kiwi fruit and spread it over the cream. Cut the passion fruit open, scoop out the juice and seeds and scatter over the kiwi fruit.

6   Serve cut in slices.

'O ruddier than the cherry,
O sweeter than the berry,
O nymph more bright
Than moonshine night
Like kidlings blithe and merry.'

John Gay